Advances in Computation: Theory and Practice
Volume 15

PARALLEL AND DISTRIBUTED SCIENTIFIC AND ENGINEERING COMPUTING:

PRACTICE AND EXPERIENCE

ADVANCES IN COMPUTATION: THEORY AND PRACTICE

Volume 15 – Parallel and Distributed Scientific and Engineering Computing: Practice and Experience
Yi Pan and Laurence Tianruo Yang
ISBN 1-59033-956-8

Volume 14 – Technology Supporting Business Solutions
Rafael Corchuelo, Antonio Ruiz-Cortés and Robert Wrembel
ISBN 1-59033-802-2

Volume 13 – Implementation of Term Rewriting-Based Programming Languages
Nadia Nedjah and Luiza de Macedo Mourelle
ISBN 1-59033-645-3

Volume 12 – Practical Application of Parallel Computing
Laurence Tianruo Yang and Marcin Paprzycki
ISBN 1-59033-532-5

Volume 11 – Numerical Solution of Nonlinear Elliptic Problems via Preconditioning Operators: Theory and Applications
IFaragó and JKarátson
ISBN 1-59033-376-4

Volume 10 - Constructive Methods for Parallel Programming
Sergei Gorlatch and Christian Lengauer
ISBN 1-59033-364-0

Volume 9 - Imaging and Vision Systems: Theory, Assessment and Applications
Jacques Blanc-Talon and Dan CPopescu
ISBN 1-59033-033-1

Volume 8 - Machines that Learn to Play Games
Johannes Furnkranz and Mirsolav Kubat
ISBN 1-59033-021-8

Volume 7 - Scientific Computing and Applications
Peter Minev and Yanping Lin
ISBN 1-59033-027-7

Volume 6 - Weak Intelligence: Through the Principle and Paradox of Multiple Knowledge
Matjaz Gams
ISBN 1-56072-898-1

Volume 5 - Parallel Program Development for Cluster Computing: Methodology, Tools and Integrated Environments
José CCunha, Peter Kacsuk and Stephen CWinter
ISBN 1-56072-865-5

Volume 4 - Structured Matrices: Recent Advances and Applications
Dario Andrea Bini, Eugene Tyrtyshnikov and Plamen Yalamov
ISBN 1-56072-890-6

Volume 3 - Recent Trends in Numerical Analysis
Donato Trigiante
ISBN 1-56072-885-X

Volume 2 - High Performance Algorithms for Structured Matrix Problems
Peter Arbenz, Marcin Paprzycki, Ahmed Sameh and Vivek Sarin
ISBN 1-56072-594-X

Advances in Computation: Theory and Practice
Volume 15

PARALLEL AND DISTRIBUTED SCIENTIFIC AND ENGINEERING COMPUTING:

PRACTICE AND EXPERIENCE

YI PAN AND LAURENCE TIANRUO YANG
EDITORS

Nova Science Publishers, Inc.
New York

Production Coordinator:
Coordinating Editor/Graphics: Tatiana Shohov
Graphics: Levani Chlaidze
Senior Production Editors: Susan Boriotti and Donna Dennis
Production Editors: Marius Andronie and Rusudan Razmadze
Office Manager: Annette Hellinger
Editorial Production: Maya Columbus, Aloysha Klestov, Vladimir Klestov, Matthew Kozlowski and Lorna Loperfido
Circulation: Ave Maria Gonzalez, Vera Popovic, Luis Aviles, Jonathan Boriotti, Alexandra Columbus, Raymond Davis, Cathy DeGregory, Melissa Diaz, Magdalena Nuñez, Marlene Nuñez, Jeannie Pappas and Frankie Punger
Communications and Acquisitions: Serge P. Shohov

Library of Congress Cataloging-in-Publication Data
ISBN 1-59033-956-8

400 Oser Ave, Suite 1600
Hauppauge, New York 11788-3619
Tele. 631-231-7269Fax 631-231-8175
e-mail: Novascience@earthlink.net
Web Site: http://www.novapublishers.com

Printed in the United States of America

CONTENTS

Introduction vii
Yi Pan and Laurence Tianruo Yang

SECTION 1: NUMERICAL ALGORITHMS 1

Row-Column Versus Vector-Radix: A Case Study of Two Parallel 2D Fourier Transform Algorithms 3
H. Martin Büecker

A Numerical Study of Some Parallel Algebraic Preconditioners 9
Xing Cai and Masha Sosonkina

A Model Reduction Web Environment for Very Large Linear Dynamical Systems 23
Peter Benner, Rafael Mayo, Enrique S. Quintana-Ortí and Gregorio Quintana-Ortí

Implementation of Multiple-Precision Parallel Division and Square Root on Distributed-Memory Parallel Computers 35
Daisuke Takahashi

Modelling the Runtime of Scientific Programs on Parallel Computers 51
Thomas Rauber and Gudula Rünger

SECTION 2: PARALLEL APPLICATIONS 67

Parallelization and Analysis of the Linkmap Program 69
N. Lopez-Benitez, A. Rai, K. Kothari and S. E. Poduslo

Methods for Parallel Simulations of Surface Reactions 85
S.V. Nedea, J.J. Lukkien, P.A.J. Hilbers and A.P.J. Jansen

Multi-Teraflops Studies of the Magnetic Structure of FeMn Alloys on Parallel Computers 99
A. Canning, B. Ujfalussy, T. C. Schulthess, X.-G. Zhang, W. A. Shelton, D. M. C. Nicholson, G. M. Stocks, Yang Wang and T. Dirks

Evaluation of the Speedup of a Distributed Groundwater Simulator Dispersion System on a Dual-Processor Beowulf Network 109
Mario Donato Marino

New Mesh Generating Adapted to Parallel Systems: PVM Implementation Issue 119
Andrei Doncescu

Implementing and Evaluating an Efficient Dynamic Load-Balancer for Distributed Molecular Dynamics Simulation 131
Naohito Sato and Jean-Marc Jézéquel

SECTION 3: CLUSTER AND GRID APPLICATIONS 145

Improving Quality of Service for Application Clusters 147
Sophia Corsava and Vladimir Getov

Increasing the Throughput of Available Resources Using Management Tools Based on Grid Technologies 163
Patricia González, María J. Martín, José C. Mouriño and Ramón Doallo

A Grid-Based RPC System for Medical Imaging 177
M. Bertero, P. Bonetto, L. Carracciuolo, L. D'Amore, A. R. Formiconi, M. R. Guarracino, G. Laccetti, A. Murli and G. Oliva

Grid Environment with Web-Based Portal Access for Air Quality Modelling 191
Barbara Chapman, Hari Donepudi, Yupeng Li, Priya Raghunath, Yonghong Yan, Babu Sundaram and Jiwen He

Coordination in Utility Managed Multi-Agent Groups 209
Fernanda Barbosa, José C. Cunha, Omer F. Rana, and Steven J. Lynden

Index 221

Introduction

In the not too distant future, every researcher and professional in science and engineering fields will have to understand parallel and distributed computing. With hyperthreading in Intel processors, hypertransport links in AMD processors, multi-core silicon in today's high-end microprocessors from IBM and emerging cluster and grid computing, parallel and distributed computers have moved into the mainstream of computing. To fully exploit these advances in computer architectures, researchers and professionals must start to design parallel or distributed software, systems and algorithms for their scientific and engineering applications. Parallel and distributed scientific and engineering computing has become a key technology which will play an important part in determining, or at least shaping, future research and development activities in many academic and industrial branches.

We would like to use this edited book to report the recent important advances in the area of parallel and distributed computing for science and engineering applications. This book contains selected best papers from prestigious workshops such as PACT-SHPSEC, IPDPS-PDSECA and ICPP-HPSECA together with some invited papers from prominent researchers around the world. The book is basically divided into three main sections. We believe all of these chapters not only provide novel ideas, new experimental results and handful experience in this field, but also stimulate the future research activities in the area of parallel and distributed computing for science and engineering applications.

Section 1: Numerical Algorithms

In the first chapter, the parallelization of two different methods to compute the complex discrete two-dimensional Fourier transform is investigated by *Bücker*. *Cai et al.* present a numerical study of several parallel algebraic preconditioners, in chapter 2 to speed up the convergence of distributed Krylov iterative solvers for large-scale linear systems. In chapter 3, *Benner et al.* describe a prototype web service for model reduction of very large-scale linear systems, with dimension in the order of millions of states, which includes a user-friendly interface designed so that the computation can be easily performed via the http protocol. *Takahashi* describes efficient parallel algorithms for multiple-precision division and square root operations of more than several million decimal digits on distributed-memory parallel computers in chapter 4. In the final chapter of the section, *Rauber and Rünger* demonstrate that the runtime functions can be used to model the computation and communication behavior of complete scientific programs by investigating the parallel implementation of a solution method for ordinary differential equations.

Section 2: Parallel Applications

Linkage analysis uses information from family pedigrees to map and locate disease genes on particular chromosomes. In chapter 6, *Lopez-Benitez et al.* provides a parallel implementation of the Linkmap program, one of the four programs in Linkage/ Fastlink, for a heterogeneous environment, using a static and a dynamic strategy for task allocation. In chapter 7, *Nedea et al.* study the opportunities for parallelism for the simulation of surface reactions by introducing the concept of a partition and by presenting new simulation methods based on Cellular Automaton using partitions. *Canning et al.* describe multi-teraflops studies of the magnetic structure of FeMn alloys on massively parallel computers in chapter 8. In chapter 9, *Marino* evaluates how much the increasing of the input parameters influences the speedups, comparing the predicted theoretical with the practical speedup when the Distributed Groundwater Simulator Dispersion System (DGWSDS) runs on a dual processor Beowulf network. Surfaces play an important role in 3D computer graphics applications. Subdivision surfaces are valued in geometric modeling applications for the representation of objects of arbitrary topological type in a form that is easy to design render and deform. In chapter 10, *Doncescu* presents different algorithms of subdivision and compression applied on this type of surfaces and their corresponding parallel implementations. *Sato et al.* propose in chapter 11 an efficient dynamic load-balancing scheme for parallel molecular dynamics simulation on distributed memory machines.

Section 3: Cluster and Grid Applications

In chapter 12, *Corsava et al.* present a software system that manages quality of service for Unix-based distributed application clusters. The aim of chapter 13 is to build a dynamic virtual high throughput platform made up of heterogeneous individual machines available in a given instant of time in a work--center. In order to achieve this objective, *González et al.* propose a low—intrusive monitor and scheduler system layered on top of an already existing Grid-based structure. In chapter 14, *Bertero et al.* describe MedIGrid, an application that enables nuclear doctors to transparently use high performance computers and storage systems for the PET/SPECT (Positron Emission Tomography/Single Photon Emission Computed Tomography) image processing, management, visualization and analysis. *Chapman et al.* in chapter 15 discuss the needs of an air quality modeling project to address several modern environmental health concerns and describe the campus grid environment that they have built to support this effort. A two stage approach to co-ordination in a multi-agent society is presented by *Barbosa et al.* in chapter 16. An example based on resource sharing within a computational grid is used to illustrate how these two approaches may be combined.

Acknowledgments

Of course, the proposed division into sections is one of the possible partitioning strategies. The represented areas, as well, are not an exaustive representation of the world of paralell and distributed scientific and engineering computing. Nonetheless, they represent the rich and useful practice and experience, that we have the pleasure of sharing with the readers. We would like to thank the authors, for their contributions, and patience in assisting us. Finally, the fundamental work of all the reviewers is also very warmly acknowledged.

Yi Pan
Georgia State University, USA
Laurence Tianruo Yang
St. Francis Xavier University, Canada

Section 1: Numerical Algorithms

In: Parallel and Distributed Scientific and Engineering Computing ISBN 1-59033-956-8
Editor: Y. Pan and L.T. Yang, pp. 3-8

ROW-COLUMN VERSUS VECTOR-RADIX: A CASE STUDY OF TWO PARALLEL 2D FOURIER TRANSFORM ALGORITHMS

H. MARTIN BÜECKER*

Abstract. The parallelization of two different methods to compute the complex discrete two-dimensional Fourier transform is investigated. The row-column method uses successive one-dimensional Fourier transforms along each dimension whereas the vector-radix method recursively computes two-dimensional Fourier transforms of lower sizes. Each method is examined with respect to independent computational parts that can be done in parallel. Performance results on a distributed memory computer with up to 16 processors are given demonstrating that the vector-radix method is attractive compared to the more widely used row-column method.

Key words. Fast Fourier transform, Two-dimensional, Parallel algorithms, Distributed memory, Hypercube

1. Introduction. Without any doubt, a family of algorithms collectively referred to as the *fast Fourier transform* (FFT) has been essential for progress in a truly-diverse range of scientific and engineering disciplines. Examples include astronomy, spectral methods for partial differential equations, medical imaging, error-correcting codes, and pattern recognition, to name a few. The FFT is not a discipline-related technique but a "big analytic hammer" [13] used as a broad instrument of mathematical analysis. This hammer is brought into play when one is looking for the discrete Fourier transform (DFT) of a one-dimensional sequence of N complex numbers. The FFT is a family of algorithms to efficiently compute the DFT using $O(N \log N)$ operations. Prior to the rediscovery of the FFT in the mid 1960s [5], all known algorithms for computing the DFT required $O(N^2)$ operations.

The two-dimensional DFT of N^2 complex numbers is ubiquitous in digital signal and image processing [6, 11]. As in the one-dimensional case, there is a more efficient technique than the straightforward $O(N^4)$ approach. The two-dimensional FFT does this job using only $O(N^2 \log N)$ operations. While the variety of different FFT algorithms for the one-dimensional case is already remarkable, see the excellent book [12], the diversity of algorithms is even richer in two dimensions. Furthermore, the number of different FFT variants increases when parallelism is taken into account; see [4] where a common framework for sequential and parallel FFT algorithms is presented.

In this note, two different approaches for the 2D FFT on a distributed memory computer are investigated. The row-column method uses successive 1D FFTs along each dimension whereas the vector-radix method recursively computes 2D FFTs of lower sizes. The row-column method is more widely used in parallel implementations [1, 7, 9] than the vector-radix method [1, 3, 10]. Hybrids of the two approaches have also been studied [14]. The purpose of this note is to emphasize the advantages of the vector-radix method in a parallel environment by making publicly available the results of the institutional report [2] in a condensed form.

In § 2, the row-column method and the vector-radix method are briefly reviewed. Their parallel implementations are sketched in § 3. Finally, we summarize the findings in the last section.

2. Two-dimensional FFT Algorithms. The one-dimensional discrete Fourier transform of length N maps complex numbers $x(k)$, for $0 \le k < N$, to

$$X(j) = \sum_{k=0}^{N-1} W_N^{kj} x(k), \qquad 0 \le j < N, \tag{2.1}$$

*Institute for Scientific Computing, Computer Science Department, RWTH Aachen University, 52056 Aachen, Germany, (buecker@sc.rwth-aachen.de).

where, with $i = \sqrt{-1}$, the symbol $W_N = e^{-\frac{2\pi i}{N}}$ denotes an Nth root of unity. A straightforward approach, hereafter denoted by 1D-DFT(N), would need $O(N^2)$ complex operations. Notice that, in all the operation counts given in this note, the cost of generating the powers of the root of unity is neglected; that is, the pre-computation of all W_N^{kj} values is assumed.

Under the assumption $N = 2^n$, the FFT reduces the complexity for computing (2.1) to $O(N \log N)$. The main idea of the FFT is to convert a transform of length N into two transforms of length $N/2$. In formulae, the 1D-FFT(N) is based on the splitting

$$X(j) = X_{\text{ev}}(j) + W_N^j X_{\text{od}}(j), \qquad 0 \le j < N/2, \tag{2.2}$$

$$X(j + N/2) = X_{\text{ev}}(j) - W_N^j X_{\text{od}}(j), \qquad 0 \le j < N/2, \tag{2.3}$$

where the symbols $X_{\text{ev}}(j)$ and $X_{\text{od}}(j)$ denote the 1D-DFT($N/2$) of the even indexed numbers $x_{\text{ev}}(k) = x(2k)$ and odd indexed numbers $x_{\text{od}}(k) = x(2k+1)$, respectively, for $0 \le k < N/2$. The splitting is then applied recursively in a divide-and-conquer fashion. See [12] for the derivation of (2.2) and (2.3) and how the recursion is ended. Note that, in each level of the recursion, the number of transforms is doubled and their length is halfed. Therefore, equations (2.2) and (2.3) are called radix-2-butterfly operation.

The two-dimensional Fourier transform of an $N \times N$ array of complex numbers $x(k_1, k_2)$, for $0 \le k_1, k_2 < N$, is defined by

$$X(j_1, j_2) = \sum_{k_1=0}^{N-1} \sum_{k_2=0}^{N-1} W_N^{k_1 j_1} W_N^{k_2 j_2} x(k_1, k_2), \qquad 0 \le j_1, j_2 < N. \tag{2.4}$$

The straightforward $O(N^4)$ approach is denoted by 2D-DFT($N \times N$).

The row-column approach for computing (2.4) is based on the reformulation

$$X_{\text{row}}(k_1, j_2) = \sum_{k_2=0}^{N-1} W_N^{k_2 j_2} x(k_1, k_2), \qquad 0 \le k_1, j_2 < N, \tag{2.5}$$

$$X(j_1, j_2) = \sum_{k_1=0}^{N-1} W_N^{k_1 j_1} X_{\text{row}}(k_1, j_2), \qquad 0 \le j_1, j_2 < N. \tag{2.6}$$

For a fixed k_1, equation (2.5) represents a 1D-DFT(N) with respect to the index k_2, i.e., rows of $x(k_1, k_2)$. Analogously, for a fixed j_2, equation (2.6) is nothing but a 1D-DFT(N) of the columns of $X_{\text{row}}(k_1, j_2)$. Thus, a 2D-DFT($N \times N$) can be computed by first transforming N rows by 1D-DFTs(N) followed by transforming N columns by 1D-DFTs(N). If $N = 2^n$ row and column transforms can be computed by 1D-FFTs(N) leading to an $O(N^2 \log N)$ algorithm called row-column 2D-FFT($N \times N$). It is fairly easy to derive a column-row version that first transforms columns and then rows.

Another approach to efficiently compute (2.4) is based on generalizing the above splitting idea from one dimension to two dimensions. To this end, assume $N = 2^n$ and decompose the array x into the even and odd indexed numbers in each dimension, i.e.,

$$x_{\text{ev, ev}}(k_1, k_2) = x(2k_1, 2k_2), \tag{2.7}$$

$$x_{\text{od, ev}}(k_1, k_2) = x(2k_1 + 1, 2k_2), \tag{2.8}$$

$$x_{\text{ev, od}}(k_1, k_2) = x(2k_1, 2k_2 + 1), \tag{2.9}$$

$$x_{\text{od, od}}(k_1, k_2) = x(2k_1 + 1, 2k_2 + 1), \tag{2.10}$$

where $0 \le k_1, k_2 < N/2$. Moreover, analogous to the one-dimensional case, let the upper case X with corresponding subscripts denote their 2D-DFT($N/2 \times N/2$), for instance

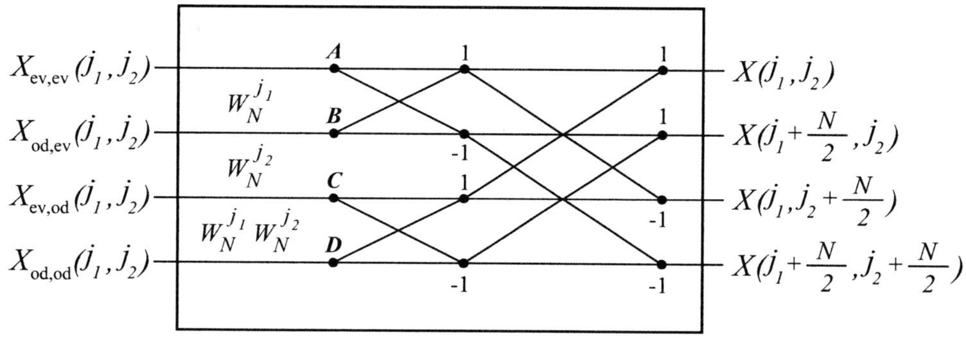

FIG. 2.1. *Schematic illustration of a vector-radix-(2 × 2)-butterfly. After computing the auxiliary quantities A, B, C, and D by four complex multiplications with the corresponding roots of unity, eight complex additions are carried out.*

$X_{\text{ev, ev}}(j_1, j_2)$ is used for the transform of $x_{\text{ev, ev}}(k_1, k_2)$. Then, using the auxiliary quantities

$$\begin{aligned}
A &= X_{\text{ev, ev}}(j_1, j_2),\\
B &= W_N^{j_1} X_{\text{od, ev}}(j_1, j_2),\\
C &= W_N^{j_2} X_{\text{ev, od}}(j_1, j_2),\\
D &= W_N^{j_1} W_N^{j_2} X_{\text{od, od}}(j_1, j_2),
\end{aligned}$$

the two-dimensional analogue of the splitting (2.2)–(2.3) is given by

$$X(j_1, j_2) = (A + B) + (C + D), \qquad 0 \le j_1, j_2 < N/2, \tag{2.11}$$

$$X(j_1 + N/2, j_2) = (A - B) + (C - D), \qquad 0 \le j_1, j_2 < N/2, \tag{2.12}$$

$$X(j_1, j_2 + N/2) = (A + B) - (C + D), \qquad 0 \le j_1, j_2 < N/2, \tag{2.13}$$

$$X(j_1 + N/2, j_2 + N/2) = (A - B) - (C - D), \qquad 0 \le j_1, j_2 < N/2. \tag{2.14}$$

Thus, a 2D-DFT($N \times N$) is converted into four 2D-DFTs($N/2 \times N/2$) and additional cost to recombine their results. Figure 2.1 shows (2.11)–(2.14) pictorially. Since, in each dimension, the number of transforms is duplicated and their length is halved, this operation is called vector-radix-(2 × 2)-butterfly. The two-dimensional splitting is then applied recursively leading to an $O(N^2 \log N)$ algorithm called vector-radix 2D-FFT($N \times N$). A more detailed description of the vector-radix method is given in [2], including the derivation of (2.11)–(2.14), graphical illustrations, and an operation count showing that the leading constant in the complexity of the vector-radix method is smaller than that of the row column method; more precisely, the vector-radix method saves 25% of complex multiplications compared to the row-column method.

3. Parallel Implementations. The two-dimensional FFT algorithms are implemented on an Intel iPSC/860 hypercube, a distributed memory computer with 16 nodes using Release 4.0 of the Portland Group's Fortran compiler. Throughout the experiments, it is assumed that $N = 2^n$ and the actual values used for the performance results are $N \in \{32, 64, 128, 256, 512\}$. The serial computation of the roots of unity is accelerated by exploiting their symmetry properties [2].

In the row-column method, the N row transformations are independent of each other and can be carried out in parallel. So are the N column transformations. Note that the results of the row transformations serve as input to the column transformations and, therefore, no row can be transformed simultaneously with any column. A coarse-grain parallelization consists in computing the one-dimensional transforms in parallel. A fine-grain approach parallelizing the radix-2-butterfly operations occurring in the one-dimensional transforms is discussed in [8] and will not be considered because, here, the number of processors p is small compared to N. In the parallel implementation, N/p rows are initially distributed to each processor. Assume that some serial implementation of an in-place one-dimensional FFT transforming data stored in contiguous memory cells, say a row of a Fortran array, is available. Then, the array initially storing the original data $x(k_1, k_2)$ has to be transposed before the column transforms are carried out. The complete row-column method consists of the following steps. Each processor computes N/p serial 1D-FFTs(N) of the rows of $x(k_1, k_2)$ first. After a parallel transposition of the resulting data, each processor ends with N/p serial 1D-FFTs(N) of the columns of $X_{\text{row}}(k_1, j_2)$ that are now stored as rows. Any serial one-dimensional FFT can be used for the row and column transformations. The parallel implementation whose results are depicted in Fig. 3.1 uses the Stockham-FFT that turns out to be the fastest in terms of execution time among several FFT variants due to Pease and Cooley-Tukey described in [2]. Notice that the speedup is measured with respect to the execution time of a serial 2D-FFT($N \times N$) using the Stockham-FFT for the one-dimensional transforms of rows and columns.

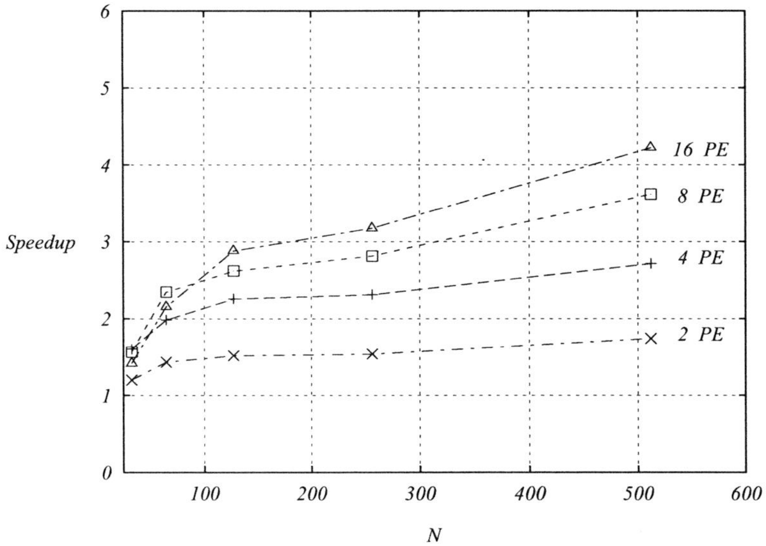

FIG. 3.1. *Speedup of the row-column method of a 2D-FFT($N \times N$).*

For the parallelization of the vector-radix method, one may use all the techniques well known from the one-dimensional case. The underlying recursion can be represented by a complete quaternary tree with $n = \log N$ levels depicted in Fig. 3.2. Here, a rectangle represent a two-dimensional Fourier transform and solid lines are used to denote the data dependence involved in recombining the results. A level $0 \leq i \leq n-1$ represents 4^i transforms 2D-FFTs($N/2^i \times N/2^i$). The data decomposition (2.7)–(2.10) shows that the four two-dimensional transforms of lower sizes are carried out with respect to disjoint data. Therefore, a Fourier transform on any level of the recursion can be computed in parallel with any other transform on the same level. Given four processors, a reasonable choice is to parallelize the four 2D-transforms on level 1 of the recursion; that is, each processor performs a single serial 2D-FFT($N/2 \times N/2$). Given 16 processors, level 2 representing 16 transforms 2D-FFTs($N/4 \times N/4$) is adequate for parallelization. If the number of processors is a power of 2 but not a power of 4, each processor computes two transforms on the appropriate level. For instance, if two processors are used each processor computes two transforms 2D-FFTs($N/2 \times N/2$) on level 1. In general, for p processors, all transforms on

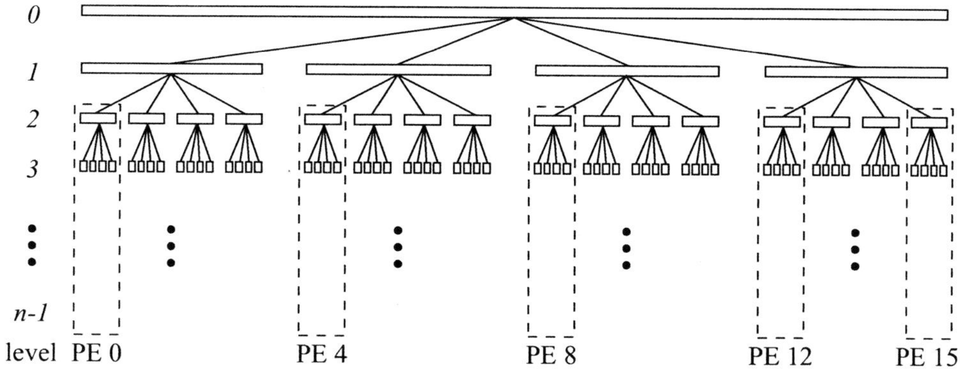

FIG. 3.2. *Schematic illustration of the parallelization of the vector-radix method. For $p = 16$ processors, transforms on level 3 are computed in parallel. Computations in subtrees marked with dashed rectangles are performed local on each processor.*

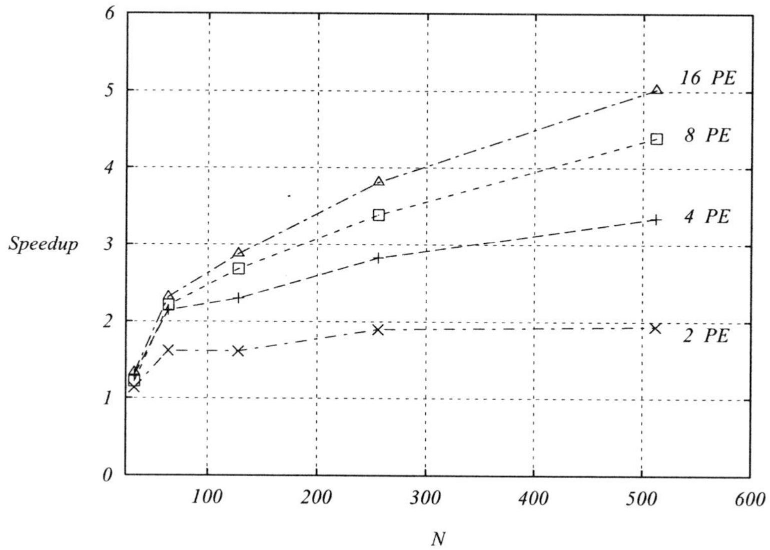

FIG. 3.3. *Speedup of the vector-radix method of a 2D-FFT($N \times N$).*

level $\lceil \log p/2 \rceil$ are computed in parallel. If $\log p$ is divisible by 2, each processor computes one transform otherwise two. The remaining transforms on level $\lceil \log p/2 \rceil - 1$ to level 0 could be parallelized using fewer processors in a similar fashion. However, the parallel implementation whose results are given in Fig. 3.3 carries out these transforms on a single processor because of the expected high communication cost. The speedup in this figure is measured with respect to the execution time of a serial vector-radix 2D-FFT($N \times N$).

4. Discussion and Concluding Remarks. In the row-column method, the two-dimensional Fourier transform is converted into several one-dimensional FFTs along both dimensions. In contrast, the vector-radix method recursively computes two-dimensional FFTs of lower sizes. Given a serial code for a one-dimensional FFT, the parallel row-column method is easy to implement on a distributed memory computer. Interprocessor communication is only required during a global matrix transposition. However, a parallel transposition may be extremely time-consuming because, at the same time, all processors have to send and receive data, potentially leading to network congestion. On the contrary, the vector-radix method can be parallelized using techniques known from parallelizing one-dimensional FFTs. The performance results given here demonstrate that the vector-radix method offers potential when the number of processors is increased and deserves more attention than it currently receives. Note that the row-column method is by far the most widely used two-dimensional FFT. One of the reasons is that its implementation consists simply of calling one-dimensional FFTs. The implementation of the vector-radix method on the other hand is more complicated, though a straight forward generalization of the ideas in the one-dimensional case. The results given in this note which are detailed in [2] suggest to take into account the vector-radix method in a parallel environment.

Acknowledgments. This work was initiated by Friedel Hoßfeld, Central Institute for Applied Mathematics (ZAM), Forschungszentrum Jülich GmbH. The author is grateful to ZAM for providing a stimulating research environment. The work was continued while the author was visiting the Mathematics and Computer Science Division, Argonne National Laboratory, supported by the Mathematical, Information, and Computational Sciences Division subprogram of the Office of Advanced Scientific Computing Research, U.S. Department of Energy, under Contract W-31-109-Eng-38.

REFERENCES

[1] R. K. ASBURY, *2D and 3D FFTs on the Intel IPSC/2 – A Distributed Memory, Multi-Processor Supercomputer*, in CA-DSP 89. 1989 International Symposium on Computer Architecture and Digital Signal Processing, vol. 2, Hong Kong, Oct. 1989, IEE, pp. 80–92.

[2] M. BÜCKER, *Zweidimensionale Schnelle Fourier–Transformation auf massiv-parallelen Rechnern*, Berichte des Forschungszentrums Jülich Jül–2833, Forschungszentrum Jülich GmbH, Jülich, Nov. 1993. In German.

[3] C. Y. CHU, *Comparison of Two-Dimensional FFT Methods on the Hypercube*, in Third Conference on Hypercube Concurrent Computers and Applications, G. Fox, ed., vol. 2, Pasadena, Jan. 1988, ACM, pp. 1430–1437.

[4] E. CHU AND A. GEORGE, *FFT algorithms and their application to parallel processing*, Linear Algebra and its Applications, 284 (1998), pp. 95–124.

[5] J. W. COOLEY AND J. W. TUKEY, *An algorithm for the machine calculation of complex Fourier series*, Mathematics of Computation, 19 (1965), pp. 297–301.

[6] D. E. DUDGEON AND R. M. MERSEREAU, *Multidimensional Digital Signal Processing*, Prentice-Hall, Englewood Cliffs, 1984.

[7] H. J. EHOLD, W. N. GANSTERER, H. KARNER, D. F. KVASNICKA, AND C. W. UEBERHUBER, *High performance Cholesky and FFT algorithms in HPF*, Tech. Report AURORA TR1999–10, Technical University of Vienna, 1999.

[8] L. H. JAMIESON, *Characterizing Parallel Algorithms*, in The Characteristics of Parallel Algorithms, L. H. Jamieson, D. B. Gannon, and R. J. Douglass, eds., MIT Press, Cambridge, 1987, pp. 65–100.

[9] S. L. JOHNSSON AND R. L. KRAWITZ, *Cooley-Tukey FFT on the Connection Machine*, Parallel Computing, 18 (1992), pp. 1201–1221.

[10] H. KUNIEDA AND K. ITOH, *Parallel 2D-FFT Algorithm on Practical Multiprocessor Systems*, in Transputer/Occam Japan 3, Proceedings of the Third Transputer/Occam International Conference, T. L. Kunii and D. May, eds., Tokyo, May 1990, IOS Press, pp. 77–89.

[11] J. S. LIM, *Two-Dimensional Signal and Image Processing*, Prentice-Hall, Englewood Cliffs, 1990.

[12] C. V. LOAN, *Computational Frameworks for the Fast Fourier Transform*, vol. 10 of Frontiers in Applied Mathematics, SIAM, Society for Industrial and Applied Mathematics, Philadelphia, 1992.

[13] D. N. ROCKMORE, *The FFT: An algorithm the whole family can use*, Computing in Science & Engineering, 2 (2000), pp. 60–64.

[14] Y.-T. WANG AND Z.-S. WANG, *Implementation of two-dimension FFT on massively parallel processing system DAWN1000*, in Proceedings SPIE. Parallel and Distributed Methods for Image Processing, H. Shi and P. C. Coffield, eds., vol. 3166, SPIE, 1997, pp. 352–359.

In: Parallel and Distributed Scientific and Engineering Computing ISBN 1-59033-956-8
Editor: Y. Pan and L.T. Yang, pp. 9-21

A NUMERICAL STUDY OF SOME PARALLEL ALGEBRAIC PRECONDITIONERS

XING CAI* AND MASHA SOSONKINA†

Abstract. We present a numerical study of several parallel algebraic preconditioners, which speed up the convergence of distributed Krylov iterative solvers for large-scale linear systems. The studied algebraic preconditioners are of two types. The first type includes simple block preconditioners using incomplete factorizations or preconditioned Krylov solvers on the subdomains. The second type is an enhancement of the first type in that Schur complement techniques are added to treat subdomain-interface unknowns. We use these parallel algebraic preconditioners in solving linear systems that arise from discretizing a suite of partial differential equations. The numerical experiments show that the scalability properties of the preconditioners are highly problem dependent, and a Schur complement-based preconditioner is favorable for achieving good overall performance. The experiments have used a software code that interfaces two mathematical software packages: Diffpack, an object-oriented computational environment for solving PDEs, and pARMS, a library of distributed-memory iterative solution techniques for large sparse linear systems.

Key words. Parallel solution of PDEs, Systems of linear equations, Parallel algebraic preconditioners, Domain decomposition, Schur complement

1. Introduction. Solving systems of linear equations is a topic of fundamental importance for the numerical solution of partial differential equations (PDEs). Almost all the numerical strategies rely on solving systems of linear equations on the form:

$$Ax = b. \tag{1.1}$$

In (1.1), A is often referred to as the system matrix, b is called the right-hand side vector, and vector x contains the unknowns. In this paper, we only consider linear systems that arise from the standard discretization techniques, i.e., finite elements, finite differences and finite volumes. The system matrix A is sparse in such cases, meaning that the number of nonzeros per row is small. Discretization on a very fine computational grid will result in a linear system that has a very large number of unknowns. Traditional direct solution methods for (1.1), such as Gaussian elimination, will become inapplicable due to high operation counts, large storage demand and high sensitivity to computer round-off errors. Large-scale linear systems are therefore better handled by iterative methods, especially the so-called Krylov subspace solvers; see e.g. [7].

If the grid resolution keeps increasing, the dimension of A will eventually become so large that one single processor will have trouble handling the entire linear system. This makes the use of parallel computers mandatory. Of course, another perhaps more important motivation for adopting parallel computers in solving PDEs is to save time by using more processors. Krylov subspace methods are in fact easily parallelized, because they involve only three types of kernel operations: vector addition (or update), inner-product between two vectors, and matrix-vector product. Once the unknowns of (1.1) are partitioned among the processors, see Section 1.1 below, the three types of kernel operations can be parallelized by running local computations on each processor, plus inter-processor communication when necessary.

1.1. Distributed sparse linear systems. A natural way of partitioning the unknowns of (1.1) is to use the idea of *domain decomposition* [11], which partitions a global

*Simula Research Laboratory & University of Oslo, P.O. Box 1080, Blindern, 0316 Oslo, Norway (xingca@simula.no). This author has received support from The Research Council of Norway (Programme for Supercomputing) through a grant of computing time.

†University of Minnesota, Duluth, MN 55812, USA (masha@d.umn.edu). The work of this author was supported in part by NSF under grants NSF/ACI-0000443 and NSF/INT-0003274, and in part by the Minnesota Supercomputing Institute.

solution domain Ω into a set of subdomains. Such a partitioning implies a partitioning of the rows of A. The grid points that lie on the boundary of a subdomain are called *interdomain interface points*, whereas the other grid points of a subdomain are called *internal points*; see Fig. 1.1. We remark that the solid curves in Fig. 1.1 represent "cutting lines" that divide the grid points disjointly among the subdomains. (Note that there are no grid points lying on the cutting lines.) We also observe that only the interdomain interface points have direct couplings with the external interface points that belong to neighboring subdomains. These interface points need to exchange values by communication during a parallel matrix-vector product.

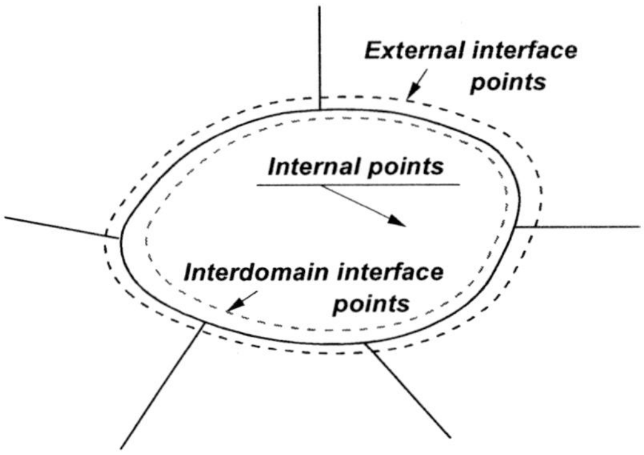

FIG. 1.1. *A subdomain that arises from domain decomposition.*

Here we have an important observation. There is no need to first build up the global linear system (1.1) by a discretization on the entire Ω, and then divide the rows of A among the processors. A better approach is to decompose Ω first and assign one subdomain (and its associated subgrid) to each processor. Thereafter, each processor carries out discretization on its own subdomain to produce the designated rows of A. These rows constitute a subdomain matrix. This "distributed discretization" approach avoids construction and storage of the global matrices/vectors. So the global linear system (1.1) only exists logically and we work with *a distributed sparse linear system* instead. Each processor thus handles only sub-matrices and sub-vectors associated with a subdomain.

A high-quality partitioning scheme should first divide the grid points evenly and disjointly among the subdomains. Although an external interface point (see Fig. 1.1) is the "responsibility" of a neighboring subdomain, it is beneficial for a subdomain to include all its external interface points into its local data structure. In this way, the rows of A that correspond to the interdomain interface points can be built without the need for inter-subdomain communication. This can be viewed as allowing a minimum amount of overlap between neighboring subdomains. In other words, each subdomain includes its external interface points in its local data structure, but is not responsible for finding the solution on these points. More overlap between subdomains is strictly speaking not necessary for parallelizing Krylov subspace methods. However, an increased overlap may help to produce better parallel preconditioner, as is well known for the so-called overlapping domain decomposition methods; see e.g. [11].

Based on the above distributed discretization approach, the global linear system $Ax = b$ does not need to exist physically. Instead, each subdomain handles its own *local* linear system. The linear algebra operations of a distributed Krylov solver are carried out by running local linear algebra operations *collectively*, using inter-subdomain communication when necessary.

1.2. Preconditioner and convergence. It is well known that the difficulty of solving a linear system, which arises from discretizing a PDE, grows as the grid resolution increases. For example, an elliptic PDE typically produces a system matrix A with a condition number of order $\mathcal{O}(h^{-2})$, where $1/h$ characterizes the grid resolution. The number of iterations needed by a Krylov subspace solver is typically of order $\mathcal{O}(h)$. To achieve faster convergence, we can use preconditioned iterations. That is, we may, e.g., solve an equivalent system

$$M^{-1}Ax = M^{-1}b, \tag{1.2}$$

where M is the preconditioner that approximates A in some way; see e.g. [7]. The work of a preconditioner can be roughly described as: Given a vector v, compute $w = Mv$.

Distributed Krylov solvers require parallel preconditioners. However, an extra difficulty in parallel solution of PDEs is that a good sequential preconditioner may not function equally well in the parallel setting. It is thus our purpose to study the behavior of the so-called parallel algebraic preconditioners. The term "algebraic" means that we only use the entries in A and its nonzero pattern. No knowledge of the underlying PDE is used during preconditioning. Neither will we use discretizations on additional computational grids, such as in geometric multigrid methods or two-level additive Schwarz methods (see e.g. [11]).

2. Parallel Algebraic Preconditioners. We adopt the framework of a distributed sparse linear system, as has been described in Section 1.1. Each subdomain vector x_i of local unknowns is split into two parts: the sub-vector u_i of internal variables and the sub-vector y_i of interdomain interface variables. The right-hand side vector b_i is split accordingly into two sub-vectors f_i and g_i,

$$x_i = \begin{pmatrix} u_i \\ y_i \end{pmatrix} ; \quad b_i = \begin{pmatrix} f_i \\ g_i \end{pmatrix} . \tag{2.1}$$

The subdomain matrix A_i residing on processor i is block-partitioned according to this splitting, leading to

$$A_i = \begin{pmatrix} B_i & F_i \\ E_i & C_i \end{pmatrix} . \tag{2.2}$$

In this setup, the local linear system can be rewritten as:

$$\begin{pmatrix} B_i & F_i \\ E_i & C_i \end{pmatrix} \begin{pmatrix} u_i \\ y_i \end{pmatrix} + \begin{pmatrix} 0 \\ \sum_{j\in\mathcal{N}_i} E_{ij}y_j \end{pmatrix} = \begin{pmatrix} f_i \\ g_i \end{pmatrix}, \tag{2.3}$$

where the term $E_{ij}y_j$ represents the contribution to the local system from the neighboring subdomain j, and $\mathcal{N}_i$ is the set of neighboring subdomains for subdomain i.

Parallel block preconditioners are the simplest algebraic preconditioning strategy, where each subdomain *independently* finds its local solution w_i by approximately solving a subdomain linear system formed by A_i and a given local vector v_i. The values on the interface points are then exchanged between neighboring subdomains. The subdomain systems can be solved in different ways, e.g., by a local (preconditioned) Krylov solver. Another simpler subdomain solver is to use the forward-backward procedure associated with an incomplete LU-factorization (ILU). We will use, in particular, a zero fill-in ILU (denoted ILU(0)) or a dual-threshold ILU (denoted ILUT); see [7].

Schur complement techniques refer to methods that iterate only on the interdomain interface unknowns, implicitly using internal unknowns as intermediate variables. Schur complement systems are derived by eliminating u_i from the local system (2.3). By noticing that $u_i = B_i^{-1}(f_i - F_iy_i)$, we get

$$S_iy_i + \sum_{j\in\mathcal{N}_i} E_{ij}y_j = g_i - E_iB_i^{-1}f_i \equiv g_i', \tag{2.4}$$

where S_i is the *local* Schur complement,

$$S_i = C_i - E_i B_i^{-1} F_i. \tag{2.5}$$

By assembling all the local Schur complement systems (2.4), we can get a *global* Schur complement system for all the interface unknowns. This global Schur complement system has a natural block structure:

$$\begin{pmatrix} S_1 & E_{12} & \dots & E_{1p} \\ E_{21} & S_2 & \dots & E_{2p} \\ \vdots & & \ddots & \vdots \\ E_{p1} & E_{p-1,2} & \dots & S_p \end{pmatrix} \begin{pmatrix} y_1 \\ y_2 \\ \vdots \\ y_p \end{pmatrix} = \begin{pmatrix} g_1' \\ g_2' \\ \vdots \\ g_p' \end{pmatrix}. \tag{2.6}$$

The diagonal blocks in this system, the matrices S_i, are dense in general. The off-diagonal blocks E_{ij} are sparse. More compactly, the global Schur complement system (2.6) can be written as

$$Sy = g',$$

where all the subdomain interface variable vectors $y_1, y_2, \dots, y_p$ are stacked into a long vector y. The matrix S is called the global Schur complement matrix. An idea proposed in [8] is to exploit methods that *approximately* solve (2.6) and use them in preconditioners for (1.1). Such a Schur complement based parallel algebraic preconditioner can be expressed by the following algorithm:

ALGORITHM 2.1. *Schur complement based preconditioner*

1. *Compute local right-hand sides:* $g_i' = g_i - E_i B_i^{-1} f_i$.
2. *Solve* $Sy = g'$ *approximately.*
3. *Solve* $B_i u_i = f_i - F_i y_i$.

Note that f_i in the above algorithm should be considered as a given local vector for the preconditioner, rather than the local right-hand side vector in the original system (2.3). Now let us consider Step 2 in more detail. First, we rewrite (2.6) as a preconditioned system with the diagonal blocks:

$$y_i + S_i^{-1} \sum_{j \in \mathcal{N}_i} E_{ij} y_j = S_i^{-1} \left[g_i - E_i B_i^{-1} f_i \right] \quad \text{for all } i. \tag{2.7}$$

This can be viewed as a block-Jacobi preconditioned version of (2.6). This global system can be solved by a GMRES-like accelerator, requiring a solve with S_i on subdomain i in each iteration. An ILU factorization of S_i can be easily extracted from an ILU factorization of A_i. Specifically, if A_i is of the form (2.2) and is factored as $A_i = L_i U_i$, where

$$L_i = \begin{pmatrix} L_{B_i} & 0 \\ E_i U_{B_i}^{-1} & L_{S_i} \end{pmatrix} \quad \text{and} \quad U_i = \begin{pmatrix} U_{B_i} & L_{B_i}^{-1} F_i \\ 0 & U_{S_i} \end{pmatrix},$$

then, $L_{S_i} U_{S_i}$ is equal to the local Schur complement S_i. So an ILU factorization of A_i provides an approximation of S_i. There are, of course, other techniques for approximating S_i, see e.g. [8].

In [5], an algebraic recursive multilevel solver (ARMS) [9], which acts on A_i, has been used to extract an approximation of the local Schur complement S_i. The construction of ARMS starts with defining "group-independent sets" in each subdomain. A group-independent set is a set of groups of unknowns such that there is no coupling between unknowns that belong to any two different groups [10]. An illustration is shown in Fig. 2.1 for a simple case with two subdomains. The solid curve in the middle contains no vertices, it

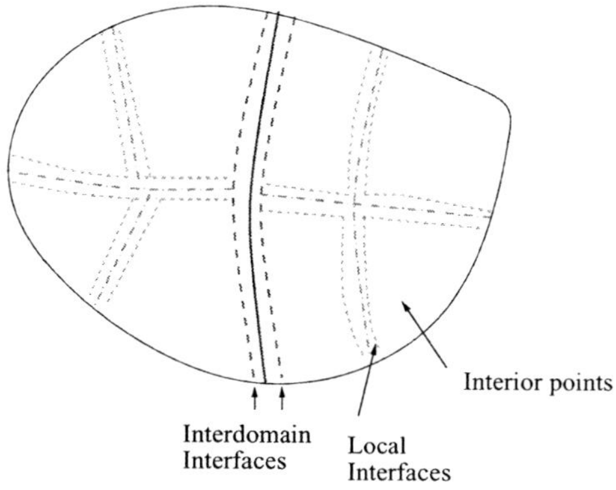

FIG. 2.1. *A two-level group-independent set.*

only illustrates the separation of the two subdomains. On each subdomain, an independent set reordering is applied locally. In Fig. 2.1, local interfaces denote the unknowns that separate the group independent sets. The local system with matrix A_i can be reordered such that the rows corresponding to local and interdomain interface unknowns are placed after the rows corresponding to the group independent set unknowns. With such a permutation, the Schur complement includes both types of the interface unknowns. We call this larger Schur complement the *expanded Schur complement.*

An advanced parallel algebraic preconditioner is thus to use a Krylov solver, preconditioned by a distributed ILU(0), for the global expanded Schur complement system. Such a Schur complement based preconditioner normally produces better convergence than a simple parallel block preconditioner. In particular, this Schur complement based preconditioner, denoted as *Schur*$_2$ in Section 4.4, can use ARMS as an approximate subdomain solver.

3. A Suite of PDEs with Test Cases. In this section, we present a suite of four PDEs. We have deliberately chosen these PDEs, which are simple in the mathematical formulation, but of great importance for many complicated mathematical models. It is therefore hoped that the numerical results presented in Section 5 will be of interest for many. We have also taken care to select test cases involving 2D/3D computations on uniform, structured, and unstructured computational grids. Although we use finite elements exclusively for the discretization, the resulting linear systems have similar properties as those arising from other discretization techniques, e.g., finite differences.

3.1. Poisson equation. Poisson equation is the simplest elliptic PDE and reads

$$-\nabla^2 u = f, \tag{3.1}$$

where f is prescribed.

Test Case 1. The Poisson equation (3.1) is considered in the 2D unit square. The right-hand side f is chosen as $f(x,y) = xe^y$, and $u(x,y) = -xe^y$ is given on the entire boundary $\partial\Omega$.

Test Case 2. The Poisson equation (3.1) is considered in the 3D unit cube. The right-hand side f is chosen as $f(x,y,z) = x(y^2+z^2)e^{yz}$, and $u(x,y,z) = -xe^{yz}$ is given on the entire boundary $\partial\Omega$.

Test Case 3. The Poisson equation (3.1) is considered in a special 2D domain depicted in Fig. 3.1. The right-hand side f and the boundary condition are the same as in Test Case 1. We use an unstructured 2D computational grid that has 521,185 points and 1,040,256 triangular elements. The computational grid is obtained from an adaptive grid refinement process, so the grid resolution varies greatly across Ω. We remark that Fig. 3.1 shows in fact a much coarser "predecessor" of our actual computational grid.

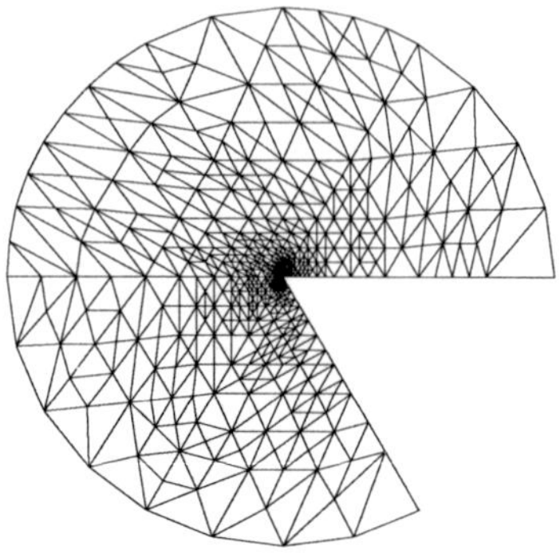

FIG. 3.1. *The solution domain and grid for Test Case 3; the Poisson equation.*

3.2. Heat conduction. The following parabolic PDE is the simplest model of heat transfer in a homogeneous medium:

$$\frac{\partial u}{\partial t} = k\nabla^2 u, \tag{3.2}$$

where constant k denotes the heat conductivity.

Test Case 4. The 3D unit cube is used as the spatial solution domain Ω. We choose $k = 1$ and use an implicit time-stepping scheme for solving (3.2), i.e.,

$$\frac{u^l - u^{l-1}}{\Delta t} = \nabla^2 u^l \;\Rightarrow\; u^l - \Delta t\,\nabla^2 u^l = u^{l-1}, \tag{3.3}$$

where the superscript l denotes the time level number. We note that the resulting system matrix A is on the form

$$A = M + \Delta t\, K, \tag{3.4}$$

where matrix M is often referred to as the *mass matrix* and K arises from discretizing $-\nabla^2 u^l$. Moreover, we choose $\Delta t = 0.05$ and let $u^0(x, y) = \sin(\pi x)\sin(\pi y)$ be the initial condition. As boundary conditions, we use $u = 0$ on the side of $x = 1$ and $\frac{\partial u}{\partial n} = 0$ on the rest of $\partial\Omega$.

3.3. Convection-diffusion equation. For a stationary convective flow that is also affected by diffusion, its mathematical model reads as follows,

$$\vec{v} \cdot \nabla u = \nabla^2 u, \tag{3.5}$$

where the constant vector $\vec{v}$ has magnitude v and an direction angle θ, i.e., $\vec{v} = (v\cos\theta, v\sin\theta)$. The magnitude v indicates the relation between convection and diffusion.

Test Case 5. We consider the convection-diffusion equation in the 2D unit square. The following boundary conditions are used: the normal derivative of u is zero on the right side ($x = 1$) and top side ($y = 1$). On the bottom side ($y = 0$) we have $u = 0$, whereas the left size ($x = 0$) is divided into two parts:

$$u = \begin{cases} 0 & x = 0,\ 0 \le y \le \frac{1}{4}, \\ 1 & x = 0,\ \frac{1}{4} < y \le 1. \end{cases}$$

By choosing $v = 1000$, we make the test case convection-dominated. The angle of $\vec{v}$ is chosen as $\theta = \pi/4$. Note that the boundary condition is discontinuous on $x = 0$, resulting in a rather sharp discontinuity of the solution that lies on a line starting from $(x = 0, y = 0.25)$ with an angle $\theta = \pi/4$; see Fig. 3.2. Due to the dominating convection, we have to use one type of upwind weighting functions, see [4], resulting in an unsymmetric system matrix A.

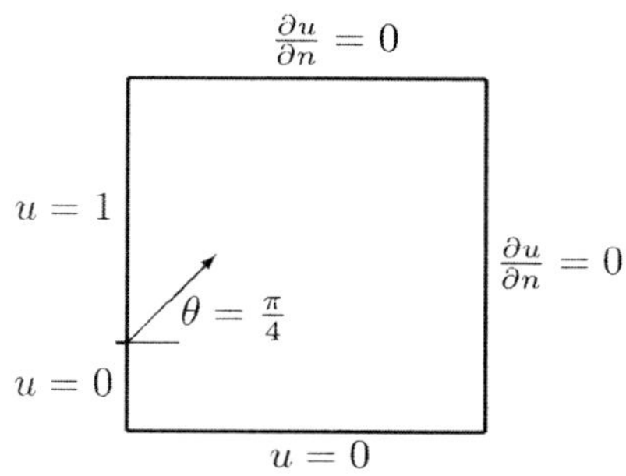

FIG. 3.2. *The solution domain of Test Case 5; the convection-diffusion equation.*

3.4. Linear elasticity. For an elastic body subject to a volume load, the displacement field $\vec{u}$ can be described by the following vector PDE that is of the elliptic type:

$$-\mu\Delta\vec{u} - (\mu + \lambda)\nabla(\nabla \cdot \vec{u}) = \vec{f}, \tag{3.6}$$

where μ and λ are elasticity constants, $\vec{f}$ is a given vector function representing the volume load; see e.g. [11].

Test Case 6. We study the displacement field $\vec{u} = (u_1, u_2)$ inside one quarter of an elastic ring, which has inner radius 1 and outer radius 2; see Fig. 3.3. We use a curvilinear structured computational grid consisting of triangular shaped elements. For the boundary condition, the stress vector is specified on the entire boundary $\partial\Omega$ except on Γ_1 and Γ_2, where $u_1 = 0$ on Γ_1 and $u_2 = 0$ on Γ_2.

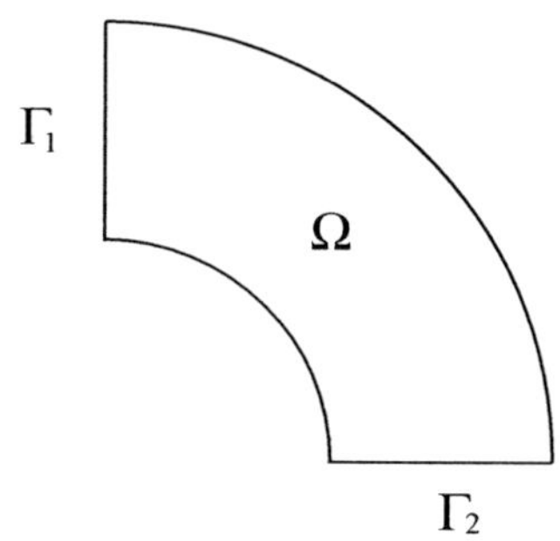

FIG. 3.3. *The solution domain for Test Case 6; the linear elasticity equation.*

4. Experiment Setup.

4.1. Software. We will use a "composite" parallel code for running simulations of the test cases presented in Section 3. More specifically, two software packages–*Diffpack* and *pARMS*–are coupled together. Diffpack (see [2, 4]) is an object-oriented computational environment with a special emphasis on solving PDEs. A Diffpack simulator is typically set up using C++ objects of classes that are provided by hierarchically designed libraries. Diffpack has a rich collection of classes representing grids, fields, finite element discretization tools, matrices, vectors, Krylov solvers, preconditioners, convergence monitors, and many more. Parallelization of a sequential Diffpack simulator can be easily done by using a special add-on parallel toolbox, which contains functionalities for grid partitioning, communication pattern recognition, and inter-processor MPI communication routines that are associated with parallel Krylov iterations. We refer to [1] for more details.

pARMS (see [6]) is a library of parallel iterative solution methods for large sparse linear systems. Its main feature is a large collection of state-of-the-art parallel algebraic preconditioners based on various incomplete factorization techniques, recursive multilevel strategies, and Schur complement solvers. The reason for coupling together the two software packages is to equip Diffpack with modern parallel algebraic preconditioners. In the resulting "composite" code, Diffpack is responsible for the overall parallel computing framework, finite element discretization, control of Krylov iterations, whereas pARMS is responsible for performing the parallel algebraic preconditioning operations based on incomplete LU factorizations with nonzero fill and/or inner iterations. Note that the simplest preconditioner, block Jacobi with zero fill and no inner iterations on the subdomains, is supplied by Diffpack.

Due to Diffpack's object-oriented design, it is quite easy to incorporate an "alien" code. In our case of using pARMS as new parallel preconditioners inside Diffpack, it suffices to write a small wrapper class, as a subclass of the generic preconditioner class in Diffpack. The function of this small wrapper class is to initiate the pARMS data structure, and shuffle data between Diffpack and pARMS every time a preconditioning operation needs to be carried out by the pARMS code.

4.2. Hardware. We have used two quite different parallel computing systems for running the simulations. One system is a low-end Linux cluster using Pentium III 1GHz processors and a fast Ethernet-based network. We have obtained exclusive access to run all the simulations on this relatively small parallel computer. The other system is a high-end SGI Origin 3800 machine using R14000 600MHz processors. Due to a restricted access to this parallel computer, we have only run a few selected simulations.

4.3. Measurements. In all the experiments to be presented in Section 5, we record the number of FGMRES iterations (with $m = 20$, see [7]), which is needed to achieve a *fixed* convergence criterion. More precisely, the 2-norm of the residual vector should be reduced by a factor of 10^6, compared with its initial value. For Test Case 4, we only run one time step so the initial guess of the solution is the initial condition of the PDE. For all the other test cases, we use zero initial values for all the unknowns except those associated with Dirichlet boundary conditions. The obtained iteration counts reveal the convergence speed of different parallel algebraic preconditioners when applied to different test cases. We have used a *general* grid partitioning scheme (based on Metis [3]) for all the simulations. We remark that due to different random number generators on the two different parallel computing systems, the global computational grid is in fact partitioned differently on the Linux cluster than on the Origin 3800 machine.

In addition, we record the *wall-clock time* consumption of the preconditioned parallel FGMRES solver. For every test case, these measurements are used to compare the overall computational performance of the different algebraic preconditioners. However, we remark that wall-clock time measurements are highly sensitive to the work load level of a parallel computing system. (The Origin 3800 machine has often been heavily loaded during our experiments.) Certain care should therefore be taken when interpreting these timing results.

For each test case, we use a *fixed global problem size* and let the preconditioner type and the number of processors P vary. When parallel speed-ups are considered, a fixed global problem size normally favors a smaller value of P, because the communication overhead is relatively low compared with the local computation. However, an opposite effect may occur if P exceeds a threshold such that the subdomain problems become small enough to be handled efficiently by the cache sitting on the an individual processor.

4.4. Notation. We use the following symbols to denote four different parallel algebraic preconditioners:

- *Schur*$_1$: A Schur complement based preconditioner where the global Schur complement system is solved approximately using five distributed global GMRES iterations preconditioned by block Jacobi, see (2.7). The associated subdomain solver is a forward-backward solve with the ILUT factors formed using the fill-in parameter equal to 20 and the drop tolerance of 10^{-4}.
- *Schur*$_2$: A Schur complement based preconditioner where the *expanded* global Schur complement system is solved approximately using five distributed global GMRES iterations preconditioned by a global ILU(0). The expanded Schur complement system arises from a two-level ARMS, which also works as the approximate subdomain solver. This comprehensive parallel preconditioner requires an extensive amount of inter-subdomain communication during its setup phase.
- *Block*$_1$: A simple block preconditioner, existing in Diffpack and using ILU(0) as the approximate subdomain solver.
- *Block*$_2$: A simple pARMS block preconditioner using ILUT with fill-in of 20 and drop tolerance of 10^{-4} as the approximate subdomain solver.

5. Numerical Results.

5.1. Results for test case 1. We use a distributed FGMRES solver and a fixed 2D global grid with 1001 × 1001=1,002,001 points. The following FGMRES iteration counts and wall-clock time measurements (in seconds) are obtained on the Linux cluster:

	Schur$_1$		*Schur*$_2$		*Block*$_1$		*Block*$_2$	
P	#itr	time	#itr	time	#itr	time	#itr	time
2	102	350.26	101	552.55	1188	1630.04	198	438.09
4	110	188.38	110	331.74	1371	1040.74	346	382.92
8	140	124.33	108	165.82	1008	425.18	352	200.26
16	146	76.70	104	100.59	977	223.31	315	102.65

We see that *Schur*$_1$ has the best overall computational performance for this test case, despite that *Schur*$_2$ has slightly faster in terms of iteration numbers and more stable convergence behavior. However, *Block*$_1$ has the best scalability with respect to wall-time per iteration. We have also tested *Schur*$_1$ and *Block*$_2$ on the Origin 3800 machine with the following results:

	Schur$_1$		*Block*$_2$	
P	#itr	time	#itr	time
8	121	303.34	270	118.34
16	145	190.14	386	83.89
32	167	153.31	511	122.70
64	184	88.78	840	98.96

We can see that the growth of iterations for *Schur*$_1$ is of moderate speed, whereas *Block*$_2$ requires many iterations for large values of P. We remark that the very poor wall-clock time measurements are due to the heavy load on the Origin 3800 machine, which ought to produce better measurements because of its more powerful processors and faster communication network. The different iteration counts for $P = 8$ and $P = 16$ are due to the different random number generators used in the grid partitioning scheme, as explained in Section 4.3.

5.2. Results for test case 2. We use a distributed FGMRES solver and a fixed 3D global grid with 101 × 101 × 101=1,030,301 points. The following results are obtained on the Linux cluster:

	Schur$_1$		*Schur*$_2$		*Block*$_1$		*Block*$_2$	
P	#itr	time	#itr	time	#itr	time	#itr	time
2	60	307.25	70	790.69	93	273.15	74	254.11
4	60	161.77	70	441.38	97	154.90	81	137.82
8	60	88.89	70	275.94	103	89.68	87	81.45
16	61	53.60	69	196.27	110	50.77	93	45.21

We can see that all the four preconditioners produce quite fast convergence, where *Schur*$_1$ and *Schur*$_2$ show very stable iteration counts. Unlike the previous test case, the *Block*$_2$ preconditioner produces the best overall computational performance, while *Block*$_1$ also performs better than both *Schur*$_1$ and *Schur*$_2$ for this test case. We have also tested *Schur*$_2$ and *Block*$_2$ on the Origin 3800 machine with the following results:

	Schur$_2$		*Block*$_2$	
P	#itr	time	#itr	time
16	70	310.40	94	39.86
32	68	114.76	103	43.83
64	67	91.74	110	26.71

We can see that the iteration counts remain stable with *Schur*$_2$, whereas the iteration number growth for *Block*$_2$ is moderate.

5.3. Results for test case 3. We use a distributed FGMRES solver and a fixed global unstructured grid with $521,185$ grid points. The following results are obtained on the Linux cluster:

	Schur$_1$		*Schur*$_2$		*Block*$_1$		*Block*$_2$	
P	#itr	time	#itr	time	#itr	time	#itr	time
2	148	223.20	74	256.54	1206	846.30	199	202.19
4	150	117.80	74	120.20	1451	530.48	171	88.87
8	152	66.07	74	70.60	1266	280.46	309	86.98
16	154	41.55	74	43.36	1163	155.06	337	51.83

The Schur complement based preconditioners again show their advantage for this test case.

5.4. Results for test case 4. We use a distributed FGMRES solver and a fixed 3D global grid with $101 \times 101 \times 101$=1,030,301 points. The following results are obtained on the Linux cluster:

	Schur$_1$		*Schur*$_2$		*Block*$_1$		*Block*$_2$	
P	#itr	time	#itr	time	#itr	time	#itr	time
2	91	466.73	116	1332.34	165	475.84	129	436.84
4	93	251.02	115	794.15	166	257.60	132	224.83
8	93	139.57	114	473.67	164	139.88	137	131.49
16	95	85.91	113	322.01	168	80.30	148	73.45

For this 3D test case, all the preconditioners produce quite stable iteration counts. However, *Block*$_2$ seems to have the best performance with respect to the overall computational performance.

5.5. Results for test case 5. We use a distributed FGMRES solver and a fixed 2D global grid with 1001×1001=1,002,001 points. The following results are obtained on the Linux cluster:

	Schur$_1$		*Schur*$_2$		*Block*$_1$		*Block*$_2$	
P	#itr	time	#itr	time	#itr	time	#itr	time
2	11	36.84	27	150.88	285	428.94	29	64.36
4	17	29.16	29	94.71	291	227.30	54	61.31
8	14	12.22	29	53.77	297	131.66	38	21.87
16	16	8.15	30	30.69	298	75.53	40	14.46

We see that the *Schur*$_1$ preconditioner is a clear "winner" in the overall computational performance. Low iteration counts for $P = 32$ and $P = 64$ that are obtained on the Origin 3800 machine (see the table below) also seem to support the same observation.

	Schur$_1$		*Schur*$_2$		*Block*$_1$		*Block*$_2$	
P	#itr	time	#itr	time	#itr	time	#itr	time
8	15	13.96	27	35.72	296	75.30	32	55.10
16	17	25.13	not converged		297	49.25	39	28.35
32	20	21.97	30	20.11	318	38.63	78	19.57
64	23	13.93	30	13.94	309	13.13	92	18.19

Again, some of the wall-clock time measurements show traces of strong influence of heavy work load on the Origin 3800 machine. We remark that we "gave up" on *Schur*$_2$ when it did not help the FGMRES solver to converge for $P = 16$ on the Origin 3800 machine. This seems to be caused by an unfortunate grid partitioning result, since *Schur*$_2$ works fine on the Linux cluster for $P = 16$.

5.6. Results for test case 6. We use a distributed FGMRES solver and a fixed global curvilinear structured grid with 481×481 grid points, where each grid point is associated with two unknowns. The following results are obtained on the Linux cluster:

	Schur$_1$		*Schur*$_2$	
P	#itr	time	#itr	time
2	302	889.84	238	1224.90
4	556	840.66	193	544.26
8	724	572.28	280	404.59
16	620	280.70	299	255.06

This test case is clearly the "toughest" for the parallel algebraic preconditioners. The *Block*$_1$ and *Block*$_2$ preconditioners have trouble producing satisfactory convergence.

5.7. Scalability and grid resolution. One question that can be asked is: how well do the parallel algebraic preconditioners behave with respect to the grid resolution? To answer this question, we coarsen the global computational grid twice for both Test Case 1 and 2. The measurements obtained on the Linux cluster are listed in the following two tables. We remark that we use the same FGMRES solver and the same fixed convergence criterion, see Section 4.3.

Test Case 1; # global grid points: 251×251								
	Schur$_1$		*Schur*$_2$		*Block*$_1$		*Block*$_2$	
P	#itr	time	#itr	time	#itr	time	#itr	time
2	33	6.92	21	7.23	250	25.82	89	12.05
4	36	4.71	22	6.02	307	16.04	119	9.16
8	40	3.12	21	5.35	319	9.59	163	6.82
16	43	2.49	23	6.39	291	6.49	180	5.29
Test Case 1; # global grid points: 501×501								
	Schur$_1$		*Schur*$_2$		*Block*$_1$		*Block*$_2$	
P	#itr	time	#itr	time	#itr	time	#itr	time
2	50	41.73	45	56.58	727	251.49	148	80.30
4	54	26.46	46	34.20	424	83.29	212	64.90
8	59	16.33	45	18.16	669	76.93	259	43.71
16	71	13.21	46	19.69	491	31.82	291	27.22

Test Case 2; # global grid points: $26 \times 26 \times 26$								
	Schur$_1$		*Schur*$_2$		*Block*$_1$		*Block*$_2$	
P	#itr	time	#itr	time	#itr	time	#itr	time
2	15	1.35	17	2.82	23	1.39	21	1.15
4	14	0.91	16	3.37	26	0.95	25	0.83
8	14	0.68	14	2.12	26	0.63	26	0.61
16	15	0.66	13	4.00	29	0.59	28	0.52
Test Case 2; # global grid points: $51 \times 51 \times 51$								
	Schur$_1$		*Schur*$_2$		*Block*$_1$		*Block*$_2$	
P	#itr	time	#itr	time	#itr	time	#itr	time
2	26	15.50	31	37.39	45	18.36	42	16.84
4	26	9.50	30	24.49	51	11.17	46	10.23
8	26	5.95	28	15.07	53	7.09	51	6.23
16	26	4.14	28	14.22	55	4.13	54	4.07

We observe that, for both Test Case 1 and 2, a higher grid resolution means more iterations of the distributed FGMRES solver for all the four parallel algebraic preconditioners.

5.8. Effect of the subdomain shape. We have so far always used a general partitioning scheme that does not produce subdomains in the shape of rectangles or boxes, even if the global computational grid is uniform. Do we get more rapid convergence if the subdomains are of simple shapes? To answer this question, we try Test Case 2 again. This time we use a simple grid partitioning scheme that produces the subdomains as small boxes. The resulting FGMRES iteration counts and wall-clock time measurements, which are obtained on the Linux cluster for $P = 16$, are listed in the following table. We also compare them with the earlier measurements obtained by using a general grid partitioning scheme.

	Schur$_1$		*Schur*$_2$		*Block*$_1$		*Block*$_2$	
P	#itr	time	#itr	time	#itr	time	#itr	time
Test Case 2; general grid partitioning								
16	61	53.60	69	196.27	110	50.77	93	45.21
Test Case 2; simple grid partitioning								
16	63	50.91	70	193.81	109	47.79	93	43.01

We observe that the change in iteration counts is hardly noticeable. However, the simple grid partitioning scheme produces better balanced subdomains, such that the communication overhead is lower. This explains the slightly better wall-clock time measurements. However, we should remember that such a simple grid partitioning is *only* applicable to global computational grids in the shape of rectangles or boxes.

5.9. Comparison with additive Schwarz. It may be argued that an additive Schwarz preconditioner (see e.g. [11]) is an algebraic block preconditioner. But we choose to view additive Schwarz preconditioners differently, because they normally use more than the minimum amount of overlap (see Section 1.1). In addition, their convergence depends greatly on the so-called *coarse grid corrections* (CGCs), which require an extra discretization on another global grid with very low grid resolution.

In the table below, we report the number of GMRES iterations and wall-clock time needed by an additive Schwarz preconditioner on the Linux cluster for Test Case 1. We remark that we use a simple partitioning scheme to produce subdomains as small rectangles. The amount of overlap in both x- and y-direction is about 5% of the side length of the subdomains. The global coarse grid has a fixed size: 5×17, and the coarse grid level linear system is solved by Gaussian elimination. The subdomain solver in use is one Conjugate Gradient (see e.g. [7]) iteration accelerated by a special FFT-based preconditioner.

Test Case 1; global grid: 1001×1001				
	Additive Schwarz without CGCs		*Additive Schwarz* with CGCs	
P	#itr	time	#itr	time
2	26	88.86	13	47.84
4	33	61.80	18	37.50
8	65	64.04	26	29.97
16	115	56.24	39	23.36

We see that, when CGCs are not used, this additive Schwarz preconditioner has a dangerously rapid growth of iteration counts. However, with the help of CGCs, the additive Schwarz preconditioner clearly converges faster than all the four parallel algebraic preconditioners.

6. Concluding Remarks. The coupling of pARMS with Diffpack has proved to be beneficial to enhancing convergence of the linear systems, which frequently arise in the applications considered by Diffpack. Our six test cases are of course insufficient for drawing any definitive conclusions on the general numerical behavior of the parallel algebraic preconditioners that have been considered in this paper. However, the following observations seem to hold:

- The *Schur*$_1$ preconditioner seems to be the best choice, with respect to the overall computational performance. It has quite stable iteration counts, which are somewhat independent of P. Moreover, it has an acceptable scalability with respect to processor numbers, due to the relatively small overhead associated with solving the global Schur complement system.

- The $Schur_2$ preconditioner has the most stable iteration counts with respect to P. This preconditioner is good at achieving satisfactory convergence, but not overall computational performance.
- The $Block_1$ and $Block_2$ preconditioners have very good scalability of parallel performance, if we consider the computational cost per iteration with respect to P. However, $Block_1$ has often very slow convergence.
- None of the four parallel algebraic preconditioners is able to produce iteration counts that are independent of the grid resolution.
- All the four parallel algebraic preconditioners are quite insensitive to the shape of subdomains.
- Parallel algebraic preconditioners normally have advantages such as ease of use and independence of underlying PDEs. However, better convergence may be achieved by preconditioners that utilize discretizations on additional computational grids, as shown in Section 5.9.

REFERENCES

[1] X. Cai and H. P. Langtangen. *Developing parallel object-oriented simulation codes in Diffpack.* In H.A. Mang, F.G. Rammerstorfer, J. Eberhardsteiner, editors, *Proceedings of Fifth World Congress on Computational Mechanics, Vienna, Austria, July 2002.*
[2] Diffpack Home Page: http://www.nobjects.com/.
[3] G. Karypis and V. Kumar. *Metis: Unstructured graph partitioning and sparse matrix ordering system.* Tech. Rep., Dept. of Computer Science, Univ. of Minnesota, 1995.
[4] H. P. Langtangen. *Computational Partial Differential Equations - Numerical Methods and Diffpack Programming.* Textbooks in Computational Science and Engineering. Springer Verlag, 2nd edition, 2003.
[5] Z. Li, Y. Saad, and M. Sosonkina. *pARMS: A parallel version of the algebraic recursive multilevel solver.* Tech. Rep. UMSI-2001-100, Minnesota Supercomputer Institute, 2001.
[6] pARMS Home Page: http://www-users.cs.umn.edu/~saad/software/pARMS.
[7] Y. Saad. *Iterative Methods for Sparse Linear Systems.* PWS publishing, New York, 1996.
[8] Y. Saad and M. Sosonkina. *Distributed Schur complement techniques for general sparse linear systems.* SIAM J. Sci. Comput. 21(4):1337–1356, 1999.
[9] Y. Saad and B. Suchomel. *ARMS: An algebraic recursive multilevel solver for general sparse linear systems.* Tech. Rep. umsi-99-107-REVIS, Minnesota Supercomputer Institute, 2001.
[10] Y. Saad and J. Zhang. *BILUM: Block versions of multi-elimination and multi-level ILU preconditioner for general sparse linear systems.* SIAM J. Sci. Comput. 20:2103–2121, 1999.
[11] B. Smith, P. Bjørstad, and W. Gropp. *Domain Decomposition: Parallel Multilevel Methods for Elliptic Partial Differential Equations.* Cambridge University Press, New York, 1996.

In: Parallel and Distributed Scientific and Engineering Computing ISBN 1-59033-956-8
Editor: Y. Pan and L.T. Yang, pp. 23-33

A MODEL REDUCTION WEB ENVIRONMENT FOR VERY LARGE LINEAR DYNAMICAL SYSTEMS*

PETER BENNER†, RAFAEL MAYO‡, ENRIQUE S. QUINTANA-ORTÍ‡ , AND GREGORIO QUINTANA-ORTÍ‡

Abstract. We describe a prototype web service for model reduction of very large-scale linear systems, with dimension in the order of millions of states, that includes a user-friendly interface designed so that the computation can be easily performed via the HTTP protocol. Access via a web browser isolates the user of the service from the complexities of installing and using the parallel model reduction codes and the maintenance of the hardware. In case the routines are found to be appropriate for the problem the user needs to solve, the library can be then downloaded and installed on the user's own computing resources.

This paper illustrates the major issues of the access procedure by means of graphical examples, and describes the structure and implementation of the remote model reduction service. The service is offered in a cluster of Linux machines.

Key words. Linear-time invariant systems, Model reduction, Web execution environment, Web-computing, Clusters

1. Introduction. The development of the Internet and its popularization via the world wide web (www) is producing a tremendous impact in our society. The www is nowadays employed to consult databases, retrieve documents, submit jobs to remote systems, and access a large number of services which is continuously growing. The extension of these services has recently reached the area of scientific computing in projects like NetSolve [4], LAPK (http://lapk3.hsc.usc.edu/lapk), the SLICOT Web Environment [16], NPACI (https://hotpa-ge.npaci.edu), CACTUS (http://www.cactuscode.org), and EOT-PACI (http://www.eot.org), among others. Many of these efforts can be generically classified as problem-solving environments or computational science portals [18]. A related, extensive survey of applications of web-computing and grid-computing can be consulted, e.g., in [10].

In this paper we further explore the www and the HTTP protocol as a means of offering an enhanced service for scientific computing to a certain cluster of the scientific and engineering community. Specifically, we offer a computational service for model reduction of large-scale linear systems, with potentially even millions of states, on a parallel cluster. The idea here is to provide an easy way for remote users to interact with the model reduction codes via the www so that the service becomes a demonstrator of the capabilities of the parallel model reduction library. Note that a usual case is that of a user with a problem that needs to be solved, who has to search for a likely solver (in the form of a code or a library), read the manuals, install the application (after having solved compatibility problems with the compiler, operating system, or even architecture), write the interface programs, and run it just to then discover that the code is not the appropriate one to solve his/her problem.

Thus, the main advantage of providing this service via the www is that the end-user remains completely isolated from the complexities of the software and the hardware system, and the maintenance of both. Then, in case the routines are evaluated as satisfactory by the user, the library itself can be downloaded and installed on any (parallel) architecture

*Peter Benner was supported by the DFG Research Center "Mathematics for key technologies" (FZT 86) in Berlin. Rafael Mayo, Enrique S. Quintana-Ortí, and Gregorio Quintana-Ortí were supported by the project CTDIA/2002/122 of the *Generalitat Valenciana* and the project PI-1B2001-14 of the *Fundació Caixa-Castelló/Bancaixa*.

†Institut für Mathematik, MA 4-5, Technische Universität Berlin, 10623 Berlin, Germany, benner@math.tu-berlin.de.

‡Depto. de Ingeniería y Ciencia de Computadores, Universidad Jaume I, 12.071 Castellón Spain, {mayo,quintana,gquintan}@icc.uji.es.

with MPI and the appropriate parallel numerical libraries (basically, BLAS, LAPACK, and ScaLAPACK [2, 9]).

The problem considered here, model reduction, is of fundamental importance in many modeling and control applications involving continuous linear time-invariant (LTI) dynamical systems in state-space form:

$$
\begin{array}{rclll}
\dot{x}(t) & = & Ax(t) + Bu(t), & t > 0, & x(0) = x^0, \\
y(t) & = & Cx(t) + Du(t), & t \geq 0.
\end{array}
\tag{1.1}
$$

Here, $A \in \mathbb{R}^{n \times n}$ is the state matrix, $B \in \mathbb{R}^{n \times m}$, $C \in \mathbb{R}^{p \times n}$, $D \in \mathbb{R}^{p \times m}$, $x^0 \in \mathbb{R}^n$ is the initial state of the system, and the number of states, n, is known as the state-space dimension (or the order) of the system. The transfer function matrix (TFM) associated with the system is defined by $G(s) = C(sI - A)^{-1}B + D$. Hereafter, we assume that A is stable, i.e., the spectrum of A is contained in the open left half plane. This implies that the system is stable, i.e., has no poles in the closed right half plane.

The model reduction problem consists in finding a reduced-order LTI system,

$$
\begin{array}{rclll}
\dot{\hat{x}}(t) & = & \hat{A}\hat{x}(t) + \hat{B}\hat{u}(t), & t > 0, & \hat{x}(0) = \hat{x}^0, \\
\hat{y}(t) & = & \hat{C}\hat{x}(t) + \hat{D}\hat{u}(t), & t \geq 0,
\end{array}
\tag{1.2}
$$

of order r, $r \ll n$, and associated TFM $\hat{G}(s) = \hat{C}(sI - \hat{A})^{-1}\hat{B} + \hat{D}$ which approximates $G(s)$. The reduced-order model can then replace the original high-order system in subsequent calculations including, e.g., the design of the controller [22], thus saving valuable hardware resources.

Model reduction of large-scale stable linear systems (n in the thousands) arises, among others, in control of large flexible mechanical structures or large power systems, and weather simulation (storm surge forecast and perturbation evolution); see, e.g., [11, 12, 13, 17, 23]. Very large-scale linear systems, with state-space dimension n as large as 10^6, are common in circuit simulation and VLSI design, air quality simulation, etc. [3]. These systems often present a sparse (unstructured or banded) state matrix A.

In general, model reduction methods for LTI systems with dense state matrices have a computational cost of $\mathcal{O}(n^3)$ floating-point arithmetic operations (flops) and require storage for $\mathcal{O}(n^2)$ numbers. While current desktop computers provide enough computational power to reduce models of order n in the hundreds using libraries like SLICOT[1] or the MATLAB control-related toolboxes, large-scale applications clearly require the use of advanced computing techniques. The approach proposed in PLiCMR[2] [7, 8] is to employ dense model reduction methods on parallel computers, thus allowing for larger problems to be reduced. Nevertheless, none of these approaches exploit nor preserve the sparsity of the state matrix and therefore the dimensions of the largest systems they can deal with is quite limited.

The model reduction approach considered in this paper is based on the so-called state-space truncation and requires, at a first stage, the solution of two large Lyapunov equations whose coefficient matrix is the state matrix of the system. These equations are solved via a low-rank iteration [20, 25] which only involves numerical computations such as the solution of linear systems and matrix-vector products. The success of these Lyapunov solvers relies in the use of efficient routines that exploit the sparsity of the coefficient matrix. Once the equations are solved, the reduced-order system is obtained using a slightly modified version of the balanced truncation (BT) method [7, 24], which only requires dense linear algebra operations on much smaller data matrices.

---

[1] Available from `http://www.win.tue.nl/niconet/NIC2/slicot.html`.

[2] Available from `http://spine.act.uji.es/~plicmr.html`.

The paper is structured as follows. In Section 2 we briefly revisit the methods for model reduction of very large linear systems, including the square-root BT method and the low-rank solvers for the Lyapunov equations arising in state-space truncation. The usage, structure, and implementation details of the web service are introduced in Section 3. There graphical examples are employed to illustrate the procedure to access the service. Concluding remarks and possible future extensions of the service follow in the final Section.

2. Model Reduction of Very Large Linear Systems.

2.1. The square-root BT method. Our routines are based on BT model reduction [21, 26, 27, 28]. BT belongs to the family of absolute error methods, which try to minimize $\|\Delta_a\|_\infty = \|G - \hat{G}\|_\infty$. Here, $\|G\|_\infty$ denotes the $\mathcal{L}_\infty$- or $\mathcal{H}_\infty$-norm of a stable, rational matrix function defined as

$$\|G\|_\infty = \operatorname*{ess\,sup}_{\omega \in \mathbb{R}} \sigma_{\max}(G(\jmath\omega)), \tag{2.1}$$

where $\jmath := \sqrt{-1}$ and $\sigma_{\max}(M)$ denotes the largest singular value of the matrix M. In the continuous-time case, a reduced-order model computed by BT approximates the original one well at high frequencies ($\omega \to \infty$), with a perfect match at $\omega = \infty$.

BT methods are strongly related to the controllability Gramian W_c and the observability Gramian W_o of the system (1.1), given by the solutions of two "coupled" Lyapunov matrix equations:

$$AW_c + W_cA^T + BB^T = 0, \tag{2.2}$$
$$A^TW_o + W_oA + C^TC = 0. \tag{2.3}$$

As the coefficient matrix in the equations, A, is assumed to be stable, W_c and W_o are positive semidefinite and therefore can be factored as $W_c = S^TS$ and $W_o = R^TR$. The factors S and R can be the *Cholesky factors* (square and triangular) of the Gramians or *full-rank factors* (possibly rectangular and full).

Efficient Lyapunov solvers that exploit the sparsity of the coefficient matrix A are described in the next subsection.

Consider now the singular value decomposition (SVD) of the product

$$SR^T = U\Sigma V^T = [\,U_1\ U_2\,]\begin{bmatrix} \Sigma_1 & \\ & \Sigma_2 \end{bmatrix}[\,V_1\ V_2\,]^T, \tag{2.4}$$

where U and V are orthogonal matrices, and $\Sigma = \operatorname{diag}(\sigma_1, \sigma_2, \ldots, \sigma_\ell)$ is a diagonal matrix containing the singular values of SR^T. Here, $\ell = \max\{s, r\}$, where $S \in \mathbb{R}^{s\times n}, R \in \mathbb{R}^{r\times n}$. The singular values $\sigma_1, \ldots, \sigma_\ell$ are known as the *Hankel singular values* of the system. If $\sigma_r > \sigma_{r+1} = 0$, then r is the state-space dimension of a minimal realization of the system.

Next, a reduced system of order r is determined by partitioning the diagonal matrix Σ into $\Sigma_1 = \operatorname{diag}(\sigma_1, \sigma_2, \ldots, \sigma_r)$ and $\Sigma_2 = \operatorname{diag}(\sigma_{r+1}, \sigma_{r+2}, \ldots, \sigma_\ell)$, so that, hopefully, a large gap exists between σ_r and σ_{r+1}. A conformal partition of U and V is induced by the partitioning of Σ.

The square-root BT method determines then the reduced-order model of order r as

$$\begin{array}{rcl} \hat{A} & = & T_lAT_r, \\ \hat{B} & = & T_lB, \\ \hat{C} & = & CT_r, \quad \text{and} \\ \hat{D} & = & D, \end{array} \tag{2.5}$$

with the projection matrices T_l and T_r given by

(2.6)
$$\begin{array}{rcl} T_l &=& \Sigma_1^{-1/2} V_1^T R \quad \text{and} \\ T_r &=& S^T U_1 \Sigma_1^{-1/2}. \end{array}$$

The realization of order r computed by the square-root BT algorithm satisfies the error bound

(2.7)
$$\|\Delta_a\|_\infty := \|G - \hat{G}\|_\infty \leq 2 \sum_{i=r+1}^{n} \sigma_i.$$

This allows an adaptive choice of the size of the reduced-order model if a given upper bound for the error is to be satisfied.

2.2. Low rank solution of Lyapunov equations. In this subsection we revisit the Lyapunov solvers introduced in [20, 25]. These iterative algorithms benefit from the usual low-rank property of the right-hand side matrix to provide low-rank approximations to a Cholesky or full-rank factor of the solution matrix. These approximations can reliably substitute S and R in the computation of (2.4) and (2.6).

Specifically, given an "l–cyclic" set of (complex) shift parameters $\{p_1, p_2, \ldots\}$, $p_k = \alpha_k + \beta_k \jmath$, such that $p_k = p_{k+l}$, the cyclic *low-rank alternating direction implicit* (LR-ADI) iteration proposed in [25] can be reformulated as follows:

(2.8)
$$\begin{array}{rcl} V_0 &=& (A + p_1 I_n)^{-1} B, \\ S_0 &=& \sqrt{-2\,\alpha_1}\; V_0, \\ V_{k+1} &=& V_k - \delta_k (A + p_{k+1} I_n)^{-1} V_k, \\ S_{k+1} &=& [S_k \;,\; \gamma_k V_{k+1}]\,, \end{array}$$

where $\gamma_k = \sqrt{\alpha_{k+1}/\alpha_k}$, $\delta_k = p_{k+1} + \overline{p_k}$, $\overline{p_k}$ is the conjugate of p_k, and I_n denotes the identity matrix of order n. On convergence, after $k_{\max}$ iterations, a low-rank matrix $\tilde{S}$ of order $n \times k_{\max} m$ is computed such that $\tilde{S}\tilde{S}^T$ approximates $W_c = S^T S$. An analogous iteration provides a low-rank approximation $\tilde{R}$ of R. The use of direct linear system solvers [15] (based, e.g., on the LU or Cholesky factorization) here is appealing as the same coefficient matrix is involved in iterations k and $k+l$. Therefore, the computed factorization can be re-used several times as long as sufficient workspace is available to store l (sparse) factorizations.

The performance of iteration (2.8) strongly depends on the selection of the shift parameters. In practice, the set $\{p_1, p_2, \ldots, p_l\}$ should be chosen so that it is closed under complex conjugation (i.e., if p_k is a selected shift parameter, so is $\overline{p_k}$). In case the eigenvalues of A are real, the optimal parameters can be computed explicitly [30, 31]. Otherwise, an optimal solution is not known. A heuristic procedure is proposed in [25] to compute parameters by approximating the largest eigenvalues of A and A^{-1}. The procedure is based on an Arnoldi iteration [19] involving A and A^{-1}. For further details on the convergence of the LR-ADI iteration and the properties of the heuristic selection procedure, see [25]. Preliminary results of a parallel Lyapunov equation solver based on the LR-ADI method are reported in [5].

It should be emphasized that, though mathematically equivalent, the methods just described for solving (2.2)-(2.3) and (2.4) significantly differ from standard methods used in the MATLAB toolboxes or SLICOT [29]. First, the proposed LR-ADI iteration for the solution of the coupled Lyapunov equation exploits the sparsity in the coefficient matrix. Besides, as we are using low-rank approximations to the full-rank or Cholesky factors, the computation of the SVD in (2.4) is usually much more efficient: instead of a computational cost of $\mathcal{O}(n^3)$ when using the Cholesky factors, this approach leads to an $\mathcal{O}(k_{\max}^2 \cdot m \cdot p \cdot n)$ cost where, in model reduction, often $m, p \ll n$; see [7]. This latter advantage is shared by the routines in our dense parallel model reduction library PLiCMR [7, 8]. However, PLiCMR is not able to exploit the sparsity of the coefficient matrix.

2.3. Parallelization. The LR-ADI iteration and the computation of the acceleration shifts basically require linear algebra operations like matrix-vector products and the solution of linear systems. Our approach for dealing with these matrix operations is based on the use of parallel linear algebra libraries. Specifically, in case sparse matrices are involved, we propose to employ codes like SuperLU [14] or MUMPS [1] to compute LU-like factorizations of the matrices $A + p_k I_n$ and keep the factors if sufficient storage is available. In case the coefficient matrix is dense or banded we use the LU factorization routines in the parallel dense linear algebra library like ScaLAPACK [9]. Note that for full dense coefficient matrices the methods in PLiCMR (see [8] for a description of the library and [6] for a web environment similar to the one described here) are to be preferred as the Lyapunov equation solvers used there have quadratic convergence rate as opposed to (super-)linear convergence of the ADI method at a comparable cost of the remaining computational steps.

Figure 2.1 shows the relation between our library of methods for model reduction, SpaRed, and the underlying parallel linear algebra libraries. All the model reduction codes in the library are written using the C programming language following an approach that could be roughly classified as object-oriented.

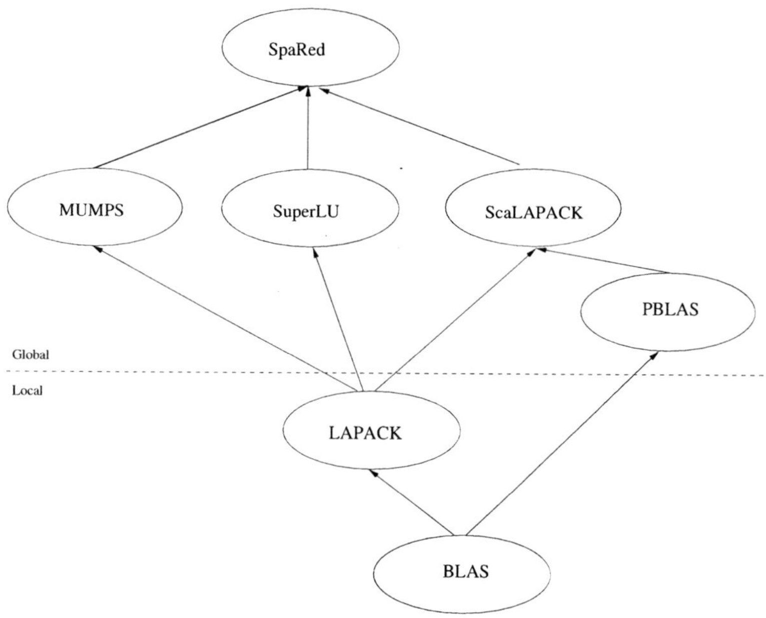

FIG. 2.1. *SpaRed and the underlying libraries.*

3. Web Service. In this section we describe both the access procedure and the structure and implementation of the prototype service for model reduction via the www. This service is provided on a cluster of computers, running the Linux (Suse 7.0) operating system, at the University Jaume I.

3.1. Accessing the service. Our computational web service for model reduction is provided at http://spine.act.uji.es/~plicmr/SpaRedW3/SpaRedW3.html. On entry (see Figure 3.1), the user is offered the possibility of registering to access the service, perform model reduction on a given system, check the status of submitted jobs, obtain information on the cluster load, etc.

The actual access to the service is performed through the job submission form (see Figure 3.2). In this form the user is requested to specify the parameters of the job, which can be grouped as follows:

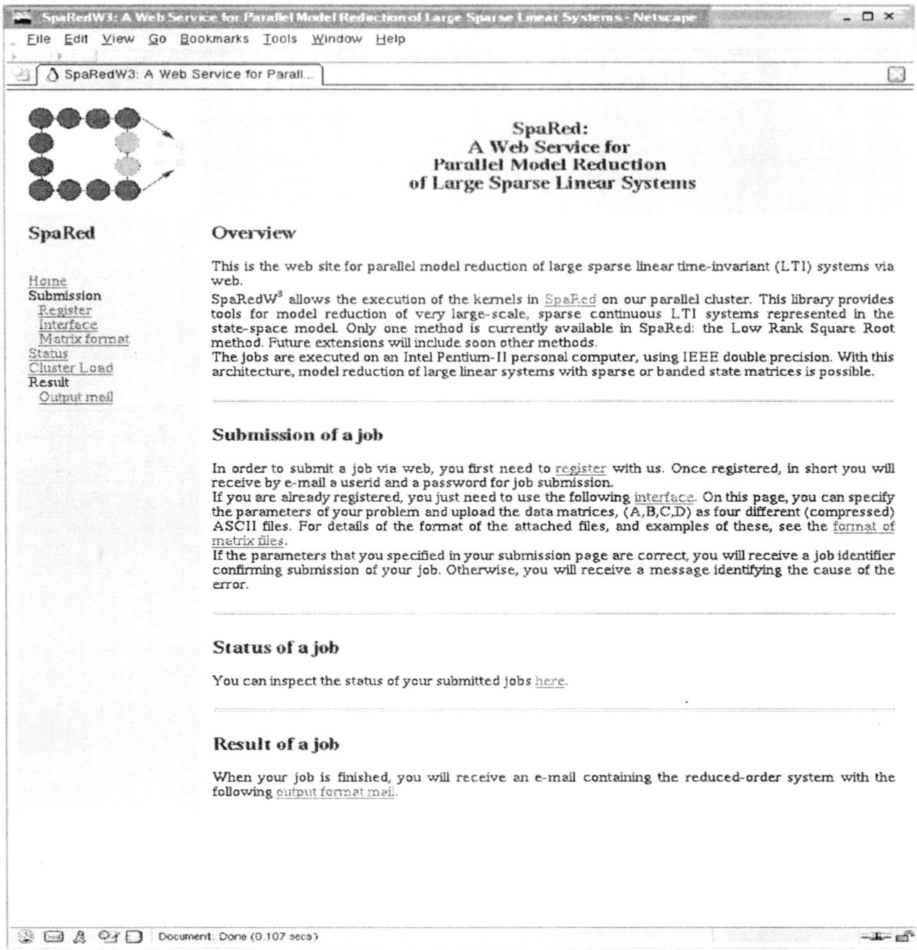

FIG. 3.1. *Access to the parallel model reduction service.*

- Validation of access: An identifier (parameter 1 in the job submission form or, for short, P1) and a password (P2), both provided via e-mail on registration, allow identification of the responsible of the requests. This identification is merely for statistical purposes as no real encryption of these data is performed.
- System parameters: The model dimensions, n, m, and p (P6, P7, and P8, respectively), and the type of matrix entries (P15), real or complex; also, the class of state matrix (P14) which, in the current implementation of the service, can be dense, symmetric/unsymmetric banded, or sparse.
- Reduced-order system parameters: Here the user is given the choice (P5) to either select a fixed order r for the reduced system (P9), or allow the order to be automatically determined using tolerance thresholds (P10 and P11).
- Numerical methods: Only the low rank square-root method (P3), a variant of the BT method that solves the Lyapunov equations using the LR-ADI iteration, is currently available. Future extensions will also provide the possibility of selecting the solver for the linear systems of equations, depending on the properties of the state matrix. Notice that this is specially interesting when sparse matrices are involved, as the performance of the model reduction methods strongly depends on the linear system solver that is selected [15].

- Execution environment: The recommended number of nodes of the cluster to participate in the execution of the job (P12), and the e-mail address (P16) where the results should be returned to.
- Data: The files with the system matrices and the compression tool (P13) employed for their preprocessing.

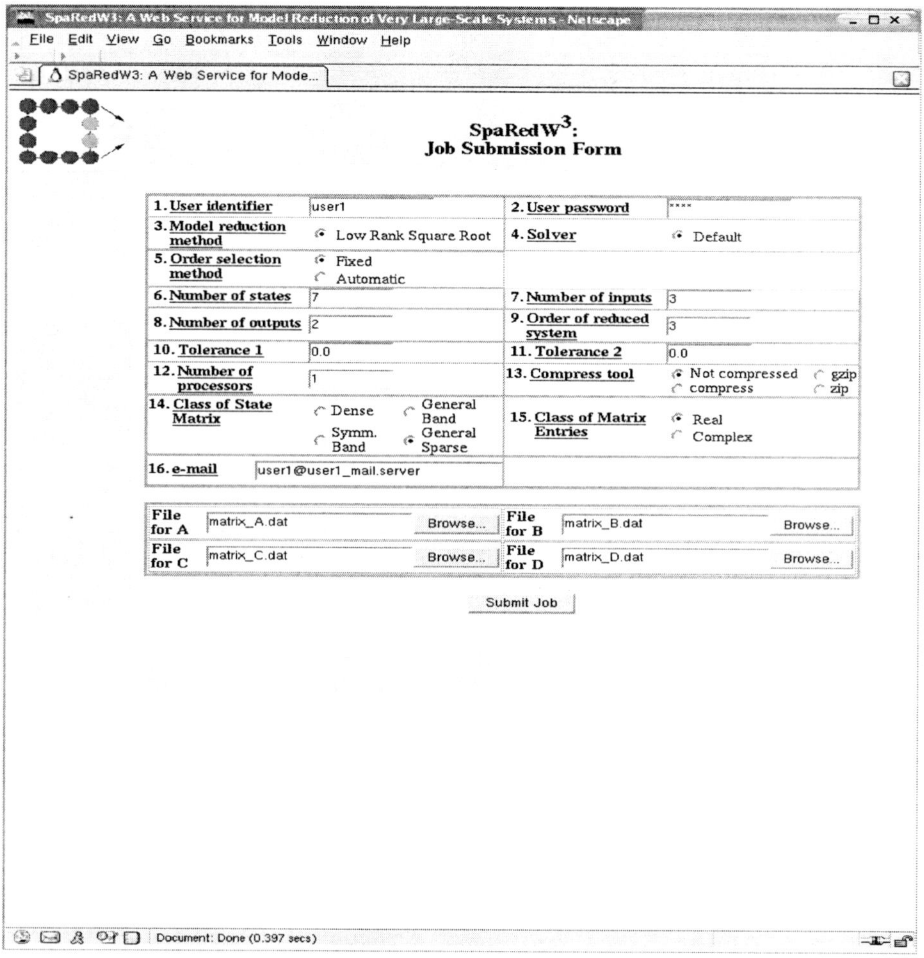

FIG. 3.2. *Job submission form.*

The same form can be used to upload the data matrices from the local file system. The structure of the file containing the data depends on the class of the matrix. Thus, column-major order is compulsory for all but the sparse matrices; files for banded matrices only include the diagonals within the band; files for symmetric matrices only contain the upper triangular part; and sparse matrices are stored in compressed column (or Harwell-Boeing) format [15]. As an example, in Figure 3.3 we show the contents of a file containing a square matrix of order $n = 6$ with $nnz = 4$ non-zero entries in sparse format:

$$\begin{bmatrix} -0.42 & 0 & 0 & 0 & 0 & 0 \\ 0 & 0 & 0.1 & 0 & 0 & 0 \\ 0 & 0 & 0 & 0 & 0 & 0 \\ 0 & -0.36 & -0.58 & 0 & 0 & 0 \\ 0 & 0 & 0 & 0 & 0 & 0 \\ 0 & 0 & 0 & 0 & 0 & 0 \end{bmatrix} \tag{3.1}$$

In particular, the first line of the file specifies the value of *nnz*. This is followed by the matrix stored using the compressed column format: the $n + 1$ entries of vector `colptr`, the *nnz* entries of vector `rowind`, and the *nnz* entries of the matrix. The indices of both vectors start at zero following the convention of the C programming language.

```
    4
    0
    1
    2
    2
    4
    4
    4
    0
    1
    3
    3
-4.2e-01
 1.0e-01
-3.6e-01
-5.8e-01
```

FIG. 3.3. *Contents of a file specifying the matrix in (3.1) in sparse format.*

```
1.  JOB ID. = 00011
    (METHOD='LRSR', SOLVER='default',
     ORDSEL='F', N=7, M=3, P=2, NR=3,
     TOL1=0.0, TOL2=0.0,
     NP=1, COMPRESS='NO')
2.  NR = 3
3.  NHSV = 3
4.  NP = 1
5.  TIME = 0.3507E+1
6.  INFO = 0
```

FIG. 3.4. *Text of an e-mail with the results of a job submission.*

In order to reduce the size of the data files that need to be transfered, compressed data files using several standard compression tools are accepted (e.g., `zip` and `gzip`).

The results of the execution are returned via e-mail, with the matrices of the reduced system as attached files (compressed with the same tool that was used on the data files). The text of the e-mail contains a few lines with the following data:

- The job identifier that was assigned to the user's job after submission. This parameter is followed by a compact description of the parameters of the job.
- The order of the resulting reduced-order system.
- The number of computed Hankel singular values.
- The number of processors that were used to execute the job.
- The wall-time required to execute the job.
- The info result (or status) from the execution of the routine.

Figure 3.4 shows an example of the text of the e-mail that is returned to the user after the job is finished.

Our model reduction service is connectionless in that any data that is submitted to the system is only stored while the reduction of the system is being performed and until the response is returned to the user. A connection-oriented (or session-oriented) service presents some advantages: for instance, the system could keep the user's data, allowing thus to perform interactive model reduction more efficiently (the data only needs to be sent once and remains stored in the system as long as the session is open). This is the approach adopted, e.g., in [16]. However, this translates much of the burden of the client-server (user-web service) interaction to the server side, apart from leading to much more complex failure recovery. Therefore, we prefer the connectionless approach, as the goal of the web service is still to serve as a rapid testbed of our parallel model reduction routines.

3.2. Structure and implementation. The model reduction web server is composed of several PHP programs and the PBS (portable batch system) job control system. In the previous implementation, the service was accessed via a set of CGI programs, written in a shell script programming language. In the current version the CGI programs have been replaced by PHP codes. The web server includes a management system so that job requests are processed using no external procedures, as was necessary in the CGI-based variant.

Thus, the job submission form includes PHP code that is directly interpreted by the web server. The code is in charge of validating the data of the request and, in case the request is correct, create a pair of files necessary for job submission: a text file with the definition of the job parameters, and a submission shell-script specifying the number of nodes to participate in the execution and the path of executable program and data files. Next, the job is submitted to the job management system that is controlled by PBS.

From then on it is the responsibility of PBS to monitor the execution of the job. This queuing system consists of a server process which is executed in the cluster server and a client process running in each node of the cluster. The scheduler determines when a job begins its execution in the cluster using a FIFO strategy. The number of actual jobs that can be simultaneously in execution in the cluster is limited by the number of available nodes, due to the exclusive use application processes make of the Myrinet network interface cards. The client processes are in charge of receiving and executing job requests and also keep the PBS server informed of the current status of the node (basically, down, idle, or busy),

The submission shell-script maintains information on the actions that are to be performed in response to the user request when the job is finished. This code is implemented in PHP and is responsible for locating the results, composing an e-mail with those data, and sending back the response. Both the parameters of the job submission (except for the data matrices) and the results of the execution are sent as part of this message.

Figure 3.5 summarizes the actors and actions of the web service.

4. Concluding remarks and future work. We have described a web service for parallel model reduction of very large linear systems. By providing a remote access, the end-user is given a computational tool to reduce large-scale systems and/or to test the numerical reliability of the reduced-order models produced via these methods. Moreover, in case the methods are found to be appropriate for the problems to be solved, the parallel library can be then downloaded and installed on any parallel platform with the appropriate underlying libraries.

Future extensions of this work will include the estimation of the absolute error $\|\Delta_a\|_\infty$ as part of the reduction procedure, the possibility of selecting among different linear system solvers and/or new state-space truncation methods for model reduction, the availability of the model reduction routines via an RPC interface (like, e.g, in NetSolve), and the development of a connection-oriented service, capable of storing the user data for efficient interactive model reduction.

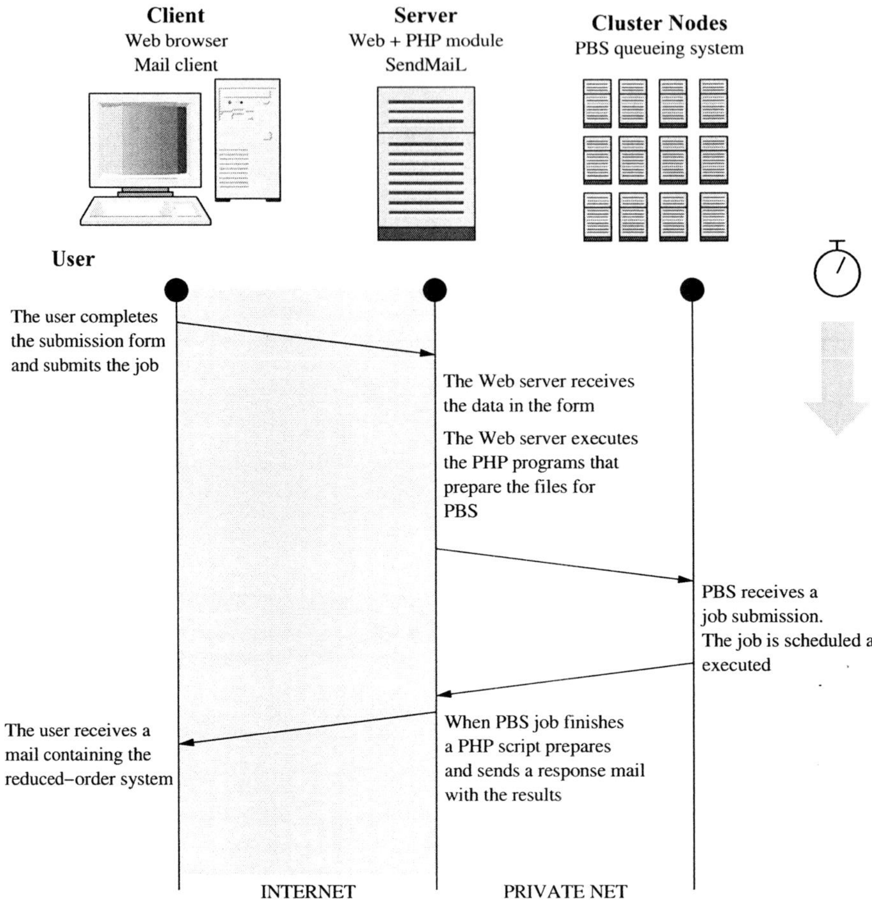

FIG. 3.5. *Actors and actions involved in processing a service request for model reduction.*

REFERENCES

[1] P. Amestoy, I. Duff, J. Koster, and J.-Y. L'Excellent, *MUMPS: a general purpose distributed memory sparse solver*, in Proc. PARA2000, 5th International Workshop on Applied Parallel Computing, 2000, pp. 122–131.

[2] E. Anderson, Z. Bai, C. Bischof, J. Demmel, J. Dongarra, J. Du Croz, A. Greenbaum, S. Hammarling, A. McKenney, and D. Sorensen, *LAPACK Users' Guide*, SIAM, Philadelphia, PA, third ed., 1999.

[3] A. Antoulas, *Lectures on the Approximation of Large-Scale Dynamical Systems*, SIAM Publications, Philadelphia, PA, to appear.

[4] D. Arnold, S. Agrawal, L. Blackford, J. Dongarra, M. Miller, S. Vahdiyar, K. Sagi, and Z. Shi, *Users's guide to NetSolve*, Tech. Report UT-CS-01-467, University of Tennessee at Knoxville, Computer Science Dept., Knoxville, TN, 2001. Available from `http://icl.cs.utk.edu/netsolve`.

[5] R. Badía, P. Benner, R. Mayo, and E. Quintana-Ortí, *Solving large sparse Lyapunov equations on parallel computers*, in Euro-Par 2002 – Parallel Processing, B. Monien and R. Feldmann, eds., no. 2400 in Lecture Notes in Computer Science, Springer-Verlag, Berlin, Heidelberg, New York, 2002, pp. 687–690.

[6] P. Benner, R. Mayo, E. Quintana, and G. Quintana-Ortí, *Enhanced services for remote model reduction of large-scale dense linear systems*, in PARA'02 Conference on Applied Parallel Computing, Espoo (Finland), 2002, J. Fagerholm, J. Haataja, J. Järvinen, M. Lyly, P. Raback, and V. Savolainen, eds., no. 2367 in Lecture Notes in Computer Science, Springer-Verlag, Berlin,

Heidelberg, New York, 2002, pp. 329–338.
[7] P. Benner, E. S. Quintana-Ortí, and G. Quintana-Ortí, *Balanced truncation model reduction of large-scale dense systems on parallel computers*, Math. Comput. Model. Dyn. Syst., 6 (2000), pp. 383–405.
[8] ———, *State-space truncation methods for parallel model reduction of large-scale systems*, Parallel Computing, to appear.
[9] L. Blackford, J. Choi, A. Cleary, E. D'Azevedo, J. Demmel, I. Dhillon, J. Dongarra, S. Hammarling, G. Henry, A. Petitet, K. Stanley, D. Walker, and R. Whaley, *ScaLAPACK Users' Guide*, SIAM, Philadelphia, PA, 1997.
[10] R. Buyya, *High performance cluster computing: Programming and applications*, Prentice-Hall, Upper Saddle River, NJ, 1999.
[11] Y. Chahlaoui and P. Van Dooren, *A collection of benchmark examples for model reduction of linear time invariant dynamical systems*, SLICOT Working Note 2002–2, Feb. 2002. Available from `http://www.win.tue.nl/niconet/NIC2/reports.html`.
[12] J. Cheng, G. Ianculescu, C. Kenney, A. Laub, and P. M. Papadopoulos, *Control-structure interaction for space station solar dynamic power module*, IEEE Control Systems, (1992), pp. 4–13.
[13] P. Chu, B. Wie, B. Gretz, and C. Plescia, *Approach to large space structure control system design using traditional tools*, AIAA J. Guidance, Control, and Dynamics, 13 (1990), pp. 874–880.
[14] J. Demmel, J. Gilbert, and X. Li, *SuperLU User's Guide*. Available from `http://www.nersc.gov/~xiaoye/SuperLU.html`.
[15] I. Duff, A. Erisman, and J. Reid, *Direct methods for sparse matrices*, Oxford Science Publications, Oxford, UK, 1993.
[16] E. Elmroth, P. Johansson, B. Kågström, and D. Kressner, *A Web computing environment for the SLICOT library*, SLICOT Working Note 2001–2, `http://www.win.tue.nl/niconet/`, June 2001.
[17] L. Fortuna, G. Nummari, and A. Gallo, *Model Order Reduction Techniques with Applications in Electrical Engineering*, Springer-Verlag, 1992.
[18] G. Fox, *Introduction to Web computing*, Computing in Science & Engineering, 3 (2001).
[19] G. Golub and C. Van Loan, *Matrix Computations*, Johns Hopkins University Press, Baltimore, third ed., 1996.
[20] J.-R. Li and J. White, *Low rank solution of Lyapunov equations*, SIAM J. Matrix Anal. Appl., 24 (2002), pp. 260–280.
[21] B. Moore, *Principal component analysis in linear systems: Controllability, observability, and model reduction*, IEEE Trans. Automat. Control, AC-26 (1981), pp. 17–32.
[22] G. Obinata and B. Anderson, *Model Reduction for Control System Design*, Communications and Control Engineering Series, Springer-Verlag, London, UK, 2001.
[23] C. Paul, *Analysis of Multiconductor Transmission Lines*, Wiley–Interscience, Singapur, 1994.
[24] T. Penzl, *Algorithms for model reduction of large dynamical systems*, Tech. Report SFB393/99-40, Sonderforschungsbereich 393 *Numerische Simulation auf massiv parallelen Rechnern*, TU Chemnitz, 09107 Chemnitz, FRG, 1999. Available from `http://www.tu-chemnitz.de/sfb393/sfb99pr.html`.
[25] ———, *A cyclic low rank Smith method for large sparse Lyapunov equations*, SIAM J. Sci. Comput., 21 (2000), pp. 1401–1418.
[26] M. Safonov and R. Chiang, *A Schur method for balanced-truncation model reduction*, IEEE Trans. Automat. Control, AC–34 (1989), pp. 729–733.
[27] M. Tombs and I. Postlethwaite, *Truncated balanced realization of a stable non-minimal state-space system*, Internat. J. Control, 46 (1987), pp. 1319–1330.
[28] A. Varga, *Efficient minimal realization procedure based on balancing*, in Prepr. of the IMACS Symp. on Modelling and Control of Technological Systems, vol. 2, 1991, pp. 42–47.
[29] ———, *Model reduction software in the SLICOT library*, in Applied and Computational Control, Signals, and Circuits, B. Datta, ed., vol. 629 of The Kluwer International Series in Engineering and Computer Science, Kluwer Academic Publishers, Boston, MA, 2001, pp. 239–282.
[30] E. Wachspress, *The ADI model problem*, 1995. Available from the author.
[31] ———, *ADI iteration parameters for the Sylvester equation*, 2000. Available from the author.

In: Parallel and Distributed Scientific and Engineering Computing ISBN 1-59033-956-8
Editor: Y. Pan and L.T. Yang, pp. 35-49

IMPLEMENTATION OF MULTIPLE-PRECISION PARALLEL DIVISION AND SQUARE ROOT ON DISTRIBUTED-MEMORY PARALLEL COMPUTERS

DAISUKE TAKAHASHI*

Abstract. We present efficient parallel algorithms for multiple-precision division and square root operations of more than several million decimal digits on distributed-memory parallel computers. It is well known that such operations can be reduced to multiple-precision addition, subtraction, and multiplication by using Newton iteration. In this paper, a parallel implementation of *floating-point real* FFT-based multiplication is used because a key operation in fast multiple-precision arithmetic is multiplication. We also parallelized an operation for releasing propagated carries and borrows in multiple-precision addition, subtraction, and multiplication. More than 206 billion decimal digits of π were computed on a Hitachi SR8000 distributed-memory parallel computer (128 nodes, 1 TFLOPS peak performance) with a computing elapsed time of 83 hours 28 minutes which includes the time for verification.

Key words. Multiple-precision arithmetic, Fast Fourier transform, Newton iteration, Distributed memory parallel computers

1. Introduction. Several software packages are available for multiple-precision computation [7, 8, 25, 3, 14]. At present, GNU MP [14] is probably the most widely used package due to its greater functionality and efficiency. Smith offers a similar package, featuring improved performance for certain transcendental functions [25].

Another package that is currently available is MPFUN, by Bailey [3]. One of the key features of the MPFUN package is that it is optimized for vector supercomputers and RISC processors.

In order to perform high-speed multiple-precision calculations, vector processing oriented implementations have been proposed [16, 8, 3]. However, the processing speed and the size of the main memory of vector computers are becoming saturated. Therefore, parallel processing by a distributed-memory parallel computer is proposed as one of the solutions for fast multiple-precision calculations.

The computation time of multiple-precision division and square root operations is considerably longer than that of addition, subtraction, or multiplication. There are a number of methods to perform division and square root operations [18, 19]. It is well known that multiple-precision division and square root operations can be reduced to multiple-precision addition, subtraction, and multiplication by using Newton iteration [19]. This scheme requires $O(M(n))$ operations, where $M(n)$ is the number of operations for an n-digit multiplication.

Parallel implementation of multiple-precision arithmetic on a shared-memory machine was reported by Weber [27]. Weber modified the MPFUN package [3] to run in parallel on a shared-memory multiprocessor. However, a complete solution of the sequential bottleneck in the normalization of the result (i.e. carry/borrow propagation) is not presented in that paper, nor are multiple-precision division and square root operations discussed therein.

Parallel implementation of Karatsuba's multiplication algorithm [17, 19] was proposed by Cesari and Maeder [9] on a distributed-memory parallel computer. Karatsuba's algorithm is known as the $O(n^{\log_2 3})$ multiplication algorithm.

However, multiple-precision multiplication of n-digit numbers can be performed in $O(n \log n \log\log n)$ operations by using the Schönhage-Strassen algorithm [24], which is based on the fast Fourier transform (FFT) [11].

*Institute of Information Sciences and Electronics, University of Tsukuba, 1-1-1 Tennodai, Tsukuba, Ibaraki 305-8573, Japan (daisuke@is.tsukuba.ac.jp).

```
      SUBROUTINE SEQADD(IA,IB,IRADIX,N)
      INTEGER IA(N),IB(N)
      ICARRY=0
      DO I=N,2,-1
        ITEMP=IA(I)+IB(I)+ICARRY
        ICARRY=ITEMP/IRADIX
        IA(I)=ITEMP-ICARRY*IRADIX
      END DO
      IA(1)=IA(1)+IB(1)+ICARRY
      RETURN
      END
```

FIG. 1.1. *Multiple-precision sequential addition.*

```
      SUBROUTINE PARAADD(IA,IB,IC,IRADIX,N)
      INTEGER,DIMENSION(N) :: IA,IB,IC
      IA(1:N)=IA(1:N)+IB(1:N)
      DO WHILE (ANY(IA(2:N) .GE. IRADIX))
        IC(N)=0
        IC(1:N-1)=IA(2:N)/IRADIX
        IA(2:N)=IA(2:N)+IC(2:N)-IC(1:N-1)*IRADIX
        IA(1)=IA(1)+IC(1)
      END DO
      RETURN
      END
```

FIG. 1.2. *Multiple-precision parallel addition.*

In multiple-precision multiplication of several thousand decimal digits or more, FFT-based multiplication is the fastest method. FFT-based multiplication algorithms are known to be good candidates for parallel implementation.

Fagin [13] used the Fermat number transform (FNT) [1] for large integer multiplication on the Connection Machine CM-2. FNT uses many modulo operations, which are slow due to the integer division process. Thus, we used *floating-point real* FFT-based multiplication for multiple-precision multiplication on distributed-memory parallel computers.

Parallel computation of $\sqrt{2}$ up to 1 million decimal digits was performed by Char et al. [10] on a network of workstations. However, multiple-precision parallel division was not presented in this paper, and a parallel version of Karatsuba's multiplication algorithm was used.

Section 2 describes the parallelization of multiple-precision addition, subtraction, and multiplication by a single-precision integer. Section 3 describes the parallelization of multiple-precision multiplications. Section 4 describes the parallelization of multiple-precision by a single-precision integer. Section 5 describes the parallelization of multiple-precision division and square root operations. Section 6 presents the experimental results. Section 7 describes the calculation of π to 206, 158, 430, 000 decimal digits on a Hitachi SR8000. We provide some concluding remarks in section 8.

2. Parallelization of Multiple-Precision Addition, Subtraction, and Multiplication by Single-Precision Integer. The arithmetic operation counts for n-digit multiple-precision sequential additions, subtractions, and multiplications by a single-precision integers is clearly $O(n)$. However, releasing the carries and borrows in these operations is a major factor po-

```
      SUBROUTINE SKIPNORM(IX,IC,IRADIX,N)
      INTEGER,DIMENSION(N) :: IX,IC
      DO WHILE (ANY(IX(2:N) .GT. IRADIX))
        IC(N)=0
        IC(1:N-1)=IX(2:N)/IRADIX
        IX(2:N)=IX(2:N)+IC(2:N)-IC(1:N-1)*IRADIX
        IX(1)=IX(1)+IC(1)
      END DO
      DO WHILE (ANY(IX(2:N) .EQ. IRADIX))
        IE=1
        DO I=2,N
          IF (IX(I) .EQ. IRADIX) IE=I
        END DO
        IS=1
        DO I=2,IE-1
          IF (IX(I) .LT. IRADIX-1) IS=I
        END DO
        IX(IS)=IX(IS)+1
        IX(IS+1:IE-1)=IX(IS+1:IE-1)-(IRADIX-1)
        IX(IE)=IX(IE)-IRADIX
      END DO
      RETURN
      END
```

FIG. 1.3. *Parallel normalization with the carry skip method.*

tentially obstructing parallelization.

For example, a FORTRAN 77 program of multiple-precision sequential addition is shown in Figure 1.1. Here, `ICARRY` is a variable to store carry, `ITEMP` is a temporary variable and `IRADIX` is a radix of multiple-precision numbers. We assume that the input data has been normalized as 0 ~ `IRADIX-1`, and is stored in arrays `IA` and `IB`.

In this program, the value of `ICARRY` recurrently decides the value of `ITEMP` at line 5, then the program can not be parallelized because of data dependency.

The algorithm shown in Figure 1.2 is one that enables us to parallelize the releasing of the carries and borrows. We assume that the input data has been normalized to 0 ~ `IRADIX-1`, and stored in arrays `IA` and `IB`.

We perform multiple-precision addition without the propagation of carries at line 3. Results are checked with (`IA(2:N)` ≥ `IRADIX`) at line 4. If the value of each element of the array `IA(2:N)` is greater than or equal to `IRADIX`, we have to compute the carries in line 6 and release the carries in lines 7 and 8. Here, `IC` is a working array to store carries.

At the time of releasing carries, the propagation of the carries is not relevant. Since the carries are not completely corrected, the `DO WHILE` loop is repeated until each element in the array `IA(2:N)` is less than `IRADIX`.

We assume that the input data has been normalized to 0 ~ `IRADIX-1`, and stored in arrays `IA` and `IB`. In the case of `IRADIX` $= 10^8$, the probability of having two consecutive carries is $0.5 \times (1/10^8)^2 = 5 \times 10^{-17}$. Thus, this algorithm performs the propagation operations successfully. When the propagation of carries repeats, as in the case of $0.99999999 \cdots 9 + 0.00000000 \cdots 1$, we have to use the carry skip method [20].

A Fortran 90 program of multiple-precision parallel normalization with the carry skip method is shown in Figure 1.3. We assume that the input data has been normalized to 0 ~ `IRADIX-1`, and stored in array `IX`. We perform *incomplete* normalization as 0 ~ `IRADIX` in lines 3 ∼ 8. Note that the `DO WHILE` loop in line 3 is repeated twice, at most. The range for carry skipping is decided from line 10 to line 17. Finally, we perform carry skipping from line 18 to line 20. Array `IC` is the working array to store carries.

The same methods can be applied to multiple-precision parallel subtraction and multiplication by a single-precision integer.

3. Parallelization of Multiple-Precision Multiplication. In this paper, we use multiple-precision multiplication based on the *floating-point real* FFT.

For *floating-point real* FFT-based multiplication, we can use the "balanced representation" [12], which tends to yield reduced errors for the convolutions we intended to perform. In this technique, an n-digit multiplicand $x = \sum_{i=0}^{n-1} x_i B^i$ with radix B is represented as follows:

$$x = x'_0 + x'_1 B + x'_2 B^2 + \cdots + x'_{n-1} B^{n-1}, \ |x'_i| \le \left\lfloor \frac{B}{2} \right\rfloor .$$

A key operation in FFT-based multiple-precision parallel multiplication is the FFT and normalization, on which a significant proportion of the total computation time is spent.

We use an efficient parallel FFT algorithm in the FFT-based multiple-precision parallel multiplication.

The normalization of results in FFT-based multiple-precision parallel multiplication is essentially the same as the parallel processing of carries in multiple-precision addition, subtraction, and multiplication by a single-precision integer. Thus, the normalization can also be parallelized.

4. Parallelization of Multiple-Precision Division by Single-Precision Integer. The multiple-precision division by a single-precision integer is also used in the multiple-precision arithmetic, which is much faster than the division by a multiple-precision number.

We discuss the multiple-precision arithmetic with radix B for the division of an n-digit integer by a 1-digit integer, giving an n-digit quotient and a 1-digit remainder. For simplicity, we assume that we are working with a non-negative integer.

Let us define an n-digit dividend $u = \sum_{i=1}^{n} u_i B^{n-i}$ and a 1-digit divisor v in radix B notation, where $0 \le u_i < B$ and $1 \le v < B$.

The quotient q can be expressed as follows:

$$q = \lfloor u/v \rfloor = \sum_{i=1}^{n} q_i B^{n-i}, \tag{4.1}$$

where $0 \le q_i < B$.

The partial remainder r_i and the overall remainder r can be expressed as follows:

$$r_i = u_i - v q_i, \qquad i = 1, 2, \cdots, n, \tag{4.2}$$

$$r = u - vq \equiv r_n, \tag{4.3}$$

where $0 \le r_i < v$.

Then, the partial quotient q_i and the partial remainder r_i can be expressed as follows:

$$q_i = \lfloor (B r_{i-1} + u_i)/v \rfloor, \qquad i = 1, 2, \cdots, n, \tag{4.4}$$

$$r_i = (B r_{i-1} + u_i) \bmod v, \qquad i = 1, 2, \cdots, n. \tag{4.5}$$

Note that equation (4.5) includes the first-order recurrence.

The first-order recurrence can be evaluated sequentially from the definition of the recurrence by the following serial FORTRAN 77 code:

```
R(1)=MOD(U(1),V)
DO I=2,N
  R(I)=MOD(B*R(I-1)+U(I),V)
END DO
```

where R and U have been declared as arrays.

We can apply the parallel cyclic reduction method [15] to the equation (4.5).

The parallel cyclic reduction algorithm can be implemented in a parallel form of Fortran 90 as follows:

```
BMOD=MOD(B,V)
R(1:N)=MOD(U(1:N),V)
DO L=1,CEILING(LOG2(N))
  IF (BMOD .EQ. 0) EXIT
  R(1:N)=MOD(BMOD*EOSHIFT(R(1:N),-(2**(L-1)))+R(1:N),V)
  BMOD=MOD(BMOD**2,V)
END DO
```

where R and U have been declared as arrays.

If BMOD mod V $= 0$, the DO loop above is exited. In particular, when b is a multiple of v, the arithmetic operation count is $O(n/P)$ on parallel machines with P processors. Also, when b is not a multiple of v, the upper bound of the arithmetic operation count of this algorithm is $O((n/P)\log n)$.

Finally, we can obtain the quotient q in parallel by the following Fortran 90 program:

```
Q(1:N)=INT((B*EOSHIFT(R(1:N),-1)+U(1:N))/V)
```

where Q, R and U have been declared as arrays.

5. Parallelization of Multiple-Precision Division and Square Root Operations.

5.1. Newton iteration. In division, the quotient of a and b is computed as follows. First, the following Newton iteration is employed, which converges to $1/b$:

$$x_{k+1} = x_k(2 - bx_k). \tag{5.1}$$

To obtain the value of a/b, we have to calculate $a \cdot (1/b) = a/b$. These iterations are performed by doubling the precision for each iteration.

Square roots are computed by the following Newton iteration, which converges to $1/\sqrt{a}$:

$$x_{k+1} = \frac{x_k}{2}(3 - ax_k^2). \tag{5.2}$$

To obtain the value of $\sqrt{a}$, we have to calculate $(1/\sqrt{a}) \cdot a = \sqrt{a}$. These iterations are also performed by doubling the precision for each iteration.

Here, we discuss the sequential computation time of n-digit division and square root operations. Let us consider an n-digit number X with radix B.

$$X = \sum_{i=0}^{n-1} x_i B^i, \tag{5.3}$$

where $0 \le x_i < B$.

Each iteration of a multiple-precision division includes two multiple-precision multiplications, and that of a multiple-precision square root operation includes three multiple-precision multiplications. At the i-th iteration, it is sufficient to work with an accuracy of $O(2^i)$. In this sense, the Newton iteration is self-correcting. Thus, the computation time of sequential processing $T_s(n)$ is as follows:

$$T_s(n) = \sum_{i=0}^{\log_2 n} c_{\text{mult}} M(n/2^i) + M(n) \approx (2c_{\text{mult}} + 1) \cdot M(n),$$

where $c_{\text{mult}} = 2$ (in division) or $c_{\text{mult}} = 3$ (in square root), and $M(n)$ is the number of operations for an n-digit FFT-based multiplication. Throughout this paper, we assume $M(n) = O(n \log n \log\log n)$.

5.2. Parallelization. To compute the n-digit multiple-precision arithmetic by Newton iteration of (5.1) and (5.2), it is necessary to perform multiple-precision parallel addition, subtraction, and multiplication on parallel computers which have P processors. For these operations, we can apply the parallel algorithm given in previous sections.

5.3. Arithmetic operation counts.

5.3.1. Arithmetic operation counts for block distribution. Given that the arithmetic operation count of n-digit multiple-precision parallel addition, subtraction, and multiplication by a single-precision integer is $O(n/P)$, no consideration of these is made in this paper.

In the case of the block distribution, n-digit multiple-precision numbers are distributed across all P processors. We denote the corresponding index at processor m $(0 \le m \le P-1)$ as i $(m = \lfloor i/\lceil n/P \rceil \rfloor)$ in (5.3).

Thus, the arithmetic operation count of the block distribution $T_{\text{calc}}^{\text{block}}(n, P)$ is as follows:

$$\begin{aligned} T_{\text{calc}}^{\text{block}}(n, P) &= \sum_{i=0}^{\log_2 \frac{n}{P}} c_{\text{mult}} M(2^i) + \sum_{i=1}^{\log_2 P} c_{\text{mult}} \cdot \frac{1}{2^i} M(n \cdot 2^i/P) \\ &\quad + \frac{1}{P} M(n) \\ &\approx \frac{1}{P}(c_{\text{mult}} \log_2 P + 2c_{\text{mult}} + 1) M(n). \end{aligned} \tag{5.4}$$

5.3.2. Arithmetic operation counts for cyclic distribution. In the case of the cyclic distribution, n-digit multiple-precision numbers are distributed across all P processors. We denote the corresponding index at processor m $(0 \le m \le P-1)$ as i $(m = i \bmod P)$ in (5.3).

Thus, the arithmetic operation count of the cyclic distribution $T_{\text{calc}}^{\text{cyclic}}(n, P)$ is as follows:

$$\begin{aligned} T_{\text{calc}}^{\text{cyclic}}(n, P) &= \sum_{i=0}^{\log_2 P} c_{\text{mult}} \cdot \frac{1}{2^i} M(2^i) + \sum_{i=1}^{\log_2 P} c_{\text{mult}} \cdot \frac{1}{P} M(n \cdot 2^i/P) \\ &\quad + \frac{1}{P} M(n) \\ &\approx \frac{1}{P}(2c_{\text{mult}} + 1) M(n). \end{aligned} \tag{5.5}$$

By comparing (5.4) and (5.5), we can conclude that the arithmetic operation count of the cyclic distribution is less than that of the block distribution.

5.4. Communication time for parallel processing (normalization). We consider the communication time of the normalization part (see Figure 1.3) of multiple-precision multiplication. We assume a message passing model.

5.4.1. Communication time of block distribution. In the normalization of the block distribution, processor m has to send the carry of one digit to the neighboring processor $(P + m - 1) \bmod P$.

Let us assume that the latency of communication is L, the bandwidth is W, and the number of iterations at the `DO WHILE` loop of Figure 1.3 is c_{norm}. Then the communication time of the block distribution $T_{\text{comm}}^{\text{block}}(n,\, P)$ is as follows:

$$\begin{aligned} T_{\text{comm}}^{\text{block}}(n,\, P) &= c_{\text{norm}}\left\{(c_{\text{mult}} \log_2 P)\left(L + \frac{1}{W}\right) + \left(L + \frac{1}{W}\right)\right\} \\ &= L \cdot \left\{c_{\text{norm}}(c_{\text{mult}} \log_2 P + 1)\right\} + \frac{1}{W} \cdot \left\{c_{\text{norm}}(c_{\text{mult}} \log_2 P + 1)\right\}. \end{aligned} \tag{5.6}$$

5.4.2. Communication time of cyclic distribution. In the cyclic distribution, in order to reduce the communication time, we realign the distributed data from the cyclic distribution to the block distribution before normalization. We realign the distributed data from the block distribution to the cyclic distribution after normalization. In the normalization of the cyclic distribution with realignment, processor number m has to send the carry of one digit to the neighboring processor $(P + m - 1) \bmod P$.

Let us assume that the latency of communication is L, the bandwidth is W, and the number of iterations at the `DO WHILE` loop of Figure 1.3 is c_{norm}. Then the communication time of the realignment (cyclic $\leftrightarrow$ block) with all-to-all communication $T_{\text{comm}}^{\text{align}}(n,\, P)$ is as follows:

$$T_{\text{comm}}^{\text{align}}(n,\, P) = (P - 1)\left(L + \frac{1}{W} \cdot \frac{n}{P^2}\right). \tag{5.7}$$

In each iteration of (5.1) and (5.2), the realignment with all-to-all communication of twice (i.e., cyclic $\rightarrow$ block and block $\rightarrow$ cyclic) is necessary. The communication time of the normalization with realignment from the cyclic distribution to the block distribution $T_{\text{comm}}^{\text{cyclic}}(n,\, P)$ is as follows:

$$\begin{aligned} T_{\text{comm}}^{\text{cyclic}}(n,\, P) = T_{\text{comm}}^{\text{block}}(n,\, P) &+ c_{\text{mult}} \sum_{i=0}^{\log_2 n} 2T_{\text{comm}}^{\text{align}}(2^i,\, P) \\ &+ 2T_{\text{comm}}^{\text{align}}(n,\, P). \end{aligned} \tag{5.8}$$

By comparing (5.6) and (5.8), we can see that the communication time of the block distribution is less than that of the cyclic distribution.

5.5. Total computational time. Here, we consider the total computation time for multiple-precision parallel division and square root operations.

5.5.1. Total Computational Time of Block Distribution. The total computational time of the block distribution $T_{\text{total}}^{\text{block}}(n,\, P)$ is as follows:

$$T_{\text{total}}^{\text{block}}(n,\, P) = T_{\text{calc}}^{\text{block}}(n,\, P) + T_{\text{comm}}^{\text{block}}(n,\, P). \tag{5.9}$$

5.5.2. Total Computational Time of Cyclic Distribution. The total computational time of the cyclic distribution $T_{\text{total}}^{\text{cyclic}}(n,\, P)$ is as follows:

$$\begin{aligned} T_{\text{total}}^{\text{cyclic}}(n,\, P) &= T_{\text{calc}}^{\text{cyclic}}(n,\, P) + T_{\text{comm}}^{\text{block}}(n,\, P) \\ &\quad + c_{\text{mult}} \sum_{i=0}^{\log_2 n} 2T_{\text{comm}}^{\text{align}}(2^i,\, P) + 2T_{\text{comm}}^{\text{align}}(n,\, P). \end{aligned} \tag{5.10}$$

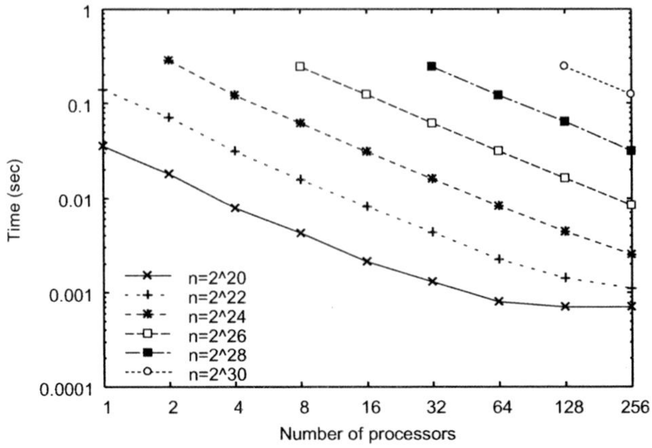

FIG. 5.1. *Execution time of multiple-precision parallel division by a single-precision integer* ($\pi/2$), n = *number of decimal digits.*

By comparing (5.9) and (5.10), we can conclude that the total computational time of the cyclic distribution is less than that of the block distribution when

$$T_{\text{total}}^{\text{cyclic}}(n, P) - T_{\text{total}}^{\text{block}}(n, P) = \left\{T_{\text{calc}}^{\text{cyclic}}(n, P) - T_{\text{calc}}^{\text{block}}(n, P)\right\} + c_{\text{mult}} \sum_{i=0}^{\log_2 n} 2T_{\text{comm}}^{\text{align}}(2^i, P) + 2T_{\text{comm}}^{\text{align}}(n, P) < 0 \tag{5.11}$$

follows from (5.9) and (5.10).

We have derived the following formula to establish the condition that satisfies equation (5.11):

$$M(n) > \frac{4c_{\text{mult}} + 2}{c_{\text{mult}} \log_2 P}\left(LP^2 \log_2 n + \frac{n}{W}\right)$$

follows from (5.4), (5.5), (5.7) and (5.11).

6. Experimental Results. In order to evaluate our multiple-precision parallel division and square root algorithms, the decimal digit n and the number of processors P were varied. We averaged the elapsed times obtained from 10 executions of the multiple-precision parallel division by a single-precision integer ($\pi/2$, $\pi/3$), multiple-precision parallel division ($\sqrt{2}/\pi$) and multiple-precision parallel square root ($\sqrt{\pi}$). We note that the respective values of n-digit π and $\sqrt{2}$ were prepared in advance. The selection of these values has no particular significance here, but was convenient to establish definite test cases, the results of which were used as randomized test data.

A Hitachi SR2201 (1024 PEs, 256 MB per PE, 300 MFLOPS per PE, 256 GB total main memory size, communication bandwidth 300 MB/sec both ways per link, and 307.2 GFLOPS peak performance) was used as the distributed-memory parallel computer. In the experiment, we used 1 PE$\sim$256 PEs. The original program is written in FORTRAN 77 with MPI.

The radix of the multiple-precision number is 10^8. The multiple-precision number is stored in the array of 32-bit integers. Each input data word is split into two words upon entry to FFT-based multiplication.

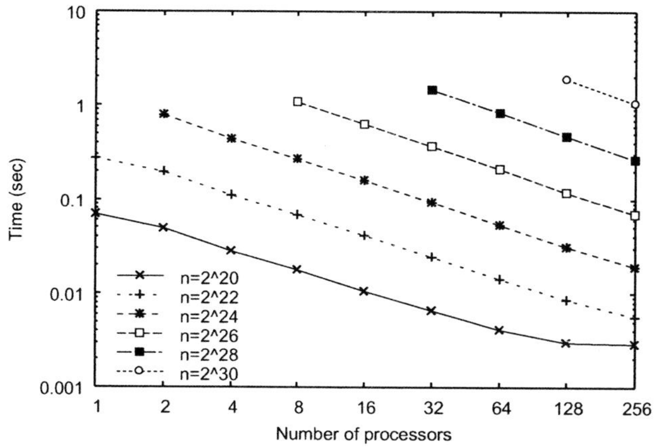

FIG. 5.2. *Execution time of multiple-precision parallel division by a single-precision integer ($\pi/3$), n = number of decimal digits.*

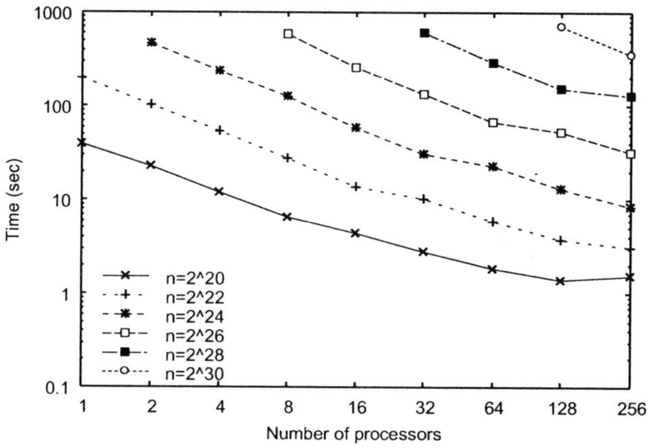

FIG. 5.3. *Execution time of multiple-precision parallel division ($\sqrt{2}/\pi$, block distribution), n = number of decimal digits.*

Figure 5.1 shows the average execution times of multiple-precision parallel division by a single-precision integer, $\pi/2$. For $n = 2^{20}$ and $P > 64$, we can clearly see that communication overhead dominates the execution time. We note that the arithmetic operation count is $O(n/P)$ in the division of $\pi/2$, because the radix ($= 10^8$) is a multiple of the divisor ($= 2$).

Figure 5.2 shows the average execution times of the multiple-precision parallel division by a single-precision integer, $\pi/3$. For $n = 2^{20}$ and $P > 64$, we can clearly see that communication overhead dominates the execution time. We note that the arithmetic operation count is $O((n/P)\log n)$ in the division of $\pi/3$, because the radix ($= 10^8$) is not a multiple of the divisor ($= 3$).

The calculation of $\pi/2$ is up to 8.4 times faster than that of $\pi/3$ when $n = 2^{30}$ and $P = 256$. This is because the computation of $\pi/2$ has less arithmetic operations $O(n/P)$ compared with $\pi/3$.

In Figures 5.3 and 5.4, we compare the average execution times of multiple-precision parallel divisions ($\sqrt{2}/\pi$). We can see that the performance of the cyclic distribution is better than that of the block distribution. In particular, for $n = 2^{30}$ and $P = 256$, the cyclic distribution runs approximately 7.5 times faster than the block distribution, as shown in Figures 5.3 and 5.4. This is mainly because the arithmetic operation time in the case of the

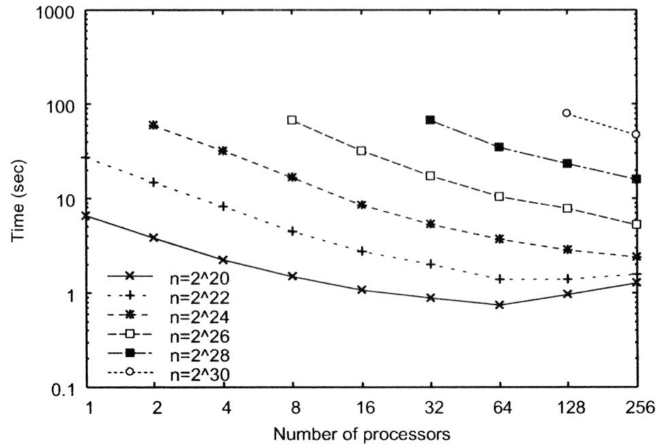

FIG. 5.4. *Execution time of multiple-precision parallel division ($\sqrt{2}/\pi$, cyclic distribution), $n =$ number of decimal digits.*

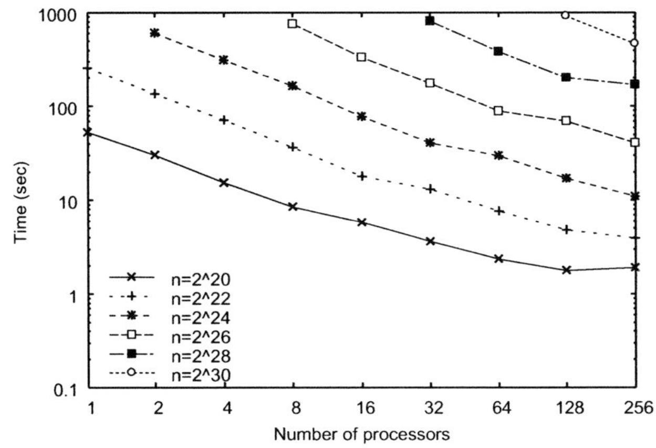

FIG. 5.5. *Execution time of multiple-precision parallel square root ($\sqrt{\pi}$, block distribution), $n =$ number of decimal digits.*

cyclic distribution is shorter. This result indicates that the cyclic distribution is preferable to the block distribution.

In Figure 5.4, for small digits $n = 2^{20} \sim 2^{22}$ and $P > 64$, we can clearly see that communication overhead dominates the execution time. This is due to the fact that the cyclic distribution requires realignment with all-to-all communication. All execution times of the cyclic distribution are less than those of the block distribution, as shown in Figures 5.3 and 5.4.

Figures 5.5 and 5.6 show a comparison of the average execution times of multiple-precision parallel square root operations ($\sqrt{\pi}$). Similarly to the multiple-precision parallel division, we can see that the performance of the cyclic distribution is better than that of the block distribution. For $n = 2^{30}$ and $P = 256$, the cyclic distribution runs approximately 8.6 times faster than the block distribution, as shown in Figures 5.5 and 5.6. As Figures 5.5 and 5.6 indicate, the tendency of the observed results is almost the same as that shown in the results of Figures 5.3 and 5.4.

We can conclude that the cyclic distribution with realignment is efficient for Newton iteration based multiple-precision division and square root operations.

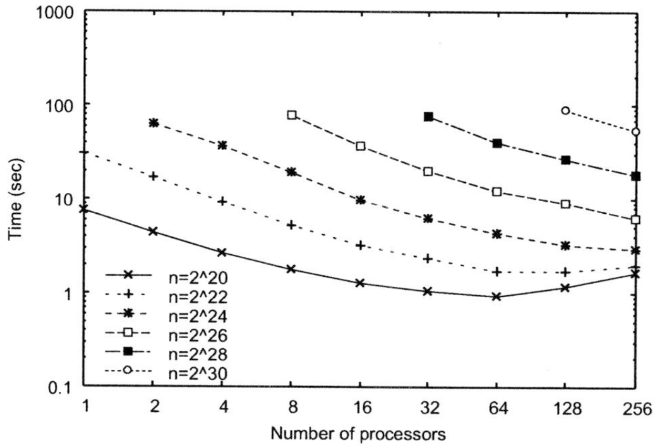

FIG. 5.6. *Execution time of multiple-precision parallel square root ($\sqrt{\pi}$, cyclic distribution), n = number of decimal digits.*

7. 206, 158, 430, 000 **Decimal Digits of π Calculation on Hitachi SR8000.** The computation of π to a high precision has a long history and several computations have been performed [4]. The development of new programs suited to the calculation of π and high speed computers with a large memory have thrown more light on this fascinating number.

We have computed π to more than 206 billion decimal digits by using the formula of the improved Gauss-Legendre algorithm and verified the results through improved Borweins' quadratically convergent algorithm for π on the Hitachi SR8000 distributed-memory parallel computer at the University of Tokyo.

7.1. Algorithms for π.

7.1.1. The Gauss-Legendre algorithm: main algorithm. The theoretical basis of the Gauss-Legendre algorithm for π is explained in the references [6, 23, 5].

We employed the following improved Gauss-Legendre algorithm for π [22]:

$A := 1;\ B := 1/2;\ T := 1/2;\ X := 2;$
while $A - B > 10^{-n}$ **do begin**
  $W := A * B;\ A := (A + B)/2;$
  $B := \sqrt{W};\ A := (A + B)/2;$
  $T := T - X * (A - B);\ X := 2 * X$
  end;
return $(A + B)/T$.

Here, A, B, T and W are full-precision variables and X is a double-precision variable.

In each iteration, multiple-precision multiplication of once can be reduced by improving the original Gauss-Legendre algorithm.

7.1.2. Borweins' quadratically convergent algorithm: verification algorithm. Borweins' quadratically convergent algorithm [5] is explained as following scheme. Let $a_0 = 6 - 4\sqrt{2}$ and $y_0 = \sqrt{2} - 1$. Iterate the following calculations:

$$y_{k+1} = \frac{1 - (1 - y_k^4)^{1/4}}{1 + (1 - y_k^4)^{1/4}}, \tag{7.1}$$

$$a_{k+1} = a_k(1 + y_{k+1})^4 - 2^{2k+3} y_{k+1}(1 + y_{k+1} + y_{k+1}^2). \tag{7.2}$$

Then a_k converges quadratically to $1/\pi$. Here, precisions for a_k and y_k must be more than the desired digits. This algorithm was used for the main 29 million decimal digit calculation by Bailey [2].

We employed the following improved Borweins' quadratically convergent algorithm for π:

$A := 6 - 4\sqrt{2};\ Y := 17 - 12\sqrt{2};\ X := 2;$
while $Y > 10^{-n/4}$ **do begin**
  $Y := 1 - \dfrac{2}{1 + (1 - Y)^{-1/4}};\ B := Y^2;$
  $W := (1 + 2 * Y + B)^2;\ Y := B^2;$
  $A := A * W - X * (W - (1 + 2 * B + Y));$
  $X := 4 * X$
  end;
if $Y < 10^{-n/2}$ **then begin**
  $W := 1 + Y/2;\ A := A * W - X * (Y/8)$
  end
else if $Y < 10^{-n/3}$ **then begin**
  $B := Y^2;\ W := 1 + Y/2 + 11 * B/32;$
  $A := A * W - X * (Y/8 + 5 * B/64)$
  end
else begin
  $B := Y^2;$
  $W := 1 + Y/2 + 11 * B/32 + 17 * B * Y/64;$
  $A := A * W - X * (Y/8 + 5 * B/64 + 15 * B * Y/256)$
  end;
return $1/A$.

Here, A, B, W and Y are full-precision variables and X is a double-precision variable.

In each iteration, the four multiple-precision multiplications and three square operations can be reduced by improving the original Borweins' quadratically convergent algorithm.

7.2. Layout of storage. A multiple-precision number is stored with cyclic distribution in the array of 32-bit integers. The radix selected for the multiple-precision numbers is 10^8. Each input data word is split into two words upon entry to the FFT-based multiplication. To perform FFT-based multiplication of $3 \times 2^{36} \approx 206$ billion decimal digit numbers, at least 2592 GB of main memory should be available. It was impossible to obtain 206 billion decimal digits through in-core (on main memory) operations because of the 896 GB main memory limit on the Hitachi SR8000 distributed-memory parallel computer.

Thus, we performed 3×2^{32} point real FFT for $3 \times 2^{33} \approx 25.7$ billion decimal digit multiplications on main memory. Then, we used Karatsuba's multiplication algorithm for $3 \times 2^{36} \approx 206$ billion decimal digit multiplications. These schemes needed approximately 865 GB and 817 GB of main memory for working storage for the Gauss-Legendre and Borweins' quadratically convergent algorithms, respectively.

Conversely, in Borweins' quadratically convergent algorithm, we performed 3×2^{32} point real FFT for $3 \times 2^{33} \approx 25.7$ billion decimal digit multiplications in main memory. These schemes needed approximately 816 GB of main memory for the working storage. In order to increase speed or reduce elapsed time, the amount of main memory available is crucial. To perform $n = 3 \times 2^m$ point FFTs, a radix-2, 3 and 5 parallel FFT was used [26].

7.3. Results of π 206,158,430,000 decimal digit calculation. The calculations of π by Gauss-Legendre algorithm and Borweins' quadratically convergent algorithm were performed on the Hitachi SR8000 distributed-memory parallel computer (128 nodes, 8 GB per node, 8 GFLOPS per node, 1 TB total main memory size, communication bandwidth 1 GB/sec per link, and 1 TFLOPS peak performance).

The node processor of the SR8000 is a 4 ns PowerPC node with major enhancements by Hitachi. Each node contains eight RISC microprocessors which have the "Pseudo Vector Processing" (PVP) feature [21]. This allows data to be fetched from main memory in a pipelined manner without stalling the succeeding instructions. The result is that data is fed from memory into the arithmetic units as effectively as in a vector supercomputer.

Eight processors are coupled to form one processing node all addressing a common part of the memory. The nodes on the SR8000 are interconnected through a multidimensional crossbar network.

The original program is written in FORTRAN 77 with MPI.

Main program run:

Job start	: 18th September 1999 19:00:52 (JST)
Job end	: 20th September 1999 08:21:56 (JST)
Elapsed time	: 37:21:04
Main memory	: 865 GB (= 6.758GB * 128)
Algorithm	: Gauss-Legendre algorithm

Verification program run:

Job start	: 26th June 1999 01:22:50 (JST)
Job end	: 27th June 1999 23:30:40 (JST)
Elapsed time	: 46:07:50
Main memory	: 817 GB (= 6.383 GB * 128)
Algorithm	: Borweins' quadratically convergent algorithm

The decimal numbers of π and $1/\pi$ from 206,158,429,981-st to 206,158,430,000-th digits are:

π : 22144 96687 55157 30964
$1/\pi$: 96680 12734 08711 53514.

The main computation took 37 iterations of the improved Gauss-Legendre algorithm for π, to yield $3 \times 2^{36} = 206,158,430,208$ digits of π. This computation was checked with 18 iterations of improved Borweins' quadratically convergent algorithm for $1/\pi$, followed by a reciprocal operation.

A comparison of these output results gave no discrepancies except for the last 45 digits due to the normal truncation errors.

8. Conclusion. In this paper, we implemented fast multiple-precision calculation of division and square root operations on distributed-memory parallel computers.

Multiple-precision division and square root operations can be reduced to multiple-precision addition, subtraction, and multiplication by using Newton iteration.

In parallel implementation of Newton iteration based multiple-precision division and square root operation, there is a trade-off between load balance and communication overhead with distributed memory parallel computers. This is because Newton iteration is performed by doubling the precision for each iteration. It was found that the cyclic distribution with realignment is quite efficient for Newton iteration based multiple-precision division and square root operation.

We have succeeded in parallelizing the basic routines of division and square root operation in multiple-precision arithmetic on the distributed-memory parallel computers.

The presented multiple-precision parallel arithmetic algorithms that made it possible to compute more than 206 billion decimal digits of π computed on a Hitachi SR8000.

Acknowledgments. The author wish to thank Prof. Yasumasa Kanada at the University of Tokyo for running more than 206 billion decimal digits of π computations on the Hitachi SR8000.

REFERENCES

[1] R. C. AGARWAL AND C. S. BURRUS, *Fast convolution using Fermat number transforms with applications to digital filtering*, IEEE Trans. Acoust., Speech, Signal Processing, ASSP-22 (1974), pp. 87–97.

[2] D. H. BAILEY, *The computation of π to 29,360,000 decimal digits using Borweins' quartically convergent algorithm*, Math. Comput., 50 (1988), pp. 283–296.

[3] ———, *Algorithm 719: Multiprecision translation and execution of FORTRAN programs*, ACM Trans. Math. Softw., 19 (1993), pp. 288–319.

[4] L. BERGGREN, J. BORWEIN, AND P. BORWEIN, eds., *Pi: A Source Book*, Springer-Verlag, New York, 2nd ed., 2000.

[5] J. M. BORWEIN AND P. B. BORWEIN, *Pi and the AGM — A Study in Analytic Number Theory and Computational Complexity*, Wiley, New York, 1987.

[6] R. P. BRENT, *Fast multiple-precision evaluation of elementary functions*, Journal of the ACM, 23 (1976), pp. 242–251.

[7] ———, *Algorithm 524: MP, A Fortran multiple-precision arithmetic package*, ACM Trans. Math. Softw., 4 (1978), pp. 71–81.

[8] D. A. BUELL AND R. L. WARD, *A multiprecise integer arithmetic package*, The Journal of Supercomputing, 3 (1989), pp. 89–107.

[9] G. CESARI AND R. MAEDER, *Performance analysis of the parallel Karatsuba multiplication algorithm for distributed memory architectures*, Journal of Symbolic Computation, 21 (1996), pp. 467–473.

[10] B. CHAR, J. JOHNSON, D. SAUNDERS, AND A. P. WACK, *Some experiments with parallel bignum arithmetic*, in Proc. 1st International Symposium on Parallel Symbolic Computation, 1994, pp. 94–103.

[11] J. W. COOLEY AND J. W. TUKEY, *An algorithm for the machine calculation of complex Fourier series*, Math. Comput., 19 (1965), pp. 297–301.

[12] R. CRANDALL AND B. FAGIN, *Discrete weighted transforms and large-integer arithmetic*, Math. Comput., 62 (1994), pp. 305–324.

[13] B. S. FAGIN, *Large integer multiplication on hypercubes*, Journal of Parallel and Distributed Computing, 14 (1992), pp. 426–430.

[14] FREE SOFTWARE FOUNDATION, *The GNU MP Home Page*. http://www.swox.com/gmp/.

[15] R. W. HOCKNEY AND C. R. JESSHOPE, *Parallel Computers*, Adam-Hilger, Bristol, 1981.

[16] Y. KANADA, *Vectorization of multiple-precision arithmetic program and* 201,326,000 *decimal digits of π calculation*, in Proc. Supercomputing '88, vol. 2, 1988, pp. 117–128.

[17] A. KARATSUBA AND Y. OFMAN, *Multiplication of multidigit numbers on automata*, Doklady Akad. Nauk SSSR, 145 (1962), pp. 293–294.

[18] A. H. KARP AND P. MARKSTEIN, *High-precision division and square root*, ACM Trans. Math. Softw., 23 (1997), pp. 561–589.

[19] D. E. KNUTH, *The Art of Computer Programming, Vol. 2: Seminumerical Algorithms*, Addison-Wesley, Reading, MA, 3rd ed., 1997.

[20] M. LEHMAN AND N. BURLA, *Skip techniques for high-speed carry propagation in binary arithmetic units*, IRE Trans. Elec. Comput., EC-10 (1961), pp. 691–698.

[21] K. NAKAZAWA, H. NAKAMURA, T. BOKU, I. NAKATA, AND Y. YAMASHITA, *CP-PACS: A massively parallel processor at the University of Tsukuba*, Parallel Computing, 25 (1999), pp. 1635–1661.

[22] T. OOURA, *Improvement of the π calculation algorithm and implementation of fast multiple-precision computation*, Transactions of the Japan Society for Industrial and Applied Mathematics, 9 (1999), pp. 165–172. (in Japanese).

[23] E. SALAMIN, *Computation of π using arithmetic-geometric mean*, Math. Comput., 30 (1976), pp. 565–570.

[24] A. SCHÖNHAGE AND V. STRASSEN, *Schnelle Multiplikation grosser Zahlen*, Computing (Arch. Elektron. Rechnen), 7 (1971), pp. 281–292.

[25] D. M. SMITH, *Algorithm 693: A FORTRAN package for floating-point multiple-precision arithmetic*, ACM Trans. Math. Softw., 17 (1991), pp. 273–283.

[26] D. Takahashi and Y. Kanada, *High-performance radix-2, 3 and 5 parallel 1-D complex FFT algorithms for distributed-memory parallel computers*, The Journal of Supercomputing, 15 (2000), pp. 207–228.

[27] K. Weber, *An experiment in high-precision arithmetic on shared memory multiprocessors*, SIGSAM Bulletin, 24 (1990), pp. 22–40.

In: Parallel and Distributed Scientific and Engineering Computing ISBN 1-59033-956-8
Editor: Y. Pan and L.T. Yang, pp. 51-65

MODELLING THE RUNTIME OF SCIENTIFIC PROGRAMS ON PARALLEL COMPUTERS

THOMAS RAUBER* AND GUDULA RÜNGER†

Abstract. Message-passing programs for parallel machines with distributed address space using communication operations of portable communication libraries such as PVM and MPI guarantee portability for most of the parallel machines available. But due to specific implementations of the runtime libraries on each specific platforms, the same program may have different runtimes on different machines, i.e., the efficiency is often not portable. Quantitative results about the runtimes of point-to-point and collective communication operations on specific parallel machines can therefore be helpful for the application programmer to select an efficient program version.

We show that the execution time of PVM and MPI communication operations can be modelled by runtime functions that depend on communication parameters of the application and the target platform. As example, we consider the Cray T3D and T3E machines. We demonstrate that the runtime functions can be used to model the computation and communication behavior of complete programs by investigating the parallel implementation of a solution method for ordinary differential equations. As application, we use this method for solving a discretized time-dependent reaction-diffusion equation.

Key words. Performance modelling, Scientific computing, Numerical analysis, Cray T3D, Cray T3E, PVM, MPI.

1. Introduction. The message passing paradigm is a popular parallel programming model used for distributed memory machines (DMMs). Typical application programs come from the area of scientific computing in the natural sciences and engineering. The portability problem for message-passing programs was solved by developing portable message passing standards like PVM or MPI which are now available for a large variety of parallel machines and are widely accepted by many application programmers. But to find an efficient parallel version of an algorithm still often takes a lot of time for programming and measuring different parallel implementations of the algorithm. This is caused by the fact that parallel algorithms on DMMs show a complicated runtime behavior caused by the overheads of explicit communication or synchronization and load imbalances. Thus the efficiency of a parallel program is not portable and using a different machine may require to select a different implementation variant to reach similar efficiencies.

In this article, we investigate and compare single-transfer and collective communication operations both in isolation and in the context of complete message passing application programs. The collective communication operations include single-broadcast, multi-broadcast, scatter, gather and reduction operations. For each operation we consider several realization variants using the PVM or MPI environment. The realizations exploit only mechanisms of the environment available to the application programmer, like buffering options or an explicit splitting of messages into pieces.

The contribution of this paper is (i) to investigate the most efficient variant of collective communication operations using PVM or MPI on the Cray T3D and T3E, (ii) to provide a modelling of the communication behavior for these variants, and (iii) to verify the performance prediction mechanism in the context of complex relationships between communication and computation within large scientific programs. The timings of the collective communication operation allow a comparison of different realization within the libraries. The runtime prediction provides functions in closed form in the spirit of the function for single-to-single transfer which is linear in the message size and which is valid for a large number of parallel machines. The functions depend on several parameters including application as well as machine parameters. The values of the parameters are determined by curve

*Department of Mathematics, Physics and Computer Science, University of Bayreuth, Germany (`rauber@uni-bayreuth.de`).

†Computer Science Department, Chemnitz University of Technology, Chemnitz, Germany (`ruenger@informatik.tu-chemnitz.de`).

fitting using the least-squares method. The resulting runtime formulas describe the communication time quite accurately (the average deviation is below 10%). The results of the experiments and the modelling can be used in compiler tools, in parallelizing compilers or directly by the application programmer. The performance of message passing programs may depend strongly on the choice of the specific communication environment, and the specific realization of a collective communication operation within this environment. A knowledge of the runtime behavior of such communication operations can have a great influence on the design process of efficient parallel programs. Runtime predictions using parameterized formulas for communication operation were also proposed by [11] and, independently, by [10, 21] for phase-structured programs. [11] derives formulas for the Thinking Machines CM-2 whereas [10, 21] mainly consider the IBM SP-2 using the native MPL (message-passing library) runtime system.

The integration of the runtime formulas into a cost model allows us to predict the runtimes for entire application programs quite accurately. We have used the operations in a library of example programs including numerical methods for the solution of linear and nonlinear algebraic or ordinary differential equations, as they are needed in a large number of industrial or physical applications such as computational fluid dynamics. The library includes Newton methods, Runge-Kutta (RK) methods and extrapolation methods, see, e.g., [14, 15]. The implementation strategies range from pure data-parallel, mixed task-data parallel to pure task-parallel implementations, but also include different numerical execution orders (not changing the numerical behavior). We demonstrate the prediction mechanism for an iterated RK method applied to different ordinary differential equations (ODEs) arising from the discretization of partial differential equations. As execution platforms we have used Cray T3D and Cray T3E machines with 512 nodes. The method also works for other homogeneous machines including cluster machines with identical nodes.

Section 2 gives an overview of the architecture of the Cray T3D and T3E. Section 3 describes the timings for communication operations. Section 4 provides runtime function in closed form of selected communication operations and Section 5 verifies the runtime functions by applying the modelling to iterated RK methods. Section 6 concludes.

2. Overview of the T3D and T3E. The Cray T3D and T3E are DMMs with up to 2048 *processing elements* (PEs) [1, 4, 17]. For the T3D, each PE contains a DEC Alpha 21064 microprocessor (clocked at 150 MHz) with an 8 KB instruction cache and an 8 KB data cache. The T3E uses an Alpha 21164 microprocessor clocked at 300 MHz (T3E-600), 450 MHz (T3E-900) or 600 MHz (T3E-1200) with an 8 KB direct-mapped instruction and data cache and an 96 KB three-way associative on-chip L2 cache. One *processing element node* comprises two PEs and a network interface; the nodes are connected by a three-dimensional torus network. The network is composed of communication links and network routers which transfer packets through the communication links. The six communication links of each node are able to simultaneously support hardware transfer rates of 300 MB/s for the T3D and 600 MB/s for the T3E. The routers contain an X-dimension switch, a Y-dimension switch, and a Z-dimension switch which control the flow of packets through the different dimensions using the routing information of the packet. Although the memory is physically distributed, a logically shared memory is provided, i.e., any microprocessor can access data in the local memory of any other PE without involving the microprocessor in that PE. Each virtual address is converted into a logical node number, PE number, and local address offset. If the PE number matches the PE number of the generating PE, a local memory access is performed. If the numbers do not match, a remote memory access is initiated by sending the PE number and the local address offset to the network interface.

A remote memory read can be performed by the function `shmem_get()` from the Shared Memory Access (SMA) library [3]. This function copies a number of words from the local memory of a specified PE to the memory of the calling PE. A remote memory write can be performed using `shmem_put()` which copies a number of words from the memory of the calling PE into the memory of a specified PE. None of these calls changes the entries of the data cache of the remote processor. The startup time for both calls lies between 1 and 2 μs. The bandwidth for `shmem_put()` is 120 MB/s. The bandwidth for `shmem_get()` is 60 MB/s because a remote load consists of a request followed by a remote write by the remote PE to the calling PE.

For the T3E, the access to remote data is performed via 640 E-registers. The latency for an access to local and remote memory is 283 ns or 1500 ns, respectively. The sustained bandwidth to local and remote memory is 630 MB/s and 300 MB/s, respectively [4].

3. Runtime of PVM and MPI operations. For single-transfer operations, we compare the following variants realized in PVM [7]:

Realizations for single-to-single transfer in PVM			
	send	receive	package-mode
(s_1)	*pvm_send*	*pvm_recv*	*PvmDataDefault*
(s_2)	*pvm_psend*	*pvm_recv*	*PvmDataDefault*
(s_3)	*pvm_psend*	*pvm_precv*	*PvmDataDefault*
(s_4)	*pvm_send*	*pvm_recv*	*PvmDataInPlace*
(s_5)	piecewise *pvm_send*	*pvm_recv*	*PvmDataInPlace*
(s_6)	*pvm_send*	*pvm_precv*	*PvmDataInPlace*

The *PvmDataInPlace* option can be used only with the standard *pvm_send* operation. The experiments with the piecewise send operations cut the messages into pieces and send them one after another. This is motivated by the way in which the PVM runtime system sends messages: If the message contains less than *PvmDataMax* bytes, a remote store operation is used by the sending processor. If the message contains more than *PvmDataMax* bytes, the sending processor sends the address of the data block to be sent with a remote store. The receiving processor uses a remote load to get the data.

Figure 3.1 (top) shows the resulting execution time in seconds for different message sizes on a T3E-600. The runtimes are obtained on a 4 processors partition with processor 0 sending data to processor 3. For small messages of up to 8192 bytes, we can observe that the *psend/precv* combination leads to the smallest execution time, whereas for medium and long messages the *PvmDataInPlace* variant with *pvm_precv* is the fastest because the copy operation to internal system buffers is avoided. The T3D shows a similar behavior except that the results change at 4096 bytes instead of 8192 bytes.

For the MPI library [8], we consider four variants of single-transfer operations:

Realizations for single-to-single transfer in MPI		
	send-operation	receive-operation
(s_7)	*MPI_Send*	*MPI_Recv*
(s_8)	piecewise *MPI_Send*	*MPI_Recv*
(s_9)	synchronous *MPI_Ssend*	*MPI_Recv*
(s_10)	buffered *MPI_Bsend*	*MPI_Recv*

Figure 3.1 (bottom) shows the resulting execution time (in seconds) on the T3E. Again, the runtimes are obtained on a 4 processors partition with processor 0 sending data to processor 3. The piecewise send operation is not shown in the figure, since the execution times are not competitive. For small messages of up to 8192 byte, the buffered send variant is slightly faster than the other variants. But for larger message sizes, the synchronous send operation is the fastest. A comparison shows that the PVM operations are usually slower than the MPI operations.

For the single-broadcast operation which sends the same message from one processor to all other processors involved, the following variants are considered for PVM:

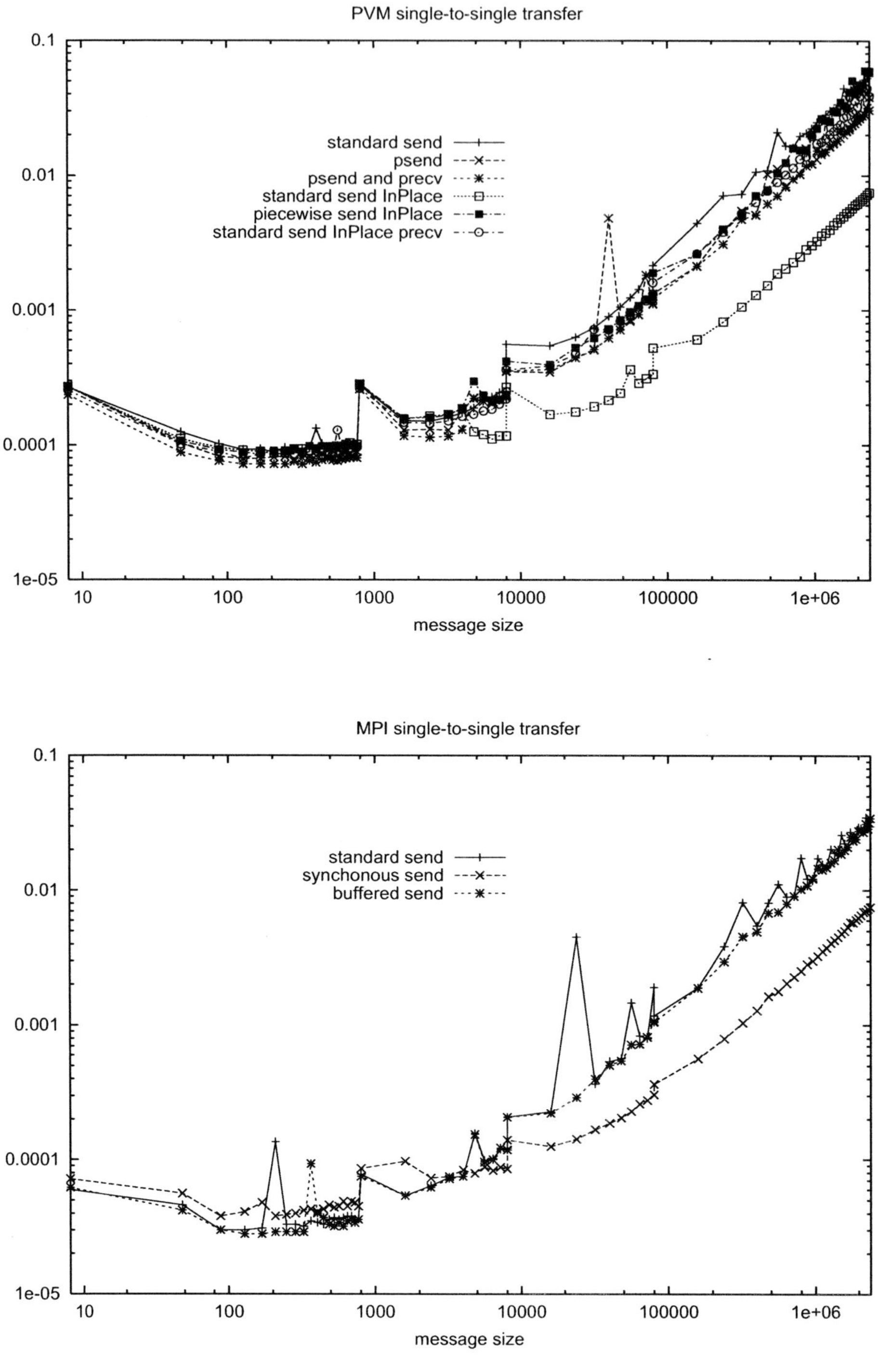

FIG. 3.1. Runtime for single-transfers on the T3E using PVM (top) and MPI (bottom).

Realizations for single-broadcast-operation in PVM			
	send	receive	package-mode
(sb_1)	*pvm_bcast*	*pvm_recv*	*PvmDataDefault*
(sb_2)	*pvm_psend*	*pvm_recv*	*PvmDataDefault*
(sb_3)	*pvm_bcast*	*pvm_precv*	*PvmDataInPlace*
(sb_4)	*pvm_bcast*	*pvm_recv*	*PvmDataInPlace*
(sb_5)	piecewise *pvm_bcast*	*pvm_recv*	*PvmDataInPlace*
(sb_6)	piecewise *pvm_bcast*	*pvm_precv*	*PvmDataInPlace*

Considering the execution time of PVM broadcast operations on 256 processors of the T3D and T3E for different messages sizes, we observe that for small message sizes of up to 4096/8192 byte, all variants except the *pvm_psend* variant have nearly the same execution time. Figure 3.2 (top) shows the results for the T3E. For larger message sizes, the piecewise operations show the best performance, i.e., it is better to split a large broadcast message into small pieces than to send it as one large message. The difference is more than a factor of 10 for messages of more than 1 Megabyte. This is usually not expected for DMMs. The explanation for this behavior is as follows: PVM initiates remote load operations by the receiving processor for messages with more than *PvmDataMax* bytes. A PVM *pvm_bcast* operation is implemented as a series of send operations from the broadcasting processor to the receiving processors. For messages with more than *PvmDataMax* bytes, the broadcasting processor sends only its address and each of the receiving processors performs a remote load. For larger numbers of receiving processors, this can lead to network contention since all receiving processors try to access the broadcasting processor at the same time. The situation can be avoided by splitting larger messages into pieces of *PvmDataMax* bytes because each piece is then transmitted by remote store operations of the broadcasting processor without contention. For MPI, only *MPI_Bcast()* is measured. A comparison between the *MPI_Bcast()* operation and the (piecewise) PVM broadcast operations shows that the MPI operations are faster than the PVM operations.

A comparison of the runtimes for accumulation operations with maximum reduction using PVM and MPI for 256 processors of the T3D with *pvm_reduce* and *MPI_Reduce*, respectively, shows that for small message sizes the PVM operation is much faster than the MPI operation. For larger message sizes, both operations have about the same runtime, but the MPI operation shows much more fluctuations than the PVM operation. For messages of more than 8000 bytes, the difference is usually below 10%. For the T3E, the runtimes are about the same for all message sizes.

A comparison of scatter and gather operations using PVM and MPI for 256 processors of the T3D and T3E with *pvm_scatter()*, *pvm_gather()*, *MPI_Scatter()*, and *MPI_Gather()*, respectively, shows that the PVM gather operation is faster than the MPI gather operation for small messages with up to 1000 bytes contributed by each processor, see Figure 3.2 (bottom). For larger messages, both the PVM and the MPI implementation have about the same execution time. The MPI scatter operation is faster than the PVM scatter operation for all message sizes.

For multi-broadcast operations, each processor contributes a data block, i.e., the total size of the message collected is obtained by adding up the size of the individual data blocks. Because there is no multi-broadcast operation directly available in PVM, we compare implementations of the operation in which each participating processors executes a single-broadcast operation. For these single-broadcast operation, we use the variants introduced above. The variant that uses a modified broadcast with *pvm_psend* to all sending processors and standard *pvm_recv* by the receiving processors is not competitive, because the runtime is one order of magnitude larger than all other variants. As a second realization of a multi-broadcast, we use a variant in which one processor executes a gather operation using *pvm_gather()* and broadcasts the complete message with the fastest single-broadcast variant (piecewise with *pvm_precv* and *PvmDataInPlace*) available to the other processors. A piecewise execution of the gather operation has about the same runtime than a normal gather operation. A comparison of the different variants shows that the gather implementation exhibits the smallest execution time, independent from the size of the data to be collected.

For MPI, the following variants are considered:

- each processor executes a standard broadcast operation with *MPI_Bcast*;
- the MPI operation *MPI_Allgather* is used;
- each processor executes a standard broadcast operation with *MPI_Bcast* but the single broadcast messages are split into pieces of 4096 bytes.

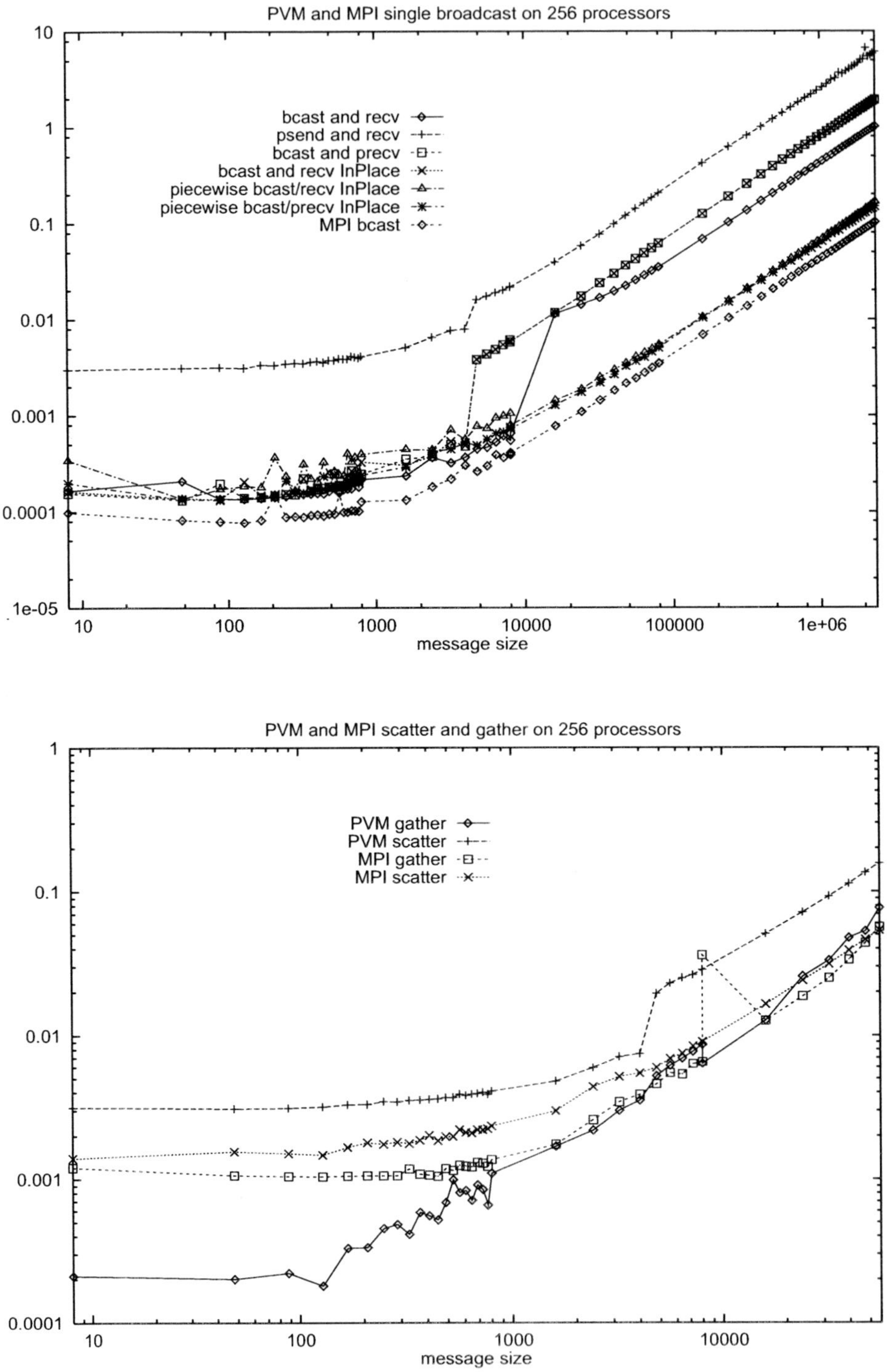

FIG. 3.2. Runtime for single broadcast, scatter and gather operations on a T3E.

A comparison shows that the implementation with *MPI_Allgather* exhibits the smallest execution time, independently from the size of the data to be collected.

Comparing the execution of multi-broadcast operations realized with PVM and MPI for different message sizes, we observe that for small messages of up to about 400 byte, the PVM implementation with *pvm_gather()* has the smallest execution time; for larger messages, the MPI implementation with *MPI_Allgather()* is faster.

4. Modelling the Communication Behavior. In this section, we show how the runtimes of the collective communication operations on the T3D and T3E can be modelled by runtime formulas that depend on various machine parameters including the number of processors, the bandwidth of the interconnecting network, and startup times for the corresponding operations. We present the modelling for the fastest variants of PVM and MPI communication operations, respectively. The runtime behavior of the other variants can be modelled similarly. The corresponding PVM and MPI operations can be modelled by the same runtime function but with different coefficients. This is, e.g., not the case for the IBM SP2, since the PVM and MPI broadcast operations show a different dependence on the number of executing processors (linearly or logarithmically, respectively). The runtime functions are summarized in Table 4.1. The value b is the message size in bytes and p is the number of processors. For different variants, different coefficient values have to be used which is identified by an additional parameter V denoting the specific variant in the following. The specific values for the coefficients $\tau(V)$, $t_c(V)$, $\tau_1(V)$, and $\tau_2(V)$ are given below. The values result from curve fitting with the least-squares method.

operation	runtime formula
single-transfer	$t_{s2s}(b) = \tau + t_c \cdot b$
single-broadcast	$t_{sb}(p, b) = \tau \log(p) + t_c \cdot \log(p) \cdot b$
single-accumulation	$t_{sb}(p, b) = \tau \log(p) + t_c \cdot \log(p) \cdot b$
multi-broadcast	$t_{mb}(p, b) = \tau_1 + \tau_2 \cdot p + t_c \cdot p \cdot b$

TABLE 4.1
Runtime formulas for single-to-single transfer and collective communication operations.

Single transfer:. The runtime for a single-to-single transfer is modeled by a linear function $t_{s2s}(b, V) = \tau(V) + t_c(V) \cdot b$, where $\tau(V)$ denotes a *startup time* and $t_c(V)$ denotes the *byte-transfer time* for the specific implementation V. (The byte-transfer time is the inverse of the effective bandwidth.) The values of the coefficients $\tau(V)$ and $t_c(V)$ are determined from measured runtimes for messages of sizes between 8 bytes and 2.4 MBytes with the least squares method. The values of the parameter for the standard PVM send, the PVM send with `precv` and `PvmDataInPlace`, the standard MPI send, and the synchronous MPI `Ssend` are:

Coefficients for runtime formula of single-transfer					
		T3D		T3E	
	message transfer variant	$\tau(V)$	$t_c(V)$	$\tau(V)$	$t_c(V)$
(s_1)	PVM send/recv	256.4 μs	0.0396 μs	331.5 μs	0.0230 μs
(s_2)	PVM psend/recv	205.0 μs	0.0392 μs	237.7 μs	0.0140 μs
(s_3)	PVM psend/precv	184.6 μs	0.0393 μs	114.4 μs	0.0128 μs
(s_4)	PVM PvmDataInPlace	196.6 μs	0.0305 μs	118.9 μs	0.0030 μs
(s_6)	PVM PvmDataInPlace precv	181.6 μs	0.0276 μs	109.9 μs	0.0158 μs
(s_7)	MPI standard	127.0 μs	0.0323 μs	357.0 μs	0.0138 μs
(s_9)	MPI `Ssend`	111.7 μs	0.0078 μs	55.7 μs	0.0031 μs
(s_10)	MPI `Bsend`	94.2 μs	0.0032 μs	-53.7 μs	0.0132 μs

A comparison between the predicted and measured runtimes for PVM and MPI single-transfer operations shows that the predictions fit the measured runtimes quite accurately, especially for large message sizes. For small message sizes, the deviation can be quite large, because we use a single linear function for the prediction. The prediction can be made more accurate for this case by using a piecewise linear function, see [5]. A simple and natural way to do this is to use a piecewise-linear function for messages of up to 4096/8192 bytes and another function for larger messages. The reason for this separation is the message transfer protocol of the T3D/T3E which specifies that for messages of up to 4096/8192 bytes, the sending processor performs a *shmem_put()* operation whereas for larger messages, the receiving processor performs a *shmem_get()* operation. This results in the following parameter values for the standard PVM send, the PVM send with *precv* and *PvmDataInPlace*, the standard MPI send, and the synchronous MPI *Ssend*:

Coefficient for runtime formula of single-transfer					
		T3D		T3E	
	message transfer variant	$\tau(V)$	$t_c(V)$	$\tau(V)$	$t_c(V)$
(s_1)	PVM standard small	184.2 μs	0.0483 μs	109.3 μs	0.0185 μs
	PVM standard large	311.1 μs	0.0411 μs	770.4 μs	0.0227 μs
(s_6)	PVM InPlace precv small	150.8 μs	0.0336 μs	107.9 μs	0.0152 μs
	PVM InPlace precv large	147.4 μs	0.0281 μs	-744.0 μs	0.0182 μs
(s_7)	MPI standard small	63.86 μs	0.0417 μs	38.87 μs	0.0116 μs
	MPI standard large	201.6 μs	0.0339 μs	991.9 μs	0.0134 μs
(s_9)	MPI Ssend small	79.81 μs	0.0231 μs	47.41 μs	0.0063 μs
	MPI Ssend large	134.6 μs	0.0078 μs	57.30 μs	0.0031 μs

Single-broadcast and accumulation:. The modelling of single-broadcast operations is performed with the formula from Table 4.1. The logarithmic dependence on the number p of processors is used because the broadcast transmissions are based on broadcast trees with logarithmic depth. The same formula can also be used for the prediction of single-accumulation operations. Again, the values of the parameters $\tau(V)$ and $t_c(V)$ are determined from a set of measured runtimes with the least squares method.

Coefficients for single broadcast and accumulation				
	T3D		T3E	
variant	$\tau(V)[\mu s]$	$t_c(V)[\mu s]$	$\tau(V)[\mu s]$	$t_c(V)[\mu s]$
PVM piecewise broadcast (sb_5)	53.65	0.0130	-18.99	0.0093
MPI_Bcast	31.26	0.0153	96.96	0.0059
PVM_Reduce	17.15	0.036	28.43	0.022
MPI_Reduce	87.10	0.036	95.10	0.021

As an example, Figure 4.1 compares the predicted and measured runtimes for PVM and MPI single-accumulation operations. For the PVM broadcast, the piecewise variant with the *PvmDataInPlace* option is used. Again, the predicted runtimes fit the measured runtimes quite accurately.

Multi-broadcast and gather/scatter:. The predictions for multi-broadcast operations are made using the formula from Table 4.1, which increases linearly with the message size and the number of processors. This formula can also be used for the prediction of scatter and gather operations. The resulting coefficients are shown in the following table.

Coefficient for gather/scatter/multi-broadcast						
	T3D			T3E		
transfer variant	$\tau_1[\mu s]$	$\tau_2[\mu s]$	$t_c[\mu s]$	$\tau_1[\mu s]$	$\tau_2[\mu s]$	$t_c[\mu s]$
PVM multi-bcast	43.16	2.84	0.098	-88.83	92.65	0.063
MPI multi-bcast	12.18	19.85	0.061	0.90	0.67	0.030
PVM gather	12.70	0.76	0.065	21.70	-1.39	0.004
MPI gather	81.53	6.74	0.064	12.95	2.65	0.004
PVM scatter	87.54	24.01	0.016	8.83	10.85	0.011
MPI scatter	11.73	11.97	0.008	0.54	6.25	0.004

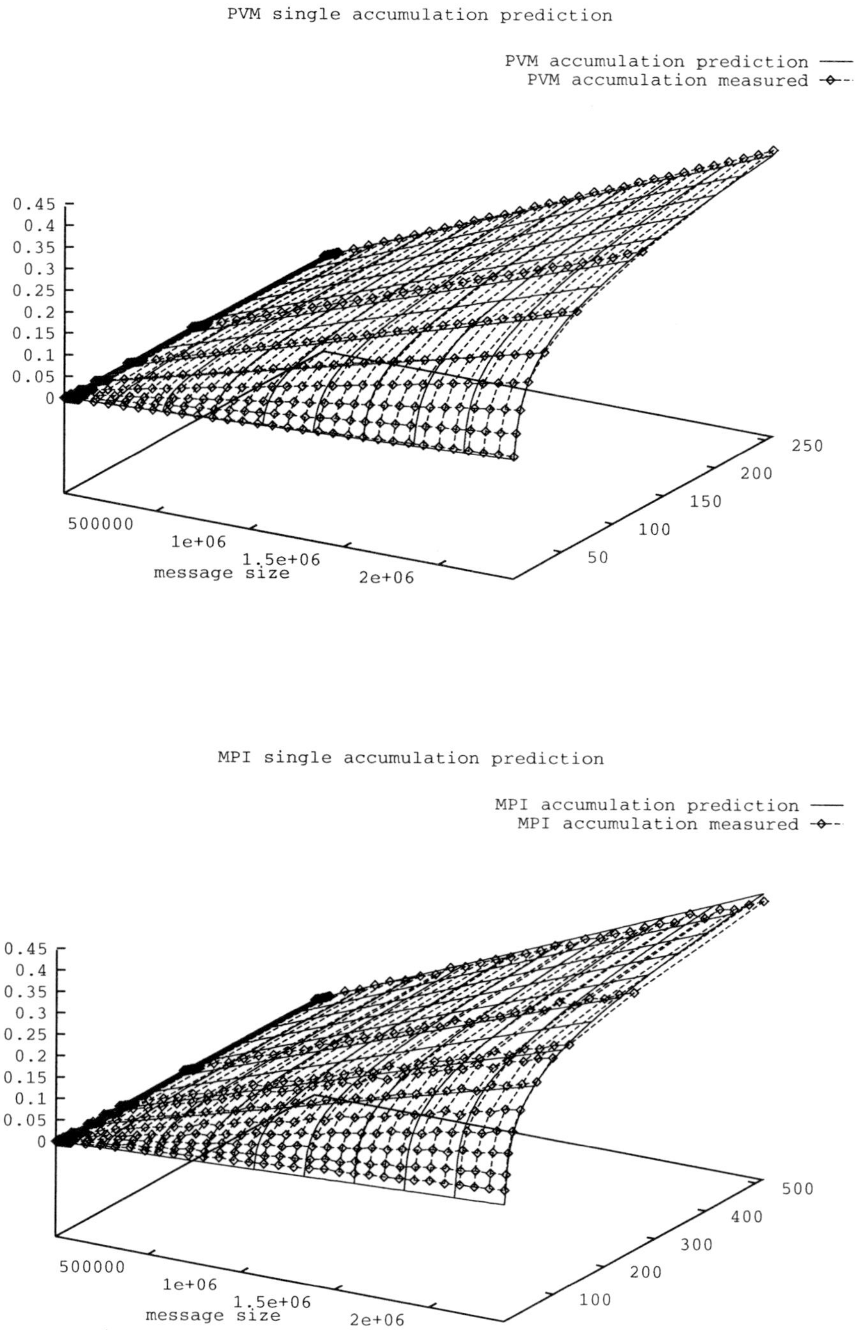

FIG. 4.1. Predicted and measured runtimes for PVM and MPI single-accumulation operations with maximum reduction on the T3E.

5. Application to Solution Methods for ODEs. The runtime predictions for entire programs is based on the modelling of the communication behavior and the computation time from which a runtime formula for the entire program is built up. The combination of the runtimes of different communication and computation times depends on the specific parallel programming model. We use a hierarchical two-level parallel programming model combining control and data parallelism which is suitable for most algorithms from numerical analysis [13, 5]. A detailed description can be found in [13, 16]. Other approaches supporting a mixed task and data parallelism like the Paradigm compiler [2, 12] or the Fx compiler [18, 19] differ not only in the way how they exploit the mixed parallelism but especially in the cost model.

We demonstrate the prediction method for a solution method for ODEs, the iterated Runge-Kutta method (IRK method). The IRK method is an explicit one-step method for the solution of initial value problems $y'(x) = f(x, y(x))$ with a given $y(x_0) = y_0$ where $y : \mathbb{R} \to \mathbb{R}^n$ is the unknown solution function and $f : \mathbb{R} \times \mathbb{R}^n \to \mathbb{R}^n$ is an application-specific function which is nonlinear in the general case.

IRK methods are new solution methods for ODEs that have been derived from classical RK methods for execution on parallel machines [20]. They are based on s-stage implicit RK methods which require the solution of an implicit equation system to determine s stage vectors $v_1, \ldots, v_s$ for the computation of the next approximation vector. Iterated RK methods iterate this (potentially non-linear) equation system for a fixed number of times m producing approximations $v^l_{(j)}$, $j = 1, \ldots, m$, of the stage vectors v_l, $l = 1, \ldots, s$. The approximations $v^l_{(m)}$, $l = 1, \ldots, s$, with the highest accuracy are used for the computation of the next approximation of the solution function (denoted by $y^{(m)}_{\kappa+1}$) according to the corresponding computation scheme:

$$v^l_{(0)} = f(y_\kappa), \qquad l = 1, \ldots, s$$

(5.1) $$v^l_{(j)} = f(y_\kappa + h_\kappa \sum_{i=1}^{s} a_{li} v^i_{(j-1)}), \quad l = 1, ..., s, j = 1, ..., m$$

(5.2) $$y_{\kappa+1} = y_\kappa + h_\kappa \sum_{l=1}^{s} b_l \, v^l_{(m)}.$$

(5.3) $$y^{(m-1)}_{\kappa+1} = y_\kappa + h_\kappa \sum_{l=1}^{s} b_l \, v^l_{(m-1)}$$

Additionally, a second approximation $y^{(m-1)}_{\kappa+1}$ with a lower accuracy is computed to perform the stepsize control. The resulting computation scheme is an *explicit* Runge-Kutta method which is suitable for the solution of non-stiff ODEs. The advantage of the iterated RK methods for parallel execution is that the iteration system (5.1) of size $s \cdot n$ consists of s independent function evaluations that can be performed in parallel [14]. For systems of differential equations, an additional data parallelism can be exploited.

The algorithms provides several possibilities for a parallel implementation. The computations of the stage vectors in one iteration j of the stage-vector computation can be performed on subsets of processors at the same time (group implementation) or by all processors one after the other (consecutive implementation). A consecutive implementation results in the computations and communications given in Figure 5.1. The vectors σ denote the approximations to the stage vectors. In contrast to Equations (5.1)–(5.3), a delayed function evaluation with $f(\sigma^i_{(j)}) = v^i_{(j)}$ is used. The implementation is executed on a DMM with p processors for an ODE system of size n and right hand side f. The number m of IRK iterations is determined from the order r of the underlying (implicit) Runge-Kutta method as $m = r - 1$. The parallel execution of the stepsize control requires the execution of a broadcast and a gather operation. If the error resulting from the current stepsize is too large, the stepsize is rejected and the approximation solution is recomputed with a smaller stepsize.

The runtime of the consecutive execution from Figure 5.1 with p processors without the

```
forall processors q do
  for  l = 1,...,s
    initialize all components of σ^l_(0);
for  j = 1,...,m do
  forall processors q do {
    for  i = 1,...,s do
      compute ⌈n/p⌉ components of f(σ^i_(j−1));
    for  l = 1,...,s do
      compute ⌈n/p⌉ components of σ^l_(j);
      multi-broadcast ⌈n/p⌉ comp. of σ^l_(j);
  }
forall q do {
  for  l = 1,...,s do
    compute ⌈n/p⌉ components of f(σ^l_(m));
  compute ⌈n/p⌉ components of y_(κ+1);
  multi-broadcast ⌈n/p⌉ components of y_(κ+1);
}
stepsize control;
```

FIG. 5.1. Consecutive implementation of the IRK method.

stepsize control can be modelled by the formula

$$T_{dp}(n,p) = \left(m \left\lceil \frac{n}{p} \right\rceil s + \left\lceil \frac{n}{p} \right\rceil \right) (2s+1)\, t_{op} + \left(ms \left\lceil \frac{n}{p} \right\rceil + s \left\lceil \frac{n}{p} \right\rceil \right) T_f + n\, s\, t_{op}$$

for the computation time where T_f denotes the time for the evaluation for one component of f and t_{op} denotes the time for the execution of an arithmetic operation. Each processor has to compute n/p components of the argument vector and n/p components of f. Since f is not given in advance, the complete argument vector has to be made available to each processor with a multi-broadcast operation. For the communication time, the following formula is used:

$$C_{dp}(n,p) = s\, m\, t_{mb} \left(p, \left\lceil \frac{n}{p} \right\rceil \right) + t_{mb} \left(p, \left\lceil \frac{n}{p} \right\rceil \right).$$

For the runtime tests, we use an IRK method that is based on a 3-stage Radau method of order five. Using $m = 4$ corrector iterations, we obtain an IRK method of order five. To evaluate the predictions, we consider the application of the IRK method to ODE systems with two different classes of right hand side functions f:

- each component of **f** has fixed evaluation costs that are independent of the system size (sparse function), i.e., the evaluation time of the entire function f consisting of n components increases linearly with the size of the ODE system.
- The evaluation costs of each component of **f** depend linearly on the system size (dense function), i.e., the evaluation time of the entire function f increases quadratically with the size of the ODE system.

Both cases may occur when solving systems of time-dependent partial differential equations. The discretization of the spatial derivatives of a two–dimensional reaction-diffusion equation (Brusselator with diffusion)

$$\frac{\partial u}{\partial t} = 1 + u^2 v - 4.4u + \alpha \left(\frac{\partial^2 u}{\partial x^2} + \frac{\partial^2 u}{\partial y^2} \right)$$
$$\frac{\partial v}{\partial t} = 3.4u - u^2 v + \alpha \left(\frac{\partial^2 v}{\partial x^2} + \frac{\partial^2 v}{\partial y^2} \right)$$

n	p=2	p=4	p=8	p=16	p=32	p=64	p=128	p=256
100	0.05	0.03	0.017	0.015	0.018	0.028	0.053	0.102
500	1.27	0.65	0.34	0.176	0.102	0.073	0.076	0.117
1000	5.15	2.60	1.33	0.695	0.369	0.216	0.158	0.161
1500	11.44	5.78	2.92	1.488	0.769	0.423	0.265	0.216
2000	20.28	10.23	5.16	2.635	1.342	0.715	0.423	0.312
3000	45.60	22.84	11.53	5.814	2.975	1.563	0.862	0.562
5000	126.40	63.23	31.75	16.02	8.159	4.215	2.202	1.263

n	p=2	p=4	p=8	p=16	p=32	p=64	p=128	p=256
100	0.06	0.03	0.020	0.017	0.022	0.037	0.076	0.164
500	1.29	0.65	0.33	0.176	0.102	0.079	0.097	0.174
1000	5.11	2.56	1.28	0.656	0.349	0.204	0.161	0.207
1500	11.46	5.73	2.88	1.452	0.743	0.410	0.265	0.261
2000	20.35	10.18	5.10	2.562	1.320	0.697	0.410	0.335
3000	45.73	22.87	11.45	5.754	2.898	1.483	0.822	0.544
5000	126.89	63.46	31.75	15.92	8.011	4.071	2.131	1.204

TABLE 5.1
Measured (top) and predicted (bottom) runtimes for the iterated RK method applied to a dense ODE system on a T3D.

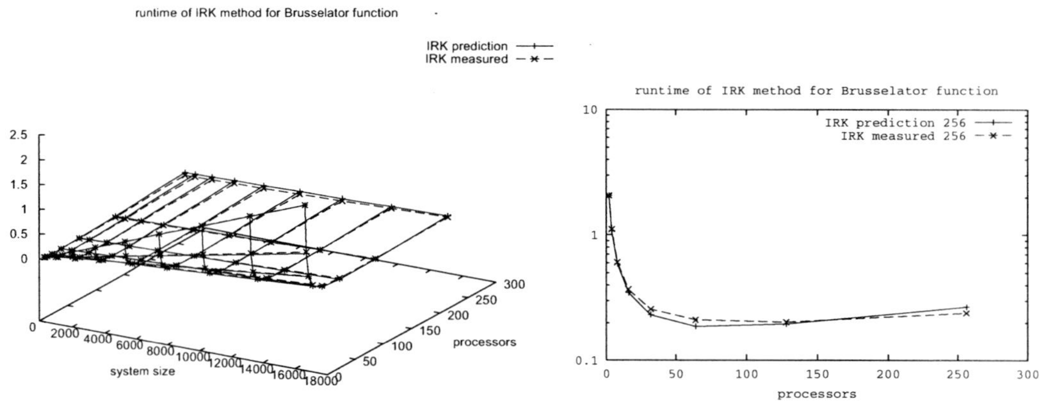

FIG. 5.2. Runtimes of the IRK method for the sparse ODE systems on the T3D.

results in a function $\mathbf{f}$ with a constant computational effort for each component [9]. The standard discretization of the spatial derivatives on an uniform grid with mesh size $1/(N-1)$ leads to an ODE system of dimension $n = 2N^2$:

$$\frac{du_{ij}}{dt} = 1 + u_{ij}^2 v_{ij} - 4.4u_{ij} + \alpha(N-1)^2 \left(u_{i+1,j} + u_{i-1,j} + u_{i,j+1} + u_{i,j-1} - 4u_{i,j}\right)$$

$$\frac{dv_{ij}}{dt} = 3.4u_{ij} - u_{ij}^2 v_{ij} + \alpha(N-1)^2 \left(v_{i+1,j} + v_{i-1,j} + v_{i,j+1} + v_{i,j-1} - 4v_{i,j}\right).$$

For $\alpha = 0.002$ and a small or medium number of grid points, this is a non-stiff system and the IRK method is appropriate [9]. A function $\mathbf{f}$ with system size depending evaluation costs arises when solving nonlinear partial differential equations with Fourier–Galerkin methods.

The dense and sparse ODE functions are chosen for the runtime tests because the IRK method shows different characteristics for these functions. For dense functions, the IRK

n	p=2	p=4	p=8	p=16	p=32	p=64	p=128	p=256
242	0.03	0.019	0.013	0.013	0.017	0.028	0.053	0.104
882	0.11	0.06	0.04	0.026	0.026	0.034	0.058	0.108
1922	0.24	0.13	0.07	0.049	0.041	0.045	0.067	0.115
3362	0.42	0.23	0.13	0.080	0.062	0.061	0.078	0.127
5202	0.65	0.35	0.19	0.121	0.089	0.082	0.094	0.140
7442	0.93	0.50	0.27	0.170	0.123	0.107	0.114	0.157
10082	1.26	0.67	0.37	0.229	0.163	0.137	0.139	0.179
13122	1.64	0.88	0.48	0.295	0.206	0.172	0.170	0.206
16562	2.07	1.11	0.60	0.369	0.257	0.211	0.203	0.239

n	p=2	p=4	p=8	p=16	p=32	p=64	p=128	p=256
242	0.03	0.018	0.014	0.014	0.020	0.037	0.075	0.163
882	0.11	0.060	0.036	0.027	0.028	0.043	0.080	0.168
1922	0.24	0.13	0.07	0.048	0.042	0.053	0.067	0.174
3362	0.42	0.22	0.12	0.078	0.060	0.066	0.089	0.184
5202	0.65	0.34	0.19	0.115	0.084	0.083	0.099	0.196
7442	0.93	0.49	0.27	0.160	0.113	0.103	0.112	0.211
10082	1.26	0.66	0.36	0.214	0.147	0.128	0.148	0.227
13122	1.64	0.86	0.47	0.276	0.187	0.156	0.170	0.246
16562	2.06	1.08	0.59	0.346	0.230	0.187	0.196	0.268

TABLE 5.2
Measured (top) and predicted (bottom) runtimes for the iterated RK method applied to a sparse ODE system on a T3D. The average deviation is 10.3 %.

method shows a good scalability to large number of processors and a small communication overhead, such that the execution time is dominated by the computation time of the method. Thus, the comparison shows how good the computation time can be predicted. For sparse functions, the communication overhead is increasing with the number of processors and for larger numbers of processors, the execution time is completely dominated by the communication time. Thus, the comparison shows how good the communication time can be predicted.

Tables 5.2 and 5.1 compare the measured (top) and predicted (bottom) runtimes of the IRK method on the T3D. Table 5.2 shows the runtimes for a sparse Brusselator function f_B which has a constant evaluation time $T_{f_B} = 7.1\mu s$ on one processor of the T3D. Table 5.1 shows the runtimes for a dense function f_S which has evaluation time $T_{f_S} = 0.66n\ \mu s$ where n is the size of the ODE system. For dense functions, the difference between the predicted and measured runtimes of the IRK method usually lies below 5%. For sparse functions, the maximum difference is 15%, but is much smaller in most cases. Figure 5.2 illustrates the prediction for sparse ODE systems. The left part of the figure shows the dependence of the runtime on the size of the ODE system *and* the number of processors whereas the right parts show the dependence of the runtime on the number of processors for the largest system size tested (16562 for sparse ODE systems). The right diagrams are given with a logarithmic scale to show the difference between the measured and predicted runtimes more clearly.

6. Conclusions. This article has shown that the modelling of collective communication operations can be done with simple formulas in closed form. The formulas can be used by application programmers to estimate the communication overhead of their algorithms which can help them to tune the algorithms without time-consuming runtime tests such that the communication overhead is minimized. A combination of the performance prediction for the communication operations with a performance prediction for the computational effort can lead to an a priori estimation of the prospective gain of a parallel implementation. Thus, the programmer can decide on the benefits of a parallel implementation before actually performing it. Another advantage of runtime formulas in closed form is that optimization methods can be used in designing efficient implementations which minimize both the communication overhead and the load imbalance.

An important application area for analytical performance prediction mechanisms are compilers for DMMs [18, 12, 6]. These compilers assist the programmer in generating an efficient parallel implementation. To make suggestions for the design of a parallel implementation, e.g., a selection of a data distribution, the compiler has to have access to a powerful performance prediction tool to estimate the effects of different parallel versions. The compiler can estimate the computations of a program by an analysis of the intermediate representation. The runtimes of the arithmetic operations can be derived from an appropriate machine description. The runtimes of the communication operations can be derived as described in this article.

Acknowledgment. We would like to thank the Edinburgh Parallel Computing Centre for giving access to the T3D and the NIC John von Neumann-Institut für Computing in Jülich, Germany, for giving access to their Cray T3E.

REFERENCES

[1] G.S. Almasi and A. Gottlieb. *Highly Parallel Computing* . Benjamin/Cummings, 1994.
[2] P. Banerjee, J. Chandy, M. Gupta, E. Hodge, J. Holm, A. Lain, D. Palermo, S. Ramaswamy, and E. Su. The Paradigm Compiler for Distributed-Memory Multicomputers. *IEEE Computer*, 28(10):37–47, 1995.
[3] K. Cameron, L.J. Clarke, and A.G. Smith. CRI/EPCC MPI for CRAY T3D. Technical report, Edinburgh Parallel Computing Centre, 1995.
[4] D.E. Culler, J.P. Singh, and A. Gupta. *Parallel Computer Architecture: A Hardware Software Approach.* Morgan Kaufmann, 1999.
[5] R. Foschia, T. Rauber, and G. Rünger. Modeling the Communication Behavior of the Intel Paragon. In *Proc. 5th Symp. on Modeling, Analysis and Simulation of Computer and Telecommunication Systems (MASCOTS'97)*, IEEE, pages 117–124, 1997.
[6] I. Foster and K.M. Chandy. Fortran M: A Language for Modular Parallel Programming. *Journal of Parallel and Distributed Computing*, 25(1):24–35, April 1995.
[7] A. Geist, A. Beguelin, J. Dongarra, W. Jiang, R. Manchek, and V. Sunderam. *PVM Parallel Virtual Machine: A User's Guide and Tutorial for Networked Parallel Computing.* MIT Press, Cambridge, MA, 1996. Zugeh"orige Webseite: www.netlib.org/pvm3/book/pvm_book.html.
[8] W. Gropp, S. Huss-Ledermann, A. Lumsdaine, E. Lusk, B. Nitzberg, W. Saphir, and M. Snir. *MPI: The Complete Reference, Vol.2: The MPI Extensions.* MIT Press, Camdridge, MA, 1998.
[9] E. Hairer, S.P. Nørsett, and G. Wanner. *Solving Ordinary Differential Equations I: Nonstiff Problems.* Springer–Verlag, Berlin, 1993.
[10] K. Hwang, Z. Xu, and M. Arakawa. Benchmark Evaluation of the IBM SP2 for Parallel Signal Processing. *IEEE Transactions on Parallel and Distributed Systems*, 7(5):522–536, 1996.
[11] S. Johnsson. Performance Modeling of Distributed Memory Architecture. *Journal of Parallel and Distributed Computing*, 12:300–312, 1991.
[12] S. Ramaswamy. *Simultaneous Exploitation of Task and Data Parallelism in Regular Scientific Applications.* PhD thesis, University of Illinois at Urbana-Champaign, 1996.
[13] T. Rauber and G. Rünger. Deriving Structured Parallel Implementations for Numerical Methods. *Microprocessing and Microprogramming*, 41:589–608, 1996.
[14] T. Rauber and G. Rünger. Parallel Iterated Runge–Kutta Methods and Applications. *International Journal of Supercomputer Applications*, 10(1):62–90, 1996.
[15] T. Rauber and G. Rünger. Parallel Solution of Stiff Ordinary Differential Equations. In T. Yang, editor, *Parallel Numerical Computations with Applications*, pages 33–51. Kluwer, 1999.
[16] T. Rauber and G. Rünger. A Transformation Approach to Derive Efficient Parallel Implementations. *IEEE Transactions on Software Engineering*, 26(4):315–339, 2000.
[17] Cray Research. Architectural overview of the CRAY T3D. Technical report, Cray Research, Inc., 1994.
[18] J. Subhlok, D. O'Hallaron, T. Gross, P. Dinda, and J. Webb. Communication and memory Requirements as the basis for Mapping Task and Data Parallel Programs. In *Proceedings of Supercomputing '94*, 1994.
[19] J. Subhlok and B. Yang. A New Model for Integrating Nested Task and Data Parallel Programming. In *8th ACM SIGPLAN Symp. on Principles & Practice of Parallel Programming*, pages 1–12, 1997.
[20] P.J. van der Houwen and B.P. Sommeijer. Parallel Iteration of high–order Runge–Kutta Methods with stepsize control. *Journal of Computational and Applied Mathematics*, 29:111–127, 1990.

[21] Z. Xu and K. Hwang. Early Prediction of MPP Performance: SP2, T3D and Paragon Experiences. *Parallel Computing*, 22:917–942, 1996.

Section 2: Parallel Applications

In: Parallel and Distributed Scientific and Engineering Computing ISBN 1-59033-956-8
Editor: Y. Pan and L.T. Yang, pp. 69-84

PARALLELIZATION AND ANALYSIS OF THE LINKMAP PROGRAM

N. LOPEZ-BENITEZ, A. RAI, K. KOTHARI* AND S. E. PODUSLO†

Abstract. Linkage analysis uses information from family pedigrees to map and locate disease genes on particular chromosomes. A recombination fraction denoted as θ is estimated as a measure of crossing over between two loci. Sequential genetic algorithms have many successful applications in very different domains, but they have a major drawback in their utilization. The availability of large family pedigrees has increased both computational demands and analysis time. To address these shortcomings and to study new more efficient models, parallel platforms are being used for genetic programs. Linkage is a software package for performing genetic likelihood calculations; Fastlink is an improved, faster version. This work provides a parallel implementation of the Linkmap program (one of the four programs in Linkage/Fastlink) for a heterogeneous environment, using a static and a dynamic strategy for task allocation. The parallelization scheme has also been implemented in a 56-node SGI Origin 2000 machine.

Key words. Parallelization, Task allocation, Task graphs, High performance computing, Genetic linkage

1. Introduction. Linkage analysis uses information from family pedigrees to map and locate disease genes on particular chromosomes. Several computer packages have been written for these linkage computations and most published linkage studies use one of these programs. Linkage is a sophisticated analysis software package which evaluates the likelihood of a given pedigree under different assumptions about the recombination fraction between two loci [1]. It contains four related programs: Lodscore, Ilink, Linkmap and Mlink for the probability computations [2]. Sequential algorithmic improvements have been made to this package which are now integrated into Fastlink [3].

Because of the basic purpose of Linkmap/Fastlink is to find the location of the disease gene with respect to other markers, the *recombination* fraction denoted as θ is used as the measure of linkage between two loci. This fraction varies from $\theta = 0$ for loci right next to each other to $\theta = 0.5$ for loci far apart [4]. Linkage will yield the pedigree likelihood for a value of θ. However, the use of large family pedigrees has greatly increased both the computational demands and analysis time. To address these shortcomings and to study new and more efficient models, parallel platforms are being used for linkage analysis. Parallelization can be achieved at two levels: at an algorithmic level which makes an improvement in the basic statistical calculations strategy, and at the code level where the code is analyzed and rearranged for potential parallelism [5]. In this context Treadmarks is a parallel programming system that allows programs written in a shared-memory style to run on a network of Unix workstations [6].

In this report a parallel model of Linkmap in the Fastlink program using code level parallelization is formulated. The model concentrates on distributing different likelihood computations for various recombination fractions on different computers. The model was implemented using a message-passing interface. Performance prediction and evaluation of this model was also carried out using TG-GUI, a user-interface designed to evaluate task graphs using simulation [8] or a numerical tool [9]. The purpose of a task graph representation is two-fold: (a) predict performance under different heuristics and (b) exploit a possible parallelism in a multi-computing environment. Once the task graph of a system is obtained, using the precedence relationships between tasks, a strategy to allocate parallel tasks to a collection of processors can be applied. A task graph representation of the LINKAGE program has permitted its evaluation under different heuristics. Typical heuristics [10], [11] that have been used are the following:

* Department of Computer Science, Texas Tech University, Lubbock, TX 79409 (nlb@cs.ttu.edu).
† Department of Neurology, Institute of Molecular Medicine and Genetics, Medical College of Georgia, Augusta, GA 30912 (sposuslo@mail.mcg.edu).

(i) Largest Task First (LTF): This heuristic will assign a task having the largest execution time to a randomly selected processor and marks that task as assigned. A task from the remaining task list is selected for the next assignment until all the tasks are assigned.

(ii) Shortest Estimated Execution Time First (SEETF): A task is selected at random from the task set and assigned to a processor that executes the task in the minimum time.

(iii) Minimum Finish Time (MFT): This heuristic takes into account the precedence constraints on the tasks. A randomly selected task T_i is assigned to a processor P_j that minimizes the finish time of the task in a deterministic simulated execution, where the finish time of a task is given by the minimum sum of the execution time and the next instance in which processor P_j becomes free.

Efficient scheduling of tasks is critical to achieving high performance in parallel systems. The objective of scheduling is to map the task onto processors and order their execution so that task precedence requirements are satisfied and a minimum schedule length is obtained [12]. Thus, various schemes need can be evaluated before a model can be implemented. This report also discusses details about the implementation of the parallel model in a heterogeneous network of workstations (NOW) environment and in SGI 2000 machine with 56 processors and 56 Gbytes of main memory. Relevant implementation issues are discussed and the results obtained in each case are analyzed.

2. Parallelization of Linkmap. Linkmap is legacy software that offers proven functionality for small pedigrees; however, its performance becomes unacceptably low for large family pedigrees when executing in a single processor environment. Therefore, a feasible parallel implementation must address the issue of providing not only higher performance but a desirable level of scalability to make an optimal use of the processing resources available. The following steps summarize a procedure followed toward the parallelization of Linkmap:

1. Analysis of the serial code to:

(i) identify sections of code that are computing and data intensive. These sections of code become possible targets for parallelization,

(ii) fine tune code for an optimal use of cache memory. Reduction of cache traffic is essential particularly for sections of code, serial and parallel that are data intensive.

2. Analysis of the parallelizable section of code previously identified considering:

(i) the type of architecture,

(ii) the number of processors available,

(iii) the underlying network and the application communication demands, and

(iv) suitable allocation schemes.

3. Implementation and experimentation. Steps two and three minimize possible problems that may be encountered due to the code design limitations. A useful tool involves the simulation of a suitable parallel model to predict performance of a given allocation scheme under different network architectures and load conditions. Parallelism and data dependencies between tasks are captured with a task graph-based model. A task graph is used with Linkmap to experiment with several selected assignment heuristics.

The sequential Linkmap code was first analyzed to find parallel components that can be distributed for simultaneous execution on different processors [16]. Profiling tools were used for the analysis of the source code for potential performance/time bottlenecks by identifying those sections of the code which are frequently executed and those likely to take longer to execute [17].

3. Methodology. Partitioning [18] implies dividing a problem into components that may execute concurrently with the primary goal of achieving scalability. Determining how a partition scales gives an indication of the maximum computing power that can be utilized without loss of performance. For the Linkage program the (θ vectors) of the program were divided and operated (performed likelihood calculations) on each part concurrently. Also, the notion of achieving higher granularity (ratio of computation to communication) was used in choosing a specific loop (outermost loop) from a nest of loops for achieving better parallelism. Sun Workshop's Looptool takes a "< *binary* > *.looptimes*" file as a parameter to draw the loop graph chart [19]. This file was created by compiling the source file with the "-Zlp" compiler option and then executing the binary thus created; i.e.,

Source.c —(Compile with -Zlp)→ Binary —(Execute)→ Source.lopptimes

A "linkmap.looptimes" was thus created and a graph using this file was obtained. Three nested loops of interest were found: a loop corresponding to line 488 and to line 730 in the file linkmap.c, and to line 1546 in the file comlike.c [20]. Using a profiling tool the following computationally intensive loops were identified [19]:

```
ipedloop(){
        do { /*Loop 1*/
                —
                iterpeds();
                —
        } (while <condition>);
}
iterpeds() {
        for() { /*Loop 2*/
                —
                likelihood();
                —
        }
}
```

Thus, effectively there is a nest of two loops that could be expressed as:

for all θ vectors
for all pedigrees
perform likelihood calculation

where the outermost loop (loop1) calls the function iterpeds(), which is in turn responsible for the actual likelihood computations. The inner loop (loop2) corresponds to the number of pedigrees, i.e., likelihood calculations performed for each pedigree. For a small number of pedigrees the number of iterations was also very small. Initial estimations revealed that distributing the inner iterations would incur more synchronization overhead offsetting any gain achieved. It was also found that if the number of iterations of the outer loop is greater than the number of processors (which is usually the case), then distributing the iterations of the inner loop would result in overhead and no gain. Analysis of the outer loop (loop1) yielded a do-while loop, that computes the θ vector (from a user-given data set) and then estimates the maximum likelihood for this vector for all pedigrees. These calculations are performed by the function *likelihood()*. The loop also calculates the loop-breaking conditions dynamically, i.e., in each pass, after the likelihood calculation, it checks whether the breaking condition had been reached. Functionally, the loop is of the form:

```
do {
    Calculate θ vector;
    Update probabilities for this θ vector (likelihood());
    Update condition for stopping;
```

```
while(condition is valid)}
```

For allocation purposes it is necessary to predetermine the total number of iterations the loop goes through in a given data set. Also, needed beforehand are the set of θ vectors for which the likelihood is to be calculated. This is required so that different θ vectors can be allocated to different processors. For this purpose, the "while" loop was simulated and converted into a partitionable "for" loop of the form:

```
for(theta_cnt = 0; theta_cnt¡num_of_iter;theta_cnt ++){
   /*Load the θ vector calculated by the simulator() for this iteration into
   gtheta[] to provide the same environment to the rest of the loop */
   for(k = 0; k ¡ mlocus -1 ; k ++)
        gtheta[k] = parArray[theta_cnt][k];
   likelihood(gtheta);
}
```

The removal of data dependencies required the introduction of some extra variables of the same type as that of the data involved in the dependency. To verify that dependencies were removed the loop was executed in a random manner. That is, iterations were run in no particular order and the results were compared with those obtained when run sequentially. The two results were found to be exactly the same. In the usual sense, if any iteration of the loop depended on any other iteration, then the results would have been erroneous. However, this random-iteration technique does not verify dependencies 100%. For example, an array addition of the form:

```
for ( i = 0; i ¡ 6 ; i ++) Var = array[ i ] + Var;
```

would yield correct results even if the iterations were calculated in a random fashion, but may give incorrect results when different iterations are run on separate computers simultaneously. In our case all iterations were independent of each other.

To formulate a parallel model of Linkmap the code was represented as one task from the point where the program began its execution i.e., the main() function in the file *commoncode.c* in Fastlink, to the point it reached the 'for' loop (function *iterpeds()* in the file *linkmap.c*). Then, the iterations of the 'for' loop were represented as 'n' independent tasks. Finally, all these iteration-tasks joined to end the program execution. Thus, the Linkmap program can be expressed as the following pseudocode:

```
main() {
     PreLoop_code ; /* master thread */
     For loop with "n" iterations; /* "n" independent worker threads */
}
```

The corresponding task graph is shown in Fig. 3.1. The number of tasks $T_1 ... T_N$ shown varies from data set to data set. The task T_M will initiate and collect results from all other tasks. In linkage analysis a data set involves two files: a *.ped* file that contains the pedigree details and the *.dat* file that contains the recombination fraction vector details. Implementation involves distributing concurrent tasks on a cluster of available computers. The message passage interface (MPI) library was used to explicitly send and execute tasks on different processors.

Two different implementation strategies to parallelize the above 'for' loop were adopted. In the first implementation, the number N of iterations of a loop were just divided by a number P of available processors, and sets of iterations were formed with N/P iterations in each set. The advantage of this strategy is that it is fairly simple to design and implement and is suited for an environment where all computers are of homogeneous speeds and loads. However, in a heterogeneous system allocating an equal number of iterations to all machines limits the overall efficiency of the partition because of the time taken by the slowest machine to execute its set of iterations. Moreover, the load at each machine changes with time. Thus, this strategy may end up having the slowest processor performing calculations while much faster processors are idle. In the second implementation, a "manager-worker" dynamic style of task allocation was used [5]. Instead of allocating sets of iterations to any processor, a processor is made a manager executing T_M to allocate exactly one iteration to every other processor (worker) in the system. The workers execute their iteration and as soon as they finish, results are sent to the manager along with the request for another iteration. The manager keeps allocating iterations in this manner, until all iterations are executed. This ensures that the processor with greater efficiency gets a larger number of iterations. Also, a processor with the greatest load will automatically perform fewer iterations. One problem with this strategy as such, is that the manager does not participate in calculations; it just waits for the workers to finish. A variation was implemented, in which the manager was made to calculate along with the workers. Since the manager has to receive/allocate iterations to the workers as well as to calculate, the fastest computer in the network was assigned as the manager. Therefore, a thread was also created in this machine to perform calculations. The implementation is outlined as follows:

```
Total number of iterations = N;
Total number of processors = P;
My rank in the cluster = my_rank;
Number of θ results that processor zero has received = recvTheta;
Number of θ that processor zero has allocated to workers = thetaVector;
Start(){
    if ( my_rank != 0 ){
        while(1) {
            Receive thetaVector;
            Calculate likelihood for this vector;
            Send results to processor 0;
        }
    }
    if (my_rank == 0){
        thetaVector = 0, recvTheta = 0;
        for ( procs = 1; procs ¡ P; procs++){
            Send thetaVector to procs;
            thetaVector++;
        }
        while(1){
            Receive results from any of the workers;
            recvTheta ++;
            Send thetaVector to the worker which sent results;
            Store results received in the output file;
            if (thetaVector ¡ N-1) thetaVector ++;
            if (recvTheta ¡ N ) break;
        }
        Send "stop-signal" to all worker processors;
    }
}
```

The first 'if' loop is executed by the worker processors until no more θ's are received from the master which is ranked zero. The second 'if' loop is executed only by processor zero. It first initializes the indexes, then it sends θ vectors to different processors, and

TABLE 4.1
Average Execution time (in seconds) of tasks on all processors (1 to 6)

Tasks	1	2	3	4	5	6
T_M	0.0937	0.1333	0.1257	0.000136	0.0001127	0.3473
T_1	174.9467	205.7513	178.103	282.2495	131.142	287.312
T_2	197.629	350.547	338.897	315.7495	147.142	610.615
T_3	206.7396	354.309	326.974	310.249	148.857	674.732
T_4	199.578	346.363	342.738	316.999	149.428	687.535
T_5	200.4077	349.853	330.017	314.249	151.2855	681.15
T_6	203.279	346.101	401.722	311.4995	150.14271	688.921

collects results from worker processors. The first worker to deliver results receives another θ vector and the results are saved. This distribution of θ stops only when the master has received N calculations of θ. It then sends an abort signal to all workers. The manager and a worker thread were created on processor '0' by specifying this in a MPI configuration file. If this file had two entries for one processor, two threads were created on that computer by MPI and both threads were treated as individual processes with separate ranks in the cluster. Therefore, the worker thread on processor '0' executes iterations under "if (my_rank != 0)" and the manager thread under "if (my_rank == 0)". This strategy adjusted itself according to the heterogeneity of the machines available.

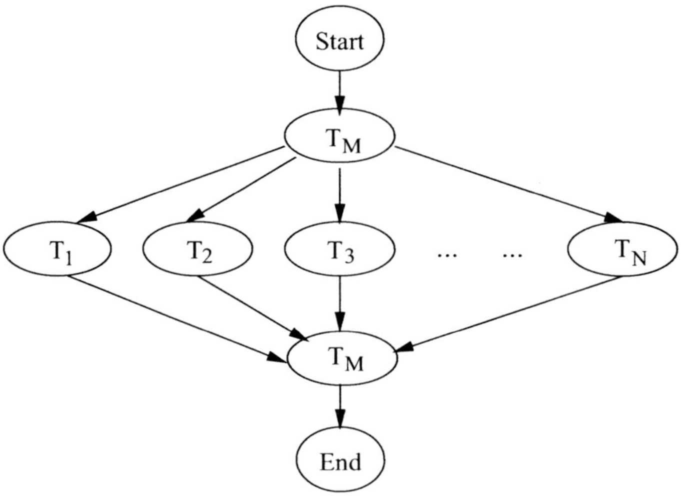

FIG. 3.1. *Task Graph of Parallelized Linkmap*

4. NOW:Simulation and Experimental Results. The actual implementation was carried out for two different strategies (an ad-hoc static and a dynamic allocation). The results obtained were compared with the sequential run and are reported in [13] and [14]. The dynamic and ad-hoc static heuristics were applied under various machine combinations and different load conditions. The ad-hoc static heuristic was also simulated and compared with actual results. The near equal execution times in this case validate the accuracy of the simulation tool.

Experiments were conducted on six computers, three DEC Alphas (machines 1, 2, and 3), one dual Pentium processor (machine 4), an Intel Pentium 200MHz (machine 5), and a SUN SPARC (machine 6). Two data sets were used for the experiments. The first data set had one family (one pedigree), 55 family members, and 21 markers. LINKMAP was run by

TABLE 4.2
Linkmap predicted execution times (in minutes)

No of processors	MFT	LTF	SEEFT
2(machines 1,2)	13.1	23.34	19.73
3(machines 13)	11.02	17.455	19.71
4(machines 14)	9.77	15.712	19.692
5(machines 15)	9.5	10.45	19.68

TABLE 4.3
Linkmap execution times (in minutes)

Fastest Sequential	Parallel ad-hoc static	Parallel Dynamic	Parallel simulation
31.97	16.43	16.38	17.3825

placing marker 1 between or beside markers 17, 14 and 9. The measured average execution times of all the tasks in the first data set on all the processors is shown in Table 4.1. The Dual Pentium Pro-processor had the fastest execution time while the Sun Sparc was the slowest. The TG GUI provided an implementation of the three different static heuristics previously mentioned: Minimum Finish time (MFT), Largest Task First (LTF) and Shortest Effective Execution Time First (SEETF). Simulation results assuming a normal distribution are shown in Table 4.2 for two, three, four and five processors.

The static and dynamic strategies were tested in various processor combinations under different loads. Measurements were tabulated to compare the observed speedup with the maximum possible speedup. In a heterogeneous environment the maximum possible speedup is estimated adding the normalized execution times of all computers involved in the calculation. Normalization is obtained with respect to the fastest machine. The observed speedups (T_{seq}/T_{par}) were also estimated with respect to the fastest sequential time.Five distinct cases were considered:

Case a: Two DEC-Alphas, (machines 2 and 3) with almost equal processing speed and negligible load, inferred by the near equal execution times shown in Table 1. The sequential execution time of Linkmap in machine 2 took 32.55 minutes and in machine 3 took 31.97 minutes. The parallel execution times are listed in Table 4.3 along with the best sequential and simulated time. The simulation results compare close enough with the measured execution times. This shows the feasibility of using simulation to analyze several allocation schemes before any actual implementation. The speedup obtained for the dynamic heuristic is shown in Table 4.4 against the maximum possible speedup. The speedup achieved (both dynamic and static) was almost equal to the maximum possible speedup, ensuring that both processors executed equal number of iterations in both schemes.

Case b: The DEC-Alphas (1 and 3) had different processing speeds and negligible loads. As shown in Table 4.4, the dynamic allocation achieved greater speedup. The static strategy allocated equal numbers of iterations to both machines. One iteration for the first dataset on machine 1 took between 2.8 to 3.33 minutes and one iteration on 3 took approximately 5 minutes. Thus out of the six iterations, three iterations were calculated by 1 in about ten minutes whereas 3 took fifteen minutes. The total time was dictated by the time taken by the slowest processor to perform its set of iterations; the static strategy yielded results in 15.25 minutes. Hence, machine 1, the faster of the two managed to finish four iterations while two iterations were performed by 3.

Case c: The three DEC-Alphas (1-3), were used with negligible load. It is clear that the dynamic heuristic almost equals the maximum possible speedup. While the static scheme

TABLE 4.4
Speedup: Dynamic vs Static

Case	Processors	Ideal	Dynamic	Static
a	2,3	1.982	1.952	1.945
b	1,3	1.62	1.614	1.257
c	1,2,3	2.189	2.05	1.997
d	1,2,3*	1.962	1.958	0.58
e	4,5,6	1.739	1.68	0.915

performed poorly with two computers, it performed almost equal to the dynamic scheme in the case of three computers since the slowest processor calculated three iterations in the former case as compared with only two iterations in the latter case.

Case d: When one of the processors was heavily loaded, a different pattern of results was obtained. The static implementation yielded poor results because even the heavily loaded processor received an equal number of iterations to calculate. In this situation the maximum possible speedup for three processors was less than that for two processors and the dynamic allocation almost equals the ideal performance.

Case e: Five processors were used. The static scheme failed because of the heterogeneity in the speed of the machines, whereas the dynamic scheme yielded better results.

5. Origin 2000: Implementation Issues. A second data set has 3 families (3 pedigrees), with 51, 60, and 55 family members and 15 markers. LINKMAP was run by placing marker 15 between or beside markers 8, 9 and 10. The data set was very computation intensive and a sequential run of this data set on the fastest DEC-Alpha took 93 hours to complete. Parallel execution time on the three computers took about 34 hours. In addition, for the first set only modest speedups were obtained as complete parallelism can not be achieved with only six nodes. Furthermore, the idea of attaining parallelism by distributing the various θ values was effective but the implementation falls short of providing all the user-required details expected from the sequential Linkmap legacy code. Therefore, the parallel design of Linkmap was implemented in the Origin 2000 (O2K) machine. The results obtained correspond to 21 iterations with a 19-fold speedup using only 22 processors. Implementations issues are addressed in the next paragraphs.

5.1. Tuning single processor performance. Tuning execution in a single processor is important because there can be operations such as square roots or floating point divisions which consume a lot of CPU time. Floating-point division operations were located in the file *commoncode.c* of the Linkmap program. Various profiling tools such as *perfex* and *speedshop* (ssrun) were used to locate these operations; *Perfex* was helpful in identifying in a first-pass program-wide performance issues; *speedshop* was useful in carrying out focused experiments for identifying procedures that have problems [22]. For example, if *a.out* is the name of an executable file of interest, perfex is run as follows:

perfex -a -x a.out

This command provides the number of instructions of each type and the time spent in floating-point operations. *Speedshop* was then used to conduct various experiments like PC (Program Counter) sampling and floating point exception tracing. Speedshop is used with the command:

ssrun -fpcsamp a.out

This command generates a file called *a.out.fpcsamp* that can be used by a profiling tool called *prof* to report statistics collected by *ssrun.* To run prof the following command was used:

prof a.out.fpcsamp

After observing that on floating-point operations, only the quotient part of these divisions was required for further calculations, division operations were carried out as repeated subtractions. The number of machine cycles required for each floating point division operation is almost five times greater than those required by a subtraction operation. And since the computational process requires a large number of floating point division operations, this change resulted in a considerable efficiency in the execution time of the sequential version of Linkmap.

5.2. Cache management. Each CPU in the O2K machine has a private cache memory of 4 MB (also referred to as L2 cache). To improve performance, the CPU always fetches and stores data in its cache. When the CPU refers to data that is not present in the cache, there is a delay while a copy of the data is fetched from memory into the cache [21]. Use of cache memory in an efficient manner is crucial for a better performance of data intensive applications. The machine will first look in the primary cache (referred to as L1 cache; which is usually very small and more expensive) to satisfy a load request. If the requested data item is not found in the primary cache, then a reference to the secondary cache (L2 cache) is made. If the request to the secondary memory also fails, then the Translation Look-aside Buffer (TLB) is searched to map the required virtual address to a physical location in main memory. If a TLB miss occurs, the requested data item is not in main memory and it needs to be brought into main memory from secondary memory. This operation incurs a lot of overhead as reflected in the latency involved in accessing secondary memory. The Linkmap program reads huge arrays of the order of 200×200 for matrix multiplication in the file linkmap.c for intermediate calculations. Consider the following example:

$$
\begin{aligned}
& for(j = 0; j < 200; j++) \\
& \quad for(i = 0; i < 200; i++) \\
& \qquad C[i][j] = C[i][j] + A[i][j] \times B[i][j]
\end{aligned}
$$

Data access for two-dimensional arrays results in a large number of TLB misses because *C* language stores arrays in row major form. When *perfex* was run for the same input file of one family and four markers, the number of TLB misses reported is 232700. Cache blocking or tiling breaks up data structures that are too big to fit in the cache. The example above shows that when the matrices A, B and C get bigger, the performance of the matrix multiply routine drops significantly. To improve performance large matrices are partitioned into blocks small enough such that one block from each matrix can fit into the cache at the same time. In the Linkmap program, the 200×200 matrices were partitioned into 50×50 blocks reducing the number of TLB misses to 120542. This reduction by a factor of 2 resulted in a faster execution time. In turn the overall execution time improved as it also depends on the input file. In one case a run time of about 20 seconds was observed for a file that took originally 4 minutes for a complete execution.

5.3. Output synchronization. Consider the task graph in Fig. 3.1. Assuming six iterations the master task T_M would allocate θ values in a sequential order, i.e. from 0 to 0.5 in steps of 0.1, to the worker threads. The worker thread that runs on a processor having the least load will complete the computation first and report back to the master. However, this order of receiving likelihood results is random and not necessarily in the order of the allocation of work. This problem is further complicated by the fact that the number of iterations of the *for* loop and the number of processors available may not be the same. For example, if there are three processors available for six iterations, θ's will be allocated to three worker threads only. If processor 2 reports back first, it will receive the next θ for computation and so on until all the six θ's are exhausted. In such a case, it becomes difficult to keep track of the correct order of likelihood results. To preserve the required order, results are now buffered as they are received from the worker threads and then saved in a temporary output file in the correct order. The *Case Vision Debugger* (CVD) available on the O2K was used extensively for solving this problem [22]. This tool is a Windows style debugger that can be used to debug multiprocessing applications.

5.4. Multiple families and sex differences. The results obtained for the case of the NOW-based implementation correspond to a pedigree file consisting of a single family (the A file). A pedigree file consisting of four families (the B file) was used for experiments on the O2K. The cluster of four to five nodes of DEC Alphas failed to produce the correct output for multiple families. For the O2K machine the master thread T_M is modified to allocate work in the following manner:

$for(family = 1; family < total\_families; family++)$
    for all thetas
        perform likelihood computations

To collect results from worker threads the following code was implemented:

for all families
    for all thetas
        receive likelihood computations

So far only θ values derived from males were considered. Since male and female gametes are produced by different biological processes, the recombination rates are also different. In general males tend to have lower recombination rates than females. The θ values from females were also handled in the same way as the male θ values to solve this problem. Likelihood computations for female θ values were also carried out and collected by the master thread. A file with sex difference specifications would naturally take more time because likelihood computations need to be carried out for both male and female members of the pedigree tree.

5.5. Varying number of iterations. Linkmap determines the position of the disease gene by placing it between each of the markers of a selected set of loci. For example, if marker 1 is the disease marker and 9,14 and 17 are the other three markers in the set, there will be four runs of the Linkmap program with markers in the following order: {(1,9,14,17), (9,1,14,17), (9,14,1,17), (9,14,17,1)}.

Lod scores for different values of θ's are calculated for each run. The run having the highest Lod score for any value will give the correct order of the markers. Therefore, the analysis of $0 < \theta \leq 0.5$ in steps of 0.1 results in six iterations for all four runs. But this is not always the case. Actually the last computation of the previous run and the first computation of the next run are the same. The previous versions of the sequential Linkmap program were inefficient in that they performed this same computation twice. The redundant computation was not performed twice in Fastlink. Linkmap does not always report this computation twice in the *stream.out* file that is responsible for producing the report in a tabular format. This is critical because an incorrect output file would produce wrong results. This problem was identified and addressed with the help of Dr. Schaffer of the National Institute of Health [23]. Suppose the distance between the markers is d and the number of markers in the set is g. The space s between markers is computed as $s = d/g$, but this is an approximation in practice. When $g \times s \leq d$, the extra point is evaluated, but when $g \times s > d$, the point is skipped. The implementation of this test resulted in the correct output obtained in the *stream.out* file.

6. Experiments and Analysis. With a large number of processors available on the O2K it was possible to perform a wide range of experiments. Execution times were collected for a higher number of iterations using a varied number of processors. For comparison, execution times were also measured for the sequential Linkmap running on a DEC Alpha. All results were taken with zero loads on the DEC Alpha. Results were taken with varying loads on the O2K. All times are reported in *hh:mm:ss* format. Speedup is measured with

TABLE 6.1
Execution times for the case of 6 iterations

No. of procs.	"1F4M"	"4F3M"	"4F4M"
S1	01:00:26	00:05:39	00:38:22
S2	00:04:43	00:04:04	00:22:17
2	00:05:30	00:04:34	00:24:26
3	00:02:42	00:03:50	00:20.15
4	00:01:59	00:01:34	00:09:00
5	00:01:55	00:01:33	00:08:48
6	00:01:48	00:01:30	00:07:33
7	00:01:09	00:00:51	00:04:25

respect to the fastest serial execution that corresponds to the time taken by the serial version on the O2K. The number of iterations was considered as a basis for collecting various results. Four sets of results for 6, 11, 16 and 21 iterations are reported. These results were also reported in [15]. The experiments performed are grouped in the following cases:
Case 1 (6 iterations): The two most important factors that dictate the amount of time taken for linkage calculations are the number of markers in the set and the number of families in the pedigree file. Observing various execution times, the number of markers has a more significant impact on the analysis than the number of families. This is because each marker has a different number of alleles which accounts for the increase in computation time. Fig. 6.1 shows the speedups obtained for different numbers of processors for three different input files. The legend used is suggestive of the input file. For example, *"1F4M"* means that an input file with one family and four markers is used.

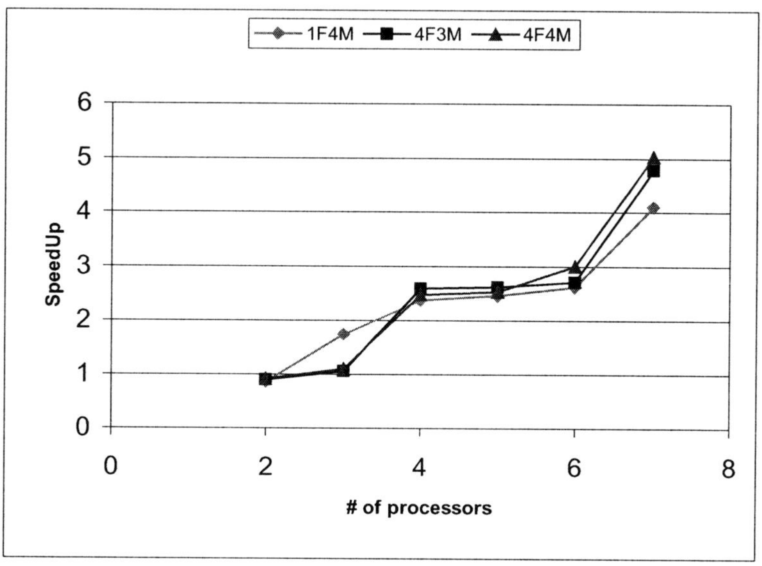

FIG. 6.1. *Speedup plots for the case of six iterations*

Referring to Fig.6.1 and Table 6.1, the following observations apply:

1. The speedup was always less than 1 when the number of processors used was 2. One processor was allocated to execute T_M. Hence, the extra communication overhead results in the speedup being less than one when compared to the serial version on the O2K.
2. Complete parallelism was obtained when seven processors were used for the case

TABLE 6.2
Execution times for the case of 11 iterations

No. of procs.	"1F4M"	"4F3M"	"4F4M"
S1	02:03:29	00:10:54	01:14:45
S2	00:09:15	00:07:50	00:43:24
2	00:09:56	00:08:21	00:44:29
3	00:05:04	00:06:36	00:40:17
4	00:04:04	00:03:35	00:21:07
6	00:02:38	00:02:36	00:15:08
8	00:01:57	00:01:51	00:08:40
10	00:01:54	00:01:32	00:08:20
12	00:01:13	00:00:50	00:04:28

of six iterations. The speedups obtained for the three different combinations of number of families and numbers of markers were 4.10, 4.78 and 5.04. These are close to the ideal speedup value of 6 that indicates that less time is spent in MPI_Send and MPI_Recv blocking calls.

3. Because loop iterations can be computed independently an increase in the number of processors will result in an increase in speedup. In addition, the communication between the master and workers is reduced because less number of tasks are assigned to each worker. This is clearly shown by the steep increase in speedup when the number of processors increased from six to seven; communication overhead was reduced drastically and the maximum possible parallelism was obtained.

4. Table 6.1 shows the execution times for the case of six iterations. $S1$ and $S2$ indicate the serial execution times on the DEC Alpha and the O2K, respectively. These times show an enormous difference between the processing time on DEC Alpha and a processor on O2K. Table 6.1 also shows that the number of markers is a more significant factor than the number of families. The execution time decreased from 00:01:09 to 00:00:51 even though the number of families increased from 1 to 4 because the number of markers decreased from 4 to 3. Similarly, the execution time increased from 00:00:51 to 00:04:25 for the case of 4 families since the number of markers increased from 3 to 4. This is a surprising result as it shows the effect of the number of markers on the computational process. The computation time change is even more dramatic on the DEC alpha machines (S1) as they are not only slower than a single processor of the O2K machine, but handle cache memory and memory swaps less efficiently.

Case 2 (11 iterations): As the number of iterations increases from 6 to 11, the precision obtained in linkage computations also increases. Fig. 6.2 shows the speedups obtained for a different number of processors for the same three input files. Maximum parallelism was obtained with twelve processors. The speedups obtained for the three different combinations of number of families and numbers of markers were 7.60, 9.40 and 9.71. These are close to the ideal speedup value of 11. Table 6.2 shows the execution times for this case. Again these results can be compared against the serial execution times on the DEC Alpha machine. These times again show an enormous difference between the processing on a single DEC Alpha machine and a single O2K processor. The execution time decreased from 00:01:13 to 00:00:50 even though the number of families increased from 1 to 4 because the number of markers decreased from 4 to 3. Similarly, the execution time increased from 00:00:50 to 00:04:28 for the case of 4 families since the number of markers increased from 3 to 4.

Case 3 (16 iterations): This case reports experiments for 16 parallel iterations. Fig. 6.3 shows the speedups obtained for the different number of processors for the same three input files mentioned above. Notice again that the speedup is always less than one when

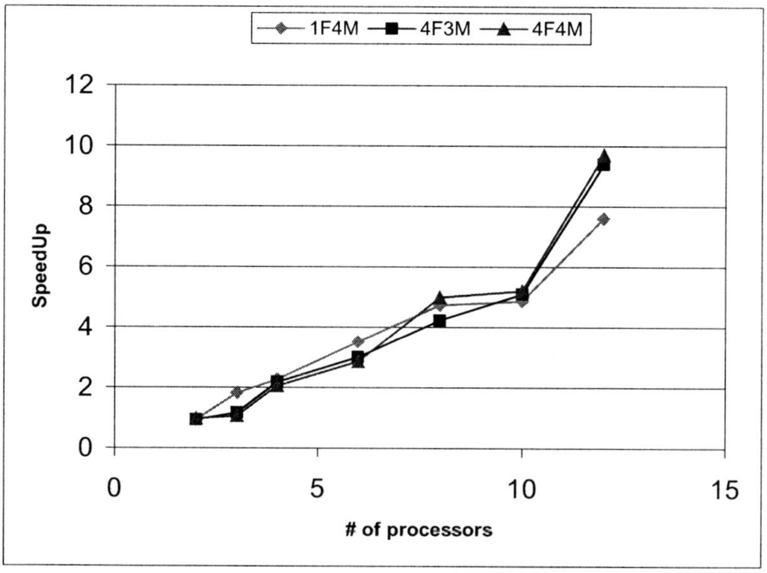

FIG. 6.2. *Speedups obtained with 11 iterations*

the number of processors used is two. Using 17 processors maximizes parallelism and all the 16 iterations are distributed at once by the master thread. This also results in a minimal communication overhead. The speedups obtained for the three different combinations of number of families and numbers of markers were 9.06, 13.66 and 14.29. Again, these are close to the ideal speedup value of 16. Table 6.3 shows the execution times. These results further emphasize the fact that the number of markers is more important than the number of families in determining the execution times. The execution time decreased from 00:01:29 to 00:00:51 when the number of families increased from 1 to 4 because the number of markers decreased from 4 to 3. Similarly, the execution time increased from 00:00:51 to 00:04:31 for the case of 4 families since the number of markers increased from 3 to 4.

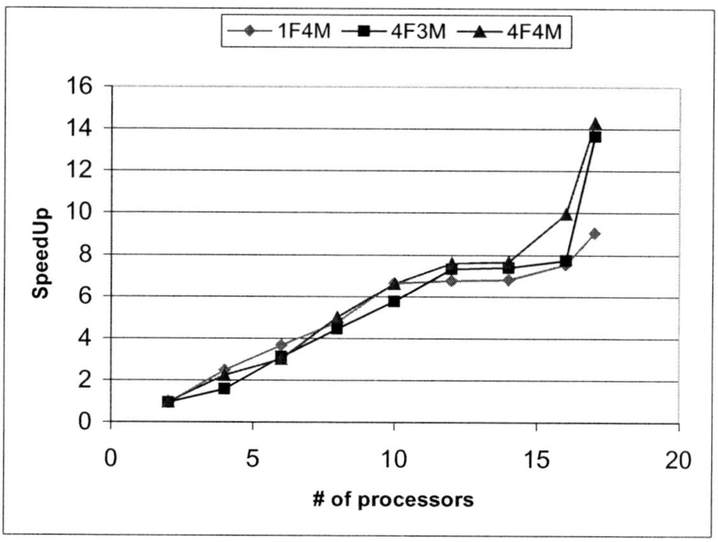

FIG. 6.3. *Speedups obtained with 16 iterations*

TABLE 6.3
Execution times for the case of 16 iterations

No. of procs.	"1F4M"	"4F3M"	"4F4M"
S1	03:07:51	00:16:09	01:51:06
S2	00:13:27	00:11:37	01:04:33
2	00:14:30	00:12:07	01:05:36
4	00:05:25	00:07:21	00:28:35
6	00:03:39	00:03:44	00:21:19
8	00:02:49	00:02:36	00:12:51
10	00:02:01	00:02:01	00:09:45
12	00:01:59	00:01:35	00:08:29
14	00:01:58	00:01:34	00:08:24
16	00:01:47	00:01:30	00:06:29
17	00:01:29	00:00:51	00:04:31

Case 4 (21 iterations): Fig. 6.4 shows the speedups obtained for different number of processors for the same three input files for 21 iterations. The use of 22 processors results in maximum parallelism. The speedups obtained for the three different combinations of number of families and numbers of markers were 12.86, 17.11 and 18.94 which are close to the ideal speedup value of 21. Note again that the speedups are not linear due to the required interactions that occurs between the master and worker threads when the number of processors is less than the number of iterations. However, the increase in speedup exhibits a good level of scalability as performance always increases with the number of processors.

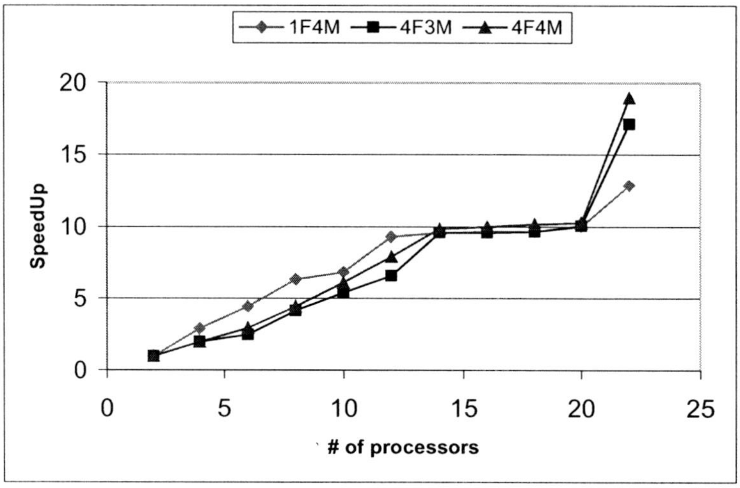

FIG. 6.4. *Speedups obtained with 21 iterations*

7. Conclusions. This research was motivated by the need of obtaining results for genetic linkage calculations in a feasible amount of time in a study of Alzheimer's disease. The results obtained showed that the number of markers is more important than the number of families in determining execution time. The following pointers are provided for future work in this area:

1. A high performance machine such as the O2K machine is able to perform likelihood computations only when the number of markers is less than or equal to four. As the number of markers increased to five, the program was not able to perform linkage calculations. The

TABLE 6.4
Execution times for the case of 21 iterations

No. of procs.	"1F4M"	"4F3M"	"4F4M"
S1	04:04:46	00:20:59	02:25:38
S2	00:19:18	00:15:07	01:24:37
2	00:19:40	00:15:23	01:24:56
4	00:06:36	00:07:36	00:42:31
6	00:04:20	00:06:06	00:28:40
8	00:03:03	00:03:37	00:19:05
10	00:02:50	00:02:48	00:13:49
12	00:02:05	00:02:18	00:10:45
14	00:02:01	00:01:35	00:08:35
16	00:02:00	00:01:35	00:08:28
18	00:02:00	00:01:34	00:08:20
20	00:01:56	00:01:30	00:08:15
22	00:01:30	00:00:53	00:04:28

cause of the bottleneck as the number of markers increased needs further research to improve the Linkmap program.

2. The master-worker model implements only one level of parallelization. The master allocates various θ values to the worker threads. Each worker thread performs all the computations for a single θ value assigned for all the families in case of a multiple family input file. One more level of parallelization can be implemented by having the worker thread distribute computations to other workers for various families. However, the amount of communication overhead involved is significantly high and may impact performance negatively even with additional processors.

3. Efficient models other than the dynamic master-worker scheme reported in this work need to be investigated for implementation on a high performance platform such as the O2K.

The parallelization of legacy software such as Linkmap involves some common general steps that guided the implementations discussed in this report. However, implementation details depend on both the application and the computing platform. In this case, while the parallelization model is simple, its implementation required on the application side, an exhaustive analysis of Linkmap. However, on the computing platform side, required the study of other factors such as floating point operations and cache memory utilization.

The master-worker scheme is dynamic in nature and supports load balancing for a faster execution. Thus, it appears to be adequate for the parallelization of the Linkage program. Geneticists using Linkmap on a parallel platform such as the Origin 2000 will be able to locate the disease gene with respect to other genes in a particular chromosome, in a matter of minutes and seconds instead of days and hours.

REFERENCES

[1] J.D. TERWILLIGER AND J. OTT, *Handbook of Human Genetic Linkage*, The Johns Hopkins University Press, Philadelphia, PA, 1994.

[2] S. DWARKADAS AND A. A. SCHAFFER AND R. W. COTTINGHAM JR. AND A. L. COX AND P. KELEHER P. AND W. ZWAENEPOEL, *Parallelization of genetic linkage analysis problems*, Human Heredity, Vol. 44, pp 127-141, 1994.

[3] R. W. COTTINGHAM JR. AND R. M. IDURI AND A. A. SCHAFFER, *Faster sequential genetic linkage computations*, Human Genetics, Vol. 53, pp 252-263, 1993.

[4] J. OTT, *Analysis of Human Genetic Linkage*, The Johns Hopkins University Press, Philadelphia, PA,

1985.

[5] K. M. Chandy and S. Taylor, *Introduction to Parallel Programming*, Jones and Bartlett, Boston, MA, 1992.

[6] C. Amza and A. L. Cox and S. Dwarkadas and P. Keleher and H Lu and R. Rajamony and W. Yu and W. Zwaenepoel, *Treadmarks: Shared Memory Computing on Networks of Workstations*, IEEE Computer, Vol. 29, No. 2, pp 18-28, 1996.

[7] P. S. Pacheco, *Parallel Programming with MPI*, Morgan Kaufman Publishers, Inc, San Mateo, CA, 1997.

[8] N. Lopez-Benitez and J. Y. Hyon , *Simulation of task graph in heterogeneous environments*, IEEE Heterogeneous Computing Workshop, 1999.

[9] N. Lopez-Benitez, *Petri-Net Based Performance-Evaluation of Distributed Homogeneous Task Systems*, IEEE Transactions on Reliability, Vol. 49, No. 2, pp. 188-198, June, 2000.

[10] D. A. Menasce and D. Saha and S. C. Da Silva Porto and D.A.FAlmeida and S. K. Tripathi, *Static and Dynamic Processor Scheduling Disciplines in Heterogeneous Parallel Architectures*, J. of Parallel and Distributed Computing, Vol. 28, pp 1-18, 1995.

[11] H. El-Rewini and T.G. Lewis and H. H. Ali, *Task Scheduling in Parallel and Distributed Systems*, Prentice Hall, 1994.

[12] H. Topcuoglu and S. Hariri and Min-You Wu, *Task Scheduling Algorithms for Heterogeneous Processors*, IEEE Heterogeneous Computing Workshop, San Juan PR, pp 3-14, April, 1999.

[13] A. Rai and N. Lopez-Benitez and J. D. Hargis and S. E. Poduslo, *Heterogeneous Parallelization of the Linkmap Program*, IEEE Proceeding of the 2000 ICPP Workshops, Toronto, Canada, pp 353-360 August, 2000.

[14] A. Rai and N. Lopez-Benitez and J. D. Hargis and S. E. Poduslo, *On the Parallelization of Linkmap from the LINKAGE/FASTLINK Package*, Computers and Biomedical Research, Vol. 33, pp 350-364, 2000.

[15] K. Kothari and N. Lopez-Benitez, and S. E. Poduslo, *High-Performance Implementation and Analysis of the Linkmap Program*, Journal of Biomedical Informatics, 34, 406-414, 2001.

[16] P. L. Miller and P. Nadkarni and J. E. Gelernter and N. Carriero and A. J. Pakstis and K. K. Kidd, *Parallelizing genetic linkage analysis: A case study for applying parallel computation in molecular biology*, Computers and Biomedical Research, Vol. 24, pp 234-248, 1991.

[17] V. Kumar and A. Grama and A. Gupta and G. Karypis, *Introduction to Parallel Computing-Design and Analysis of Algorithms*, The Benjamin/Cummings Publishing Co., Menlo Park, CA, 1994.

[18] D. E. Culler and J. P. Singh and A. Gupta, *Parallel Computer Architecture: A Hardware/Software Approach*, Morgan Kaufman Publishers, Inc, San Francisco, CA, 1999.

[19] *Sun Microsystems*, *Sun Workshop 4.0 Answerbook*, http://docs.sun.com, 1999.

[20] A. Rai, *On the Parallelization of the LINKMAP Program*, Computer Science Dept., Texas Tech University, December, 1999, Lubbock, TX.

[21] K. Dowd and C. Severance, *High Performance Computing*, O'Reilly & Associates, 1998.

[22] *SGI Global and Technical Education, Handbook for Origin 2000*, May, 2000.

[23] A. A. Schaffer, *Personal Conversation*, 2000.

[24] FASTLINK software:, *http://linkage.rockefeller.edu/software/linkage/unix/*, 2000.

In: Parallel and Distributed Scientific and Engineering Computing ISBN 1-59033-956-8
Editor: Y. Pan and L.T. Yang, pp. 85-97

METHODS FOR PARALLEL SIMULATIONS OF SURFACE REACTIONS

S.V. NEDEA, J.J. LUKKIEN, P.A.J. HILBERS* AND A.P.J. JANSEN†

Abstract. We study the opportunities for parallelism for the simulation of surface reactions. We introduce the concept of a *partition* and we give new simulation methods based on Cellular Automaton using partitions. We elaborate on the advantages and disadvantages of the derived algorithms comparing with Dynamic Monte Carlo algorithms. We find that we can get very fast simulations using this approach trading accuracy for performance and we give experimental data for the simulation of Ziff model.

Key words. Surface reactions, Partition, Cellular automaton, Dynamic monte carlo, Parallel simulation

1. Introduction . Understanding chemical reactions that take place on catalytic surfaces is of vital importance to the chemical industry. The knowledge can be used to improve catalysts thus yielding better reactors. In addition, improving the catalytic process in engines can lead to improvement of environmental conditions. Dynamic Monte Carlo simulations have turned out to be a powerful tool to model and analyse surface reactions [22, 1, 10, 21, 14, 24, 20]. In such a DMC model, the surface is described as a two-dimensional lattice of sites that can be occupied by particles. The simulation consist of changing the surface over time by execution of reactions, which are merely modifications of small neighborhoods. Simple models can be simulated easily; however, for more complicated models and for larger systems computation time and memory use become very large. One way of dealing with this is to use parallelism.

There are roughly three ways to introduce parallelism in simulations. First one may choose an existing simulation algorithm and exploit inherent concurrency. This boils down to a parallelization effort which is by no means straightforward but limited by the properties of the algorithm one starts with. General parallel methods such as the optimistic method Time Warp or the pessimistic methods suggested by Misra and Chandy can be used [15, 7, 19]. If the model (and, hence, the algorithm) does not admit much concurrency one may try to change the model. The penalty in many cases will be that such a model is less accurate but this may be acceptable. Third, the necessary statistics may be obtained from the averaging of a large number of small, independent simulations (this is, in fact, an instance of the second approach). The mathematical model for DMC simulations of surface reactions is the Master Equation ([13], see also section 2). The algorithms based on it are rather sequential in nature and do not admit an optimistic parallel simulation method like Time Warp. This is because each reaction disables many others and, hence, an optimistic method would result in frequent roll-back. Successful parallel methods therefore change the model.

The most frequently used alternative model is that of a Cellular Automaton (CA) model. The CA model [5] is inherently parallel: all sites of the lattice are updated simultaneously according to the state of the neighboring sites. The time is incremented after updating synchronously all the sites of the lattice, such that the state of a cell at time t depends on the state of the neighboring sites at time $t-1$. Each site is updated according to a transition rule dependent on the state of the neighboring sites.

There are two problems with the CA. First, all patterns (i.e., neighborhood occupations) are treated on the same footing. In practice, however, these patterns represent different reactions that proceed with a different speed. The solution is to use a so-called non-deterministic CA (NDCA) in which execution of reaction is performed with a probability dependent on

*Department of Mathematics and Computer Science, Eindhoven University of Technology, P.O. Box 513, 5600 MB Eindhoven, The Netherlands, Email: silvia@win.tue.nl

†Department of Chemical Engineering, Eindhoven University of Technology, P.O. Box 513, 5600 MB Eindhoven, The Netherlands

its rate. The second problem concerns the occurrence of conflicts. These conflicts must be resolved but they make it impossible to have a synchronous update.

In this paper we introduce and study the partitioned CA model [27, 28]. Each site of the lattice belongs to a set of a partition. These sets are chosen such that reactions concerning sites within the same set have no conflicts. If we have, for example, a von Neumann neighborhood [25], the sites can be distributed over five sets with this property. The result is that updates in the same partition can be done simultaneously.

The paper is organized as follows. In section 2 we give the mathematical description of the simulation model. DMC simulation methods and algorithms are introduced in section 3. In section 4 we give the CA and its simulation algorithm. Section 5 introduces the idea of partitioning worked out into several alternatives. Section 6 contains some experimental data. We end with some conclusions.

2. The Model. The model comprises the surface, the particles (molecules and atoms) and the reactions that take place. A picture of a model system is found in Fig. 2.1.

Lattice and set of states - Ω, D. We model the surface by a two-dimensional lattice Ω of $N=L_0$ x L_1 sites. Every site takes a value from a set D, the domain of particle types. D is a finite set and generally contains an element to indicate that a site is vacant, $D=\{*, \mathrm{A}, \mathrm{B}, \ldots\}$, where * stands for an empty site. A complete assignment of particles to sites is called a *system state* or *configuration*. Hence a configuration is a function from Ω to D.

The set of reaction types - $\mathcal{T}$. A system state can be changed into a next state through a reaction. Such a reaction is an instance of a *reaction type* at a specific site s. Occurrence of a reaction means that the particles in a small neighborhood of s are replaced by new particles. A reaction can only occur when it is enabled, i.e., when the neighborhood is occupied according to some specific pattern. A reaction type therefore specifies

1. the neighborhood that should be considered for a given site,
2. the pattern needed for the reaction type in the neighborhood (the *source pattern*),
3. the pattern that will result from occurrence of the reaction (the *target pattern*).

A reaction type therefore is a function that, when applied to a specific site s yields a collection of triples of the form (*site, source, target*). The collection specifies the neighborhood and the source and target patterns. More precisely, a reaction type Rt is a function from Ω to the subsets of Ω x D x D, $\mathcal{P}(\Omega$ x D x $D)$.

For $t \in Rt(s)$ we call the first component $t.site$, the second component $t.src$ and the third component $t.tg$. We will loosely refer to the set of first components as the neighborhood of Rt, the set of second components as the source pattern and the set of third components as the target pattern. The neighborhood of Rt is a function, Nb_{Rt}: $\Omega \to \mathcal{P}(\Omega)$, that, when applied to a site s, yields a collection of sites from Ω. This function must have the following two properties

1. the neighborhood of a site s includes s: $s \in Nb(s)$.
2. translation invariance: the neighborhood looks the same for all sites such that for any site t, $Nb(s+t) = Nb(s) + t = Nb(t) + s$.

We can now also define when a reaction type is enabled. A reaction type Rt is enabled at site s in state S when for all t in $Rt(s)$, $S(t.site) = t.src$, i.e., when the source pattern matches at s in S.

Usually, there are many reaction types and in a certain state many of them are enabled. A simulation proceeds by repeatedly selecting an enabled reaction and executing it. The new state that results from executing an enabled reaction type Rt in state S at a site s is defined as follows. Call this new state S' then

1. $S'(z) = S(z)$ if $z \notin Nb_{Rt}(s)$, i.e. z does not occur in the neighborhood of $Rt(s)$,
2. for any t in $Rt(s)$, $S'(t.site) = t.tg$.

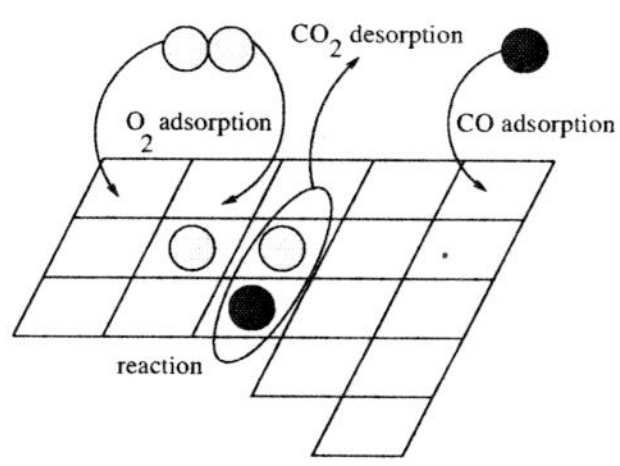

FIG. 2.1. *Reactions on a surface modelled by a two-dimensional lattice, with two types of particles,* O*(light) and* CO*(dark).*

	0	1	2	3
Rt_{CO+O}	{(s,CO,*), (s+(1,0),O,*)}	{(s,CO,*), (s+(0,1),O,*)}	{(s,CO,*), (s+(-1,0),O,*)}	{(s,CO,*), (s+(0,-1),CO,*)}
Rt_{O_2}	{(s,*,O), (s+(1,0),*,O)}	{(s,*,O), (s+(0,1),*,O)}		
Rt_{CO}	{(s,*,CO)}			

TABLE 2.1
The transformations of the reaction types that model the reactions of the system in Fig. 2.1 applied on a site s. Notice that Rt_{CO+O} *has four versions (the four possible pattern orientations);* Rt_{O_2} *has only two.*

Reaction Rates. Each reaction type Rt has a rate constant k associated with it, which is the probability per unit time that the reaction of type Rt occurs. This rate constant depends on the temperature, expressed through an Arrhenius expression $k = \nu \exp\left(\frac{-E}{k_B T}\right)$ where E is the activation energy and ν the pre-exponential factor.

Example. We give a simple example where we use the defined model to describe the surface reactions in a simple system. In this system [23], particles of type CO (carbon monoxide) may adsorb on the sites of a square lattice. Particles of type O (oxygen) may do so as well, but in the gas phase O is diatomic. The adsorption of CO has rate constant k_{CO} and the dissociative adsorption of O_2 has rate constant k_{O_2}. O_2 adsorbs at adjacent vacant sites. Adsorbed O and CO particles form CO_2 and desorb (see Fig. 2.1). The rate of formation and desorption of CO_2 is k_{CO_2}. The surface is modelled by a lattice of sites $\Omega = L_0$ x L_1, and $D=\{*,\ CO,\ O\}$. The reactions are modelled by seven reaction types that we give in Table 2.1.

For CO adsorption there is one reaction type, for O_2 adsorption there are two reaction types because two orientations are possible when the O_2 molecule dissociates. Finally, the CO_2 formation and desorption is modelled by four reaction types.

3. Simulations. Using different simulation techniques we want to study the evolution of the defined model over time. This means that we repeatedly execute enabled reactions on the lattice according to a simulation algorithm. There are basically two different approaches to simulate lattice models: Dynamic Monte Carlo (DMC) and Cellular Automata (CA).

3.1. Dynamic monte carlo. Dynamic Monte Carlo methods are used to simulate the behavior of stochastic models over time. The stochastic models of physical systems are based on a Master Equation (ME) of the form

$$\frac{dP(S,t)}{dt} = \sum_{S'} \left[k_{SS'} P(S',t) - k_{S'S} P(S,t)\right]. \tag{3.1}$$

In this equation $P(S,t)$ denotes the probability to find the system in a configuration S at time t, $k_{SS'}$ is the reaction probability of the reaction that transfers S' into S. Such a reaction is an instance of a reaction type at a particular location.

A simulation according to this equation is essentially a discrete event simulation with continuous time, where the events are the occurrences of reactions. When we assume that the rate constants do not change over time, occurrence of each event has a negative exponential distribution [1, 10]. In an abstract way, a simulation then consists of a repetition of the following steps

1. Determine the list of enabled reactions.
2. Select the reaction that is the next and the time of its occurrence.
3. Adjust the time and the lattice.
4. Continue from 1.

There are many different ways to organize these steps resulting in different algorithms. The taxonomy by Segers [11] mentions not less than 48 DMC algorithms. One of these algorithms, called the Random Selection Method (RSM) has become quite popular in the literature because of its simple implementation. It reads as follows

set time to 0;
repeat
  1. select a site s randomly with probability $1/N$;
  2. select a reaction type i with probability k_i/K;
  3. check if the reaction type is enabled at s;
  4. if it is, execute it;
  5. advance the time by drawing from
     $[1 - \exp(-NKt)]$;
until simulation time has elapsed;

We denoted with K the sum of the rate constants of the reaction types, i.e., $K = \sum_i k_i$. A single iteration of this algorithm is called a *trial* as no success is guaranteed. In the literature the connection with real time (step 5) is usually not mentioned. Since the method decouples the notion of time completely from the simulation (the time increment is drawn from a fixed distribution) there is a tendency to measure time in Monte Carlo steps. One MC step corresponds to one trial of a reaction type per lattice site on average, i.e., one MC step is N trials.

This definition of MC steps also allows comparison between time-based simulation techniques and MC step-based techniques. Thus, one MC step is equivalent to $\sum_{j=0}^{N-1} T_j$, where the time increment T_j is selected from the fixed distribution $1 - \exp(-NKt)$. This value can be drawn at the end of an MC step or at the end of the entire simulation. Without using the negative exponential distribution, method RSM can also be regarded as a time discretization of the ME. The time step is then $1/NK$.

In this paper we apply method RSM because it is a DMC method that is very similar to a cellular automaton. RSM is a purely sequential algorithm that is not well suited for parallelism. In [11, 12], Segers et al. investigated how parallelism may be used in the simulation of surface reactions. The goal was to see whether simulations that are too large to run on a sequential computer may run on a parallel computer. He proposed an approach in which coherent parts of the lattice, so-called chunks, are assigned to a number of processors. The chunks are then simulated using RSM. When reactions are across multiple lattice chunks, state information has to be exchanged. Thus, synchronization and communication techniques are required for the chunk-boundaries. His investigation shows that for parallel simulations, the overhead of the parallel algorithm is considerable because of the high communication latency of parallel computers. In order to get a significant increase in speed over the sequential algorithm the amount of work on each processor must be large

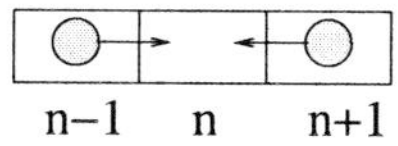

FIG. 4.1. *Conflict for simulating reactions that affect neighboring sites (such as diffusion) in a CA model. Both particle can jump to the empty site n during the same step.*

compared to the amount of communication. This trade-off is given by the volume/boundary ratio of the blocks. In this paper we explore another direction, viz., a parallel simulation algorithm that *approximates* the kinetics of the ME, thus trading accuracy for performance.

4. Cellular Automaton. Cellular Automata are a powerful tool to simulate physical and chemical systems of a high level of complexity. The CA approach is discrete in space and time. In a CA, all sites can make a reaction in each step of the simulation. For a standard Cellular Automaton the notion of real time is discarded: the decision of whether to make a reaction is based only on information local to that site. As a result, a slowly evolving reaction at some part of the lattice, has the same probability to occur as a fast reaction at another place. In order to introduce the real-time dynamics, the decision of whether to make a reaction is taken with a probability that depends on the rate constant resulting in a Non-Deterministic Cellular Automaton (NDCA). This NDCA resembles the RSM method the best. A NDCA algorithm consists of the following steps

for each step

for each site s

1. *select a reaction type i with probability* k_i/K;
2. *check whether the reaction is enabled at* s;
3. *if it is, execute it;*
4. *advance the time;*

In this algorithm, the steps in italics can be executed in parallel. In RSM and NDCA the mechanism of selecting a site is different and generates deviations in the simulation results. This happens because in a NDCA, each site is always selected during a step, while in RSM there is a non-zero probability that a site is chosen twice or more in a succession during one simulation step. This difference in selecting a site introduces biases in the rates of the reactions and causes NDCA to give degenerate results for some systems (Ising models, Single-File models, etc.) [26].

The CA approach is inherently parallel and all lattice sites can be updated simultaneously in one single time step of the simulation. However, parallelism also introduces conflicts for reactions that may disable each other. Consider, for instance, a diffusion model involving two sites. A particle at site n can jump to one of the neighboring sites if this is an empty site, while another particle from the same neighborhood could jump as well to the same empty site (see Fig. 4.1). Failure to deal with this may lead to the violation of the physical laws. We avoid erroneous simulations by adjusting the simulation model in order to avoid the conflicts that arise as a consequence of the parallel execution.

5. Cellular Automaton with Partitions. In the literature, the problem of the conflicts in parallel simulations is solved using Block Cellular Automata (BCA). The BCA uses the concept of partitioning. The sites of a CA are partitioned into a regular pattern of blocks that cover the whole space and do not overlap. A step is then applied at the same time and independently to each block. In the next step, the block boundaries are shifted such that the edges occur at a different place.

In Fig. 5.1 we have an example of using blocks in a very simple one-dimensional BCA. The only reaction rule is that the state of a site (0 or 1) becomes 0 if at least one of the neighboring sites is 0, otherwise it stays the same.

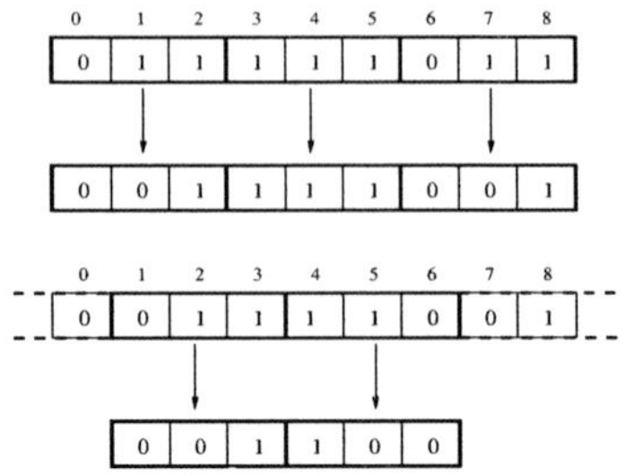

FIG. 5.1. *Example of a BCA where the transition is applied within blocks consisting of three sites.*

The lattice can be partitioned in sets of three blocks, B_0={0,1,2}, B_1={3,4,5}, B_2={6,7,8} and B'_0={0,7,8}, B'_1={1,2,3}, B'_2={4,5,6}. The blocks B'_i have been obtained by shifting the edges of the blocks B_i to the right.

To avoid the exchange of information between the blocks and the problems that might appear at the edges, we generalize this idea of a block. We define a second level of partitioning P, $P = \{P_i, 0 \leq i\}$, called *chunks*, such that these chunks are disjoint and cover the entire lattice, $\Omega = \sum_i P_i$. The chunks are chosen such that the simulation can be done for all the elements of a chunk in parallel.

For instance, for the example in Fig. 5.1 we can assign each site with a color such that the sites with the same color are in the same chunk. A partition P consists of three chunks where in P_0 are all the red labeled sites, $P_0 = \{1, 4, 7\}$, in P_1 are all the white labeled sites, $P_1 = \{0, 3, 6\}$, and in P_2 are all the blue labeled sites, $P_2 = \{2, 5, 8\}$. For the work distribution in the parallel execution we use the same blocks as before. By letting all processors execute on sites in the same chunk, the conflicts disappear.

The new definition of a partition introduces more freedom: we can assign non-adjacent sites to the chunks such that the problem with the edges between the chunks disappears. This means that the conflicts should disappear and we therefore add the following restriction.

Each site of the lattice is assigned to a chunk such that between the sites in the same chunk there are no conflicts for the given model.

This means that for all $s, t \in P_i$, $s \neq t$ and for all reaction types Rt, Rt'

$$Nb_{Rt}(s) \cap Nb_{Rt'}(t) = \emptyset.$$

As all the sites in a chunk can be simulated simultaneously, we are interested to minimize the number of these chunks of a partition (i.e., minimize $|P|$) in order to increase parallelism.

Example. We consider again the physical model used in the previous section for CO oxidation on a catalyst surface (see Fig. 2.1). From Table 2.1 we can see that the reaction types do not include more than two sites. When assigning sites to the chunks we observe that a minimum number of five chunks can be used, such that the patterns of the defined reaction types applied at the sites of these chunks do not overlap. In Fig. 5.2 we have a block of 5 x 5 lattice sites, optimally divided into a number of five chunks. We can use this block as a pattern to tile the whole lattice.

Algorithm. We give here a NDCA that uses the concept of partitions. We call it the Partitioned NDCA algorithm (PNDCA) and it reads as follows

for each step
  choose a partition P;
  for all $P_i \in P$

0	1	2	3	4
3	4	0	1	2
1	2	3	4	0
4	0	1	2	3
2	3	4	0	1

FIG. 5.2. *The lattice is split into five chunks in this case; the sites are distributed among these chunks. Sites are labelled according to the chunk they belong to. The sites into a single chunk can be updated simultaneously, giving a von Neumann neighborhood.*

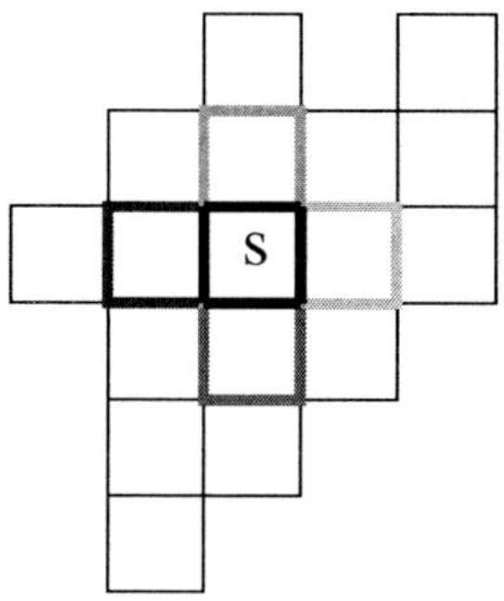

FIG. 5.3. *Overlap of the reaction patterns on the central site s for the model of* CO *oxidation.*

for each site $s \in P_i$

1. select a reaction type with probability k_i/K*;*

2. check if the reaction is enabled at s;

3. if it is, execute it;

4. advance the time;

In this algorithm, visting the sites of a chunk (steps in italics) can be done in parallel. The idea is to simulate the enabled reactions according to their rate constants visiting all the sites of the chunks P_i. This algorithm has been implemented on a parallel computer and measurements about the performance of this algorithm are given in the next section.

5.1. Opportunities for improvements. The RSM simulations differ from PNDCA simulations for the following reasons. In a PNDCA, in a step, a site can be selected only once for the simulation because a chunk is selected once per step, and in each chunk a site is selected exactly once. After the site has been selected once, the probability to select that site again in the same step is 0. In RSM there is a probability $1/N$ per iteration to select a site and a non-zero probability to choose the site again in the same step. Another reason is that while the reactions in a chunk are simulated, the enabled reactions in other chunks are postponed for execution.

The deviation can be made smaller through additional randomization and through reorganization of the steps in the algorithm. Depending on how the selection of a chunk is done, we can derive a set of algorithms. Chunks can be selected in the following ways:

1. all chunks in a predefined order,
2. all chunks randomly ordered,
3. a set of random chunks such that a chunk has a probability $1/|P|$ to be selected during a step,
4. a weighted selection according to the rates of enabled reactions in each chunk.

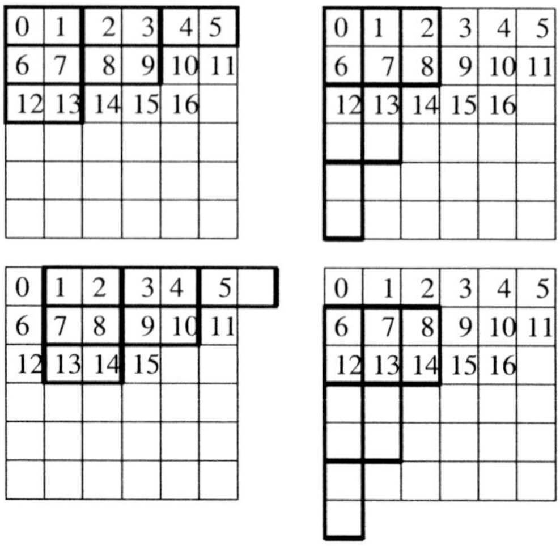

FIG. 5.4. *The four partitions of $\Omega x T$ according to the subsets T_i of reaction types, for the model of CO oxidation.*

Simulating all the chunks per step in order or randomly, introduces correlations in the occupancy of the sites. More correlations between occupancy of the sites occur as less chunks are introduced. If $|P|$ is large the algorithm performs better. If $|P| = N$ and a chunk is selected randomly, PNDCA and RSM match.

We can also vary the amount of work done per chunk through the choice of the number of trials, L. If this number is small only a relatively small amount of time is spent within the chunk resulting in a small overall deviation. This leads to the following general structure:

for each step
  choose a partition P;
  set *trials* to 0;
  repeat
    select $P_i \in P$ (probability $|P_i|/|P|$);
    select $L, 1 \leq L \leq (N - trials)$
    set *trials* to *trials* + L;
    for L *sites* $\in P_i$
      1. select a reaction type with probability k_i/K*;*
      2. check if the reaction is enabled at the site;
      3. if it is, execute it;
      4. advance the time;
  until *trials* = N

In this algorithm, visiting L sites from a selected chunk(steps marked in italics) can be done in parallel. This algorithm has been implemented on a parallel machine and more details about the measurements are given in the next section. The number of trials per chunk is smaller than the size of a chunk, $L \leq |P_i|$, and the sites to be visited in a chunk are selected randomly. We name this algorithm L-PNDCA. Through special choices of the parameters that we have introduced the L-PNDCA approaches the DMC method RSM. For example, when L is fixed at 1 or when $|P|$ assumes the extreme values 1 or N.

5.2. Another approach using partitions. The effect of the non-overlap rule is that the patterns in the model limit the choice of the partition significantly: larger patterns lead to more chunks. Since the degree of concurrency is related to the size of the chunks the non-overlap rule also limits the concurrency. By adding an additional ordering constraint

$\mathcal{T}_0$	$Rt^{(0)}_{CO+O}$, $Rt^{(2)}_{CO+O}$	$Rt^{(0)}_{O_2}$	Rt_{CO}
$\mathcal{T}_1$	$Rt^{(1)}_{CO+O}$, $Rt^{(3)}_{CO+O}$	$Rt^{(1)}_{O_2}$	-

TABLE 5.1

The new division of the reaction types in subsets $\mathcal{T}_j$, $j = 0, 1$ for the model in Fig. 2.1 applied on a site s.

we can reduce this effect as follows.

If we look at the simulation of a single chunk in the partition then this simulation proceeds by repeatedly selecting a reaction type and executing it. We re-order these steps by partitioning the set of reaction types $\mathcal{T}$ into $\sum_j \mathcal{T}_j$. The sets $\mathcal{T}_j$ are selected according to their rates and then the algorithm is executed for the reaction types in this selected $\mathcal{T}_j$. We can now do a partitioning of the set $\Omega x \mathcal{T} = \sum (P_i, \mathcal{T}_j)$. The non-overlap rule reduces to non-overlap with respect to the reactions types within $\mathcal{T}_j$ and, as a result, the partition can be done with fewer chunks. There is a trade-off however: the work per chunk is less, in principle.

Example. The patterns of the reaction types that can be enabled at a specific site s, all contain two sites positioned as in Fig. 5.3 and the site s can thus be a part of four possible pairs during a transformation. We split the set of reaction types in subsets, such that the patterns of the reaction types from a subset T_i are included in only one such pair, apart from translation. The set of reaction types is then a collection of two subsets $\mathcal{T}_j$, $\mathcal{T}=\sum_{j=0}^{1} \mathcal{T}_j$ (see Table 5.1). The new partition P is a collection of only two chunks which are constructed by skipping a row or a column each time. Fig. 5.4 illustrates the principle for our earlier example. The chunks P_i are the following: $P_0=\{0, 2, 4, 7, 9, \dots\}$, $P_1=\{1, 3, 5, 6, 8, \dots\}$. This means that for all $s, t \in P_i$, and for a given reaction type Rt, we have $Nb_{Rt}(s) \cap Nb_{Rt}(t) = \emptyset$.

Algorithm. The algorithm consists of the following steps

for each step
  for $|\mathcal{T}|$ times
    select $\mathcal{T}_j \in \mathcal{T}$ with probability $K_{\mathcal{T}_j}/K$;
    select a reaction type from $\mathcal{T}_j$ with probability $k_i/k_{\mathcal{T}_j}$;
    select $P_i \in P$
    for each site $s \in P_i$
      1. check if the reaction is enabled at s;
      2. if it is, execute it;
      3. advance the time;

This is basically the generalization of the simulation algorithm used by Kortlüke [18]. Here also the steps marked in italics can be executed in parallel. We have used here $K_{\mathcal{T}_j}$ to denote the sum of the reaction rates of the elements from the set $\mathcal{T}_j$.

6. Correctness and Performance. In order to study the correctness of our methods, we compare the kinetics of the reactions in DMC and in CA simulations. DMC is based on the following fundamental assumption known as Gillespie hypothesis:

> *If a reaction with a rate constant k is enabled in a state S, then the probability of this reaction occurring in an infinitesimal time interval of size δt is equal to $k\delta t$. The probability that more than one reaction occurs in an interval of length δt is negligible.*

The above assumption says that in any state and at any time, the probability of occurrence of an enabled reaction in a vanishingly small interval is proportional to its rate, and that the probability of two reactions occurring simultaneously is negligible [6, 8, 9].

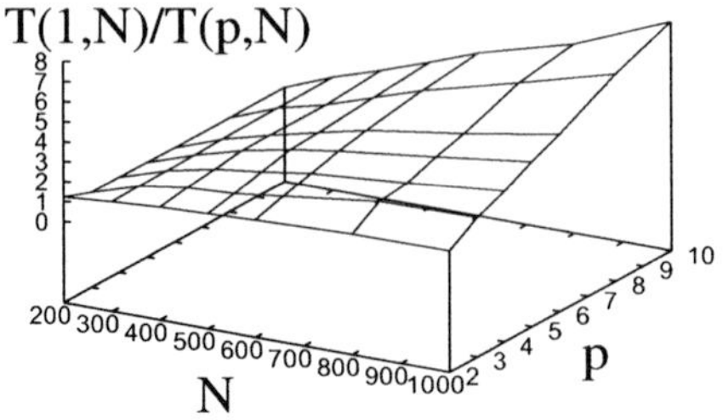

FIG. 6.1. *Speedup function on the system size N and on the number of processors p.*

A stochastic model that respects the fundamental assumption is described by a Master Equation and can be simulated using DMC methods [13, 22, 21, 1, 20, 10, 14].

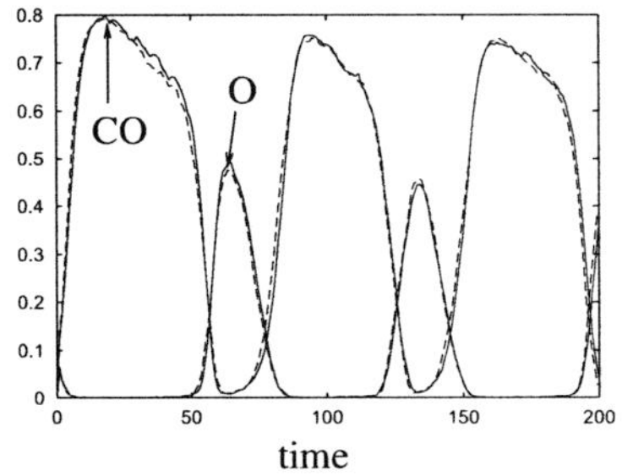

FIG. 6.2. *RSM and L-PNDCA results for the time dependence of the coverage with* CO *and* O *particles of a system of size N=100x100. The continuous line is for RSM, and the dashed line is for L-PNDCA with parameters* $m = 1$, $L = N^2$ *and* $m = N^2$, $L = 1$.

Based on the Gillespie hypothesis, Segers et al. [11] has given two criteria for the correctness of the simulation algorithms of surface reactions. These criteria suggest a way to select a site and a reaction type with a correct probability. According to these criteria, each algorithm is correct if only enabled reactions are performed and 2 conditions are satisfied:

1. the waiting time for a reaction of type i (the time that elapses before it occurs) has an exponential probability distribution ($\exp(-k_i t)$);
2. the waiting time of the next reaction type i is according to the ratio between the reaction rate constant (k_i) and the sum of the rate constants of all the enabled reactions.

In our CA methods with partitions, we have seen that the order of visiting the sites is important and can introduce correlations in the simulations. Using partitions, some sites are excluded from simulation for a certain time, while others are preferred. The same problem arises for executing the enabled reactions. Executing reaction types from a chunk, disables the enabled reactions in other chunks and introduces biases in the rates of reactions. This comes from the fact that for CA methods, the fundamental assumption does not hold. In principle, many reactions can be enabled and executed during a small time interval in a CA. Thus, CA gives results that may deviate from the DMC results.

As an example for our new methods, we consider the model used by Kuzovkov et al. [17] to study reactions on the surface including surface reconstruction. The model used is similar to our example model, the oxidation of CO on a face of Platinum(100). Adsorbates like CO can lift the reconstruction of the hexagonal structure of the top layer of Pt(100) to a square structure. CO adsorbs in both phases of the top layer. O_2 adsorbes only in the square phase.

Adsorbed CO may desorb again and O and CO may desorb associatively, forming CO_2. The behavior on the surface is the following: CO adsorbs on Pt(100) in a hexagonal phase, the surface top layer reconstructs into a square structure such that O_2 can now adsorb on the lattice. As O_2 molecules are adsorbed, CO_2 is produced and desorb liberating the lattice from particles. The surface reconstructs again to a hexagonal structure and the process is repeating: we get oscillatory behavior on the surface. We use the oscillations in the coverage with particles of the lattice for comparing our results.

The parallel algorithms used in the simulations and previously described (PNDCA, L-PNDCA) have been run on a cluster consisting of 17 PC's connected through a 100Mbit/sec fully switched ethernet network (Cisco Catalyst 3524XL 100Mbit 24-ports switch). Because of the absence of conflicts between the chunks, the approach with partitions leads to a significant increase in speedup even for not so large systems (100x100, 200x200). Each simulation consisted of a large number of steps ($N_{steps} = 1000$). In Fig. 6.1 we can see how the speedup of the PNDCA algorithm depends on the system size N and on the number of processors p. The speedup is defined as the ratio between the simulation time using 1 processor, for a system size N (T(1,N)) and the simulation time on p processors, for a system size N (T(p,N)).

We denote with m the number of chunks ($m = |P|$). In Fig. 6.2 we see that for $m = 1$, $L = N^2$ (one chunk containing all the lattice sites), and for $m = N^2, L = 1$ (N^2 chunks with one site per chunk), DMC and L-PNDCA give the same results.

For the optimal case of five chunks, we experimented with different L's. Increasing L introduces biases in the simulations. In Fig. 6.3 we illustrate this for case $L = 1$ and $L = 100$, for lattice size N=100x100. We notice that for $L = 1$, L-PNDCA gives almost the same results as DMC.

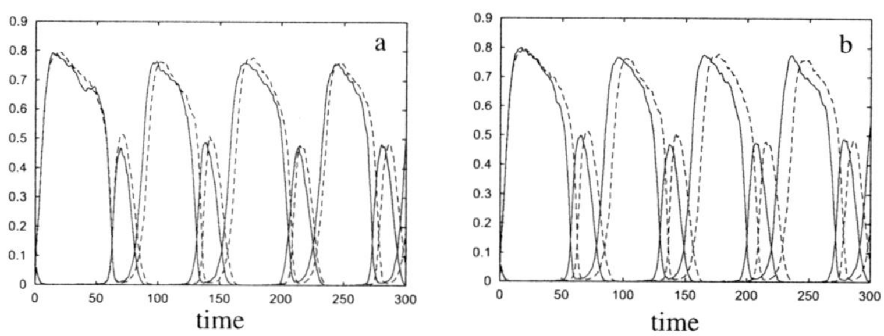

FIG. 6.3. *RSM and L-PNDCA results for the time dependence of the coverage with* CO *and* O *particles, for five chunks and N=100x100. In a) $L = 1$ and in b) L=100.*

In case a chunk is selected each time with a probability $|P_i|/|P|$, for larger values of L (e.g. L=100), the correlations have as effect the deviation in time of the oscillations from the DMC results. In this case, for very large values of L, the oscillations disappear. But, if we simulate all the chunks only once per step in a random order, we get oscillatory behavior even for very large values of L ($L = N^2/m$)(see Fig. 6.4). In this case, if we consider very fast diffusion and small probabilities for chemical reactions in the cells, the deviations are so small that DMC and L-PNDCA give similar results. We can have in this case full parallelization and very accurate results.

7. Conclusions. We have presented a collection of approximate algorithms based on the Cellular Automaton model for parallel simulation of surface reactions. We have introduced the concept of partitions in a Non-Deterministic Cellular Automaton, and we have derived a set of parameterized algorithms based on the partitions concept. The approximation in these algorithms is introduced through parameters. The Cellular Automaton is

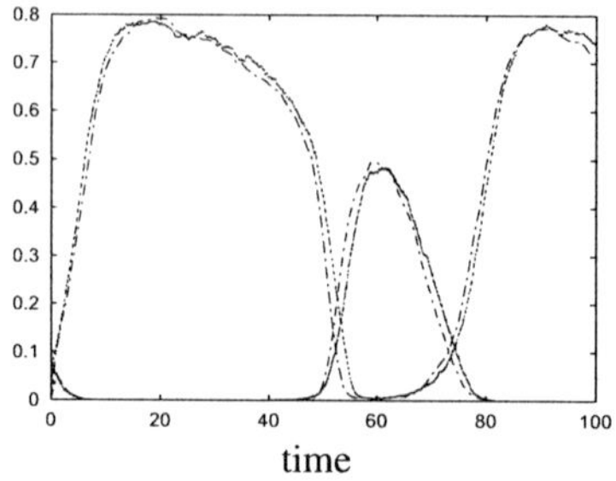

FIG. 6.4. *RSM and L-PNDCA results for the time dependence of the coverage with* CO *and* O *particles, for five chunks ($m = 5$), N=100x100, $L = N^2/m$, when all the chunks are randomly selected exactly once per step.*

already an approximate approach that can be taken as a starting point for simulation of surface reactions, but it gives results that deviate from the Master Equation. These CA algorithms simulate for the limit parameters the Master Equation, such that the accuracy of the simulations can be compared for different parameters sets. We find that we can get fast simulations using this approach trading accuracy for performance. We give an example when we can use full parallelization getting accurate results.

REFERENCES

[1] A.P.J.JANSEN, *Monte carlo simulations of chemical reactions on a surface with time-dependent reaction-rate constants*, Comput. Phys. Comm., 86 (1995), pp. 1–12.

[2] B.CHOPARD AND M.DROZ, J. Phys. A, 21 (1988), p. 205.

[3] ———, J. Stat. Phys., 64 (1989), p. 859.

[4] ———, Europhys.Lett., 15 (1991), p. 459.

[5] C.LEVERMORE AND B.BOGHOSIAN, *Springer Proceedings in Physics*, vol. 46, Springer, Berlin, ed. P. Manneville at al, 1989.

[6] D.T.GILLESPIE, *A general method for numerically simulating the stochastic time evolution of coupled chemical reactions*, J.Comput.Phys., 22 (1976), pp. 403–434.

[7] R. M. FUJIMOTO, *Time warp on a shared memory multiprocessor*, Proc. 1989 International Conference on Parallel Processing, III (1989), pp. 242–249.

[8] D. GILLESPIE, *Exact stochastic simulations of coupled chemical reactions*, J.Phys.Chem., 81 (1977), pp. 2340–2361.

[9] A. P. J. JANSEN, Comput. Phys. Commun., 86 (1995), p. 1.

[10] J.J.LUKKIEN, J.P.L.SEGERS, P.A.J.HILBERS, R.J.GELTEN, AND A.P.J.JANSEN, *Efficient monte carlo methods for the simulation of catalytic surface reactions*, Phys.Rev.E, 58 (1998), pp. 2598–2610.

[11] J.P.L.SEGERS, *Algorithms for the Simulation of Surface Processes*, Ph.D. thesis, Eindhoven University of Technology, 1999.

[12] J.P.L.SEGERS, J.J.LUKKIEN, AND P.A.J.HILBERS, *Parallel monte carlo simulation of chemical reactions: A case study.*, High-Performance Computing and Networking. Proceedings HPCN Europe 1996, 1067 (1996), pp. 235–242.

[13] V. KAMPEN, *Stochastic Processes in Physics and Chemistry*, Elsevier Science Publishers B.V., 1981.

[14] K.BINDER, *Monte Carlo methods in Statistical Physics*, Springer, Berlin, 1986.

[15] K.M.CHANDY AND J.MISRA, *Asynchronous distributed simulation via sequence of parallel computations*, Communications of the ACM, 24, no.11 (1986), pp. 39–65.

[16] O. KORTLÜKE, V. N. KUZOVKOV, AND W. VON NIESSEN, Phys. Rev. Lett., 81 (1998), p. 2164.

[17] V. N. KUZOVKOV, O. KORTLÜKE, AND W. VON NIESSEN, J.Chem.Phys., 108 (1998), p. 5571.

[18] O.KORTLÜKE, *A general cellular automaton model for surface reactions*, J.Phys. A, 31 (1998), pp. 9185–9197.

[19] D. A. REED AND A.MALONY, *Parallel discrete event simulation: The chandy-misra approach*, Proc. 1988 SCS Multiconference on Distributed Simulation, (1988), pp. 8–13.

[20] R.J.GELTEN, A.P.J.JANSEN, R. SANTEN, J.J.LUKKIEN, AND P. HILBERS, *Monte carlo simulations of surface reaction model showing spatio-temporal pattern formations and oscillations*, J.Chem.Phys., 108(14) (1998), pp. 5921–5934.

[21] R.J.GELTEN, R. SANTEN, AND A.P.J.JANSEN, *Dynamic monte carlo simulations of oscillatory hetero-*

geneous catalytic reactions, Israel J.Chem., 38 (1998), pp. 415–428.

[22] ———, *Dynamic Monte Carlo simulations of oscillatory heterogeneous catalytic reactions in P.B. Balbuena and J.M.Seminario*, Elsevier, Amsterdam, 1999.

[23] R.M.ZIFF, E.GULARI, AND Z.BARSHAD, Phys. Rev. Lett., 56 (1986), p. 2553.

[24] S.V.NEDEA, A.P.J.JANSEN, J.J.LUKKIEN, AND P.A.J.HILBERS, *Steady-state properties of single-file systems with conversion*, Phys.Rev.E, (2002).

[25] TOFFOLI AND N. MARGOLUS, *Cellular Automata Machines*, Cambbridge, MA:MIT, 1987.

[26] Y. VICHNIAC, Physica D, 10 (1984), p. 96.

[27] J. WEIMAR, *Simulation with Cellular Automata*, Logos-Verlag, Berlin, 1997.

[28] T. WORSCH, *Simulation of cellular automata*, Future Generation Computer Systems, 16 (1999), pp. 157–170.

In: Parallel and Distributed Scientific and Engineering Computing ISBN 1-59033-956-8
Editor: Y. Pan and L.T. Yang, pp. 99-108

MULTI-TERAFLOPS STUDIES OF THE MAGNETIC STRUCTURE OF FEMN ALLOYS ON PARALLEL COMPUTERS

A. CANNING*, B. UJFALUSSY†, T. C. SCHULTHESS‡, X. -G. ZHANG‡, W. A. SHELTON‡, D. M. C. NICHOLSON‡, G. M. STOCKS‡, YANG WANG§, AND T. DIRKS¶

Abstract. Massively parallel computers have been used to perform first principles spin dynamics (SD) simulations of the magnetic structure of γ-FeMn (Iron-Manganese). The code uses a novel parallel approach to solve the Kohn-Sham equations obtained from density functional theory (DFT). This approach uses limited local communications avoiding the large global communications found in other DFT based methods. This allows our code to scale efficiently to very large processor counts and large system sizes. Computationally our method can be implemented using mainly BLAS3 routines which typically run at a very high percentage of peak speed on most computers. Our large scale quantum mechanical simulations using this method, reveal new details of the orientational configuration of the magnetic moments of γ-FeMn that are unobtainable by any other means. The understanding of the magnetic structure of γ-FeMn is important in exchange bias, which involves the use of an antiferromagnetic (AFM) layer such as FeMn to pin the orientation of the magnetic moment of a proximate ferromagnetic (FM). Exchange bias is of fundamental importance in magnetic multilayer storage and read head devices. Here the equation of motion of first principles SD is used to perform relaxations of model magnetic structures to the true ground (equilibrium) state. Our code has achieved a maximum execution rate of 4.42 Teraflops on the IBM SP at the National Energy Research Scientific Computing Center (NERSC) and 4.65 Teraflops on the HP-Compaq machine at the Pittsburgh Supercomputing Center (PSC).

Key words. Parallel Computing, Materials Science, Magnetism, Spin Dynamics

1. Introduction. Massively parallel processing (MPP) computers have been used to implement first principles spin dynamics and to study the magnetic structure of complex inhomogeneous systems. The method we have used rests on three theoretical developments. The equation of motion of first principles Spin Dynamics (SD) [1], [2] which is used to relax model magnetic structures to the ground state or equilibrium T=0K configuration. Constrained density functional theory implemented within the Constrained Local Moment (CLM) model [3], [4] for calculating the magnetic structure, energy, and constraining field associated with the non-equilibrium, non-collinear, magnetic states that are required at each time step of a SD simulation. The Locally Selfconsistent Multiple Scattering (LSMS) method for performing first principles, non-collinear, constrained local moment, electronic structure calculations of a sufficiently large number of atoms for us to be able to realistically simulate the magnetic structure of such complex systems. This implementation of SD relaxation within the CLM-LSMS code has allowed us to significantly extend the work that won the Gordon Bell prize at SC98 [6] where we studied CLM states of Iron above the Curie temperature.

We have used the new LSMS code to study the ground state magnetic structure of $Fe_{0.5}Mn_{0.5}$ alloy. These first principles quantum mechanical calculations have uncovered details of the magnetic structure that cannot be obtained by any other means - either experimentally or theoretically from spin model Hamiltonians. These calculations were performed in order to shed light on the technologically important phenomenon of exchange bias which is an important ingredient in determining the utility of magnetic multi-layer Giant Magneto-Resistance (GMR) read heads for the latest generation of disc drives. Exchange bias refers to the asymmetric placement of the magnetic hysteresis loop that is induced when a ferromagnetic (FM) material such as Co is placed proximate to an antiferromagnetic

*CRD, Lawrence Berkeley National Laboratory, Berkeley, CA 94720
†Department of Physics and Astronomy, University of Tennessee, Knoxville TN 37996
‡Oak Ridge National Laboratory, Oak Ridge, TN 37831
§Pittsburgh Supercomputer Center, 4400 Fifth Avenue,Pittsburgh, PA 15213
¶IBM, Bethesda, Maryland

(AFM) material such as equiatomic FeMn alloys. While the mechanism responsible for exchange bias is unknown, it is believed that the magnetic structure at the FM/AFM interface is a key ingredient. It is therefore important to determine the lowest energy state of the AFM material (in our case FeMn) before looking at the interface. Far from the interface the AFM will be in its lowest energy state.

Our first principles studies are based on the large cell model of the face centered cubic (fcc) solid solution alloy $Fe_{0.5}Mn_{0.5}$. This alloy has long been of scientific interest in that it is an example of a compositionally disordered fcc alloy that is, nonetheless, ordered antiferromagnetically. The AFM ordering in this material is believed to be the so called "3Q" state shown in figure 1.1. It is a rare example of a peculiar AFM state in which the magnetic moments are non-collinear.

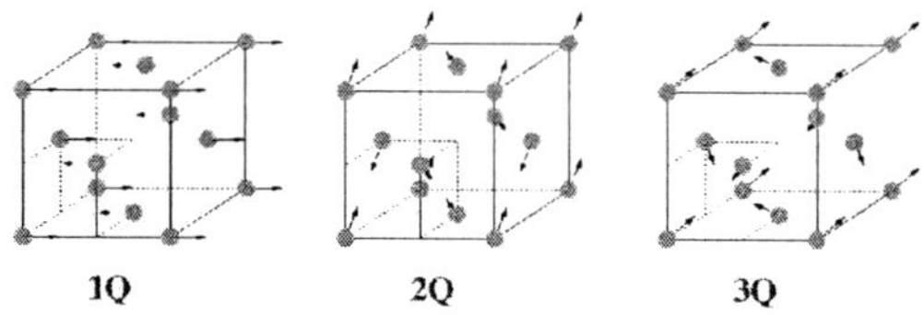

FIG. 1.1. *Candidate 1Q (left), 2Q (center), and 3Q (right) antiferromagnetic orderings of face centered cubic $Fe_{0.5}Mn_{0.5}$ solid solution alloys. The arrows show the directions of the local magnetic moments.*

More specifically, our largest unit cell model consisted of 4000 atoms on an fcc lattice populated randomly and equally with Fe and Mn. Smaller cells of 32 to 2048 atoms were also simulated. For a 256 atom system the energies of the 1Q, 2Q and 3Q structures were calculated. First principles spin dynamics([1], [2]) starting from the 3Q state were used to determine the lowest energy magnetic configuration of the system. More details of these results are presented in the section 4.2 on scientific results.

In this work the major computational problem, that of performing DFT first principles local density approximation (LDA) electronic structure calculations on large systems, is solved using the LSMS method. The basic LSMS method is an $O(N)$ LDA method that was specifically designed for implementation on MPPs. In the present work the standard LDA task of self-consistently determining the charge and magnetization densities is made more difficult by the need to also self-consistently determine site dependent magnetic fields that serve to constrain the local magnetic moments to a prescribed set of directions. This is then further compounded by the necessity of doing this for many orientational configurations of the magnetic moments as the system is evolved towards its ground state through repeated application of the equation of motion of SD.

2. Methods and Algorithms.

2.1. Methods.

2.1.1. Local density approximation. Using DFT is now the accepted way of performing first principles electronic structure and total energy calculations for condensed matter [7]. DFT is an exact theory of the ground state; the LDA converts it into a practical computational scheme. DFT-LDA replaces the solution of the many particle Schrödinger equation by the solution of a set of single particle self-consistent field (SCF) equations. The complex many body exchange and correlation effects are included through an effective exchange correlation potential. In DFT, the central quantity of interest is the charge density $\rho(\mathbf{r})$ (and, additionally, in LS(pin)DA the magnetization density $\mathbf{m}(\mathbf{r})$). For a fixed external potential (e.g. that resulting from a set of nuclei) DFT-LDA returns the ground state $\rho(\mathbf{r})$

(and $\mathbf{m}(\mathbf{r})$). For non-spin-polarized systems the SCF equations take the form:

$$\left\{ \frac{\hbar}{2m}\nabla^2 - V_{eff} + \epsilon \right\} G(\mathbf{r}, \mathbf{r}'; \epsilon) = \delta(\mathbf{r} - \mathbf{r}') \tag{2.1}$$

$$\rho(\mathbf{r}) = -\frac{1}{\pi\Omega}\int_{\Omega} d\mathbf{r} \int_{-\infty}^{\infty} d\epsilon\, G(\mathbf{r}, \mathbf{r}; \epsilon) f(\epsilon - \mu) \tag{2.2}$$

$$V_{eff} = V_{ext} + e^2 \int d\mathbf{r}' \frac{\rho(\mathbf{r}')}{|\mathbf{r} - \mathbf{r}'|} + \frac{\delta E_{xc}}{\delta\rho(\mathbf{r})} \tag{2.3}$$

The SCF algorithm proceeds as follows: an input guess $\rho^{in}(\mathbf{r})$ of the electronic charge is used in eq. 2.3 to construct an initial guess of the effective electron-ion potential $V_{eff}(\mathbf{r})$ appearing in the Schrödinger equation (eq. 2.1). The single particle Schrödinger equation is then solved to obtain the single particle wave functions or, as indicated in eq. 2.1 and as is appropriate to the multiple scattering Green's function methods used in this paper, the single particle Green's function, $G(\mathbf{r}, \mathbf{r}; \epsilon)$. Next, the output charge density $\rho^{out}(\mathbf{r})$ is obtained from eq. 2.2. Finally, a new $\rho^{in}(\mathbf{r})$ is constructed by mixing the original $\rho^{in}(\mathbf{r})$ with $\rho^{out}(\mathbf{r})$ according to some (linear or non-linear) mixing algorithm. This procedure is then iterated until $\rho^{in}(\mathbf{r})$ and $\rho^{out}(\mathbf{r})$ agree to a prescribed small tolerance. Once a SCF solution is found the total energy is obtained from:

$$E_{tot}[\rho] = E_{band} - \int d\mathbf{r}\rho(\mathbf{r})V_{eff}(\mathbf{r}) + E_{Coulomb}[\rho] + E_{xc}[\rho] \tag{2.4}$$

Clearly, LDA is a first principles, parameter free, theory of matter in that the only inputs are the atomic numbers of the constituent elements.

2.1.2. The LSMS method for non-collinear magnetism. Standard reciprocal space ($\mathbf{k}$-space) electronic structure methods for solving the LDA single particle Schrödinger equation (eq. 2.1) ultimately scale as the third power of the number of atoms, N, in the unit cell. This is due to the need to diagonalize, invert, or orthogonalize a matrix whose size is proportional to N. For the very large cells that are required for implementing SD this scaling is prohibitive. The LSMS method [5] avoids this $O(N^3)$ scaling by using real space multiple scattering theory to obtain the Green's function (eq. 2.1) and hence the electronic charge (eq. 2.2) and magnetization densities. In the LSMS method the atoms comprising the crystal are treated as disjoint electron scatterers. The multiple scattering equations are solved for each atom by ignoring multiple scattering processes outside a local interaction zone (LIZ) centered on each atom (see figure 2.1).

The potential throughout the whole space is reconstructed in the standard way by solving Poisson's equation (eq. 2.3) for a crystal electron density made up of a sum of the single site densities. For the LSMS method, the LIZ size is the central convergence control parameter. For face and body centered cubic (fcc and bcc) transition metals LIZ sizes of a few ($\sim 3-7$) neighboring atom shells are sufficient to obtain convergence of the charge and magnetization densities. Using a Cray T3E, quite precise $O(N)$ scaling of the basic LSMS method has been demonstrated previously for up to 1024 atoms (nodes) [6].

The details of the LSMS method have been described in the literature [5]. The extension to cover the case of non-collinear moment arrangements is discussed in references [3] and [4]. Here let us simply quote the two most salient formulae necessary to understand the basic algorithm. The first is the Green's function for the atom at the center of the LIZ, $\hat{\mathcal{G}}_M(\{\mathbf{e}\}_i; \mathbf{r}; \epsilon)$, which is given by

$$\hat{\mathcal{G}}_M(\{\mathbf{e}\}_i; \mathbf{r}; \epsilon) = \sum_{LL'} \hat{Z}^i_L(\mathbf{r}; \epsilon)\, [\hat{\underline{\tau}}_M(\{\mathbf{e}\}_i; \epsilon)]^{ii}_{LL'}\, \hat{Z}^i_{L'}(\mathbf{r}; \epsilon)$$

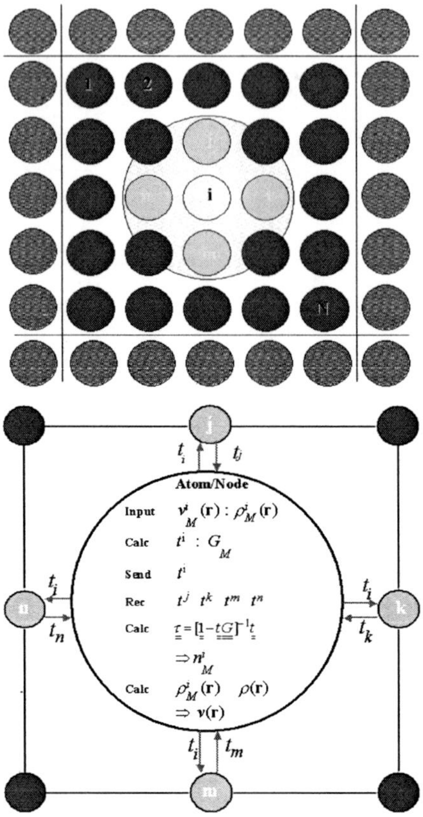

FIG. 2.1. Top: *Schematic of a parallel SCF algorithm. We envision a basic unit cell consisting of N-atoms labeled* $1, \ldots, N$ *which is periodically reproduced as indicated. About each atom, for example the* i^{th}, *we define a local interaction zone consisting of M-atoms including itself, for example labeled* i, j, k, m, n. Bottom: *Schematic of the implementation LSMS algorithm on a massively parallel computer.*

$$-\sum_L \hat{Z}_L^i(\mathbf{r};\epsilon)\hat{J}_L^i(\mathbf{r};\epsilon), \tag{2.5}$$

The second is the scattering path matrix, $\hat{\underline{\tau}}_M(\{\mathbf{e}\}_i;\epsilon)$, which describes the multiple scattering effects within the LIZ. It is given by the inverse of the KKR matrix, **M**, through

$$\hat{\underline{\tau}} = \underline{\hat{\mathbf{M}}}^{-1} \tag{2.6}$$

$$\underline{\hat{\mathbf{M}}} = \left[\, \underline{\hat{\mathbf{t}}}^{-1} - \underline{\hat{\mathbf{G}}} \,\right]. \tag{2.7}$$

In the last equation $\underline{\hat{\mathbf{t}}}$ is the t-matrix which describes the scattering from a single site and $\underline{\mathbf{G}}$ is the structure constant matrix which describes the propagation of free electrons from site to site. The above are matrices in site (i), angular momentum (L) and spin (denoted by ˆ) indices. This gives a linear dimension of $M \times L \times 2$, where M is the number of atoms in the LIZ (87 in the present work), L is a combined angular and azimuthal quantum number (16 for atoms near the center of the LIZ and 9 for the more distant ones), and the factor of 2 arises from the spin index. Not surprisingly, inversion of the KKR matrix (eq. 2.6) to obtain the scattering path matrix is the most time consuming task in the LSMS method.

2.1.3. Algorithm of *Ab initio* spin dynamics.. A general orientational configuration of atomic magnetic moments $\{\mathbf{e}_i\}$ such as is encountered during an individual time step of spin-dynamics, is not a ground state of LSDA. In order to properly describe the energetics of a general configuration it is necessary to introduce a constraint which maintains the orientational configuration. The purpose of the constraining fields is to force the local magnetization, $\mathbf{M}_i$, to point along the prescribed local direction $\mathbf{e}_i$. Note that at each site the constraining field ($\vec{B}_{cons}$) is transverse to the magnetization. The constraining field is not known *a priori*, and has to be calculated by some additional algorithm. The details of the theory and the constrained local moment (CLM) model are contained in reference [4]. The CLM state may be considered as a time freeze during the evolution of the system from a general initial state to a final state. This final state may be the ground state, as most often is, or another non-equilibrium state. We apply a simple model to describe the time-evolution process of the system between such CLM states: if the timestep is very small, the magnetic moments can be considered as classical moments of constant size. The relaxation of such moments to the ground state is then described by a Landau-Lifshitz like equation of motion of the form

$$\begin{aligned} \frac{d}{dt}\mathbf{e}_i &= \alpha \mathbf{e}_i \times (\mathbf{e}_i \times \mathbf{B}_{eff}) \\ \vec{B}_{eff} &= -\vec{B}_{cons}. \end{aligned} \tag{2.8}$$

This simple first order differential equation needs to be solved for each moment. This gives the orientational configuration for the new timestep. A new constrained LDA calculation is then performed. This is repeated until a ground state is obtained in which $\mathbf{B}_{\text{cons}} = 0$.

2.2. Parallel challenges. By making an atom (or atoms) to node (or CPU in the case of a machine that has multiple CPU's per node) mapping the LSMS is highly scalable on MPPs since each node can be assigned the work involved in setting up and inverting the KKR matrix eq. (2.6) for the atom(s) to which it is assigned. Inversion of the KKR matrix is the most time consuming step in the LSMS method. It typically takes over 80% of the total run time and is implemented in terms of complex matrix-matrix multiplies using the highly optimized BLAS routine ZGEMM.

Keeping angular momenta up to l_{max} (typically $l_{max} = 3$) the dimension of the matrix that is inverted is $2 \times (l_{max} + 1)^2 \times M$, where M is the number of atoms in the LIZ and the factor of 2 comes from the spin-index. Calculation of the charge and magnetization densities requires that each node invert this matrix for a set of energies along a contour in the complex energy plane of sufficient density to converge the necessary energy integrations. If M is smaller than the number of atoms in the system, N, this is clearly advantageous compared to conventional reciprocal space methods since these involve the inversion of a matrix of dimension $2 \times (l_{max} + 1)^2 \times N$ at a sufficient number of $\mathbf{k}$-points (a few for large systems to a few hundred for small systems) to converge necessary Brillouin zone integrals. The details of how the LSMS algorithm maps onto a parallel machine is shown in figure 2.1 (left) and explained in detail in the literature[5].

Necessary message passing involves passing of single site t-matrices for the sites/nodes in a given atom's LIZ, as well as global information regarding the total charge in the system, charge transfer and potential multipole moments. A typical run spends more than 80% of the time in BLAS3 routines and only a few percent in communications. This is a direct result of the complete rethinking of the electronic structure problem in terms of a parallel algorithm. This allows the algorithm to scale up to very large numbers of processors with the percentage of time spent in communications staying approximately constant when the number of processors increases with the number of atoms.

2.3. Special optimization issues: fast algorithms for matrix inversion. In the LSMS method each node calculates the scattering path matrix for its own atom(s). Hence, only the $L \times L$ ($L = 2(l_{max}+1)^2$) upper left block of the inverse is required, which represents the local atom's contribution to the scattering path matrix. A significant enhancement in computational performance can be achieved by taking advantage of this fact. Furthermore, the design of the inversion algorithms can be largely based on BLAS level 3 matrix-matrix multiply routines to ensure optimal performance.

The size of the KKR matrix in the LSMS approach for an LIZ size of M atoms, is $Q = ML$, where $L = 2(l_{\max} + 1)^2$ for each atom. Here for simplicity we assume that all atoms in the LIZ are calculated to the same $l_{\max}$. If different $l_{\max}$ are used this may lead to some load imbalance but if the LIZ's are large this effect will be minimal. The standard approach for the dense matrix inversion would be to apply the LU factorization of the whole matrix, which takes $\frac{1}{3}Q^3$ operations (one operation is one multiply and one add), or $\frac{2}{3}Q^3$ floating point operations, plus the forward and backward substitution for the first L columns, which take Q^2L operations or $2Q^2L$ floating point operations, for a total of

$$Q^2(\frac{2}{3}Q + 2L) = \frac{2}{3}M^3L^3 + 2M^2L^3 \tag{2.9}$$

floating point operations.

Recognizing that not the entire first L columns of the inverse are needed, we searched for a more efficient algorithm that could greatly reduce the total number of floating point operations for the calculation. The approach that we take is a variant of Strassen's [10] technique due to X.-G. Zhang [9]. If we partition a matrix of dimension Q into blocks of Q_1 and Q_2, $Q_1 + Q_2 = Q$, in the form,

$$\begin{pmatrix} A & B \\ C & D \end{pmatrix}, \tag{2.10}$$

then the top $L \times L$ diagonal block of the inverse of this matrix is also the top $L \times L$ diagonal block of the inverse of the following matrix,

$$A' = A - BD^{-1}C. \tag{2.11}$$

Thus we performed a transformation that reduced the problem from $Q \times Q$ to $Q_1 \times Q_1$. The number of operations (one multiply and one add) involved in this transformation is obviously $\frac{1}{3}Q_2^3 + Q_2^2Q_1 + Q_2Q_1^2$, which is smaller for smaller values of Q_2. However, Q_2 cannot be too small, otherwise the performance of the computer can degrade considerably due to cache misses. A reasonable choice is $Q_2 = L$ where L is typically 32 for our calculations. Thus we apply Eq. (2.11) recursively, until the size of the resulting A' is $L \times L$, at which time a simple inversion yields the desired upper $L \times L$ diagonal block of the inverse of the KKR matrix. The total number of floating point operations is,

$$\begin{aligned} & 2\sum_{m=1}^{M}\left\{\frac{1}{3}L^3 + L^2[(M-m)L] + L[(M-m)L]^2\right\} \\ &= \frac{2}{3}M^3L^3 - 2M^2L^3 + 2ML^3. \end{aligned} \tag{2.12}$$

The leading term of this result is the same as the standard LU algorithm, Eq. (2.9). However, the difference in the lower order terms of M can significantly reduce the number of operations for small M. Furthermore, since the new algorithm spends a very small fraction of the operations in inversion, ($\frac{2}{3}ML^3$ floating point operations), the majority of the operations are in matrix-matrix multiplies, it is much more easily optimized than the standard LU algorithm. For example, for a typical calculation where $L = 32$ and $M \approx 36$, we find that the new algorithm is about a factor of three faster than the standard LU on a wide range of platforms although the speedups are less significant for larger values of M.

3. Software Configuration. The Spin Dynamics (SD) version of the LSMS code is written in FORTRAN90 and is approximately 45,000 lines. The SD-LSMS code is derived from the CLM-LSMS code that won the 1998 Gordon Bell. The CLM-LSMS code for performing first principles constrained local moment (CLM) calculations is subsumed with the spin dynamics loop of the present code. The essential point being that the current generation of machines is sufficiently powerful to allow integration of the SD equation of motion over many time steps. In the present case SD time stepping is utilized to allow 'annealing' of an initial model configuration into the ground state. The CLM model is used to calculate the magnetic moments, energy, and constraining fields for the current orientational configuration. The SD equation of motion is then used to evolve the orientational configuration using the negative of the constraining field as the driving field.

In the current code message passing, which was previously distributed throughout the code and activated using a precompiler, according to the message passing interface being used - originally NX and PVM - is implemented through an interface of our own design. The specifics of message passing are relegated to a FORTRAN90 message-passing module and are implemented in both MPI and PVM. The consequence is that use of a precompiler is confined to the message-passing module and the rest of the source code does not depend on the message passing library used. Both the MPI and PVM versions of the code are used depending on the platform being used. Typically, PVM is used on work-station clusters and MPI is used on Cray T3E, IBM-SP, and HP-Compaq MPP machines.

4. Results.

4.1. Performance. In addition to performing the specific science calculations reported in the next sub-section, we performed a number of calculations on large cell models of disordered FeMn alloys designed to study the performance of the SP3 within a real application context.

The specific performance runs documented here were for large cell models of FeMn alloys made up of N×N×N repeats of the underlying face centered cubic (fcc) lattice with the 3Q alignment of magnetic moments. Since the fcc cell contains 4-atoms, cells having N=2,3,4,5,6,7,8 and 10 corresponded to simulating system sizes of 32, 108, 256, 500, 864, 1372, 2048 and 4000-atoms respectively. The NERSC IBM-SP has a total of 416 Nighthawk II SMP nodes, each with 16, 375 MHz Power3+ processors and a peak speed of 9.12 Tflops for the 380-node (6080 processors) compute partition. The largest run we could perform was on 4000 processors as there is a limit of 4096 MPI processes under the AIX operating system. The performance runs comprised of 10 self-consistent field (SCF) iterations towards convergence of the CLM state of one SD-time step. This is sufficient to amortize the start-up and shut-down (or check pointing) cost of the code and is representative of how the code is used in a scientific simulation. The start-up and shut-down time increases slowly with system size but still only accounts for $\approx$ 60 seconds of a $\approx$ 4000 second run. Internal timings embedded within the code were used to obtain execution times on the IBM SP3.

The LIZ was held fixed at 7 near-neighbor (nn) shells (87-sites) and $l_{max} = 3$ was used for the first two nn-shell and $l_{max} = 2$ for the rest which results in a KKR matrix dimension of 876×2. This LIZ size is sufficient to reliably resolve the ground state configuration.

Similar runs for a benchmark systems of bulk Iron were performed on the HP-Compaq Alphaserver at the Pittsburgh Supercomputing Center. This computer (Lemieux) has 750 HP-Compaq Alphaserver ES45 nodes and two separate front end nodes. Each computational node contains four 1-GHz processors giving the machine a peak speed of 6 Tflops. The nodes are connected together with a Quadrics interconnection network. The largest run was for a 3000 atom iron system.

The measured execution rates are shown in figure 4.1 and are compared with ideal linear scale up from the 32-processor timings. For the largest system on the SP (4000 processors)

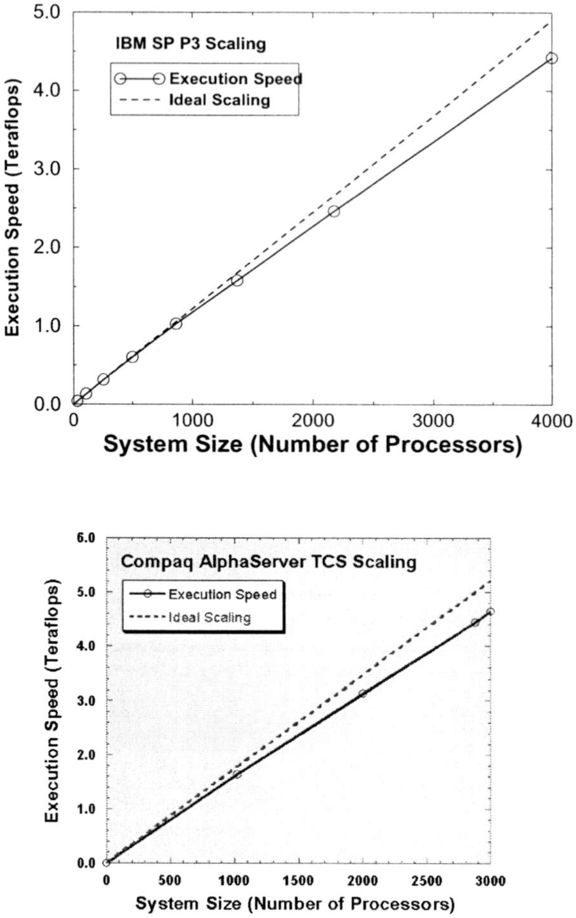

FIG. 4.1. *Execution rate of SD-LSMS code. The measured execution rates are shown as open circles and the solid line is a guide to the eye. The ideal linear scaling line (dashed line) is based on straight-line extrapolation of the 32-atom (processor) results. The performance runs on the SP were carried out during normal production cycles with an unknown mix of other jobs running of the machine. The runs on the SP are for an FeMn system while the runs on the Compaq Alphaserver are for a pure Fe system.*

the code ran at 4.42 Teraflops. On the HP-Compaq Alpha-server the code ran at 4.65 Tflops on 3000 processors for a benchmark system of 3000 iron atoms with an LIZ of 137. The high flop speeds are obtained in part by using the IBM and HP-Compaq native BLAS3 (matrix-matrix multiply) routines which run close to the peak performance of the machines for sufficiently large matrices. For very large systems a slight deviation from ideal linear scaling is observed. In each SCF loop the KKR-matrix is inverted on a mesh of 31 energies in the complex energy plane needed to perform an energy integration. The time to perform an inverse is essentially constant, independent of system size. However, the time to perform a SCF loop gradually increases from $\approx$ 380 sec. for the 32-atom system to $\approx$ 440 sec. for the 4000-atom system. Thus, the additional time results from the time required to construct the KKR-matrix. Since the size of the matrix is again constant, independent of system size, the major difference between these runs is the total number of messages being passed during the set up process. Therefore the time increase can be ascribed to the increasing cost of message passing of the single site t-matrices during the set up of the KKR matrix as the number of atoms/processors increases (see figure 2.1).

4.2. Scientific results: the magnetic structure of FeMn. The face centered cubic (fcc) solid solution alloy $Fe_{0.5}Mn_{0.5}$ has long been of scientific interest in that it is an example of a compositionally disordered fcc alloy that is, non-the-less, ordered antiferromagnetically. However, the precise nature of the antiferromagnetic state has been in dispute. Candidate antiferromagnetic states are shown in Fig. 1.1 and are labeled 1Q, 2Q, and 3Q. In the collinear 1Q structure (left) the moments point in opposing (100) directions in alternating layers, while in the non-collinear 2Q and 3Q structures the moments point in opposing (110) and (111) directions respectively. In the case of the compositionally disordered $Fe_{0.5}Mn_{0.5}$ alloy system, while the magnetic moments form a periodic ordered structure, the occupancy of the atomic sites (circles) is randomly Fe and Mn according to the 50/50 composition of the alloy. How can this be? Superficially, one would expect the disorder in the site occupancy to lead to disorder in the arrangement of the magnetic moments, if for no other reason that the local atomic moments associated with Fe and Mn sites are expected to be different.

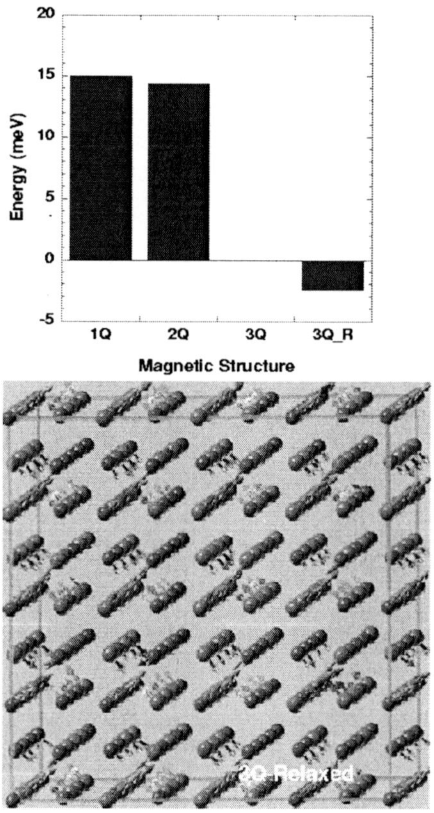

FIG. 4.2. *The top figure shows the energies of the 1Q,2Q,3Q and $3Q_R$ (3Q Relaxed) magnetic structures for the 256 atom super-cell model of $Fe_{0.5}Mn_{0.5}$ alloys. The energies are given relative to the 3Q-structures. The bottom figure shows a visualization of the ground state $3Q_R$ magnetic structure for the 256 atom super-cell model of $Fe_0.5Mn_0.5$ alloy. The arrows show the magnetic moments. The Fe (rust-spheres) and Mn (green spheres) are randomly distributed on a single underlying fcc lattice.*

In our simulations the energy of large cell models, consisting of 256-atoms of $Fe_{0.5}Mn_{0.5}$ periodically repeated, were calculated for the 1Q,2Q and 3Q states. Also, starting from the 3Q state the system was allowed to relax via first principles spin dynamics to the $3Q_R$ state (3Q Relaxed) which is lower in energy than the $3Q$ state. These $3Q_R$ state and the energies of the different states are shown in figure 4.2. The $3Q_R$ state is a new state that is even lower in energy than the the 3Q structure, which in turn is lower in energy than the 2Q and 1Q structures. This new state is 3Q only *on average* and has small fluctuations of the orientations of the site moments about the ideal 3Q orientations as well as fluctuations in the magnitudes of the local moments. Therefore, the compositional disorder in the system does lead to small disorder in the magnetic structure even though it is still 3Q on average. This may have implications for the mechanisms controlling exchange bias.

Acknowledgments. The calculations reported in this work were performed at the Pittsburgh Supercomputer Center (PSC), CCS-ORNL and at NERSC. CCS-ORNL and NERSC are supported by the Office of Science of the U.S. Department of Energy and PSC is supported by the National Science Foundation. This work was supported by the Division of Materials Sciences and Engineering, and by the Director, Office of Advanced Scientific Computing Research, Division of Mathematical Information and Computational Sciences Division, of the U.S. Department of Energy, under contract number DE-AC03-76SF00098 and subcontract DE-AC05-00OR22725 with UT-Battelle LLC.

REFERENCES

[1] V. P. Antropov et al. Phys. Rev. **54**, 1019 (1996).
[2] Q. Niu, Xindong Wang, L. Kleinman, Wu-Ming Liu, D. M. C. Nicholson, and G. M. Stocks, Phys. Rev. Letters, **83**, 207 (1999).
[3] G. M. Stocks, B. Ujfalussy, Xindong Wang, Xiaoguang Zhang, D. M. C. Nicholson, W. A. Shelton, Yang Wang, A. Canning, and B. L. Gyorffy, Phil. Mag. B **78**, 665, (1998).
[4] B. Ujfalussy, X. D Wang, D. M. C. Nicholson, W. A. Shelton, G. M. Stocks, Y. Wang, B. L. Gyorffy, J. Appl. Phys. 85, 4824 (1999)
[5] Y. Wang, G.M. Stocks, W.A. Shelton and D.M.C. Nicholson, Phy. Rev. Letters **75**, 2867 (1995).
[6] *High Performance First Principles Method for Complex Magnetic Properties*, Ujfalussy, B., Xindong Wang, Xiaoguang Zhang, D. M. C. Nicholson, W. A. Shelton, G. M. Stocks, A. Canning, Yang Wang, and B. L. Gyorffy, Proceeding of the ACM/IEEE SC98 Conference, Orlando, Florida, November 7-13, (1998). IEEE Computer Society, Los Alamitos, CA 90720-1264, CD-ROM.). First Place Gordon Bell Prize at SC98 Orlando. Proc. of SC98, Orlando, Florida, (1998).
[7] P. Hohenberg and W. Kohn, Phys. Rev. **136**, B864 (1964), W. Kohn and L. J. Sham, Phys. Rev. **140**, A1133 (1965).
[8] J. S. Faulkner and G. M. Stocks, Phys. Rev. **B21**, 3222 (1980).
[9] X.-G. Zhang, Ph.D. thesis, Department of Physics, Northwestern University (1989).
[10] V. Strassen, Numer. Math., 13, 354 (1969).

In: Parallel and Distributed Scientific and Engineering Computing ISBN 1-59033-956-8
Editor: Y. Pan and L.T. Yang, pp. 109-118

EVALUATION OF THE SPEEDUP OF A DISTRIBUTED GROUNDWATER SIMULATOR DISPERSION SYSTEM ON A DUAL-PROCESSOR BEOWULF NETWORK

MARIO DONATO MARINO *

Abstract. The Distributed Groundwater Simulator Dispersion System (DGWSDS) is a distributed simulator based on a public domain software of groundwater dispersion previously presented and studied. In this paper, our goal is to evaluate how much the increasing of the input parameters influences the speedups, comparing the predicted theoretical with the practical speedup when the simulator runs on a dual processor beowulf network. Some results show that it's better to run the simulator in 8 single processor-machine than in 4 dual-processor-machines.

Key words. Distributed, Application, Groundwater, Simulator, MPI.

1. Introduction. The movement of contaminants in groundwater is a particularly active area of research[1, 3, 4]. Models have been developed to study and simulate solute transport in groundwater systems. The research in this model is growing mainly due to the studies of weather forecast, sea streams and oil pollution.

In order to minimize the numerical errors, we are particularly interested in a numerical solution, where the partial differential equations are replaced by a set of ordinary differential equations approximated using finite differences.

The interest of a groundwater simulator is to use a computational numeric model of dispersion caused by large-scale heterogeneities within the aquifer.

The governing equation for advection-dispersion has several analytic solutions, which depend on the assumptions, boundary and initial conditions that can be seen in Anderson[1].

The simulator of the dispersion used as a basis for this work is a FORTRAN program located in sections 7.6 and 8.4 of Anderson's book[1]. It uses a computational numeric model of dispersion caused by large-scale heterogeneities within the aquifer.

The simulation of the dispersion can be prohibitive in terms of execution time depending on the number of NNODEs (number of nodes in the problem domain). The other important parameter is the NELEM, the number of elements in the grid studied. Thus, a distributed groundwater simulator dispersion system (DGWSDS) was developed in MPI [9] and some results were published[2][11].

In previous works[2, 11], the main idea of the simulator was presented and the speedups of DGWSDS were evaluated for the pairs NNODExNELEM: 1000x1000, 2000x2000 and 3000x3000.

The parameter NELEM represent the columns dimension of the matrices (for example, the ones of the paragraph above) of DGWSDS. As we will see in section 2 and 3, the NELEM dimension is divided among the nodes to implement the parallelism. If NNODE is fixed, it's possible to evaluate how the amount of computation of each node changes with NELEM. Concluding, by increasing NELEM, the slice of computation given to each processor to compute is higher, and the ratio computation x communication increases too. In this work, DGWSDS is evaluated with NNODE equals to 2000, 4000 and 6000, and NELEM from 1000 to 6000 (with step of 1000).

Nowadays, due to the decreasing of the costs of processors, Beowulf[11] networks built with dual node machines are very common. Thus, we are interested in the behavior of DG-WSDS in a dual processor network machine, i.e., how much the communication is influenced when the simulator runs on a network like this.

*Associate Researcher, Laboratory of Architecture and Basic Software of Polytechnic School of University of Sao Paulo; e-mail:mario@regulus.pcs.usp.br

Our environment of evaluation is a network of 8 PCs interconnected by a fast-Ethernet switch. Each PC is a dual processor machine, which is running Linux Redhat 8.0.

Concluding and resuming, the main goal of this paper is to show and evaluate how the speedups of DGWSDS are influenced by the variation of NELEM and also, how is the behavior of this simulator in a dual processor network system.

In section 2, the groundwater dispersion model and program are described. In section 3, our distributed implementation of this program is described. Section 4 defines the base criteria of how NELEM affects the behavior of DGSWSDS. Section 5 describes what is the behavior expected from running the simulator in a dual processor network system and discusses about the the predicted speedup. In section 6, the evaluation environment is described. Section 7 shows and discusses the results. Section 8 concludes the study.

2. Groundwater Dispersion Modeling and Simulation. Movements of contaminants in groundwater occur not only by advection but also by dispersion, which refers to mixing and spreading caused part by molecular diffusion and part by variations in velocity within the porous medium[1, 5, 6].

If a tracer slug is injected instantaneously into a uniform flow field, it disperses in the direction of flow (longitudinally) and transverses to the direction of flow (laterally). The dispersive flux in a uniform field is assumed to be proportional to the concentration gradient in the flow direction times porosity, which is known as Fickian model[1]. In a non-uniform field, the longitudinal and transverse dispersion coefficients are important; as a result, the dispersion coefficients are proportionality constant, which relate the mass flux vector to the gradient of concentration. Thus, the main directions are in the direction and perpendicular of flow. In a non-uniform flow field, the main directions vary from point to point in the problem domain.

The total max flux in some direction is the sum of the advective and dispersive fluxes. In the perpendicular direction, there is just the dispersive flux. Using the continuity of conservation, the divergence of the flux must be equal to the rate of decrease of solute concentration per unit of volume of aquifer. The total max flux is a generalization to an advection-dispersion governing equation, but not for short travel distances.

There are several solutions to solve the advection-dispersion equation. Early solutions used finite difference approximations, which sometimes contain numerical errors that can invalidate the solution. In order to minimize the numerical errors, the partial differential equation is replaced by a set of ordinary differential equations, which are approximated using finite differences. The former is more immune to numerical errors than the later.

In section 7.6 or in section 8.4 of Anderson[1], there's a program based on finite element for solving the solution dispersion in uniform flow field. This solution is valid by considering some boundary conditions and initial conditions:

- uniform groundwater field in x direction, with an average linear velocity;
- for times less than or equal to zero, the solute concentration throughout the aquifer is zero;
- for times greater than zero, calculates the concentration at the left edge of the aquifer which becomes a constant Co.

By observing this sequential program, three different blocks are observed:

block 1: generates

- nodal coordinates matrices: x, y, ns, nx and ny;
- initial conditions: cold (concentration in previous time step), cnew (concentration in actual time step), g , p and u (these three matrices are used for calculating the grid positions).
- some boundary conditions for cold and cnew.

block 2: generates global coefficient matrices: node, g, p and u. These matrices are of dimension NNODExNELEM.

block 3: solves the numerical system of equations in order to calculate the concentration for each time step. This block is done 100 times until the error is lower than a delta predefined. Each interaction of the block generally contains:

loop1) one loop based on index1 containing the block:
b[index1]=b[index1]+p[index1]*cold[index]/deltat

loop2) one loop based on index2 and index3 containing the block:
sum = sum + (g[index2] + u[index2] + p[index2]/deltat) * cnew[index3]

loop3) one loop based on index4 and index5 containing the block:
cnew[index4]=(-sum+b[index4])/(g[index5] + u[index5]+p[index5]/deltat);

In the equations above, deltat is the variation of the time, sum is an auxiliar value and the indexes are variables used to define the index of the positions manipulated inside each loop inside block 3.

3. Implementation of DGWSDS. In this section, the procedures to parallelize the sequential simulator of groundwater modelling are described. These procedures result on the distributed version of the simulator (DGWSDS).

3.1. Identification of the higher time consuming phase of the program. Since the goal is to parallelize in order to reduce the used time of the sequential version, the latter version was executed several times with different parameters. As a result of this process, the phase correspondent to the **block 3** was identified as the phase which spends most of the time.

Inside block 3, it's possible to identify some sub phases, named loop1, loop2 and loop3, explained in section 2, inside block 3. Among these phases, the ones that consume more time are:

- loop1: the sub-phase of calculation of matrix b, which is an auxiliary variable that stores some partial values, which will be used to calculate cnew,
- loop3: the sub-phase of calculation of matrices cold and cnew, which are the concentrations in present step and next step.

The two phases above mentioned were parallelized, although the loop3 is the most time consuming phase.

3.2. Parallel and sequential phases of the DGWSDS simulator. The phases which consume more time were parallelized and we followed the suggestion of Eppstein[6], i.e., the better algorithm for this problem is SPMD like. As a result, the algorithm we have implemented follows this model. The other phases are kept sequential (not parallelized).

3.2.1. Algorithm: calculation of matrix b. In this case, the following solution was adopted for each time step:

1. one of the nodes is selected to be the master;
2. the master, receiving b from all the nodes, calculates b resultant which depends of matrix p and vector cold. Since each node calculates b from matrix p, this matrix was divided in some pieces, which are manipulated in parallel by each node.

3.2.2. The phase of calculation of matrices cold and cnew (concentrations). In this case, the following solution was adopted for each time step:

1. one of the nodes is selected to be the master;
2. each node, including the master, calculates its partial sum, which is a function of the g, u, p and cnew matrices. Here was applied the same idea of the item 2 of subsection 3.2.1: the range of the columns of the matrices g, p and u was divided among the processors to improve the speedup.

3. all the nodes, except the master send its sum to the master;
4. the master, receiving the partial sums, adds them to its own sum and produces a resultant b, from which it can calculate the cnew (new concentrations) matrix;
5. the master send to all the nodes the cnew, except to itself;
6. all the nodes have their cnew actualized.

Obviously, considering that there is a master, the implementation becomes centralized. We think that it is not worthwhile to use an alternate implementation such as a tree or a butterfly[7, 8] because the message sizes are too small and there are a low number of messages sent to the server simultaneously, limited to the number of nodes that execute the program.

4. Increasing The Ratio Computation/Communication of DGWSDS. In step 2 of section 3.2.1, it's possible to notice the parallelism of DGWSDS: since matrix b was divided among the nodes, the amount of calculations by the number of nodes evolved in the computation decreases, thus decreasing the time to compute it, which benefits the speedups.

In step 2 of section 3.2.2, it's possible to notice how NELEM affects the behavior of DGWSDS: since matrices g, p and u are two-dimensional matrices, and the parallel algorithm divides NELEM among the nodes, if this parameter is increased, each node will have a large slice to compute, so the ratio computation/communication increases, improving the speedup. On the other hand, if NNODE was increased, the number of messages changed from all the nodes to the master would be increased, decreasing the speedups.

5. Running DGWSDS in a Dual Processor Network System: Prediction of the Speedup. Since our goal is to reduce the simulation times, and since our laboratory (LASB) acquired a network of dual processor machines, we used a network of dual processor nodes to evaluate our simulator.

Although our implementation is a non multithreaded implementation neither a based on processes, and considering that MPI exploits the shared memory to realize the message passing in a shared memory machine (dual processor nodes) to reduce the overheads of communication, we decided to identify how much our simulator improves its speedup if we run it on a dual processor network.

Two theoretical [14, 15] models for prediction of the speedup were developed for DGWSDS: the first for one processor running per node, and the second for two processors per node.

In the case of the first model, considering all the PCs interconnected by a network, the figure 1 shows the predicted speedup for the case of NNODE=6000, with 99% parallel algorithm, a communication cost of 0.01 and the startup cost 0.05. The efficiency of the algorithm can be changed by adjusting the problem.

In the case of the second model, considering all the PCs such as shared memory model machines interconnected by a network, the figure 1 shows the predicted speedup for the case NNODE=6000, with 99% of parallel algorithm, communication cost of 0.01 and the startup cost 0.05.

The behavior of the predicted models shows that the speedup obtained for the version with two processors per node is about twice of the version with one processor.

6. Evaluation Environment. In this section, the hardware and software required for evaluation of the performance of our distributed implementation are described.

6.1. Hardware. Our distributed implementation will be evaluated on a network of 8 nodes. Each node has the following features:

- 1GB MB of DDR133 main memory;
- Dual Athlon MP 1.8 GHz processor;
- Intel Pro/100 fast-Ethernet card.

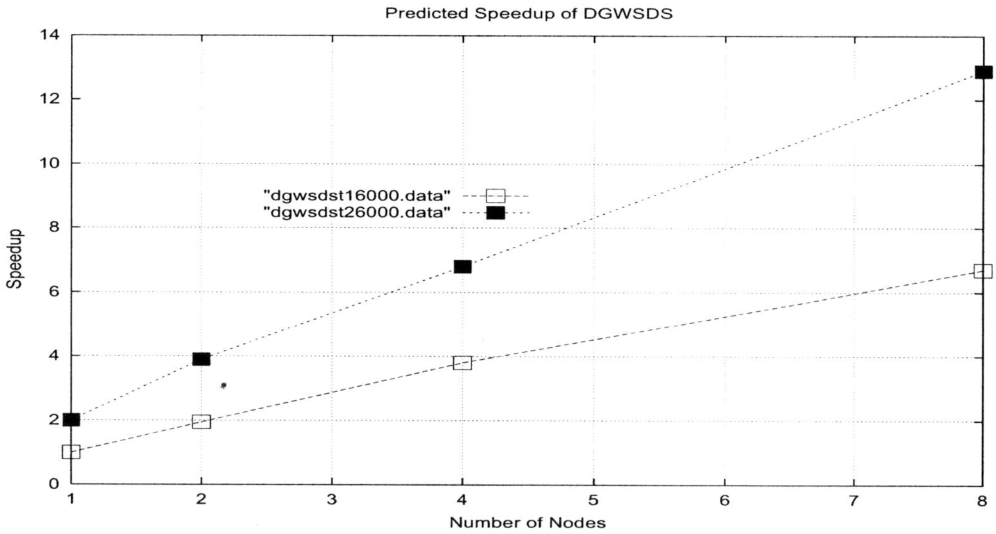

FIG. 1. *predicted speedup of DGSWSDS with NNODE=6000 for one and two processors per node*

All the PCs are interconnected by a 3Com 3300C switch.

6.2. Software. Each PC runs Red Hat Linux 8.0.

Since the international tendencies are toward [9], it was adopted to implement DGWSDS instead of [10].

The version of MPI used is Lam version 6.5.9.

The version of DGWSDS used in this experiments is 0.0.3.

DGWSDS is evaluated with NNODE equals to 2000, 4000 and 6000, and NELEM from 1000 to 6000 (with step of 1000).

7. Results. In this section the results of the speedups are shown in two situations:

- one program running per node: all the nodes are used (only one processor per node is used)
- two programs running per node: in this case, only 4 nodes (dual processor) are used in the experiments

After presenting the results for executions with one program and two programs running per node, they are compared.

An *important* notice is that for the executions with two programs per node Lam-MPI was informed that there are two CPUs, i.e., in the machine file archive, *CPU=2* was passed as a parameter.

7.1. One program running per node . In this section, the speedups of DGWSDS will be shown for one program running per node, for NNODE=2000, NNODE=4000 and NNODE=6000. For each value of NNODE, NELEM will change from 1000 to 6000.

7.1.1. One program per node, NNODE=2000. The speedups for these parameters can be observed in figure 2. By observing this figure, we notice that for NELEM=1000 and NELEM=2000, the speedups are very poor due to the low ratio computation/communication. Since the amount of calculations is proportional to NELEM, and if it assumes a low value, the number of calculations is lower compared to the amount of messages exchanged through the net. Also for these two cases, if the number of nodes is increased, the number of messages through the net is either and the speedup decreases. For NELEM=3000, the speedups are better than for NELEM=1000 and NELEM=2000. As NELEM is increased from 3000 to

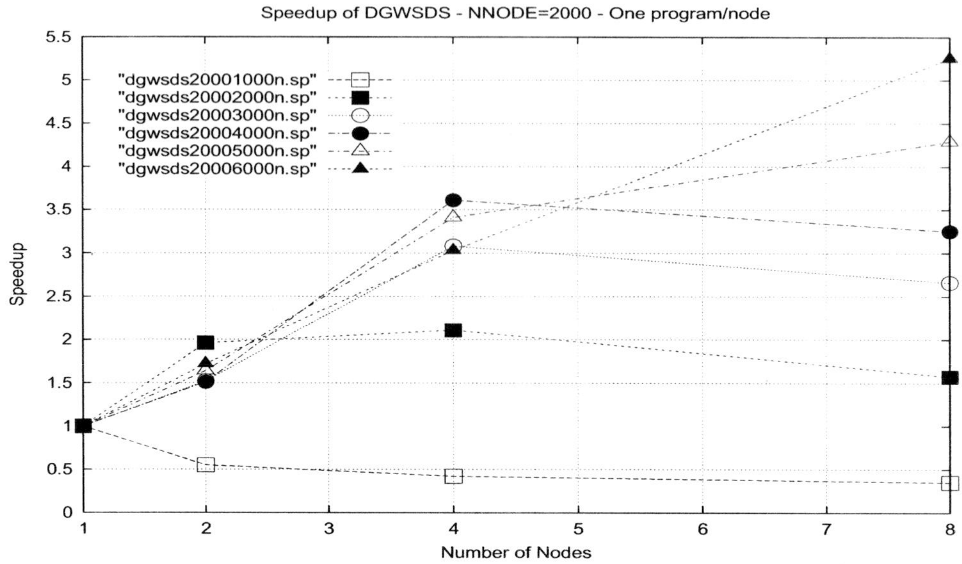

FIG. 2. *speedups for the DGWSDS, NNODE=2000, one processor per node*

6000, we notice an improvement of the speedups and they increase as the number of nodes increases, scaling better than the previous ones. For NELEM=6000 and 8 nodes, we obtain speedups up to 5.25.

7.1.2. One program per node, NNODE=4000. The speedups for these parameters can be observed in figure 3. By looking in this figure, we notice that for NELEM=1000, NELEM=2000 and NELEM=3000 the speedups are very poor due to the low ratio computation/communication. The comments done in the previous subsection with respect to NELEM and number of calculations are valid too, thus in these cases the number of calculations is lower compared to the amount of messages exchanged through the programs. In the same way, for these cases, if the number of nodes is increased, the number of messages through the net also is increased and the speedup decreases. For NELEM=3000, the speedups are better than for NELEM=1000, but poor yet. For NELEM bigger than 3000, we notice an improvement of the speedups obtained and they increase as the number of nodes increases. For NELEM=6000 and 8 nodes, we obtain speedups up to 3.75.

7.1.3. One program per node, NNODE=6000. The speedups for these parameters are in figure 4. By analyzing this figure, we notice that for NELEM=1000 the speedups are very poor due to the low ratio computation/communication. The comments done in the previous subsections with respect to NELEM and number of calculations are valid too. For NELEM bigger than 2000, we notice an improvement of the speedups obtained and they increase as the number of nodes increases. For NELEM=6000 and 8 nodes, we obtain speedups up to 6.30.

7.1.4. Comparing: NNODE=6000, predicted speedup x obtained speedup, one program per node. For NNODE=6000x6000, for one program per node, by comparing the figure 4 with figure 1, we conclude that the prediction model obtained results very closer to the practical results, thus a good predicted model.

7.1.5. Comparing: NNODE=2000, NNODE=4000 and NNODE=6000, one program per node. By comparing the speedups obtained in the previous subsections, it's possible to conclude that as NNODE is increased the speedups increase, considering one

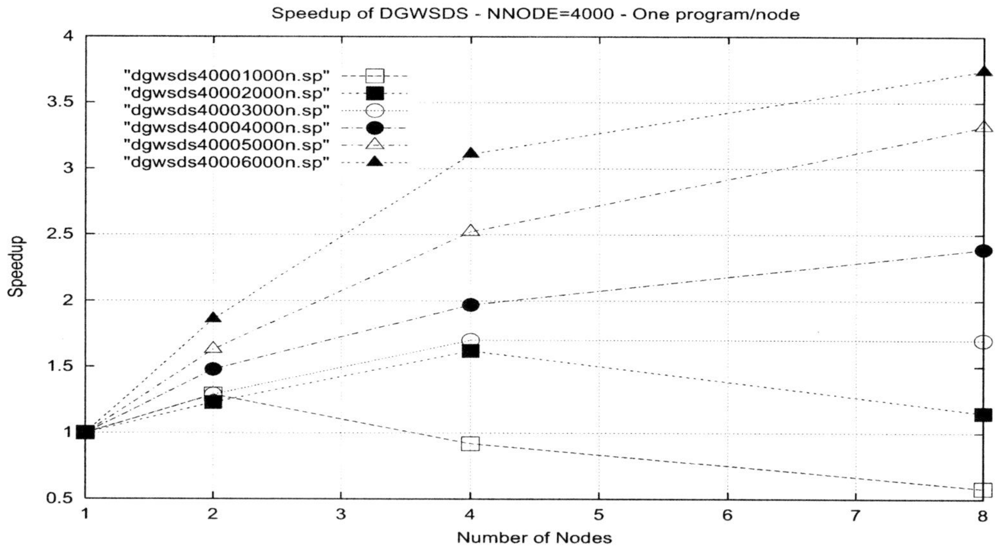

FIG. 3. *speedups for the DGWSDS, NNODE=4000, one processor per node*

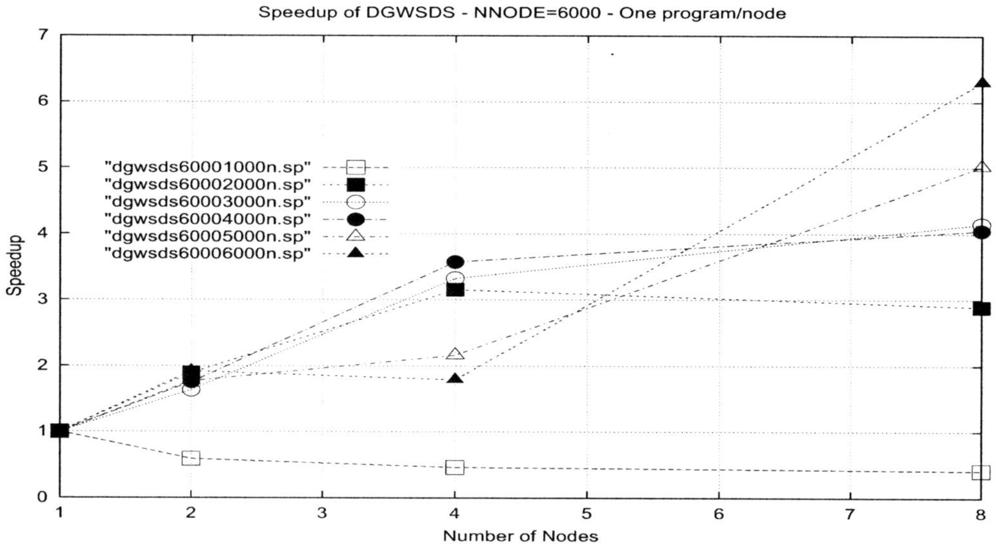

FIG. 4. *speedups for the DGWSDS, NNODE=6000, one processor per node*

program per node.

7.2. Two programs running per node. In this section, the speedups of DGWSDS will be shown for two programs running in a node, for NNODE=2000, NNODE=4000 and NNODE=6000. For each value of NNODE, NELEM will change from 1000 to 6000.

7.2.1. Two programs per node, NNODE=2000. The speedups are shown in figure 5. By observing this figure, we notice that for NELEM=1000, the speedups are very poor due to the low ratio computation/communication, even if the communication is done in the same node. In the subsection 7.3, it's discussed how communication is done in the same node and its effects. For NELEM=1000, if the number of nodes is incremented, the number of messages through the net is increased and the speedup decreases. For NELEM bigger

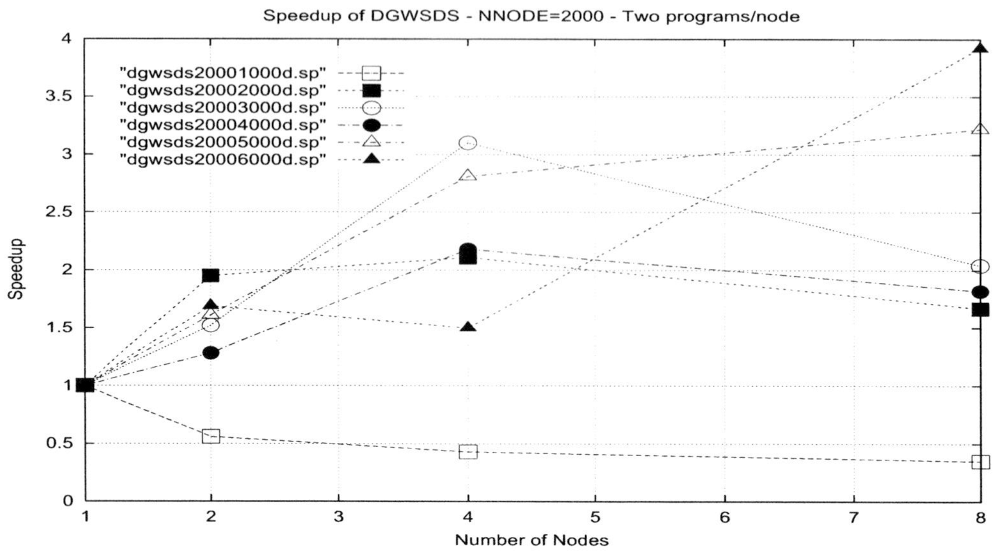

FIG. 5. *speedups for the DGWSDS, NNODE=2000, two programs per node*

FIG. 6. *speedups for the DGWSDS, NNODE=4000, two programs per node*

than 2000, the speedups increase as the number of nodes increases. For NELEM=6000 and 8 nodes, we obtain speedups up to 3.92.

7.2.2. Two programs per node, NNODE=4000. It's possible to observe the speedups in figure 6. For NELEM=1000, for the same reasons explained in the section 7.2.1, the speedups are very poor (low ratio computation/communication). For NELEM=1000, if the number of nodes is incremented, the number of messages exchanged is increased and the speedup decreases. For NELEM bigger than 1000, we notice an improvement of the speedups and they increase as the number of nodes increases. For NELEM=6000 and 8 nodes, we obtain speedups up to 4.10.

7.2.3. Two programs per node, NNODE=6000. It's possible to observe the speedups in figure 7. For NELEM=1000 and NELEM=2000, for the same reasons explained before in the section 7.2.1, the speedups are very poor (low ratio computation/communication). For NELEM=1000 and NELEM=2000, if the number of nodes is incremented, the number of messages exchanged (even the program is running in the same node) is increased and the speedup decreases. For NELEM bigger than 2000, the speedups increase as the number of nodes increases. For NELEM=6000 and 8 nodes, we obtain speedups up to 6.29.

7.2.4. Comparing: NNODE=6000, predicted speedup x obtained speedup, two program per node. For NNODE=6000x6000, for two processors per node, by comparing the figure 7 with figure 1, we conclude that the prediction model did not obtain results closer to the practical results, due to the high contention of the shared memory bus, which was not included in the respective prediction model.

7.3. Comparing the results with one program x two programs per node. Considering 8 nodes, for all NNODEs evaluated, the speedups of the programs running with two processor per node were smaller than one program per node. If the parameter CPU=2 is passed to Lam-MPI when it configures the topology (lamboot), the communication is done via shared memory, instead of through exchange messages by TCP.

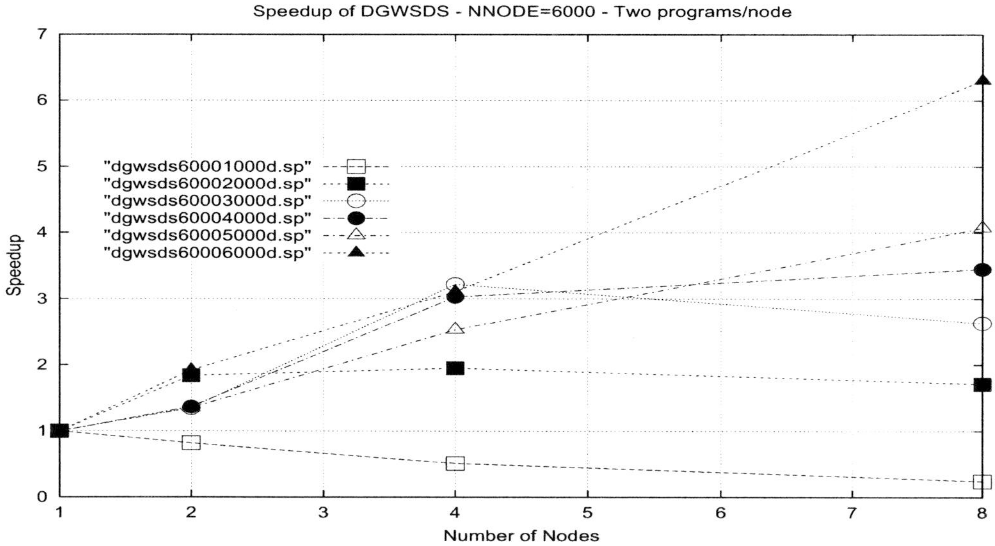

FIG. 7. *speedups for the DGWSDS, NNODE=6000, two programs per node*

When two copies of the simulator are running on the same machine, both of them access the physical shared memory of the dual processor node, causing a high contention for it. This high contention causes the saturation of the memory bus, resulting a slow access memory system, which degrades the speedup of the program. This contention could be minimized using another types of memory systems[13].

The conclusion is that, by supposing a distributed application with only one process or thread, for running it with more than one application per node in a dual machine, if the application has a high access ratio of the memory, it won't produce such as good speedups as if only one application per node was executed. This result is the opposite of the predictions of section 5, because we haven't considered the memory access system implementation of the motherboard of our dual node PCs.

8. Conclusion. We studied the speedups of a program created to simulate groundwater systems named DGWSDS. Practical speedups up to 6.3 for two types of configuration machines, one-processor and two-processors per PC. The speedups for the one-processor configuration were obtained and also, the results obtained were closed to the predicted theoretical results for one processor per node, but for the two-processor configuration, the speedups were very poor due to the high contention for the shared memory bus, which interconnects the two-processor machine.

As a conclusion of this study, the speedups increased with the increasing of one of the input parameters NELEM, both in a one-processor and on a dual-processor network of PCs. By increasing NELEM, the ratio computation/communication increases, as a consequence, the speedups increase.

Another important conclusion is that considering that our simulator is an application with only one process (it could be a thread), if it runs on a machine with two processors and if the application has a high access ratio for the memory, it won't produce such as good speedups as if only one application per node was executed. This result is the opposite of we are waiting because of the high congestion in the memory access system of the motherboards of the dual processor nodes. In addition, another prediction model taking into account the shared memory contention will be included to improve it in next comparisons.

As a suggestion of future tests, a possibility is to compare the tests with two programs/node specified with CPU=2 with the same two programs with the name of the machines doubled in the machine file of Lam-MPI. This will allow us there is any problem on MPI implementation or confirm if the memory access really is the problem for this type of machine.

Depending on the input parameters, the program's matrices can occupy too much memory. So, we're developing a technique that allow us to run the program bigger input sizes, which can help us to improve our simulations' results.

REFERENCES

[1] ANDERSON, M. P.Introduction to Groundwater Modeling - Finite Difference and Finite Element Methods, University of Wisconsin, Madison.

[2] MARINO, M.D. AND SATO, L.M., *Evaluating the Speedup of a MPI-based Distributed Dispersion Simulator for Ground Water Systems*, ICPADS2002, Taiwan, China, 2002.

[3] AHLFELD, D.P. AND HEIDARI M., *Applications of optimal hydraulic control to ground-water systems*, ASCE J. Water Resour. Plan. and Manag., 120(3), 350-365, 1994.

[4] GORELICK, S.M., *Sensitivity analysis of optimal groundwater contaminant capture curves: spatial variability and robust solutions*, in: Proceedings of the Solving Ground Water Problems with Models Conference, National Water Well Association, Denver, CO, 1987.

[5] BREDEHOEFT, J.D., REICHARD E.G. AND GORELICK S.M., *If it works, don't fix it: Benefits from regional ground-water management*, in: Proceedings of the Assessment of Models for Groundwater Resources Analysis and Management Conference, sponsored by University of Hawaii, Honolulu, Hawaii, March, 1994.

[6] EPPSTEIN, M J, GUARNACCIA, J F AND DOUGHERTY, D E, *Parallel groundwater computations using MaAl. Finite Elements in Water. Resources*, Proceedings of the International Conference, Computational Mechanics Publ, Univ of Vermont, Burlington, VT, USA, Southampton, Engl. v 1. p 713-720, 1992.

[7] BROOKS, E., *The butterfly barrier*, International Journal of Parallel Programming, vol. 15, no. 4, pp. 295–307, 1986.

[8] LUBACHEVSKY B., *Synchronization barrier and related tools for shared memory parallel programming*, in Proceedings of the 1989 International Conference on Parallel Processing, Aug., 1989, II-175–II-179.

[9] http://www.lam-mpi.org

[10] http://www.pvm.org

[11] MARINO, M.D. AND ALEIXO, L.A., A Distributed Simulator for Groundwater Systems, SPDSEC'02, Charlottesville, Virginia, September, 2002.

[12] BECKER D. AND MERKEY P., *Beowulf: Harnessing the Power of Parallelism in a Pile-of-PCs*, Proceedings, IEEE Aerospace, 1997.

[13] ANNARATONE M. AND RUHL R., *Performance Measurements of a Commercial Multiprocessor Running Parallel Code* in The 16th International Symposium on Computer Architecture, Jerusalem, Israel, pp. 307-314, May 1989.

[14] HARRISON R.W, *Implementation and Analysis of a Parallel Amortized Fast Multipole Algorithm for Molecular Modeling with MaAl*, technical Report, CS, Georgia State University, 2003.

[15] KUMAR V. AND RAO N., *Parallel Depth-First Search, Part II: Analysis*, International Journal Parallel Programming, 16:501-519, 1987.

In: Parallel and Distributed Scientific and Engineering Computing ISBN 1-59033-956-8
Editor: Y. Pan and L.T. Yang, pp. 119-129

NEW MESH GENERATING ADAPTED TO PARALLEL SYSTEMS: PVM IMPLEMENTATION ISSUE

ANDREI DONCESCU*

Abstract. This work relates to the study of three-dimensional objects covered with a formed grid of deformable unidimensional elements and valence 3. The advantages of this new type of grid are: the compression of information $3D$ for their transmission, the synthesis of objects 3D for their recognition as well as a tool adapted to the problems of measurement of deformation. The Wavelet Transformation allowed the study of this new grid for the analysis and the synthesis of images 3D at various levels of resolution. We present in this paper the different algorithms of subdivision and compression applied on this type of surfaces. All these algorithms could be parallelized due to the system of numbering of this type of meshes.

Key words. Wavelets, Voronoi, Subdivision, Compression, Parallel, PVM

1. Introduction. Surfaces play an important role in 3D computer graphics applications. Subdivision surfaces are valued in geometric modelling applications for the representation of objects of arbitrary topological type in a form that is easy to design render and deform. Recursive subdivision is a common technique for obtaining satisfactory piecewise linear approximation to smooth surfaces. The computation is repetitive, intensive and would benefit from an architecture that exploits parallelism. Hierarchical representations of the 3D surfaces provide the opportunity for multiresolution and compression. The Wavelet Transform allows a reversible transformation of the 3D surfaces. The Wavelet Transform is applied in generally on surfaces meshed by triangles, which is more adapted for polygons in 2D and in 3D. This work relates to the study of three-dimensional objects covered with a formed grid of deformable unidimensional elements and valence 3. We named this grid "Organized Voronoi" because each vertex has always 3 neighbors inspired of the C60 molecule. The most striking property of the C60 molecule is its high symmetry. There are 120 symmetry operations, like rotations around an axis or reflections in a plane, which map the molecule onto itself. This makes C60 the molecule with the largest number of symmetry operations, the most symmetric molecule. Based on a theorem of the mathematician Leonhard Euler, one can show that a spherical surface entirely built up from pentagons and hexagons must have exactly 12 pentagons. Depending on the number of hexagons, molecules of different sizes are obtained. Starting with this kind of meshes we construct different objects start-shaped or not. The advantages of this new type of grid are the compression of information 3D for their transmission, the synthesis of objects 3D for their recognition as well as a tool adapted to the problems of measurement of deformation. The Wavelet Transformation allowed the study of this new grid for the analysis and the synthesis of images 3D at various levels of resolution. We present in this paper the different algorithms of subdivision and compression applied on this type of surfaces. All these algorithms could be parallelized due to the system of numbering of this type of meshes. This implicit system of vertices numbering could be calculate at each level. Applied on Voronoi Organized Meshes the calculus time is ameliorated and the communication process between the computers is simple and smart. An efficient mesh bust be easily tessellated when a visual realism is needed , and must easily loosen when a fast but rough solution is needed. The algorithm of subdivision of surfaces has been introduced by Catmull and Clark [3] and by Doo and Sabin in 1978 [2]. They generalize the bicubic and biquadratic B-splines. In 1987 Loop [8] generalizes the quartic triangular B-splines. Rectangular patches have also been studied by Ball and Story [1] which use the Fourier Transform to find the tangent plan in singular points. Halstead, Kass and DeRose use the analysis of the eigenvalues in the determination of the

*Laboratory of Analysis and Architecture of Systems, Laboratory of Biotechnology and Bioprocesses-INSA,Avenue de Rangueil, Toulouse France (adoncesc@laas.fr)

sufficiently conditions for the convergence of the algorithm of subsection and the possibility to calculate the normal from the clean value structure.

2. Construction of the 3-connected Objects. To generate an organized mesh, three methods are proposed:

1. the radial projection,
2. the organized triangulation,
3. the union of spheres meshed on Organized Voronoi Diagram.

The first two methods are used for star-shaped surfaces. The third is more general.

1. The radial projection is inspired of the work of Kent [5] for the radial projection of a polyhedron, what allows it to have the same number of vertices between the two objects. At the end the vertices are interpolated. The quality of intermediate surface depends strongly of the process of meshing. The disadvantage is the applicability only for radial surfaces. The difference with the algorithm of Kent resides in the manner of sphere meshing. The sphere meshing is obtained from a dodecahedron subdivided by methods presented in the next paragraph. The faces are 3D solids supposed star-shaped. We project a given level of the sphere on a digitized face and our algorithm deduces other levels of meshing, but also we could generate this organization starting with triangles meshes which was submitted at same constraints allowing us the construction of the "dual" polyhedron formed by pentagons and hexagons keeping the fullerenes organization.
2. The triangulation organized uses the transformation star-triangle. In geometry, the triangulation of a surface has long been studied. A transformation triangle-star allows us the construction of the patches related by vertices of valence 3. The idea is to place the vertices representing the future pentagons in the points of maximal curvature and to construct a mesh of valence 5. Successively the recursive transformation triangle-star allows finding the future hexagons. The relationship star-triangle appears in statistical mechanics as a method allowing to solve the spin models of Ising and the Q states model of Potts. In geometry, it is imposed by the topology invariants. The connection between mathematics and physics is mainly based on the theory of fields, where, to each point is associated a variable. The approach of the theory of fields consists in considering them as them limit discreet fields, constructed on regular systems whose one makes tend the patch to zero. The model of Ising shows that the limit of this model of two dimensions is a quantum field of one dimension. The passage to the limit has tempted the researchers to interpret the models of the statistical mechanics using the theory of invariants polynomials for the vertices [6]. In geometry the triangulation of a surface was studied a long time. A transformation of the triangle-star type can allow us a construction of the grid *Organized Voronoi Diagram* with 12 pentagons and the hexagons determined by the relations of recurrence described in the chapter on the construction of the database. The methods of subdivision preserve the centers of gravity. On the basis of the idea that we can impose the centers of gravity on a star-shaped surface, an algorithm is presented:
   (a) choose 12 representative points on surface,
   (b) connect the 12 centers of gravity: each point is connected to 5 other centers of gravity by curves of surface in accordance with the graph,
   (c) insert inside each triangle determined by the centers of gravity of the points representing the future centers of gravity of the hexagons,
   (d) connect the 12 centers of gravity of the type pentagon and the 20 centers of gravity of the hexagonal type, in accordance with the graph:
   each center of gravity of the pentagon type is connected to 5 centers of gravity

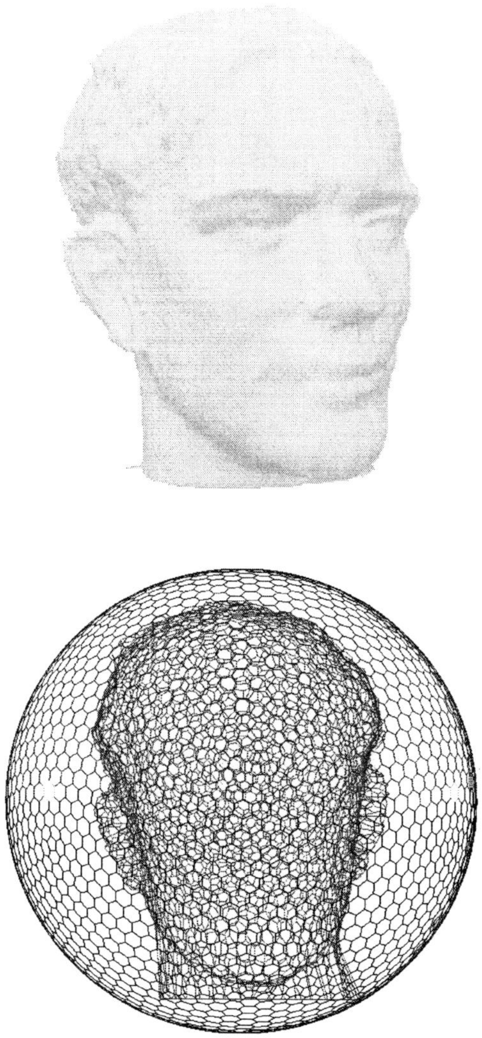

FIG. 2.1. *The radial projection*

and each centers of gravity of the hexagonal type is connected to 6 centers of gravity.

(e) iteration by transformations of the triangle-star type of the same type as those presented previously. The number of centers of gravity of the hexagonal type B_{h_i} per level $i > 0$ of triangulated surface ($i = 0$ corresponds to the icosahedron) is:

$$B_{h_i} = 10(3^i - 1) \tag{2.1}$$

and 12 centers of gravity corresponding to the future pentagons. The number of triangles T_i is :

$$T_i = 20 \times 3^i \tag{2.2}$$

(f) construction of 12 pentagons and H_i hexagons while choosing on connections

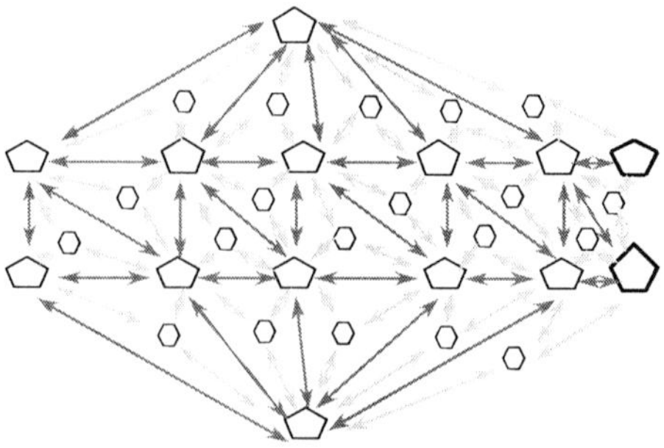

FIG. 2.2. *The graph construction*

of each centers of gravity of the points a ratio which must be lower than $\frac{l_d}{2}$, where l_d is the distance between two centers of gravity. $(\frac{l_d}{3})$.

Thus, on the level of subdivision i the number of hexagons which can be built is:

$$H_i = B_{h_i} + T_i = 10(3^i - 1) + 20 \times 3^i = 10(3^{i+1} - 1) \quad (2.3)$$

Fig. 2.2 represents the transformation triangle-star, which we will call dual-3, because each side of the triangle is divided into three parts.

3. The union of spheres uses the calculation of the skeleton 3D of a cloud of points. Spheres are placed on the skeleton, which merging forming thus polygons 6,7,8 edges. The disadvantage of this method is the important time calculation. We can notice that if the skeleton is a point, the radial projection allows to have a complete system of mesh generation. Thus, the union of spheres allows the local subsection. The difference with Ranjan and Fournier [9] , that interpolate by unions of sphere UoS (UoS is a representation of an object 3D by spheres placed in the characteristic points of an object), is the union of the Organized Voronoi mesh of the spheres and not representing by implicit surfaces.

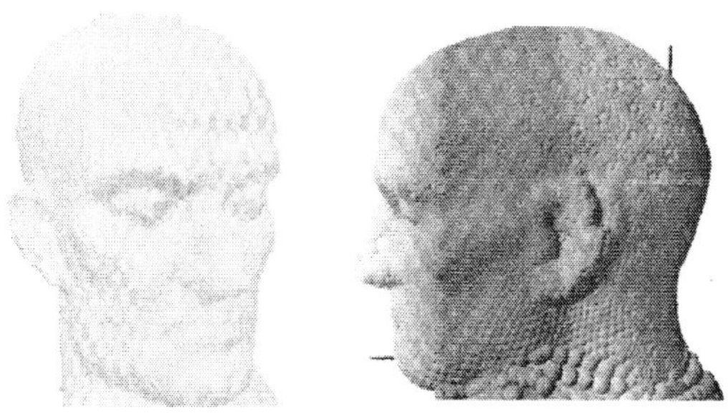

FIG. 2.3. *Head interpolation by spheres*

Euler's law

For a convex polyhedron with F faces, V vertices and E edges, Euler's law state that $V - E + F = 2$. A sphere has genus zero and if another more complex polyhedron can be obtained by deforming the shape of a sphere with N handles, then it has genus $g = N$. In this case the Euler's Law in $3D$ is $V - E + F = 2 - 2g$. For an object obtaining by Union of Sphere there are only pentagons, hexagons, heptagons or octagons, each edge is shared by two polygonal faces and three shares each vertex polygons. In this case we have:

$$F = N_5 + N_6 + N_7 + N_8 \quad (2.4)$$

(2.5) $$2E = 3V = 5N_5 + 6N_6 + 7N_7 + 8N_8$$

(2.6) $$N_5 - N_7 - 2N_8 = 12(1 - g)$$

For a torus $N_5 - N_7 - 2N_8 = 0$ and for a sphere $N_5 - N_7 - 2N_8 = 12$

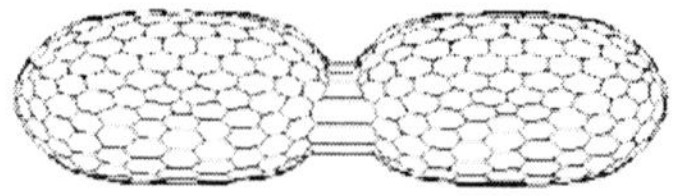

FIG. 2.4. *Fusion of two spheres*

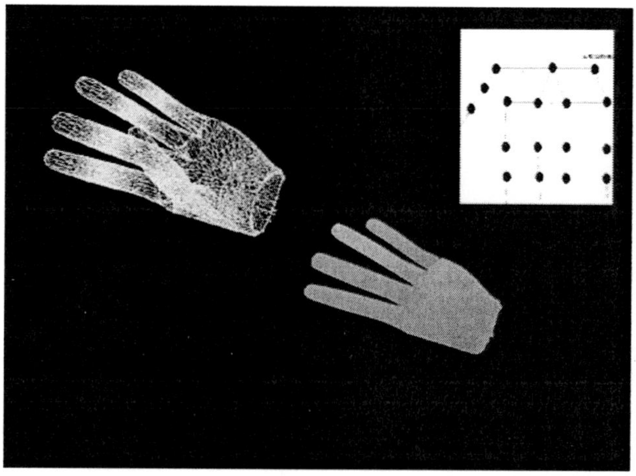

FIG. 2.5. *The mesh of the hand*

3. Subdivision of the Organized Voronoi Surfaces. Proposed algorithms are developed for surfaces having the vertices of valence 3. In this case algorithms of subdivision can be considered as methods of interpolation of gravity centers. This advantage is used for the representation of objects 3D by metaballs to the different levels of resolution. Two methods of subdivision are used.

1. The first method uses filters associated to a orthogonal basis of wavelets [4].
2. The second allows to avoid the problem, that is not again solved, the construction of the wavelets in 3D of any angle using the techniques of finite length filters. Algorithms are recursive and convergent.

Other possibility is the method of dual patches. Three centers of gravity of the faces having the same vertex in common are connected. Under this vertex, an equilateral triangle is built, then the each edge is subdividing in 3 segments determined a hexagon. The disadvantage of this method is that it does not preserves the centers of gravity of each face.

3.1. Subdivision by rotational wavelets. Let consider the next three wavelets ψ_1, ψ_2, ψ_3 having the properties:

1. compactly supported,
2. regular,
3. $\psi_3 = R(\psi_2)$ and $\psi_2 = R(\psi_1)$ where R is the matrix of rotation of angle $2\pi/3$.

The basis $2^j\psi(2^jx - k), k \in Z^2, j \in Z, \psi \in \psi_1, \psi_2, \psi_3$ is an orthogonal basis and is unconditional of $L^2(R^2)$.

The construction of a wavelet basis in $2D$ or $3D$ uses the tensorial product. Starting with $1D$ basis, the scaling function ϕ is invariant to the rotation of $2\pi/3$. The wavelets ψ_1, ψ_2, ψ_3 are defined:

$$\begin{aligned} \psi_1(x,y) &= \phi(x)\psi(y) \\ \psi_2(x,y) &= \psi(x)\phi(y) \\ \psi_3(x,y) &= \psi(x)\psi(y) \end{aligned}$$

To avoid this difficult problem a possibility is to start with the matrix formula of Wavelet Transform. In matrix form the formula of exactly reconstruction is written:

$$H^T H + G^T G = I \tag{3.1}$$

So, a matrix R composed of several R_θ is introduced. R and R_θ are orthogonal matrices $R_\theta^T R_\theta = I$, $R^T R = I$, so we can write

$$H^T R^T R H + G^T R^T R G = I \tag{3.2}$$

Using this idea we could applied it to the subdivision. The subdivision process starts to level i and behind each vertex a new hexagon is constructed (level $i+1$).

The solution is to take the center of gravity of each facet and to calculate:

$$P_{1m} = tC_g + (1-t)P_1 \tag{3.3}$$

where P_1 corresponds to a C_{g_i}, P_2 corresponds to one vertex point obtained from the first step and P_3 is obtained from this second step.

With Haar basis $t = 0.5$, P_{1m} is the middle of the segment and we can write:

$$P_{1m} = h_0 C_g + h_1 P_1 \tag{3.4}$$

where $h_0 = 0.5$, $h_1 = 0.5$ are the coefficients of the Haar filter.

After this contraction of 0.5 it is necessary to rotate the hexagon through an angle θ about a line passing through the origin with a direction u determinate by C_g.

$$\underline{\mathrm{R}}_\theta = \begin{pmatrix} u_1^2 + cos\theta(1-u_1^2) & & u_1u_2(1-cos\theta) - u_3 sin\theta & u_3u_1(1- \quad u_1u_2(1-cos\theta) + u_3 sin\theta \\ u_2^2 + cos\theta(1-u_2^2) & u_3u_2(1- & u_1u_3(1-cos\theta) - u_2 sin\theta & u_3u_2(1-cos\theta) + u_1 sin\theta \end{pmatrix} \tag{3.5}$$

where u_1, u_2, u_3 are the directive cosines for the axis origin, center of gravity.

This matrix multiplies a matrix [6x3] for hexagons and [5x3] for the pentagons. For the pentagons we rotate with a $\theta = \pi/5$ and for the hexagons with an angle $\theta = \pi/6$.

4. Database construction. We have previously described the subdivision process. This process consists of adding vertices, edges and "polygonal facets", in accordance with the following recursive relations: *Vertices :*

$V_0 = 20$ *number of vertices for the dodecahedron (level 0)*
$V_1 = 60$ *number of vertices for the truncated icosahedron (level 1)*
$V_i = 6V_{i-2} + V_{i-1} = 3V_{i-1}$ (*level* $i \geq 2$)
$V_i = 20 \times 3^i$
Facets :
Pentagons
$P_i = 12$ *level* i $i = 0, 1, 2, \ldots$
Hexagons
$H_0 = 0$ *(level 0)*
$H_1 = 20$ *(level 1)*

$H_i = 60 + 6H_{i-2} + H_{i-1}$ $\quad$ *(level* $i \geq 2)$
$H_i = V_{i-1} + H_{i-1} = 20\ 3^{i-1} + H_{i-1}$
$H_i = 20(3^{i-1} + 3^{i-2} + ... + 1) = 20\frac{3^i-1}{3-1} = 10(3^i - 1)$
Edges :
generated by Euler relation :
$V_i - E_i + F_i = 2$
which gives $E_i = V_i + F_i - 2$ *with* $F_i = P_i + H_i$
$E_i = 20\ 3^i + 12 + 10(3^i - 1) - 2 = 10 \times 3^{i+1}$

It appears that the transformation of level i to level $i+1$ keeps the number of pentagon ($P_i = 12$) because each pentagon is reproduced, keeps the number of hexagons H_i because each hexagon is reproduced, add V_i hexagons because each vertex of level i create a new hexagon in level $i+1$. It is important to remark that at each level of subdivision the number of vertices and the number of hexagons are known. The topological properties of the mesh generation lead to a system of numbering suitable for this kind of applications. In Fig. 4.1 we present this system. We remark that the old position of analyzed vertex $P1$ (level i) determine the vertices which participate at the construction of the new hexagon. For example the new position of $P1$ is $P1A$ and this new hexagon obtaining by contraction-rotation of FA involvement an edge $P1AP9A$ in the new hexagon behind $P1$. $P9A$ could be obtain taking the $P1A$ position k and decrease by 1, $k-1$. Similarly for the 3 other hexagons, with condition to have the same counter clockwise inside of the hexagons and for scour around the vertex $P1$. This system allows to parallelize the algorithm.

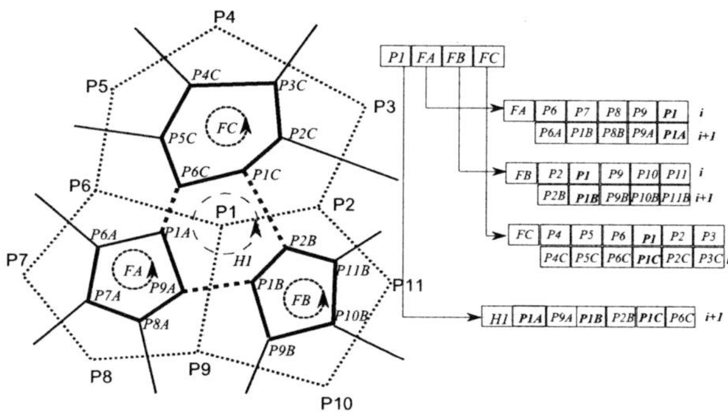

FIG. 4.1. *Numbering of vertices*

5. Compression. This method was developed in order to preserve the centers of gravity. The idea is to carry out a dilation and a rotation around the facets of level $i-2$ without being useful itself of the ramifications used by the preceding methods. For that, we sought to determine the coefficients of a filter associated with a wavelet base allowing us to dilate a polygon in its own plan. On the basis of the relation:

$$P_1 = h_0 C_g + h_1 P_{11} \tag{5.1}$$

is obtained:

$$P_{11} = \frac{P_1 - h_0 C_g}{h_1} \tag{5.2}$$

if dilation is carried out, a rotation is necessary to obtain the 3-related grid. A solution consists in calculating the medium of the segment and then:

$$P_{1m} = \frac{P_{11} + P_{22}}{2} = \frac{\frac{P_1 - h_0 C_g}{h_1} + \frac{P_2 - h_0 C_g}{h_1}}{2} \tag{5.3}$$

while replacing h_1 h_2 by 0.5 0.5, we obtain:

$$P_{1m} = P_1 - C_g + P_2 \tag{5.4}$$

This relation is directly connected to two types of known filters:

1. filters of Adelsson and Simoncelli had used the coefficients [1 2 1] and [−1 2 − 1]. During the application of these filters, we leave the signal: $\frac{-C_g}{2}, P_2, \frac{-C_g}{2}, P_3, \frac{-C_g}{2}, P_4, \frac{-C_g}{2}, P_5, \frac{-C_g}{2}, P_6, \frac{-C_g}{2}$. Thus, the centers of gravity were introduced between two nodes. The interest of this algorithm is that the filter has 3 taps. The resume is obtained with the filter [1 2 1] and by considering the cyclic convolution: $P_1 - C_g + P_2, P_2 - C_g + P_3, P_3 - C_g + P_4, P_4 - C_g + P_5, P_5 - C_g + P_6, P_6 - C_g + P_1$. Thus, the new hexagon is: $P_{1m}, P_{2m}, P_{3m}, P_{4m}, P_{5m}, P_{6m}$. The detail is obtained with the filter of coefficients [−1 2 − 1].
2. the matrices W [7] which use the splines wavelet. For the direct transform, the filters are: $[1, 2, 1]\, and\, [-1, -2, -1]$ and for the inverse transform: $[-1, 2, 1]\, and\, [-1, 2, -1]$.

Remark. This method presents the disadvantage of carrying out compression on the first $12 + h_{i-2}$ facets without taking account of the connections, from where a strong reduction in dimensions of the facets (sides) used by the transformation. On the head, a deformation of the grid is also noticed but the centers of gravity are preserved.

6. Parallel Algorithms of the Subdivision. To accelerate the computing time and to process an important data bases we present the parallel implementation is presented. For that we had used the PVM library.

The choice of PVM library was:

1. *PVM* is a portable library used to connect different type of UNIX stations allowing to form an only one.
2. *PVM* is able to work on different processors, therefore the software portability is guarantee.

The algorithm of subdivision has $O(n)$ complexity and the propagation step takes time $O(clogc)$ where c is the number of polygonal faces.

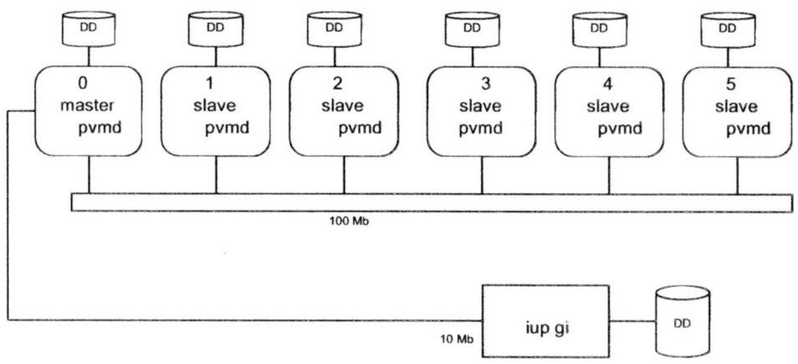

FIG. 6.1. *The implementation of PVM on the HP-9000 PA-RISC*

The algorithm of vertices numbering is implicit and presents the advantage that the file could be cut up (concerning the faces) in M parts corresponding to the number of processors chooses. In real fact on the last one we have also the integer part of the division $n/M + reste$). The global memory between the different process is managed by the master process . The coming data is synchronized by the master process figure 6.1.

In figure 6.2, we present the Master cutting up the file corresponding to the level i of subdivision in 5 parts. Each slave station gets one part to apply the method of subdivision. The new vertices had been send to the Master which determine the new numbering.

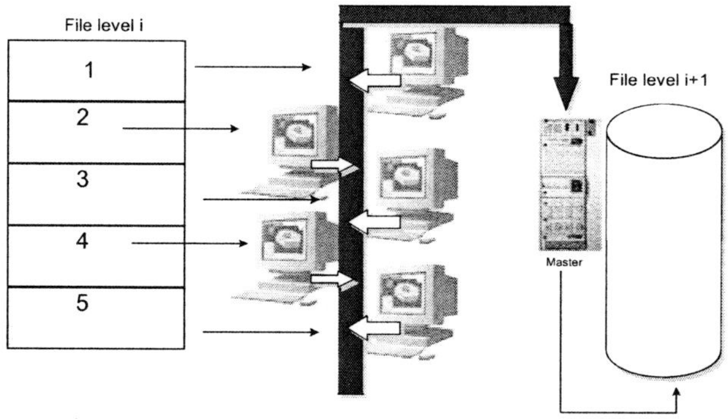

FIG. 6.2. *The implementation of PVM on the HP-9000 PA-RISC*

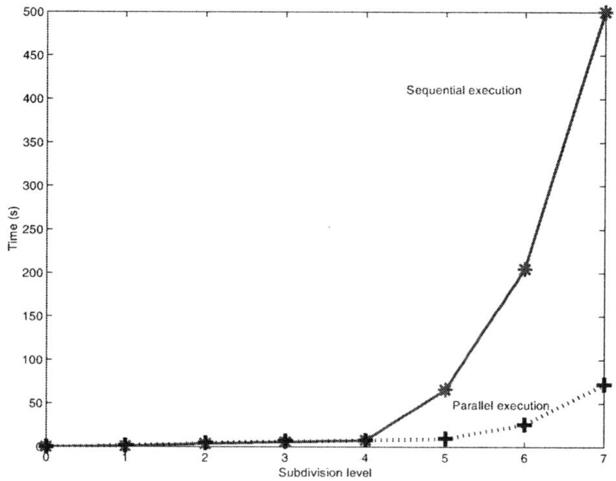

FIG. 6.3. *The comparison of the computing time between PVM on 4 HP station and an only one*

The network used to implement our algorithms is type Ethernet with a bus topology. The aces method is $CSMA/CD$. Our network is a FastEthernet at 100 Mb/s, but it presents the inconvenient to write the file of level $i+1$ on the server at 10 Mb/s. The results presented put on light that for the subdivision levels superior to 5 using PVM increase the speed.

The implementation of subdivision algorithms using rotational wavelets on the $HP-9000$ station gives the next results for the computing time and size files containing the vertices numbering:

Time

Subdivision level	Time(s)
5	10
6	26
7	72

The sizes of the files compressed using *gzip* are:

Dimension

Subdivision level	Size(Mb)
5	0.208
6	0.662
7	1.94

The results presented corresponding to the transformation from level i to level $i+1$.

7. Conclusion. This new type of mesh allows:

1. a minimal representation of objects 3D,
2. a method of implicit numbering,
3. the fast subdivision-compression of 3D data in view of their transmission,
4. the implementation on parallel systems.

With the resulting one from these results, four applications are proposed: in the field of animation and of deformation of surface (method of metamorphosis of face materialize by of sphere center with centers of gravity), -in the field of grid of object 3D (grid of a surface, with a level selected with advance, when the surface of object in the form of a cloud of point resulting of a digitizer 3D be known), -in the field of multi-media and of transmission of data (the method of subdivision and of compression allow not only of draw the object with a level of detail according to the distance observer-object, but also of decrease the number of information with time during calculations carried out on high levels of subdivision when a development tool of distributed applications such PVM is used).

The originality of these applications is due to the vertices numbering.

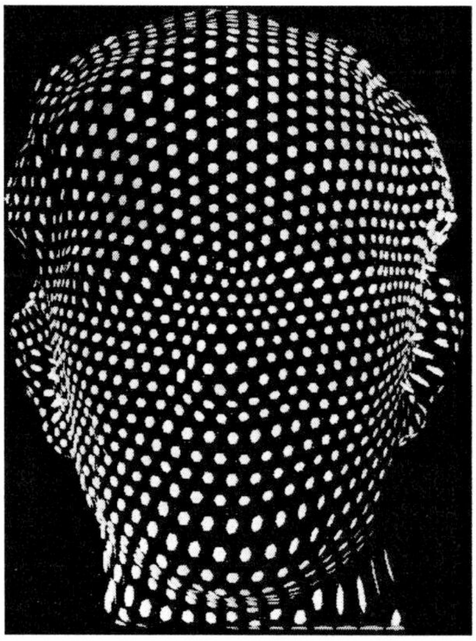

FIG. 7.1. *The progressive head construction*

This search is significant to treat all the types of surfaces having the vertices of valence 3 and thus profiting from many properties of the Voronoi Organized Mesh highlighted in this article. All the algorithms could be generalized on the Voronoi Diagram.

REFERENCES

[1] A. Ball and D. Storry. *"Behaviour of recursive division surfaces near extraordinary points"*, Computer Aided Geometric Design, 6(10), 1978.
[2] E. Catmull and J. Clark. *"Recursively generated b-spline surfaces on arbitrary topological meshes" Computer Aided Geometric Design*, 6(10), 1978.
[3] M. S. D. Doo. *"Behaviour of recursive division surfaces near extraordinary points" Computer Aided Geometric Design*, 6(10), 1978.
[4] A. Doncescu, J. P. Gourret. *"Wavelet Transform Implementation for Star-Shaped Modelling: Signal Analysis and Prediction" series Applied and Numerical Harmonic Analysis : Birkhauser Boston.*
[5] W. C. J. Kent and R. Parent. *"Shape transformation for polyhedral objects" Proceedings of SIGGRAPH '92*, 1992.

[6] V. Jones. *"A polynomial invariant for knots via von Neumann algebras" Bulletin of the American Mathematical Society*, (12):103–111, 1985.
[7] M. K. Kwong and P. Tang. *"W-matrices, nonorthogonal multiresolution analysis, and finite signals of arbitrary length" Technical report, Argone National Laboratory*, 1995.
[8] C. Loop and T. DeRose. *"Surfaces" ACM Transaction on Graphics*, 3(8), 1989.
[9] V. Ranjan and A. Fournier. *"Volume models for volumetric data" IEEE Computer*, 7(27), 1994.

In: Parallel and Distributed Scientific and Engineering Computing ISBN 1-59033-956-8
Editor: Y. Pan and L.T. Yang, pp. 131-143

IMPLEMENTING AND EVALUATING AN EFFICIENT DYNAMIC LOAD-BALANCER FOR DISTRIBUTED MOLECULAR DYNAMICS SIMULATION

NAOHITO SATO* AND JEAN-MARC JÉZÉQUEL†

Abstract. This paper proposes an efficient dynamic load-balancing scheme for parallel molecular dynamics simulation on distributed memory machines. It decomposes a spatial domain of particles into disjoint parts, each of which corresponds to a processor and dynamically changes its shape to maintain almost the same number of particles (as its load) throughout the simulation. In contrast to other similar schemes, ours requires no long-distance inter-processor communications, but only those among neighboring processors (thus little communication overhead), while it still guarantees fast reduction of any load imbalance among the processors. It owes these advantages mainly to the following features: (1) Sufficiently correct *global load information* is effectively obtained using *step-wise propagation* of appropriate information via nearest neighbor communication. (2) In addition to the global load-balancing, another load-balancing procedure is also invoked on each processor without global load information in order to *counteract any rapid increase or decrease of the load.* Thus, informations from remote processors can provide reliable values even after a certain period of delay. To evaluate the effectiveness of our scheme, we have integrated our load-balancer into the NAMD simulation system, by replacing its own load-balancing component. Preliminary experiments on a cluster of workstations connected through Myrinet switches show it successfully reduces load-imbalance through a small amount of load migration among processors.

Key words. Molecular dynamics simulation, Dynamic load balancing, Distributed memory machines

1. Introduction. Molecular dynamics simulation plays an essential role for analyzing the functionalities of large biochemical systems of macromolecules such as proteins and DNA. To trace the temporal trajectories of the particles in a system and artificially observe their interactions, the forces on the particles are accumulated at each time step of a simulation based on the predefined potentials and their geometric positions are incrementally updated by solving the equations of motion for the particles in a similar manner to an N-body simulation. Since even a simple system of a small protein surrounded by solvent molecules often consists of a very large number of unit particles (i.e. atoms), molecular dynamics simulation of realistic biochemical systems requires substantial computational resources, and therefore has been considered as an important application of parallel distributed computing.

For highly scalable parallel molecular dynamics simulation on distributed memory machines, it is crucial to effectively balance the loads (i.e. the particles) across the processing units while reducing expensive inter-processor communications for force accumulation as much as possible. To meet these efficiency criteria, the *short-range nature* of the (classical) molecular dynamics potentials is exploited. Particles are assigned to processors in a *spatial* manner, that is, particles within a close distance tend to be mapped to the same processor, so that a large part of the force accumulation can be computed without particle information from remote processors. Consequently, each time a particle on a processor updates its position to a location that is mapped to another processor, the particle then needs to be transferred to that processor to maintain the consistency of the spatial decomposition. In addition, to maintain the loads of each processor at the same size, the decomposition itself needs to be updated by shrinking overloaded parts and expanding sparse parts. In short, an effective load-balancer needs to decompose a spatial domain of particles into disjoint parts and reshape each spatial part dynamically and constantly throughout a simulation to preserve the spatial locality and the load size on each processor. From the inter-processor communication point of view, the load-balancing procedure (i.e. the "reshape" procedure) should run on each processor in a decentralized manner without any global synchronization

*IBM Research, Tokyo, Japan (hito@acm.org).
†IRISA/CNRS, Rennes, France.

to prevent the simulation from suspending, with possibly disastrous performance drawbacks in distributed environments. Further, although each processor often needs remote load information for its local selection of migrating loads, that remote information should be gathered with the least overhead through communications with a constant number of other processors.

To meet these challenges, we have developed a simple but efficient dynamic load-balancing scheme which requires no global synchronization or long-distance inter-processor communications, but only those among 'neighboring' processors, in terms of the underlying logical grid topology, and incurring little communication overhead. It only requires these loose and light-weight communications thanks to the following two features: (1) Each processor invokes a load-balancing procedure *without any global information* that reshapes the spatial parts to cancel or suppress the effect of particle motions. That is, when particles update their positions and move to the domain of some processor, the balancer shrinks the domain and expands the other domain to which those particles previously belonged. Notice that the shrinkage/expansion factor can be determined by the number of migrating particles. (2) Since it is highly likely that the local load-balancer may fail to maintain the load size in the long run (as discussed later in the chapter) and incur load imbalances, each processor runs another load-balancer based on global load information, which is obtained *through step-wise and gradual propagation* across the processors via a constant number of nearest neighbor communications. The key idea here is that, although load information reaches the processor that needs it after a certain period of delay, it can still remain relevant, primarily since the local load-balancer prevents the rapid increase or decrease of loads. As an option, we can add distinctive weights to the information propagated across the processors to control the degree of the trustworthiness of each piece of information and improve the effectiveness of the global load balancer, though we do not explore in this chapter how to determine optimal values for these weights.

As the primary advantage over other similar schemes, ours requires no long-distance inter-processor communications but only those among neighboring processors, while it still guarantees the fast reduction of any load imbalance among the processors. For examining the effectiveness of our load-balancing scheme, we have integrated the scheme into the NAMD simulation system developed at UIUC and evaluated its performance on a cluster of Myrinet-connected workstations. The approach successfully keeps balancing the loads of a acetylcholine macromolecule with a large number of surrounding solvent molecules throughout all of the simulation steps. Most notably, it only requires a much smaller amount of inter-processor communications for load balancing than those for the force accumulation, and this is sustained throughout the simulation. In terms of the overall performance, the results has been show that our scheme brings (up-to) 10% speed-up by comparing the executions with and without our scheme. In summary, our scheme has proven its strong potential for large-scale parallel molecular dynamics simulations in distributed environments.

The rest of the chapter is organized as follows: The following section provides a brief introduction of the terminology of parallel molecular dynamics simulation and discusses several major issues of concern for achieving high performance and high scalability. Section 3 proposes our load balancing scheme that combines two different strategies. Section 4 describes implementation issues, including how our scheme has been integrated with the NAMD simulation system, and Section 5 shows some results of the evaluation of our scheme. The final section provides concluding remarks and possible research directions.

2. Parallel Molecular Dynamics Simulation. This section briefly surveys parallel molecular dynamics (MD) simulation and load-balancing schemes for parallel MD simulation on distributed memory machines.

2.1. Molecular dynamics simulation. First, let us consider a system of N particles, denoted by $p_1, \ldots, p_N$, distributed over a bounded spatial domain. Let m_i, $\boldsymbol{x}_i = (x_i^1, x_i^2, x_i^3)$, $\boldsymbol{v}_i$, and $\boldsymbol{f}_i$ respectively denote the mass, the coordinates, the velocity of p_i, and the force affecting p_i $(1 \leq i \leq N)$. Then, interactions among those N particles in the system can be numerically traced as follows: At each time step of a simulation, (1) interactions among the particles are computed (through force accumulation) by using the predefined potentials (such as the van der Waals potential, the Coulomb potential, and the bond potentials), then (2) the coordinates and the velocity of each particle are updated by solving the motion equations. This procedure is repeated until the end of the simulation. Once the total force affecting p_i is accumulated, then $\boldsymbol{v}_i(t)$ and $\boldsymbol{x}_i(t)$ can be updated to $\boldsymbol{v}_i(t + \Delta t)$ and $\boldsymbol{x}_i(t + \Delta t)$ by solving $\boldsymbol{f}_i(t) = m_i \dot{\boldsymbol{v}}_i(t)$ and $\boldsymbol{v}_i(t) = \dot{\boldsymbol{x}}_i(t)$, where Δt denotes the fixed time interval between time steps. In practice, $\boldsymbol{v}_i(t + 1/2 \cdot \Delta t)$ is first computed for stability, and it is applied for computing $\boldsymbol{x}_i(t + \Delta t)$ as defined in the Leapfrog method.

2.2. Parallel molecular dynamics simulation. Molecular dynamics simulation involves natural parallelism: Interaction force can be accumulated for each particle in parallel. However, the straightforward exploitation of this parallelism results in poor performance due to the explosion of parallelism. Instead, we need to employ appropriate decompositions of particles onto processors so that each processor computes the same number of particle interactions. For parallel MD simulation, three major decomposition schemes have been proposed, namely (1) particle decomposition, (2) force decomposition, and (3) spatial decomposition.

The particle decomposition scheme statically decomposes particles into blocks and maps them onto processors [2, 7]. This is undoubtedly one of the simplest ways for guaranteeing the best load balance, though it often suffers from poor scalability due to frequent long-distance inter-processor communications in computing particle interactions.

The force decomposition scheme, in contrast, decomposes pairs of particles instead of individual particles [11, 6]. It attains high-performance only when the number of particles involved in the simulation is not too large, and therefore lacks enough scalability. See [11] for the details.

In the spatial decomposition scheme, the spatial domain of the particles is geometrically decomposed into disjoint parts, often called *subdomains*, each of which is further decomposed to small regular bounded regions, called *cells*. Since the particles dynamically change their positions, the subdomains also exchange cells with one another and retain about the same number of particles throughout the simulation [4, 7, 5, 10]. Currently, this is the most promising decomposition scheme for attaining high performance and high scalability. (See Figure 3.7.) As another spatial decomposition scheme, [9] divides the domain in an oct-tree fashion as is often employed in the parallel N-body simulation to compute the long-range interactions based on the Coulomb potential. Since high scalability plays a key role for efficient large-scale parallel molecular dynamics simulations, we developed our load-balancing scheme based on the spatial decomposition scheme.

2.3. Existing load-balancing schemes for parallel MD simulations. When employing spatial decomposition, it is crucial to develop an efficient dynamic load balancing scheme to maintain the number of particles on each processor at the same value. The efficiency of a load-balancing scheme then depends how much the communication overheads can be reduced and how optimally load can be exchanged among the processors. In the rest of this section, we briefly survey some existing work in the area of dynamic load balancing.

One of the simplest schemes is to redistribute the entire load (i.e. cells in our case) in every few time steps of a simulation. For example, [4] employs a recursive geometric bisection along the axes for cell redistribution. However, this needs global synchronization and intensive data transfer among the processors, and this often results in poor scalability.

There is another sort of load-balancing scheme in which long-distance inter-processor communication is required only in collecting load information prior to load migration. In [6], load information is propagated along linearly indexed processors by the *positional scan* operation. Each processor then determines the migrating loads locally. In [7], the destinations of the migrating loads are selected randomly. These approaches, however, still need considerable long-distance inter-processor communications, which also result in poor scalability.

In addition, the well-known *diffusion scheme* [12, 3] can also be used: Each processor exchanges loads only with its neighboring processors to reduce the differences of the load sizes among them, and this needs no long-distance inter-processor communication. The serious drawbacks of this scheme are, however, that it does not guarantee optimality of load migration and often takes a long time for reducing load imbalances among the processors.

Considering those points discussed above, we then propose a new load balancing scheme that requires little communication overheads and guarantees fast reduction of load imbalance.

3. An Efficient Load-Balancer for MD Simulation. In this section, we propose a new load-balancing scheme for parallel molecular dynamics simulation on distributed environments.

3.1. Suppressing rapid increase and decrease of loads. We describe the first part of our load-balancing scheme, which works without any global load information to keep the loads on each processor approximately the same size throughout a simulation.

As explained in the previous section, the entire spatial domain is decomposed into small bounded regions, called *cells*, and they are lumped into subdomains, each of which occupies a *simply-connected* area (i.e. its cells are contiguous to each other) in the domain as illustrated in Figure 3.7. Each subdomain is then mapped to a distinct processor. In terms of the underlying execution environments, we assume a homogeneous 3-dimensional mesh-wise network, in which processors with local memories (identical with one another) are connected through data transmission devices with the same bandwidth and latency. To identify the processors, let N_{PE}^1, N_{PE}^2, and N_{PE}^3 denote the numbers of processors along the axes, respectively, and let N_{PE} be $N_{\mathrm{PE}}^1 \times N_{\mathrm{PE}}^2 \times N_{\mathrm{PE}}^3$. We then identify each processor as $\mathrm{PE}_{\boldsymbol{i}}$, where $\boldsymbol{i} = (i_1, i_2, i_3)$ ranges over $0 \leq i_k < N_{\mathrm{PE}}^k$ for $1 \leq k \leq 3$. In the same way, let $D_{\boldsymbol{i}}$ denote the subdomain corresponding to $\mathrm{PE}_{\boldsymbol{i}}$. Given N particles and N_{PE} processors, the ideal number of particles on each processor, denoted by $\widehat{N}$, is N/N_{PE}.

Clearly, $N_{\boldsymbol{i}}$ dynamically changes its value throughout a simulation since the particles constantly update their positions due to the interactions: Let $N_{\boldsymbol{i}}(t)$, instead of $N_{\boldsymbol{i}}$, denote the number at the time t, and $\Delta N_{\boldsymbol{i}}^{\mathrm{mot}}(t)$ denote the number of particles moved into $\mathrm{PE}_{\boldsymbol{i}}$ as a result of particle interactions at t. Notice that $\Delta N_{\boldsymbol{i}}^{\mathrm{mot}}(t)$ is equal to the difference between the numbers of the incoming and the outgoing particles. Also, let $\Delta N_{\boldsymbol{i}}^{\mathrm{mig}}(t)$ (for particles being migrated) denote the number of particles to be transferred out at t by our load-balancing procedure, which is invoked after particle interactions are computed. Then, the following equation holds, where Δt denotes the time interval between time steps.

$$
\begin{aligned}
N_{\boldsymbol{i}}(t + \Delta t) &= N_{\boldsymbol{i}}(t) + \Delta N_{\boldsymbol{i}}(t) \\
\Delta N_{\boldsymbol{i}}(t) &= \Delta N_{\boldsymbol{i}}^{\mathrm{mot}}(t) - \Delta N_{\boldsymbol{i}}^{\mathrm{mig}}(t)
\end{aligned}
\tag{3.1}
$$

The aim of the load-balancing is, then, to keep $N_{\boldsymbol{i}}(t)$ close, or make it closer, to $\widehat{N}$ for all $\boldsymbol{i}$ throughout the simulation.

As a simple case, let us consider $N_{\boldsymbol{i}}$ is approximately equal to $\widehat{N}$ for all $\boldsymbol{i}$ at the beginning of a simulation. Then, the aim can be rephrased as keeping $\Delta N_{\boldsymbol{i}}(t)$ close to 0. Since each particle changes its positions by a small amount of distance at a time and may move, in most cases, to one of the neighboring subdomains, we can recover the balanced state

($\Delta N_i = 0$) by transferring loads from the overloaded subdomains (where $N_i > \widehat{N}$) to the sparse subdomains ($N_i < \widehat{N}$) exactly in the opposite manner that the particle migration has occurred among the processors.

In general, let $\Delta N^{\mathrm{mot}}_{D_i \to D_{i'}}$ denote the number of particles that have moved from D_i to $D_{i'}$ prior to the load-balancing. Then, the number of particles to be transferred out of PE$_i$, denoted by $\Delta N_i^{\mathrm{mig}_1}$, can be determined as follows, where α is a positive constant for acceleration. Figure 3.1 illustrates the procedure quantified by these equations:

$$\begin{aligned} \Delta N_i^{\mathrm{mot}} &= \sum_{i'} \left(-\Delta N^{\mathrm{mot}}_{D_i \to D_{i'}} + \Delta N^{\mathrm{mot}}_{D_{i'} \to D_i} \right) \\ \Delta N_i^{\mathrm{mig}_1} &= \alpha \cdot \Delta N_i^{\mathrm{mot}} \qquad (\alpha \le 1) \end{aligned} \tag{3.2}$$

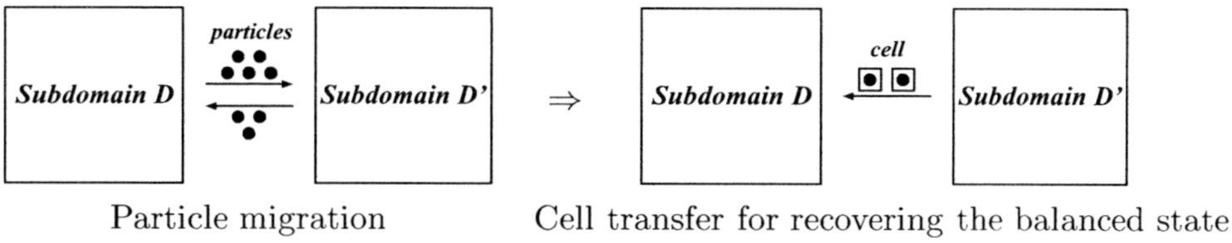

FIG. 3.1. *Load balancing – 5 particles moving from D to D′ ($\Delta N^{mot}_{D \to D'}$) and 3 particles from D′ to D ($\Delta N^{mot}_{D' \to D}$), followed by migrating 2 particles from D′ to D ($\Delta N_D^{mig_1}$).*

Clearly, this load-balancing procedure can be invoked in parallel on each processor. However, it does not always attain high performance when invoked with $\alpha = 1$, since the procedure might transfer more particles than necessary as illustrated in Figure 3.2. Further, when a particular processor holds only a small number of particles, it may not select as many particles for transfer as required by the load-balancing procedure in Equations (3.2). Therefore, α is chosen to be smaller than 1 in most cases, so that $\Delta N_i^{\mathrm{mig}_1}$ is smaller than required for perfect load balancing. Thus, we need another mechanism to adjust a possibly growing imbalance among the processors. Note that the optimal value of α depends on the conditions of each simulation and, in this chapter, we do not discuss how to determine the value.

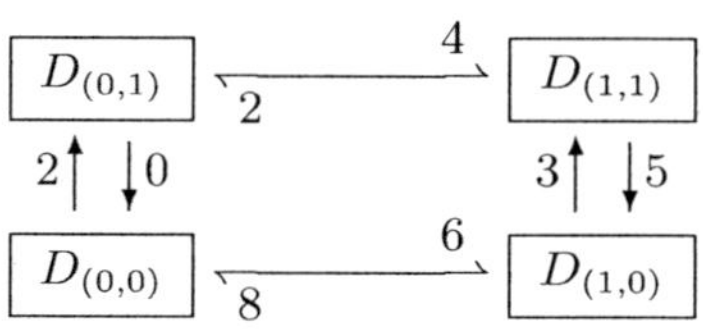

FIG. 3.2. *Loads will be transferred even though $\Delta N_i^{mot} = 0$ (for all D_i)*

3.2. Reducing load imbalance among the processors. We now describe the main part of our load-balancing scheme, which uses global load information to reduce any load imbalance among the processors and makes N_i closer to $\widehat{N}$ for all $\boldsymbol{i}$ so the processors will recover their balance.

In the same way as before, let us assume the processors and the subdomains are indexed with ($\boldsymbol{i} = (i_1, i_2, i_3)$) as PE$_{\boldsymbol{i}}$, $D_{\boldsymbol{i}}$, respectively, and PE$_{\boldsymbol{i}}$ contains $N_{\boldsymbol{i}}(t) = N_{(i_1,i_2,i_3)}(t)$ particles at the time t. Then, let us define $\delta_{\boldsymbol{i}}(t)$ as $N_{\boldsymbol{i}}(t) - \widehat{N}$, and σ^k as the integral value of δ along the k-th axis ($k = 1, 2, 3$) as follows.

$$\delta_{\boldsymbol{i}}(t) = N_{\boldsymbol{i}}(t) - \widehat{N}$$

(3.3)
$$\sigma^k_{(i_1,i_2,i_3)}(t) = \begin{cases} \sum_{i_1'<i_1} \delta_{(i_1',i_2,i_3)}(t) & (k=1) \\ \sum_{i_2'<i_2} \delta_{(i_1,i_2',i_3)}(t) & (k=2) \\ \sum_{i_3'<i_3} \delta_{(i_1,i_2,i_3')}(t) & (k=3) \end{cases}$$

Clearly, σ^k implies the total amount of imbalance on the processors that precede PE$_{\boldsymbol{i}}$ along the k-th axis. Notice that the processor (i_1, i_2, i_3) does not need the direct transmission of the δ values from its preceding processors, $(1, i_2, i_3), \ldots, (i_1-1, i_2, i_3)$ to compute $\sigma^1_{(i_1+1,i_2,i_3)}$, but it only needs $\sigma^1_{(i_1,i_2,i_3)}$ from the processor $(i_1 - 1, i_2, i_3)$ to compute $\sigma^1_{(i_1+1,i_2,i_3)} = \sigma^1_{(i_1,i_2,i_3)} + \delta_{(i_1,i_2,i_3)}$ and propagate it to the processor $(i_1 + 1, i_2, i_3)$. Thus, No matter how many processors are involved in the computation, each processor transmits load information to a neighboring processor only once along an axis. Subsequently, by using the σ values, the number of loads to be transferred out of PE$_{\boldsymbol{i}}$ along the k-th axis in the positive direction, denoted by $\Delta_k N^{\text{mig}_2}_{\boldsymbol{i}}$, and the total number to be transferred out of PE$_{\boldsymbol{i}}$, denoted by $\Delta N^{\text{mig}_2}_{\boldsymbol{i}}$, are defined as follows (where ρ is a positive constant for acceleration):

(3.4)
$$\begin{aligned} \Delta_k N^{\text{mig}_2}_{\boldsymbol{i}} &= \frac{\rho}{3} \cdot \left(\sigma^k_{\boldsymbol{i}}(t) + \delta_{\boldsymbol{i}}(t)\right) \qquad (0 < \rho \leq 1) \\ \Delta N^{\text{mig}_2}_{\boldsymbol{i}} &= \sum_{k=1,2,3} \left(-\Delta_k N^{\text{mig}_2}_{(i_1',i_2',i_3')} + \Delta_k N^{\text{mig}_2}_{\boldsymbol{i}}\right) \\ &\text{where } i_k' = i_k - 1, i_m' = i_m \ (m \neq k) \end{aligned}$$

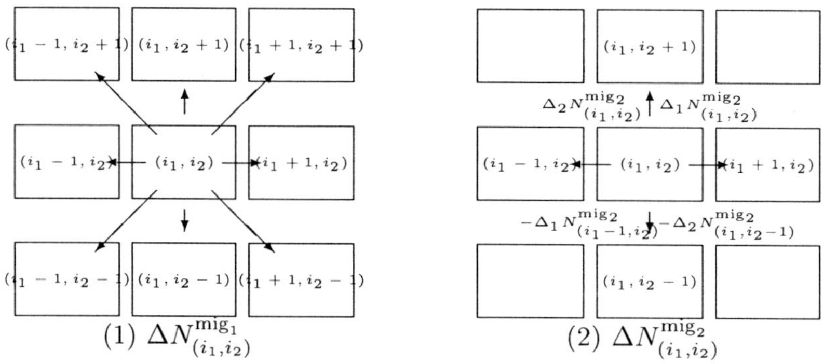

FIG. 3.3. *Particle transfer in* $D_{(i_1,i_2)}$ *— 8 and 4 adjacent processors are involved respectively in* $\Delta N^{mig_1}_{\boldsymbol{i}}$ *and* $\Delta N^{mig_2}_{\boldsymbol{i}}$ *(2 dimensional).*

As an example, let us consider a typical case of the imbalanced state as depicted in Figure 3.4 (left), where 64 particles are unevenly distributed over the 16 processors ($\widehat{N} = 4$). In this case, the global load-balancer first collects remote load information and computes $\delta_{\boldsymbol{i}}, (\sigma^1_{\boldsymbol{i}}, \sigma^2_{\boldsymbol{i}})$ and $\Delta N^{\text{mig}_2}_{\boldsymbol{i}}$ for all $\boldsymbol{i}$ as shown in the middle of the figure. When fixing $\rho = 1$ and choosing $\boldsymbol{i} = (1, 1)$, these values turn out to be: $N_{(1,1)} = 7$, $\delta_{(1,1)} = N_{(1,1)} - \widehat{N} = 3$, $(\sigma^1_{(1,1)}, \sigma^2_{(1,1)}) = (2, -1)$, $\Delta_1 N^{\text{mig}_2}_{(1,1)} = 2.5$, $\Delta_2 N^{\text{mig}_2}_{(1,1)} = 0.5$, and $\Delta N^{\text{mig}_2}_{(1,1)} = 3$. Once these are computed for all the processors, then the balancer transfers $\Delta_1 N^{\text{mig}_2}_{(i_1,i_2)}$ units of loads from the processor (i_1, i_2) to the processor $(i_1 + 1, i_2)$ and $\Delta_2 N^{\text{mig}_2}_{(i_1,i_2)}$ units from (i_1, i_2) to $(i_1, i_2 + 1)$ for each (i_1, i_2). As the result, the totally balanced state is successfully recovered as shown on the right side of the figure. Notice here that the total amount of the transferred loads (i.e. the difference of the exported loads and the incoming loads) on $PE_{(i_1,i_2)}$ is equal to $\Delta N^{\text{mig}_2}_{(i_1,i_2)}$.

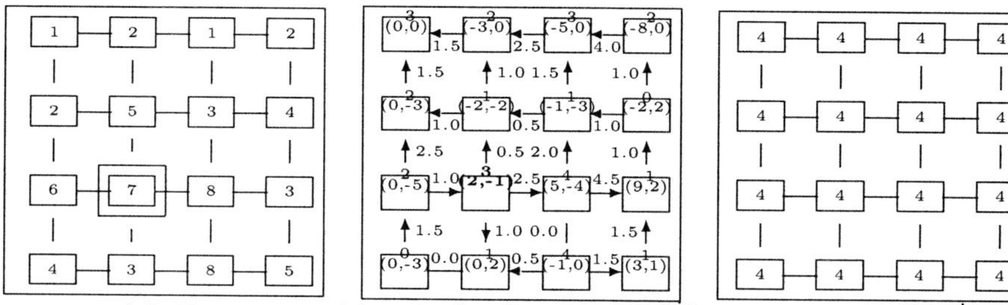

(1) $N_{\boldsymbol{i}}$ (2) $\delta_{\boldsymbol{i}}/(\sigma^1_{\boldsymbol{i}}, \sigma^2_{\boldsymbol{i}})$ and $\Delta N^{\text{mig}_2}_{\boldsymbol{i}}$ (3) $N_{\boldsymbol{i}} + \Delta N^{\text{mig}_2}_{\boldsymbol{i}}$

FIG. 3.4. *Computing* $\Delta N^{mig_2}_{\boldsymbol{i}}$ $\left(N = 64, N_{PE} = 16, \widehat{N} = 4, \rho = 1\right)$ – $PE_{(1,1)}$ *for example transfers out* $-(-1/2) = 0.5, (-1+3)/2 = 1, -(2/2) = -1, (2+3)/2 = 2.5$ *particles to its adjacent processors as defined in (3.4), so that the load imbalance shown in (1) becomes improved as in (3).*

The most important consequence of this definition of $\Delta N^{\text{mig}_2}_{\boldsymbol{i}}$ is that the load imbalance ($\delta_{\boldsymbol{i}}$) is reduced to 0 on each processor in a *monotonous and optimal* fashion for any $0 < \rho \leq 1$. In fact, after the load migration at each time step, $N_{\boldsymbol{i}}(t)$ and $\sigma_{\boldsymbol{i}}(t)$ respectively become closer to $\widehat{N}$ and 0, for any $\rho \leq 1$, as shown below.

$$\begin{aligned}
N_{\boldsymbol{i}}(t) - \Delta N^{\text{mig}_2}_{\boldsymbol{i}}(t) &= N_{\boldsymbol{i}}(t) + \left(\Delta_1 N_{(i_1-1,i_2,i_3)}(t) - \Delta_1 N_{\boldsymbol{i}}(t)\right) \\
&\quad + \left(\Delta_2 N_{(i_1,i_2-1,i_3)}(t) - \Delta_2 N_{\boldsymbol{i}}(t)\right) \\
&\quad + \left(\Delta_3 N_{(i_1,i_2,i_3-1)}(t) - \Delta_3 N_{\boldsymbol{i}}(t)\right) \\
&= N_{\boldsymbol{i}}(t) + \rho \cdot \left(-N_{\boldsymbol{i}}(t) + \widehat{N}\right) \\
&= (1-\rho)\cdot N_{\boldsymbol{i}}(t) + \rho \cdot \widehat{N} \\
\sum_{i'_k < i_k} \left(\delta_{\boldsymbol{i}'}(t) - \Delta N^{\text{mig}_2}_{\boldsymbol{i}'}(t)\right) &= \sigma^k_{\boldsymbol{i}}(t) - 3 \cdot \Delta_k N_{\boldsymbol{i}'_{\max}}(t) \\
&= (1-\rho)\cdot \sigma^k_{\boldsymbol{i}}(t)
\end{aligned}$$

where $0 \leq i'_k < i_k, i'_m = i_m \ (m \neq k), \boldsymbol{i}'_{\max} = (i_1, \ldots, i_k - 1, \ldots, i_3)$

Unfortunately, however, the definition in Equation (3.3) implies that the processor $\boldsymbol{i} = (i_1, i_2, i_3)$ obtains the load information, $\sigma^k_{\boldsymbol{i}}$ $(k = 1, 2, 3)$, after the i_k-step propagation of loads along the k-th axis, which might involve a large amount of inter-processor communications when the number of processors increases. In other words, collecting the load information as defined in Equation (3.3) needs too much long-distance inter-processor communication, which may result in poor scalability due to the heavy communication overhead. To eliminate those potential overheads and improve scalability, we replace (3.3) as follows:

(3.5)
$$\sigma^k_{(i_1,i_2,i_3)}(t) = \begin{cases} \sum_{i'_1 < i_1} c_{i_1 - i'_1} \cdot \delta_{(i'_1,i_2,i_3)}(t_{i_1 - i'_1}) & (k=1) \\ \sum_{i'_2 < i_2} c_{i_2 - i'_2} \cdot \delta_{(i_1,i'_2,i_3)}(t_{i_2 - i'_2}) & (k=2) \\ \sum_{i'_3 < i_3} c_{i_3 - i'_3} \cdot \delta_{(i_1,i_2,i'_3)}(t_{i_3 - i'_3}) & (k=3) \end{cases}$$
where $t_m \equiv t - m \cdot \Delta t, c_m \leq 1$

Notice that $\delta_{\boldsymbol{i}'}(t - ||\boldsymbol{i} - \boldsymbol{i}'|| \cdot \Delta t)$ is used instead of $\delta_{\boldsymbol{i}'}(t)$ as the load imbalance on $PE_{\boldsymbol{i}'}$ which is $||\boldsymbol{i} - \boldsymbol{i}'||$ nodes away from $PE_{\boldsymbol{i}}$. Thus, each processor only needs inter-processor communication with its adjacent processors (see Figure 3.5). Apparently, the efficiency of the load-balancing depends on the coefficients $(c_1, c_2, \ldots)$, which need to be chosen carefully for each simulation to attain high performance. Although we do not discuss how to determine such coefficients for any particular situation, it is worth mentioning that one possible criterion could be: $|c_1| > \sum_{m>1} |c_m|$. It is, indeed, quite analogous to the case of the vector computation in the linear algebra that the criterion implies positive semi-definiteness of the coefficients and sufficiently guarantees convergence to a balanced load distribution regardless of the trustworthiness of $c_m (m > 1)$. For example, defining $c_m = 2^{-1} \cdot c_{m-1}$ apparently satisfies this. (Note that as c_{m+1}/c_m becomes smaller, the load-balancing then becomes closer to that defined by the diffusion scheme discussed in the previous section.)

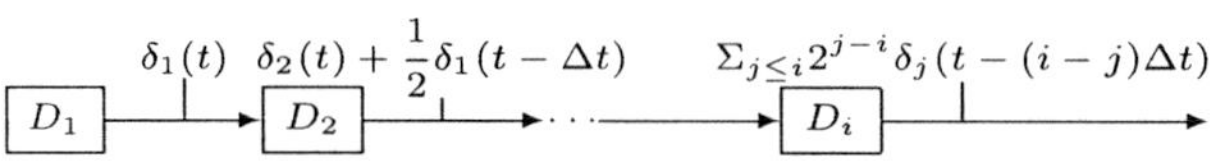

FIG. 3.5. *Propagation of load information (1-dimensional)*

To complete the formal definition of our load-balancing scheme, we only need to define ΔN_i^{mig}, the total number of particles to be transferred out of PE$_i$, with $\Delta N_i^{\text{mig}_1}$ and $\Delta N_i^{\text{mig}_2}$ as follows.

$$\Delta N_i^{\text{mig}} = \Delta N_i^{\text{mig}_1} + \Delta N_i^{\text{mig}_2} \tag{3.6}$$

We are ready to present the final form of our load balancing procedure on each processor as a combination of Equations (3.2) and (3.4): (1) On PE$_i$, ΔN_i^{mot} is computed when particles have been moved as the result of the particle interactions and $\Delta N_i^{\text{mig}_1}$ is then updated as defined in Equations (3.2). (2) The value of $\Delta N_i^{\text{mig}_2}$ is updated as defined in Equation (3.4) when σ^k $(k = 1, 2, 3)$ along the three axes are propagated to PE$_i$ as defined in (3.5). The values of σ are then updated and propagated to adjacent processors. (3) Once $\Delta N_i^{\text{mig}_1}$ and $\Delta N_i^{\text{mig}_2}$ are successfully computed, PE$_i$ then transfers out ΔN_i^{mig} of its cells to reduce its load imbalance, and it updates N_i and δ_i by using (3.1) and σ_i by using (3.5). The algorithm will be stated in a more concrete form later in this section.

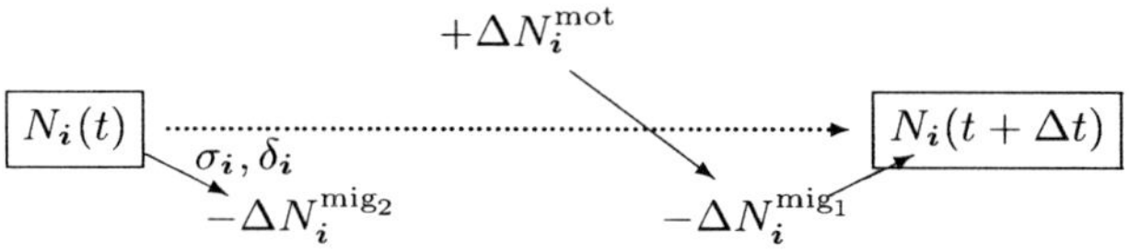

FIG. 3.6. $N_i(t) \to N_i(t + \Delta t)$ – $\Delta N_i^{mig_2}$ *is first computed on PE$_i$ by using* σ_i, *while* $\Delta N_i^{mig_1}$ *is computed after* ΔN_i^{mot} *is determined.*

3.3. Selecting loads for migration. Once the number of loads to be transferred out has been computed, each processor then selects particular loads, i.e. cells of particles, to transfer out to each of its adjacent processors. In the selection, we impose a constraint that the adjacency relations among the processors should be preserved, that is, the subdomain corresponding with each processor should share its boundary with the same adjacent subdomains throughout the simulation, as illustrated in Figure 3.7.

In order to satisfy this condition, we introduce a simple procedure for load selection: We always select cells along subdomain boundaries and transfer them out only when the adjacency relations between the processors sharing the boundaries will be preserved through the migration. Let us explain this in detail for the 2-dimensional case, though it can be easily extended to the 3-dimensional case. First, let us assume the adjacency condition holds for each processor. Then, the subdomain boundaries are then classified into two distinct

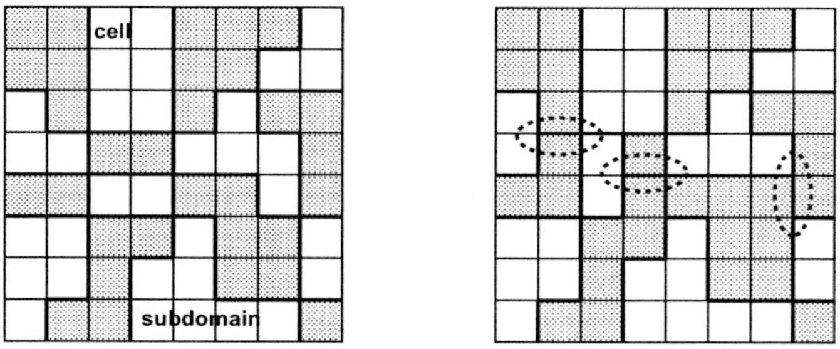

FIG. 3.7. *The adjacency constraint – The left-side case conforms to the constraint, where 64 cells are lumped to 16 processors each of which has borders only with its 'logically-neighboring' processors. The right-side case, in contrast, violates the constraint in three spots.*

groups, namely (1) those shared by 2 subdomains, and (2) those shared by 4 subdomains. In the first case, a cell along the 2-processor boundary, denoted by c, can be safely selected for migration across the boundary when the 8 cells around c belong to the two processors sharing the boundary as specified in Figure 3.8 (left). In a similar manner, two cells sharing

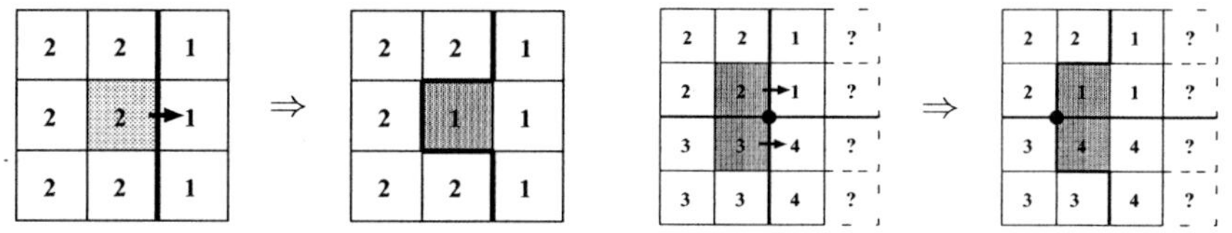

FIG. 3.8. *Examples of cell migration across a 2-processor boundary (left) or a 4-processor boundary (right) – shaded cells can be transferred through the boundaries. (the numbers in the boxes denote processor indices.)*

a 4-processor cross-point can be safely selected when the 12 cells around the two cells belong to the four processors as specified in 3.8 (right). Note that we can arbitrarily select cells that satisfy the above conditions to preserve the adjacency relationships among the processors.

As a summary of the previous discussion, we show our load-balancing scheme in a concrete procedural form as follows.

1. Transfering $\Delta N_i^{\mathrm{mot}}$ particles (Particle Interaction): Each processor computes $\Delta N_i^{\mathrm{mot}}$ as well as the force accumulation.
2. Computing $\Delta N_i^{\mathrm{mig}_1}$: The value of $\Delta N_i^{\mathrm{mig}_1}(t)$ is computed by using $\Delta N_i^{\mathrm{mot}}$ as defined in Equation (3.2).
3. Computing $\Delta N_i^{\mathrm{mig}_2}$ and $\Delta N_i^{\mathrm{mig}}$: As defined in Equation (3.4), the number of particles to be migrated out to each adjacent cell is computed by using the current values of σ_i and δ_i. Also, $\Delta N_i^{\mathrm{mig}_2}(t)$ and $\Delta N_i^{\mathrm{mig}}(t)$ are computed by using (3.4) and (3.6), respectively.
4. Updating N_i and δ_i: N_i and δ_i are updated as shown in Equation (3.1).
5. Updating σ_i and migrating loads (Load Migration): A total of $\Delta N_i^{\mathrm{mig}}$ particles are selected as specified in Section 3.3 and migrated out to the adjacent cells. The value of σ_i is also transmitted during the migration for the compution of Equation (3.5).
6. Synchronization: The time is updated by Δt (i.e. $t \leftarrow t + \Delta t$) to proceed to the next simulation step.

4. Implementation Issues. To examine the feasibility and effectiveness of our load-balancing scheme, we have developed a prototype load balancer that implements the features discussed in the previous section, and integrated it into the NAMD system, a portable parallel MD simulator developed at the University of Illinois [1]. In this section, we briefly describe the design decisions and implementation issues of our load balancer.

We have chosen NAMD (version 1.5) as the basis of our development efforts, since it uses a spatial decomposition scheme, on which our load-balancing scheme is primarily founded, and it also discloses comprehensive API information on its program modules, which simplify our efforts to integrate our load-balancing module. From the software development point of view, NAMD is designed in a highly portable and modular fashion. All of its program modules are defined and encapsulated as object-oriented class components. Thus, it hides the low level details such as the underlying architecture-dependent message-passing features while it provides a convenient way to modify its behavior or introduce new features with the smallest changes to the existing class components.

As one of its design principles, NAMD attains high portability in terms of integration of the load-balancing functionality: It includes a generic class component, called LOADBALANCE, that defines functions to be invoked during simulation. By carefully separating the MD modules and the load-balancing class, it takes into account replacing the predefined load-balancing class with another.

One serious problem with the load-balancing component, however, arose when integrating our load-balancing scheme. The component is designed to work in a *centralized fashion*. Every specified number of time steps during the simulation, each processor node collects load information (such as the number of atoms allocated to that processor) and sends the information to the unique master node. Once the master node receives information from all nodes, then it calculates redistribution of the simulation space to eliminate any load imbalances, determines for each processor the particular cells to be migrated, and sends instructions for the migrations to each processor node.

Since our primary goal is to examine the feasibility and effectiveness of our load-balancing scheme, we decided to make no change to this centralized nature of load balancing but instead replaced its cell selection procedure for migration. Although we lost a chance to examine the effectiveness of the elimination of long-distance inter-processor communications as its consequence, we could still examine how fast load imbalances can be reduced by small amounts of load migration.

5. Evaluation of the Effectiveness of our Scheme. In this section, we show some results of the evaluation of our scheme on a cluster of workstations. Although the scale of the particle system we have chosen is rather modest, the primary characteristic of our scheme – fast reduction of load-imbalance through a small amount of inter-processor communications – were demonstrated successfully.

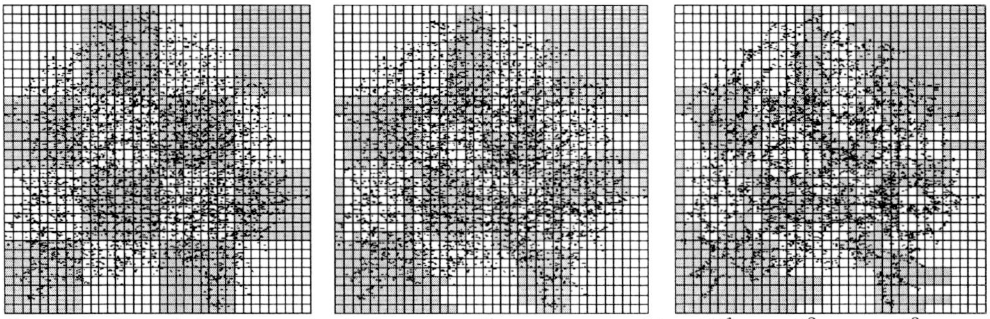

FIG. 5.1. *Snapshots from a simulation on a 16-processor machine* ($N^1_{PE} = N^2_{PE} = 4, N^3_{PE} = 1$) *at* ***t****=0,1,20 – Each cell size is almost identical with the cutoff distance. Shades in each snapshot indicate the correspondence between the cells and the 16 processors. Notice that each cell takes a column-like shape in the spatial domain* ($N^3_{PE} = 1$).

As the center of our focus, we examined how smoothly and effectively our load-balancer works in a (perfect) situation where the balancer has little restriction in selecting loads to transfer, and where each processor is assigned a large number of unit loads (i.e. cells), so that the load-balancer can easily find loads to transfer between neighboring processors to reduce the load imbalance. In Figure 5.1, the three pictures show snapshots from a simulation of a 5159-atom acetylcholine molecule (1ack) distributed over the domain. The simulation was conducted on a cluster of workstations, each of which has a Pentium III processor (500 MHz) and which are connected with each other through Myrinet switches (1.25 GB/s). Note that the simulation domain was divided into small cells whose edges were set to an (artificially short) 3 angstroms in length. This limitation had to be introduced primarily for the balancer to select transferring cells as freely as possible, and can be removed when it is applied to larger molecular systems [1].

Figure 5.2 shows the temporal changes of the normalized load sizes of the processors (i.e. load=1 implies the perfectly balanced state) and the amount of inter-processor data transfer (the number of atoms), respectively. Notice that, even though the shapes of the 16 subdomains become quite irregular after a few steps as shown in Figure 5.1, the amount of the inter-processor communications for load balancing remains at a negligible size, while that for force accumulation remains *almost the same throughout the simulation.* This strongly suggests that our scheme succeeds in a considerable reduction of the inter-processor communication. The advantage of our scheme in terms of inter-processor communication becomes even clearer when compared with the well-known particle decomposition scheme. As shown in Figure 5.2, as the simulation proceeds, the scheme needs inter-processor communication more and more frequently to adjust the load imbalance. This primarily comes from its casual manner of selecting transferring loads, as explained in Section 2.

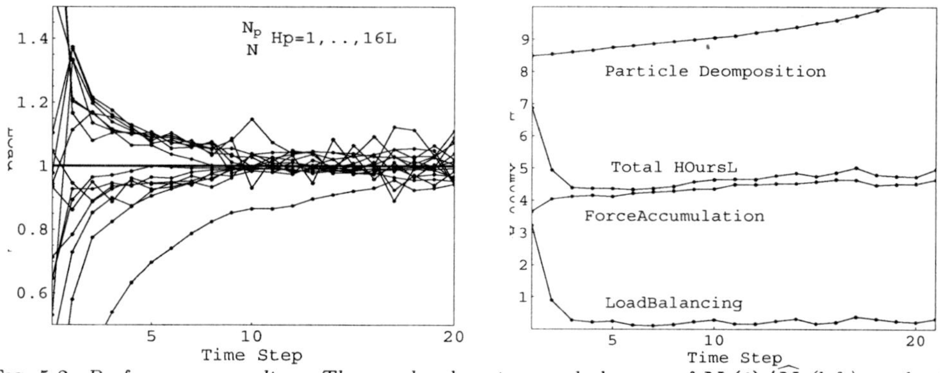

FIG. 5.2. *Performance results — The graphs show temporal changes of* $N_i(t)/\widehat{N}$ *(left) on the 16 processors and the number of atoms involved in inter-processor communication (middle) during the simulation of the 5159-atom acetylcholine (1ack).*

In terms of the overall performance, Figure 5.3 compares the performances between the simulations with and without our load-balancing mechanism. It shows that our scheme brings (up-to) 10% speed-ups of the performances. Even though this result does not at first sound very impressive, readers should note that our scheme has been integrated into the NAMD system in rather a loose manner (as described in the previous section). This result suggests, in positive terms, that our scheme has the potential to improve efficiency by 10% for any MD simulation system. In summary, we have shown that our scheme has potential for attaining effective load balancing with little overhead.

6. Discussion and Concluding Remarks. In this paper, we have proposed a new load-balancing scheme for parallel molecular dynamics simulation on distributed memory

[1]Experiments with large molecules and comprehensive analysis of their results are currently being conducted by the authors.

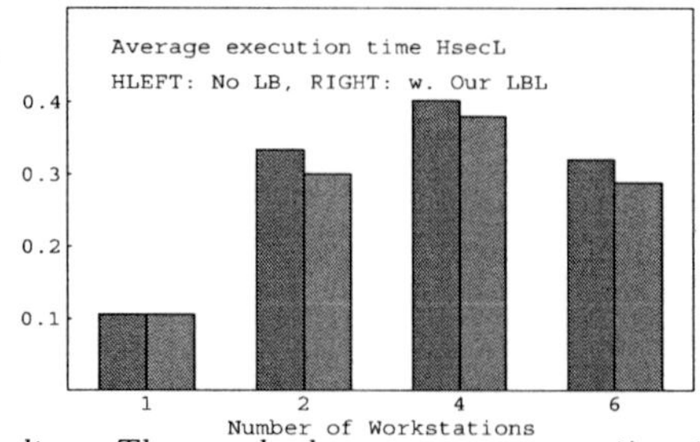

FIG. 5.3. *Performance results – The graph shows average execution time (in seconds) for each simulation step on a 1,2,4,6-node workstation cluster.*

machines, and evaluated its feasibility and effectiveness through preliminary experiments on a uniprocessor workstation.

Our scheme has several advantages over the other load-balancing schemes discussed in Section 2. A static load-balancing scheme such as one based on particle decomposition has a serious drawback for its scalability since it needs considerable inter-processor communication for force accumulation. Dynamic load-balancing schemes, in turn, typically define how to collect load information and how to select migrating loads: Our scheme allows for doing this in a local and optimal fashion. Specifically, our scheme requires inter-processor communications only among neighboring processors while it still guarantees fast reduction of load-imbalance among the processors, whereas the other existing schemes lack the optimality [7], or (more often) need rather frequent long-distance inter-processor communication [4, 6]. In fact, it is difficult to keep the amount of inter-processor communication the same size throughout a simulation with those approaches (cf. Figure 5.2).

Currently, we are undertaking efforts to show our load-balancing scheme has enough efficiency for a large scale MD simulation and high scalability in a cluster environment. Further, we also plan to port our load-balancer to another parallel MD simulation system, called PEACH [8], which is currently under development at ETL, Japan, through a collaboration with the developers of the system. Such collaboration will lead to a thorough integration of the load balancer into the simulation system. Also, since PEACH is a highly optimized Fortran program and targeted at very large scale MD simulations, it will be a promising step to show our load-balancer can really work for improving the performance of high-performance computing.

REFERENCES

[1] R. BRUNNER, J. PHILLIPS, AND L. KALE, *Scalable Molecular Dynamics for Large Biomolecular Systems*, in Supercomputing, 2000.

[2] S. DEBOLT AND P. KOLLMAN, *AMBERCUBE MD, Parallelization of AMBER's Molecular Dynamics Module for Distributed-Memory Hypercube Computers*, Journal of Computational Chemistry, 14 (1993), pp. 312–329.

[3] R. ELSAESSER, B. MONIEN, AND R. PREIS, *Diffusive Load Balancing Schemes on Heterogeneous Networks*, in the 12th ACM Symposium on Parallel Algorithms and Architectures, ACM Press, 2000, pp. 30–38.

[4] K. ESSELINK, B. SMIT, AND P. HILBERS, *Efficient parallel implementation of molecular dynamics on a toroidal network: Multi-particle potentials*, Journal of Computer Physics, 106 (1993), pp. 108–114.

[5] R. GILES AND P. TAMAYO, *A Parallel Scalable Approach to Short-Range Molecular Dynamics on CM-5*, in Scalable High Performance Computing Conference, IEEE, 1992, p. 240.

[6] D. HEGARTY AND M. KECHADI, *Topology Preserving Dynamic Load Balancing for Parallel Molecular Simulations*, in Supercomputing, IEEE, IEEE Press, Nov. 1997.

[7] J. KITOWSKI, *Distributed and parallel computing of short-range molecular dynamics*, Lecture Notes in Computer Science, 1041 (1996), p. 345.

[8] Y. KOMEIJI, M. HARAGUCHI, AND U. NAGASHIMA, *Parallel molecular dynamics simulation of a protein*, Parallel Computing, 27 (2001), pp. 977–987.

[9] K.-T. LIM, S. BRUNETT, M. IOTOV, R. MCCLURG, N. VAIDEHI, S. DASGUPTA, S. TAYLOR, AND W. GODDARD III, *Molecular Dynamics for Very Large Systems on Massively Parallel Computers: The MPSim Program*, Journal of Computational Chemistry, 18 (1997), pp. 501–521.

[10] S. LIN, J. MELLOR-CRUMMEY, B. PETTITT, AND G. PHILLIPS JR, *Molecular Dynamics on a Distributed-Memory Multiprocessor*, Journal of Computational Chemistry, 13 (1992), pp. 1022–1035.

[11] S. PLIMPTON, *Fast Parallel Algorithms for Short-Range Molecular Dynamics*, Journal of Computational Physics, 117 (1995), pp. 1–19.

[12] M. WELLEBEEK-LEMAIR AND A. REEVES, *Strategies for Dynamic Load Balancing on Highly Parallel Computers*, IEEE Tranactions on Parallel and Distributed Systems, 4 (1993), pp. 979–993.

Section 3: Cluster and Grid Applications

In: Parallel and Distributed Scientific and Engineering Computing ISBN 1-59033-956-8
Editor: Y. Pan and L.T. Yang, pp. 147-162

IMPROVING QUALITY OF SERVICE FOR APPLICATION CLUSTERS

SOPHIA CORSAVA* AND VLADIMIR GETOV†

Abstract. Quality of service (QoS) requirements, which include availability, integrity, performance and responsiveness are increasingly needed by science and engineering applications. Rising computational demands and data mining present a new challenge in the IT world. As our needs for more processing, research and analysis increase, performance and reliability degrade exponentially. In this paper we present a software system that manages quality of service for Unix based distributed application clusters. Our approach is synthetic and involves intelligent agents that make use of static and dynamic ontologies to monitor, diagnose and correct operational faults and performance problems at run time, over a private network. Finally, we provide experimental results from our pilot implementation in a production environment.

Key words. Application clusters, Distributed applications, Quality of Service, Performance

1. Introduction. Researchers, analysts, scientists and engineers, need reliable and powerful systems. Having the ability to run multiple analyzes, experiments and realistic simulations can lead to new and more comprehensive discoveries. Research scientists and engineers can properly research by performing experiments in a trial and error mode. Most researchers are led to the wrong conclusions as they are faced with processing problems. To overcome them, they reduce sample populations. Alternative scenarios cannot be investigated thoroughly and creativity cannot be fully expressed. Delivery of processing outputs and timing get adversely affected as well. Opportunities get lost this way too, if it takes months to determine which is the best processing technique for atomic energy for example. Data mining techniques, cannot be put to their full use, as by nature they are processing-intensive. The majority of database servers cannot withstand the load of running repeated comparisons of large data groups against a set of possible parameters and outcomes. Processing needs to be smooth, transparent and efficient.

Robust, dependable [1,9,18] infrastructures are very difficult to maintain. Complex environments are difficult and costly to manage and, generally speaking, complexity reduces the predictability and reliability of application services and systems [1,4,12,16]. Due to this complexity, it is usually quite difficult to identify performance problems, bottlenecks or failures promptly. Analyzing collected availability and performance data can be a time-consuming thankless task that requires pain-staking manual labor. Deciding upon a course of action to resolve failures and performance problems may take weeks and can be very costly. With the exponential growth of distributed clusters and emerging grids [8], the matching human component is simply not available. We urgently need to reconsider the way we build infrastructures and troubleshoot faults. Infrastructures, (hardware, network and software) are essential prerequisites for efficient service delivery. In this paper, we propose a solution to these problems by introducing the architectural framework for a fault-tolerant, self-managing, intelligent infrastructure for Unix-based distributed application clusters. This paper is organized as follows. In section 2 we discuss related work. In section 3 our building methodology and approach, while section 4 discusses some preliminary results from one of our implementations at a UK-based customer site.

2. Related Work. Agents have been used in service, task and resource mapping, security, event management, adaptation, information organization and retrieval among other things [20]. Examples are: RETSINA that manages adaptation in open Internet environments; RASCAL that handles service mapping and arbitration services; JAM, a belief-desire-intention agent architecture that supports goal-based reasoning with priorities; JACK

*Sophia Corsava, Harrow School of Computer Science, University of Westminster, U.K.,Email: sophiac6@yahoo.com

†Harrow School of Computer Science, University of Westminster, U.K. Email: v.s.getov@wmin.ac.uk

Intelligent Agents that provide the infrastructure for developing agents for distributed applications; OpenCybele for event, thread, and concurrency management, as well as internal event generation (send and receive). Structured troubleshooting and fault correction approaches are widely used in the application domain. These techniques include recursive restarts [6], check-pointing [17], reboot [12] and undoing old configurations [12]. The check-pointing technique allows applications to recover from the last point of failure by copying on a regular basis their status on stable storage and then retrieving it. Application recursive restarts are based on the principle of infrastructure-centric software design: move intelligence from endpoints into the supporting infrastructure. Reboot, restarts not only the application but also the underlying operating system and undoing old configurations involves restoring old backups and overwriting current assumed "invalid" settings. A newer approach is the N-layered architecture for application development that allows for resiliency and better performance [3].

A lot of important work has been done, in the areas of fault diagnosis, performance and decision-making. Current diagnostic methods include: the threshold analysis, the bottleneck analysis, the what's different analysis and the correlation analysis. In this area, a lot of important work has been done by J. Hellerstein [10]. Closely related to our work is also the very important work done by John Wilkes and R Golding on self-managing, self-configuring storage [9,18].

There are a number of tools that measure performance and monitor systems. These include BMC, HPGlance Plus, HP Measureware, SystemEdge, Sun Management Centre, TeamQuest, Landmark Performance Works, Aurora Software Sarcheck, Foglight Software RAPS, Compuware Ecotools, Datametrics Viewpoint, Metron Athene, Network Weather Service (mostly for networks) etc [7]. To our knowledge, there are no commercial tools that automatically correct performance problems.

2.1. Current problems. Distributed application clusters consist of multiple components. The sound inter-operability of these components is important for the correct functionality of the service as a whole. A common problem in large systems, is that component interdependencies are highly complex and therefore difficult to maintain. These components may be front-end web services or application GUIs, that users use to connect, and back-end processes such as databases and other applications for transaction processing. Very often, a component failure can have catastrophic results. For example, if the front-end web services fail, users cannot connect to the site and therefore cannot access the back-end database. In some cases there may be legal and ethical repercussions from distributed component failures [5,12]. Current problems for distributed application clusters could be summarized in four main categories as follows: 1) Users unable to access one or more service components, 2) Users can access service components, but they do not function properly (logical errors, bugs etc), 3) Users can access services but performance is bad, 4) Work in progress gets interrupted unexpectedly, because one or more service components (server, application, network) crash mid-way.

In addition to these problems, there are other issues that run deeper and do not allow for effective resolution. To start with, there seems to be a huge communication breakdown amongst software developers, scientists who come up with mathematical solutions to IT problems and professional support people. If the gap could be bridged, experienced support people could provide theorists with real-world information. Scientists would then have realistic material to work with instead of relying on simulations in controlled environments. Another worrying issue is that uptime claims achieved by applications and management software are unfortunately false. Detailed information on this can be found in D.Patterson's Key Note speech [12]. The simplistic measure of uptime of the "5 nines", has rarely been achieved if at all.

Measuring performance and system availability is a rather complicated task as collecting daily raw system utilization statistics is hardly adequate to determine if the system has a performance problem or not and how available it is. Currently problems include, determining the optimum performance baseline per application/server, determining the diagnostic method and decision process to use, standardizing performance data collection, deciding which measurements to use, where to keep them, for how long and how to present them in a meaningful manner so they can be assessed.

Performance problems can be classified in 4 main categories. 1) Progressive performance degradation, 2) Recurrent performance problems, 3) Expected Load spikes and 4) Unexpected performance problems. To effectively troubleshoot any problem, it is necessary to have correct input real data. This seems to be surprisingly difficult as most uptime claims are false [12], benchmarks are not realistic (as most do not consider random faults) [12], support people do not fully understand their systems and human experts are expensive and difficult to find [4,5,12,18]. As technology advances rapidly, more than one human experts need to work together to determine the problem.

Most performance/reliability measurement software is inaccurate and resource intensive as metrics change on a per case (application/server) basis [10]. Multi-component, distributed applications are not handled well because they have different measurement variables. The relationship of causal variables is subject to change from one hardware or software platform to another. Therefore we end up calculating inconsistent and inaccurate performance baselines. For example an average of 80% CPU utilization is normal for a powerful server with multiple CPUs but indicates a serious performance problem for a low specification server with only one CPU. From experiments we can see that we cannot generalize performance measurement techniques/tools [10]. Each diagnostic technique works better if it is specific to the system it monitors. There are so many frequent software and/or hardware releases that our measurement, diagnostic and decision models need to be changed to go along, every time. Finally, current techniques do not consider non-linear relationships such as the CPU run queue size with the CPU utilization for example [10].

3. Building Methodology.

3.1. Overview. Our approach involves:

1. Unix shell based intelligent agents that monitor, troubleshoot and manage distributed services within the datacenter. These agents also collect detailed system performance/availability measurements.

2. Dedicated administration servers that act as external agent coordinators in a high-availability failover configuration and share a common pool of NFS mounted disks, to avoid single points of failure.

3. A dedicated private network, where all agent related traffic goes through to avoid congesting the public LAN and

4. Static and dynamic ontologies [14]. These ontologies include :

- Static local knowledge templates(SLKTs) that contain information about what the server should be like hardware-wise, which applications it should run, all application external and internal dependencies and requirements (file systems, path names, application component startup sequences, binary location, application type, version, name, IP address, port it listens to – if any, application process names and numbers etc),
- Dynamic local service profiles(DLSPs) that are generated by each agent controlled server in regular intervals and contain information about server hardware, software, load, capacity and services.

From these ontologies, intelliagents generate i) Dynamic global service profile lists or **DGSPLs** that contain information about all running and available services across the entire datacenter. Available services are presented by ¡Server type, OS, memory and CPUs,

Application type and version, Current Load, Users logged in, Geographical Location, Site Name¿ and ii) Index static service lists or **ISSLs** that contain very basic information about each server or resource IP address and services. They can contain up to 200 entries and are manually updated.

The ontological knowledge is automatically processed by intelliagents to determine host and service status. Agents using keywords mentioned in ontologies can "understand" if there are hardware or software problems. Agents come to this conclusion by comparing values in static ontologies (SLKTs) against those in dynamic ones (DLSPs). When it is determined that there is a fault (different values, i.e. services, hardware, software or resources are unavailable), they create a flag in the flags log directory that describes it appropriately and initiate "healing" actions to repair it. Various other intelliagents that monitor applications with multiple dependencies and required resources can later check these flags and take the desired course of action in order to achieve their ultimate goals (i.e. all services, resources and hosts available and in a good state).

3.2. Assumptions. We make the following assumptions:

1. All servers are Unix-based and NTP synchronized.
2. For all applications participating in the datacenter (databases, web servers etc), we have startup and shutdown scripts.
3. Specialized application developers have provided us with tools and methodologies to test and confirm if these applications are up and running and available to be used, that have been incorporated in the agent source code and ontology definition. In addition these people have provided us with application specific connectivity time-out definitions.
4. All ontologies, templates, files and logs produced are flat ASCII files generated by I/O Unix pipes, readable by most Unix tools (operators) and human administrators.
5. The maximum load a server can successfully sustain has been provided to us by either hardware/operating system manufacturers combined with practical experience information by human experts and adapted based on our own observations.
6. All communications are based on TCP/IP.
7. We use the term application/service interchangeably in this paper, as in the context of this paper, applications are service vehicles.
8. We assume that the majority of distributed services run on physically separate unix servers.

3.3. Intelligent agents. There are a number of definitions for agents. Of them, the Wooldridge-Jennings one is the most relevant to our work. According to them, agents are software or hardware-based systems that are autonomous, interact with other agents or humans, are reactive, proactive, can take initiative and exhibit goal-directed behavior [19]. Intelligent agents or intelliagents are unix programs that monitor systems and services and wherever possible automatically correct run-time operational faults with as little downtime as possible. They are highly modular and use constraint-based causal reasoning to decide the best course of action [11]. A causal model is a triple that encodes the truth-values of sentences that deal with causal relationships. They include 1) action sentences such as A will be true if we do B, 2) counterfactuals such as A would have been different if it were not for B and 3) plain causal utterance such as A may cause B OR B occurred because of A.

Intelliagents are installed locally on each server they monitor, always at the same physical location *"/apps/intelliagents"* and are "awakened by local Unix crons every X minutes (every 5 minutes for example). Intelliagents do not use a relational database (to avoid corruptions and for simplicity), they use static and dynamic ontologies as discussed. Our intelliagents are mainly developed in bourne shell and are as likely to fail as any standard system startup script (in Unix-based systems most startup/shutdown scripts are written in bourne shell) [13]. They use Unix IPC and exit codes to communicate with the operating system. The reason why we used Unix shell is because it is very easy and fast to write scripts, change them when needed or troubleshoot them. In addition, we did not have to install additional compilers that would put more load to monitored systems, or that would compromise security in any way as is the case with JAVA or C++ based software [5,12,13]. Finally, by experience, we know that when a system is failing or is overloaded, complicated measurement/troubleshooting tools tend to stop working altogether [7,13]. It should be noted however that agents can be written in any other programming language that suits the programmer best.

Intelliagents use 2-phase locking which is a programming discipline that shows that no lock can be released, before the last lock has been obtained. This avoids them operating inconsistently by "healing" the same type of resource concurrently. All actions are logged and every time an intelliagent observes a problem and takes an action, a message is sent to human operators (usually by email). On each server a full intelliagent suite is running locally that is read-only. On each external administration server intelliagent originals are kept in a secure location. Human administrators are allowed very limited access to administration servers. Access control procedures are in place to ensure that no modifications take place without detection. Password ageing is also implemented that forces users and administrators to change them on a daily basis. The SSH [2] protocol is used, while all other connection methods (such as remsh, rlogin, rsh, telnet) are disabled by default during the server build process. This protects intelliagents, hosts and services from unauthorized accesses, intrusions and changes. This type of security was deemed necessary after we discovered experimentally that human operators were responsible for a significant amount of errors that caused 1,536 hours of cumulative downtime within 16 months at a customer site. This confirms surveys [12] reporting that 40% of downtime is due to human errors.

Whenever local intelliagents run, they produce flags in the dedicated directory on the local server disk at *"/logs/intelliagents/intelliagent_name"* to show the status of the run. A number of flags are produced with appropriate naming conventions that show what happened and exactly where the agent found a fault. Absence of these flags means that we either have an internal intelliagent problem or that they did not run at all. Administration servers monitor the creation of these flags every X+5 minutes, where X is the frequency intelliagents run, i.e. every 10 minutes (adjustable parameter). If these flags are not there, they start troubleshooting intelliagent processes. Whenever an agent detects an error it tries to fix it. All intelliagents run in parallel, in a distributed manner and do not depend on each other as each agent is started by the local Unix cron. At start-up each intelliagent checks to see if any other of the same type is running, if so it exits, i.e. you can never have two backup intelliagents running at the same time. It also removes its own flags from previous runs and old status profiles. For each application type there are customized error categories. Application health is determined by attempting to connect to them every Y minutes and run basic commands (such as a "get" on a web server process for example). This is essentially the way intelliagents communicate with applications – by trying to use them and by examining the resulting exit codes at the Unix shell.

Each intelliagent has 5 major parts: a) Monitoring, b) Diagnosing, c) Self-Healing, Action, Repair, d) Communication, Logging, e) Self-maintenance. The monitoring part is tasked to look after one particular resource or system aspect. Whenever the monitored subject does not respond as expected, the diagnosing part is invoked and goes through a series of tests to determine the root of the problem. The diagnostic procedure is done in two ways; statically and dynamically. Statically from parsing and examining error logs and flags and dynamically by the use of Unix administration commands to ensure the best possible diagnosis. Findings are recorded automatically in the dynamic ontologies. Based on these findings the self-healing portion gets activated and starts repairing the faults.

The communication part is responsible for communicating with other intelliagents and human operators. It is also responsible for logging all intelliagent activities and results. Intelliagents are classified according to their functions and tasks. Intelliagent categories include: 1) Hardware agents that look after hardware components (CPU, memory, boards etc), 2) Operating system/network agents that look after all OS and network related aspects, 3) Resource intelliagents that are responsible for managing and configuring resources such as disks, network cards, virtual memory etc, 4) Application/Service intelliagents that manage and troubleshoot local and global application/services across the datacentre and 5) Status intelliagents that dynamically generate status profiles for servers, resources and services in terms of availability, load, capacity, geographical location and site name.

3.4. Service management. Service management is handled in a what could be called unorthodox way. Each local server in the datacentre is responsible for "knowing" and taking care of its own resources and services. Its local status intelliagent is "awakened" by the Unix cron and compiles dynamically its local DLSP.

To confirm that local services are available on each server local status intelliagent invoke local service intelliagents who attempt to connect to local running services and perform very simple queries (e.g. in the case of a web server they do an http "get", for a database they connect and attempt to do a "select * from table name"). Connectivity tests and timeout baselines are provided by specialized application/service providers as discussed. If services that should be running on that server are not running, service intelliagents start troubleshooting. Their aim is to ensure that local services run at all times and if not restart them. Once they achieve this, they perform the prescribed connectivity tests again and if there is a problem they cannot resolve they notify human administrators (usually via email or SMS).

Manually created ISSPs have been experimentally proven to be the best way to maintain server information, as datacentres do not undergo drastic reconfigurations in terms of existing devices. We have moved the responsibility of monitoring services to each server locally. This has been proven to be the safest and less "resource" expensive way to keep detailed information about servers, services and resources.

3.4.1. Service intelliagents. Service intelliagents, use SLKTs to monitor and troubleshoot application/service related issues. They have detailed knowledge about local and global application/service dependencies and requirements. Every time they run, they create flags to indicate the service status (up or not) and any problems they have encountered. In figure 1, we can see how service intelliagents manage distributed application services. An example of how they check global interdependencies for distributed applications follows.

1) Service Intelliagent at startup checks if local SLKT exists. If not, it copies it from its administration server. If unsuccessful it exits and notifies operators about the problem. If the SLKT is there, it reads it and removes old flags from the log directory. Tries to connect to the local application component and runs a simple query such as "*select count from table_name*" in the case of a database. If successful it creates the flag *SVR_name.UP*. If not, checks to see if all application processes are running (all this information is retrieved from the ontology). If none are running, it creates the flag *SVR_name.STOPPED*. If all application processes are running, it checks to see if the maximum connection limit has been reached. If not and it cannot connect it creates the flag *SVR_name.FAULTED*. It stops any running application processes, and informs human operators (OPS). If more application processes are running than they should, tries to kill the obsolete ones (zombies or application processes that should not be there – any application process not in the service ontology are considered illegal). It then tries to connect to the application again. If it succeeds it creates the flag *SVR_name.UP* and informs OPS else the flag *SVR_name.FAULTED*, stops any running application processes and informs OPS. If some application processes are running, it tries to start the missing ones. It tries to connect again and if successful it creates the flag

SVR_name.UP, else the flag *SVR_name.FAULTED* stops any running application processes and informs OPS. If all application processes are running and the maximum connection limit has been reached, it tries to clear any old application connections (using commands provided by experienced application people and incorporated in the agent code). It then tries to connect again. If it succeeds it creates the flag *SVR_name.UP* and informs OPS about what it did. If it cannot connect it creates the flag *SVR_name .CLIM.MAX* and informs OPS. In any case it continues to the next step as it cannot be sure yet why there is a problem if at all.

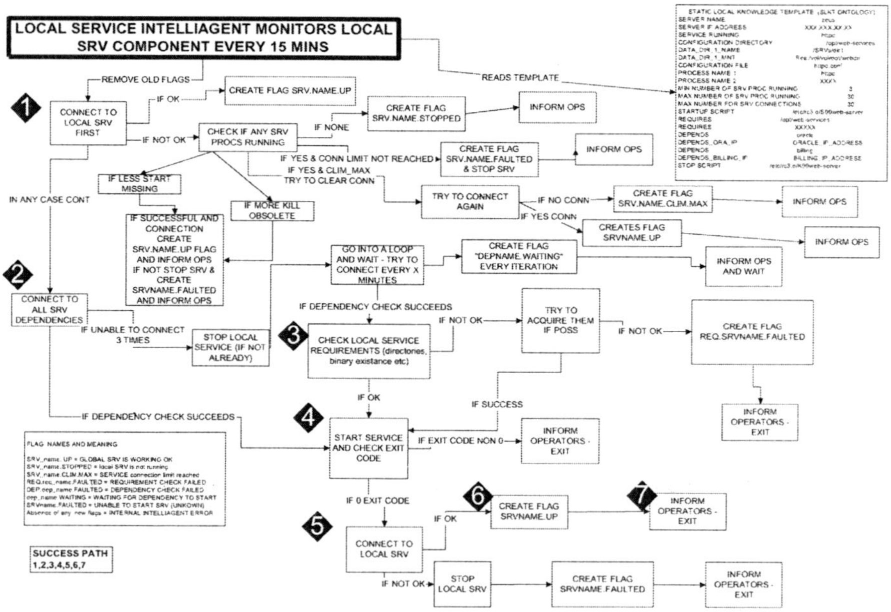

FIG. 3.1. *Local service intelliagents monitoring and correcting faults dynamically. When they cannot deal with a fault, they contact human operators and ask for help. Operators can easily add a new intelligent module to the troubleshooting process or update static ontologies accordingly.*

2) It tries to connect to the first external application dependency (i.e. the first in line distributed application component that must be running so the local application can also start), if it is unable to do this successfully for 3 consecutive times, it stops the local application if it is not stopped already. (Why? If any of the dependent components in a multi-component application is not up and running the application may end up in a very inconsistent state.) It goes into an infinite loop, where it tries to connect to the first external dependency every 5 minutes and it emails OPS through every iteration. If/When it finally succeeds, it continues likewise with the rest of the dependencies defined in the service ontology. It behaves likewise waiting for the connectivity test to succeed. If not it stays in the infinite loop and emails accordingly OPS. If/when it successfully goes through all dependency checks, it proceeds with the local requirement checking. (Note that it is not necessary for the loop to be infinite, in some cases the loop can be finite, by incorporating a small counter. As Unix shell loops of this type hardly consume any system resources, we were happy to let it run until the rest of the application components became active).

3) It checks if the local application requirements are present, i.e. mount points, application binaries etc. if not it tries to mount it with a command such as "/usr/sbin/mount -F nfs *nfs_mount_place mount_point*". If not and it is unable to satisfy them (unix administration commands are used to achieve this), it creates the flag *REQ.requirement_name.FAULTED*. It then emails OPS and exits. At that point human operators are called to intervene and

resolve the problem. They can later, easily add the resolution procedure to the agent code so that next time it knows what to do to acquire the resource.

4) If all requirement checks succeed for the local application component, it uses the startup script mentioned in the service ontology to start the component. If it starts successfully (i.e. exit code 0), it performs yet another local component connectivity test and if successful, it creates the flag *SVR_name.UP*. Finally it emails OPS. At this point it has successfully started the local application and all dependencies (pre-requisite application components) are running as well. If the application startup script returns a non-zero exit code, it stops any application process that may have started, creates the flag *SVR_name.FAULTED* and emails OPS so they can manually intervene and fix the problem. If, application dependencies are locally located, i.e. run on the same local host, the intelliagent tries to start dependencies sequentially. The sequence by which external and internal dependencies are defined in the SLKT ontology dictates the startup sequence of all distributed application components.

Intelliagents ensure the following: a) If an application component is dependent on others and these are not up and running, the local application component does not start. b) If application/service dependencies are not present, and the local application component is running, it forcefully stops it. c) They can troubleshoot the local application up to a point. c) They create meaningful flags that point human operators to the right direction and narrow down troubleshooting procedures substantially.

3.5. Performance intelliagents. Our performance measurement techniques were orientated towards workgroup aggregation. We divided our measurements into 5 main groups: 1) Operating system, 2) Network, 3) Disks, 4) Application processes and 5) User processes. Measurements were kept in a special logs directory and were classified first by server name and then by measurement group. All measurements were recorded in ASCII text files, created by Unix pipes through standard output redirection. We observed 1) I/O rates on disks and network devices, 2) processes per user name, 3) per command name and arguments, 4) per user and command name, 5) per CPU and 6) the match between network packets, port numbers and protocols. They were non-intrusive as they did not load the system they were monitoring. For each monitored resource type or workgroup, a dedicated performance intelliagent was responsible for collecting performance statistics and comparing them against pre-scripted baseline thresholds, every 10 or 15 minutes. All collected data were manipulated as text strings. Different types of measurements were associated together by matching their timestamps. Measurements were ordered by timestamp and treated as a time series to produce graphical representations of the system performance either as a whole or by component/workgroup. Each file produced by persistent state processes, was managed as a circular queue, the length of which was configurable. Every time these intelliagents run, they produced flags to indicate what happened. Every time, a threshold was exceeded they notified us via email or SMS. The tools used, were standard unix tools such as vmstat, iostat, sar, netstat, nfsstat, top etc. To determine accurately the behavior of each process, we used microstate measurements where applicable, as most modern CPUs allow for them. The accuracy of microstate measurements is microsecond resolution and the overhead is sub-microsecond (units are nanoseconds). In this way we had very accurate thread and process accounting. More about microstate accounting can be found in [7]. In figures 2 and 3 we can see how important microstate measurements are in calculating accurately system performance.

3.5.1. Baselines and thresholds.. All baselines were determined based on the hardware configuration of each system and the application type it was running. These baselines were set with the help of hardware and operating system experts, application experts who had given us expected application performance times and our own experimental observa-

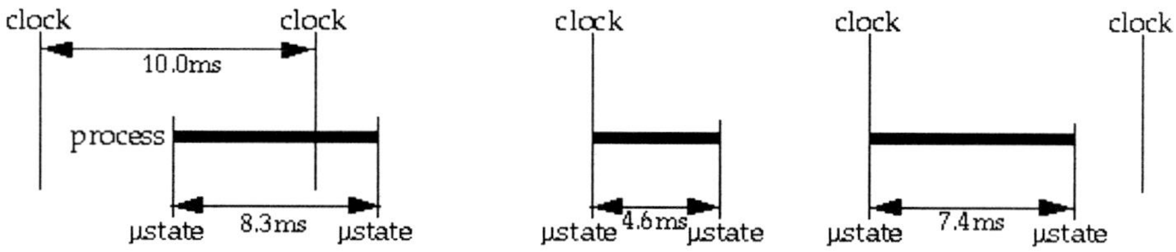

FIG. 3.2. *In the diagram above, (taken from [7]) a process wakes up, then sleeps twice. The first wake-up occurs between clock ticks. The period is interrupted by the subsequent tick, which charges a full 10 milliseconds to the process. The next two wake-ups occur as a result of the clock interrupt scheduling the process. They complete before the subsequent interrupt, so there is no charge. The true measured CPU usage is measured by microstate accounting as 8.3 + 4.5 + 7.4 = 20.3 ms. The first wake-up is overestimated; the second and third are missed completely.*

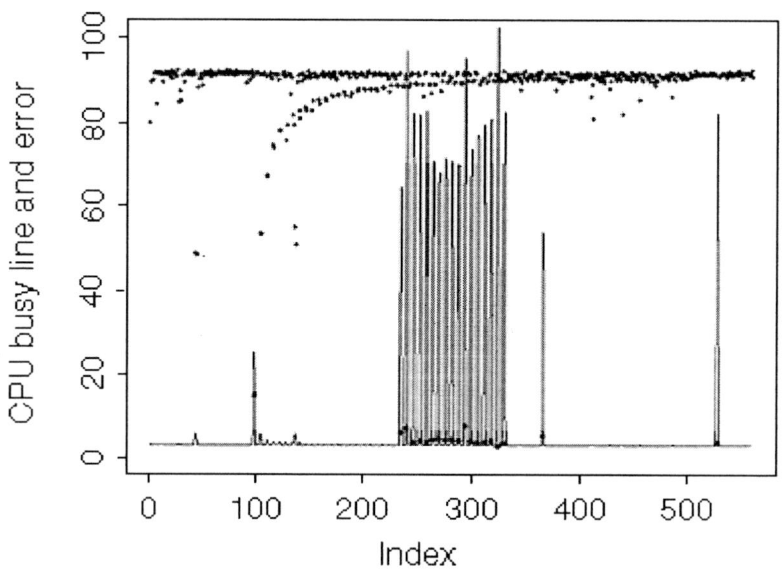

FIG. 3.3. *(Taken from [7]), Discrepancy (error) between reported (with vmstat) CPU usage versus actual CPU usage (with microstate measurements) measured over time on a SPARCstation 10 with dual 60-MHz CPUs. (CPU usage is denoted by the line, error is denoted by the dots)*

tions. Every time a baseline setting was not proven to be correct, we adjusted it accordingly manually initially. This happened quite often in the case of newly installed applications mainly. Utilization spikes occurred quite often, and in these cases we used our performance measurements to determine what was wrong. We had developed customized system builds for each hardware, operating system and application type and made sure that all the servers in the datacenter were built as such. This policy was proven very effective as we avoided known operational and performance pitfalls.

3.5.2. Operating system. The measurements we considered were: 1) Memory "sr" (scan rate), "po" (page out), page faults and free memory measurements to determine memory shortage, 2) CPU run queue, to detect any processes waiting to be served by any CPU, 3) Overall CPU idle time %, 4) Blocked processes waiting for I/O, 5) Per process CPU and memory utilization, and 6) Disk I/O and throughput. We used 30 second intervals during I/O measurements to avoid spikes in the load. We were interested in the asvc_t and wsvc_t values (read and write response times).

3.5.3. Network. For the network we considered the following measurements, 1) Network interface utilization statistics and errors, 2) Network route utilization, 3) NFS statistics, 4) TCP/IP bandwidth and end-to-end round trip latency measurements, 5) Size of incoming/outgoing network packets and TCP windows, 6) Network connection time to live and 7) Name server response (DNS, NIS, NIS+, LDAP).

3.5.4. Databases. For databases, we used scripts that had a lot of input from experienced database administrators. We used a combination of Unix tools and SQL commands to monitor and measure their performance. We considered the following measurements: 1) Time taken for a request to connect to the database, 2) Time taken for the request to be served by the database, 3) Time taken for the database to initialize, 4) Time taken for the database to shutdown, 5) Time taken for the database backup to complete, 6) Per process CPU and memory utilization, 7) Number of users connected to the database and for how long each, 8) Memory allocated at startup, 9) Database checkpoints and 10) Memory per transaction.

3.5.5. Web servers and application GUIs. For web servers and application GUIs we considered the following measurements; 1) Time taken to connect to them, 2) Time taken for the process to come back with the results of the query, 3) Per process CPU and memory utilization, and 4) Number of http/application connections and for how long each.

3.5.6. Distributed applications on different machines. For distributed applications we observed the time taken for a request to be served by the entire application from beginning to end. Every 15 to 30 minutes we initiated a dummy process to run through all application components, simulating a user and measure the total response time, in addition to the business-as-usual requests.

3.5.7. Performance intelliagent decision rules. To determine if we were dealing with a performance problem, we used some basic rules based on our experience and input provided by hardware, operating system and application experts as well as performance specialists. In addition, we followed up mailing lists on the internet where people discussed performance problems, monitoring, diagnostic and resolution techniques. The rules we came up with for performance intelliagents can be summarized [7] as follows:

1. If memory scan rate AND page outs consistently high, AND page faults are high, AND free memory is low then probable memory shortage. If the virtual memory size of a process keeps on increasing then we probably have memory leaks. Multithreaded processes with lots of wait % time on the CPU (like Java) do not actually consume it. If CPU run queues are consistently high and CPU utilization $> 80\%$ and CPU load spikes $> 90\%$ then probably we need to add more CPUs. Involuntary CPU context switches indicate the existence of a CPU bottleneck. If the CPU system time is more the CPU user time then we have an OS problem (possible corruption or bad configuration).

2. The right TCP window sizes limit high latency over links. Open TCP connections consume memory while initiating a connection uses more CPU than data transfers. If TCP retransmit rates are $> 25 - 30\%$ then we have a network problem. If TCP throughput is more than 2KB/sec then we have a network problem. If packets are dropped with a rate $> 0.5\%$/sec then we have a network problem. If incoming duplicate TCP packets $> 25\%$ then the remote host keeps on re-transmitting. If TCP port resets > 2/second then we have a possible port scanner attack. If maximum packets in the software TCP transmit queue > 0 and equal to current hardware transmit queue length then TCP window (both send and receive) need to be increased. If the number of errors is large then the receive queue must be decreased. From the NFS statistics, if badxid = retransmissions and retransmissions $> 5\%$

then the problem is with server, otherwise it is the network. If there are too many timeouts, we need to add more nfs daemons.

3. If the I/O system shows > 30%, we need to add more I/O boards, or spread evenly the load on the existing ones. Local disks with response time ($a/wsvc\_t$) > 30 msecs, then we have a performance problem. For externally attached RAIDed disks > 20 msecs response times indicate a problem.

4. If application performs badly while memory and CPU and network do not, then it is an application configuration/tuning related problem. If there are load spikes (both CPU and memory) whenever a database runs a query, the database needs more indexes and probably more stripes in the file system configuration. We need to try tuning the application/database first and if the problem insists, developers need to revisit the application source code. If a system performs badly after a configuration change, it is probably the change that caused it. If a system starts performing badly, without any additional load from anywhere (application, OS, network), then it probably has a hardware problem (other h/w components take over the load).

5. If one cannot login to a server at the Unix prompt, AND the application on that server does not respond, the server needs to be rebooted by any means possible.

6. If there are service requests in a distributed system that do not reach any of the application components, and all application components are up and running, then it is either a hardware problem or a network permission issue (i.e. firewall drops or does not allow connections).

7. If all tuning has been done and the system is built according to all hardware and software manufacturer guidelines and still performs badly, then the system has not been sized correctly for the application it runs. If servers are pre-configured and their builds optimized, they perform much better compared to out-of-the-box builds.

8. Databases are faster if they using raw UFS partitions and striped file systems. Usually 11 stripes are good for good performance. More indexes reduce the load for lookups. Big block sizes speed up sequential scans.

9. Multi-threaded web server processes, compiled on the server they are meant to run, perform far better than single-threaded out-of-the-box installations.

Wherever possible, we scripted Unix administration commands in the intelliagent code, to tune operating system kernel variables, with caution. For applications, we asked experienced application support people and developers, to provide us with tuning and troubleshooting procedures, which we scripted in the intelliagent code. This aspect of our performance intelliagent, is in progress, as it can be dangerous to change operating system or application tuning variables at run time.

4. Results. One of the sites our work was implemented was a financial company of a UK based international customer. Servers included SUN, HP, IBM and linux machines. The breakdown of machines and their functions were: 100 database servers, a mixture of Oracle and Sybase databases, running on Sun Enterprize Series 4500, and E10Ks. 55 transaction processing servers a mixture of E10Ks, Ultra 10s, linux, E450s, E220Rs HP K and T series and 60 front-end application IBM SP2 servers for user front-end financial applications. Services were distributed across these servers. All data was residing on local disks. The network was 100 Base/T ethernet for all servers.

Financial analysts used services for data-mining, financial projections, financial model evaluations, market data/trend simulations and analytical reports. The Load Sharing Facility, LSF [15] application was used for scheduling jobs against databases. Users via the application GUI, manually selected database servers to submit jobs or submitted them to be processed at a latter time, using either native LSF utilities, or Unix utilities like "cron" or "at" jobs. Computations were deployed across different geographical sites the customer had.

Market data feeds would come in from all parts of the world from international customer sites and other places such as Reuters.

The main problem the users had was that application components were failing very often and on many occasions errors were latent. They had no means to automatically correct operational faults. For them downtime meant severe financial losses as their systems needed to be available on a 24x7 basis. Stock brokers needed frequent access to databases, market trend analysis reports, forecasts, projection and simulation results, to decide how to handle end-customer investments. Because it was a high-pressure complex environment, downtime had big impacts on service integrity, safety and QoS. What was happening on a regular basis was that various application components would stop working altogether and operators did not know where to start looking. Large database jobs scheduled to run overnight would frequently crash databases and calculations would not complete. Human operators tried to resolve operational problems and faults manually. Available services would often become unavailable without any explanation and users would become increasingly frustrated. The financial company would suffer financial losses because analysts and researchers could not easily quantify and qualify financial models and analyze market trends. Operators were under immense pressure to resolve operational faults and performance problems under difficult circumstances and usually during the night and the end of financial periods.

Users used for monitoring BMC patrol and SystemEdge [7]. The environment was highly complex and faults (operational, performance and human errors) would make things much worse. Experienced administrators were "on-call" every night. Operators had the main task of notifying system administrators about fatal faults. There were many time-delays caused by operators not understanding how critical a fault was, or trying to locate the on-call people during the night. It could take up to 2 hours at a time for a service or server restart, as faults had to be diagnosed and that was difficult as services were distributed. In addition, a number of people had to be notified about the problem before any decisive action was taken (i.e. a server reboot). Often experts from more than one areas had to be called in together to decide what caused the problem. If experienced support people could not diagnose and correct remotely a fault, they were obliged to come in to work. The whole troubleshooting procedure (and subsequent downtime) could take an average of 4 hours in such cases.

End-users were becoming increasingly frustrated as they were having more downtime they could afford and the failure of one of more distributed application components would impact on service integrity. In Figure 4, one can see the detailed breakdown in hours based on the type of errors that caused downtime at the customer site for 1 year, before we implemented our software. Total downtime was 550 hours from service-related faults. 345 hours caused by databases crashing in the middle of a job, 60 hours caused by human errors, 30 hours caused by LSF errors, 40 hours from front-end user application downtime, 10 hours caused by firewall configuration/network errors, 50 hours from performance-related errors and 5 hours from services being completely unavailable (corruptions, bugs etc) and 10 hours from all types of hardware errors. After our work was implemented, downtime went down to 31 hours in total. The error distribution was, 8 hours from firewall/network related errors, 6 hours from various hardware related errors, 2 hours from human errors, 9 hours from performance errors, 1 hour from LSF errors, 3 hours from service front-end errors, 2 hours from complete service unavailability errors and 8 hours from databases crashing in the middle of a job. Intelliagents were used to monitor, troubleshoot and analyze distributed application services, servers, and performance. They were also used to automatically monitor and reschedule batch jobs if these failed. The administration servers generated dynamic global service profile lists per database type every 15 minutes on average. They managed the LSF job-scheduling tool and presented the best available database server for the batch job in a shortlist, with the best choice always first. The LSF software was configured to allow a finite number of scheduled jobs per database server and user access rights were defined at the Unix, the application/database and the LSF levels. Only specific users would submit specific types of jobs to a pre-determined group of database servers.

Performance problems were detected and dealt with much faster, as performance intelliagents created comprehensive reports about what may have caused a performance related problem and helped narrow down various possibilities. The vast majority of performance problems were corrected automatically and dynamically by running agents. The same applied for operational faults. Intelliagent error reporting/alerting mechanisms were integrated with SystemEdge and notifications were presented to operators from within the SystemEdge graphical user interface. Every time a fault was dealt with manually, we added a new troubleshooting procedure to the intelliagent source code and updated static ontologies accordingly when necessary. Despite the impressive decrease in downtime our software was unable to take care of firewall/network and hardware related errors as well as eradicate completely human errors. Faults however, were detected within the first 5 minutes of them happening (the intelliagent run frequency), as opposed to about 1 hour during day time, about 25 hours over the weekends and 10 hours from overnight jobs (data provided by the customer using BMC Patrol). The customer did not have any means to automatically monitor, detect and correct any batch job failures or global distributed cluster faults prior to our work.

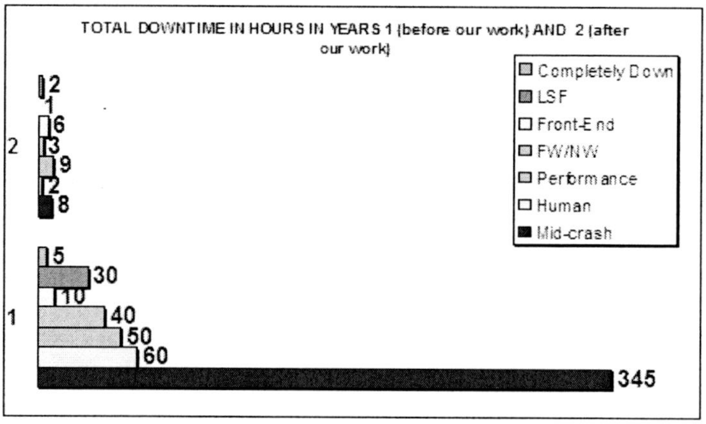

FIG. 4.1. *Breakdown of errors in hours and types for 2 years before and after our work was implemented. (Data provided by the customer)*

Intelliagents, in addition, checked every 5 minutes, if LSF processes were running (very often they would crash), if databases were up and running (likewise), the time batch jobs had left to complete (using pre-scripted LSF specific commands), if a batch job completed successfully (likewise), number of LSF scheduled jobs per database server as well as server, network and database load. They recorded all measurements and emailed summary reports to nominated administrators on a daily basis, on demand and whenever a job failed. Service intelliagents would attempt to troubleshoot and restart crashed processes and databases and they would notify human administrators accordingly. If jobs failed, intelliagents residing on the administration servers resubmitted them not based on the manual LSF settings and rules for job submissions, but based on the dynamically generated DGSPs. We had modified all ontologies to include LSF specific information such as number of jobs currently processed, jobs waiting to be processed and job number submission limit per database server. For this purpose we embedded LSF native commands in the service intelliagent source code. The reason we chose to use DGSPs, was because every time a job crashed a database there were implicit conclusions that the user who submitted the job manually either a) did not select a powerful enough server, or b) selected a server that was already overloaded, or c) the server became overloaded later from scheduled job submission, or there were d) random or otherwise errors potentially responsible for database or server crashes.

These intelliagents, were also using SLKTs to select a server of equal or higher in power than the server that failed, i.e. if the failed server had 4 CPUs, 4 GBs of RAM and was a of a specific model, their selection process would "prefer" first a server of the same model with more CPUs and memory. Choosing "randomly" a server for resubmitting a failed job, without any knowledge of its past job submission history and failures, although not ideal, significantly decreased downtime from database crashes in the middle of a job. If intelliagents were unable to allocate a server for job submission at all for any reason, or if a server had crashed, they emailed human operators to manually troubleshoot the failed machine.

Figures 5 and 6 show respectively the average CPU and memory utilization per system by intelliagents as opposed to BMC Patrol. Both cases clearly demonstrate the small percentage of system resources used by active intelliagents.

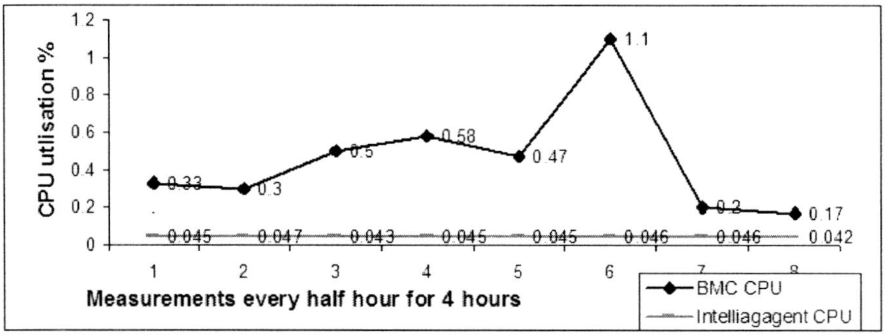

FIG. 4.2. *Intelliagent average CPU utilisation as opposed to BMC Patrol on a server at peak time.*

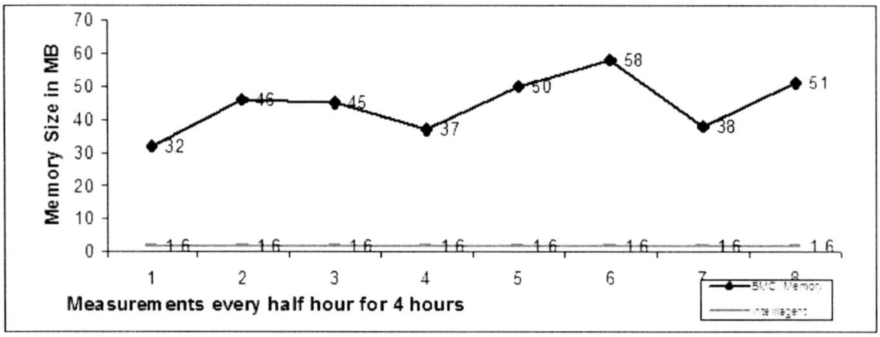

FIG. 4.3. *System Memory consumed by BMC patrol vs. intelliagents on the same server at peak time.*

5. Conclusions and Future Work. Our approach has, experimentally, increased quality of service for Unix-based multi-component distributed services. From 550 hours of total downtime within a year before any of our parts of our work were implemented, downtime went down to 31 hours in total the next year.

Our main conclusions can be summarized as follows. In the case of complex multi-component applications local application-specific detection/correction mechanisms work much better than generic troubleshooting approaches. The distributed manner intelliagents work ensures that the more components an application is consisted of, the higher the probability is it will not fail if it is managed in this way. Agent code and ontologies are easily maintainable and do not tax the system they look after because of their size and simplicity. They are not memory resident and the flags they produce pinpoint errors accurately. Automated error detection and correction techniques improve quality of service as errors are picked up faster than ever before. Methodical, structured performance measurement and collection techniques can help resolve performance related issues and bottlenecks more efficiently and effectively. Administrators can generate timelines of system behavior and observe similar behavioral patterns. In addition, they are notified automatically every time a threshold is exceeded.

Much work remains to be done, so our error detection and correction techniques are further improved and become more generic. We are also trying to reduce as much as possible manual input and generate automatically static ontologies. Performance modelling and dynamic troubleshooting of performance-related problems need further work. As we are not software developers, we used Unix-shell languages as the best and easiest way to test our theories. The intelliagent source code can be improved in that respect. Our approach, as is, at the moment cannot cater for network or obscure logical errors and needs manual input. It can however deal with latent errors up to a point, by restarting failed component applications. Extended logging of all system and intelliagent activities, ensure that human administrators have comprehensive information about all infrastructure aspects and can narrow down their search options when they do manual troubleshooting.

Our research continues in all these areas, in the hope that we'll improve our software and methodology further. Additional future work includes integrating our agent software with the grid technology. We hope the way agents generate dynamic global service lists (that contain information about all agent-enabled services) can be used in someway in the grid resource discovery and selection mechanisms for semantic grids. Intelliagents can manage quality of service very effectively for any distributed Unix application cluster, or standalone hosts by ensuring that all service components are available in the sequence they are meant to be. Service integrity and safety are protected in this way, as all interdependent distributed application components must be up and running for the distributed service to be considered healthy. If services are unavailable or take long to respond, intelliagents based on prescripted scenarios, try to restore them. If they are unable to do so, human administrators are notified so they can fix the problem. In that respect, services will not have resources vanishing unexpectedly without any explanations. Frequent monitoring ensures that service or server related faults are picked up and dealt with promptly.

REFERENCES

[1] J.-C Avizienis, Laprie and B. Randell, *Fundamental concepts of dependability* Proc. of the 3rd Information Survivability Workshop, October 2000.

[2] Daniel J. Barrett, Richard Silverman, *SSH, The Secure Shell: The Definitive Guide*, O'Reilly & Associates, February 2001.

[3] Roger Chartier, *Application Architecture: An N-Tier Approach - Part 1*, `http://www.15seconds.com/issue/011023.htm`

[4] Sophia Corsava, Vladimir Getov, *Self-Healing Intelligent Infrastructure for computational clusters*, SHAMAN workshop proceedings, ACM ISC conference, New York, June 2002.

[5] Sophia Corsava, Vladimir Getov, *Intelligent Fault-Tolerant architecture for cluster computing*, IASTED, PDCN03, Innsbruck, Austria, Feb 2003.

[6] George Candea, James Cutler, Armando Fox, Rushabh Doshi, Priyank Garg, Rakesh Gowda, *Reducing Recovery Time in a Small Recursively Restartable System*, Proceedings of the International Conference on Dependable Systems and Networks,DSN-2002, Washington, D.C., June 2002.

[7] Andrew Cockroft, *Sun Performance and Tuning*, Talk, 2001.

[8] I. Foster, C. Kesselman, S. Tuecke, *The Anatomy of the Grid: Enabling Scalable Virtual Organizations*, International J. Supercomputer Applications, 2001.

[9] Richard Golding, Elizabeth Borowsky, *Fault-tolerant replication management in large-scale dis-*

tributed storage systems, Proceedings 18th IEEE Symposium on Reliable Distributed Systems, 1999.

[10] JOSEPH HELLERSTEIN, *A comparison of Techniques for Diagnosing Performance Problems in Information Systems: Case Study and Analytic Models*, IBM Research Division, 1994.

[11] JOSEPH Y. HALPERN, *Axiomatizing Causal Reasoning*, Journal of Artificial Intelligence Research 12, 2000.

[12] D. PATTERSON, *A new focus for a new century: availability and maintainability ¿¿ performance*, Keynote speech at USENIX FAST, January 2002, `http://www.cse.ucsc.edu/~darrell/tmp/FAST/FAST\%20Keynote\%20-\%20Patterson.pdf`

[13] ELLIE QUIGLEY, *Unix Shells by example*, Prentice Hall, 1999.

[14] JOHN F. SOWA, *Knowledge Representation: Logical, Philosophical, and Computational Foundations*, Brooks Cole Publishing Co, 2000.

[15] ZHOU SONGNIAN, *LSF: load sharing in large-scale heterogeneous distributed systems*, In Proceedings of the Workshop on Cluster Computing, December 1992

[16] VERITAS, *Veritas Cluster server*, release 1.3.0, Veritas Software Corporation, 2000.

[17] KENNETH F. WONG, MARK FRANKLIN, *Checkpointing in Distributed Computing Systems*, Journal of parallel and distributed computing, vol. 35, 67-75, 1996.

[18] JOHN WILKES, AND KIMBERLY KEETON, *Automating data dependability*, 10th ACM SIGOPS European Workshop, 2002.

[19] WOOLDRIDGE AND NICHOLAS R. JENNINGS, *Agent Theories, Architectures, and Languages: a Survey*, in Wooldridge and Jennings Eds., Intelligent Agents, Berlin: Springer-Verlag, 1-22, 1995.

[20] AGENTS `http://www.agentbuilder.com/AgentTools/commercial.php`

In: Parallel and Distributed Scientific and Engineering Computing ISBN 1-59033-956-8
Editor: Y. Pan and L.T. Yang, pp. 163-175

INCREASING THE THROUGHPUT OF AVAILABLE RESOURCES USING MANAGEMENT TOOLS BASED ON GRID TECHNOLOGIES*

PATRICIA GONZÁLEZ, MARÍA J. MARTÍN, JOSÉ C. MOURIÑO AND RAMÓN DOALLO†

Abstract. The aim of this work is to build a dynamic virtual high throughput platform made up of the heterogeneous individual machines available in a given instant of time in a work–center. In order to achieve this objective a low–intrusive monitor and scheduler system layered on top of an already existing Grid-based structure is proposed. The monitoring tool indicates available/unavailable nodes to be added/removed to/from the virtual platform. The scheduler manages the distribution of jobs among the available resources. The final goal is to increase the computational capacity of the work–center in a way that is both simple and costless for the users. Results obtained using the proposed tools to run two different applications, an image modeling application and a mpi parallel air quality model simulation, prove the feasibility and efficiency of our proposal.

Key words. Distributed resources management, Monitoring, Scheduling, Grid computing, Globus.

1. Introduction. Many applications require high computational power. However, HPC environments are often difficult to access. As current computers are now faster and cheaper, most scientists have resorted to making use of small workstations or personal computers to which they have exclusive access thus compensating, to a certain extent, their lack of computational power. The global result for an institution is that now, instead of using a large mainframe, most of its computing power is carried out in several locally managed personal computers; a distributed environment is created, where each individual possesses his own resources. However, even though the computational capacity of the institution as a whole may grow, the resources available to each individual user remain very limited. Besides, since many machines may remain idle for long periods of time, the distributed computing environment can be underused and inefficient.

The aim of this work is to increase the throughput of this distributed computing environment. This objective is achieved by building a virtual computing platform using the existing Grid technology but developing new low-intrusive monitoring and scheduling tools. Specifically, we have constructed a virtual high throughput platform (VHTP from now on) using the machines available in our work-center. In our laboratories, several personal computers, linked through a local network, are idle about 40% of the day (after working hours) and up to 70%-80% during weekends. The goal is to profit from the free cycles of the personal computers as it has been done at the SETI@home project [18].

The VHTP is a dynamic and heterogeneous system: the number and the characteristics of their nodes will change along the time as each machine belongs to different users and they have different time-tables. Besides, the different users have not free access to all the machines and their disks are configured in a different way. The development of applications and tools on this kind of system is complicated by the heterogeneity and dynamic behavior of the underlying resources. In the last few years, a number of interesting projects like Globus [8], Legion [12] and UNICORE [3] have developed the software infrastructure needed for simplifying the use of distributed resources. Specifically, Globus has become a standard de facto for Grid Computing. It supports all the necessary features required to build the virtual platform such as security issues, or transfer of data files between computing nodes with different file systems, among others. The Globus toolkit consists of a set of components that can be used either separately or in groups: Globus Resource Allocation Manager

*This work has been supported by the Galician Government (Project PGIDT01-PXI10501PR) and by the EU under project CrossGrid (Ref: IST-2001-32243).

†Computer Architecture Group, University of A Coruña, Spain.({pglez,mariam,doallo}@udc.es, jmourino@mail2.udc.es)

(GRAM), Grid Security Infrastructure (GSI), Metacomputing Directory Service (MDS), Global Access to Secondary Storage (GASS), Globus Toolkit I/O, Nexus and Heartbeat Monitor (HBM). Each component provides a basic service, such as authentication, resource allocation, information, communication, fault detection, and remote data access [8].

Globus Toolkit components are designed to support the incremental development of tools and applications. We develop low-intrusive monitoring and scheduling tools on top of Globus to extract the maximum possible benefit from the virtual platform. The monitoring tool indicates available and unavailable nodes to be added or removed respectively from the virtual platform. The scheduler system carries out the distribution of jobs among the available resources increasing the throughput by means of a good load balance.

The structure of this paper is as follows: Section 2 explains the mechanism we have implemented for resource monitoring and CPU scheduling. Section 3 shows load balance and efficiency obtained when running two different real applications on the virtual platform; overhead introduced by the proposed tools is also measured. Section 4 describes related work. We give concluding remarks and explain our future work in Section 5.

2. Monitoring and Scheduling Tools. The resource management system is divided into three different components, apart from those provided by Globus framework, shown in Figure 2.1. All of these components can be replicated as required, with the exception of the Node_Server:

- Input_Point: It is an interface that allows the user to introduce its program and all the execution parameters required. The Input_Point is in charge of the user authentication and the distribution of the job submitted by the user among the resources provided by the Node_Server. First, it should obtain single sign–on capability by using the Globus certificate and obtaining a Globus proxy credential. This is done using capabilities of the GSI (Grid Security Infrastructure) Globus component. Then, it communicates with the Node_Server, requesting the necessary resources. Finally, it calls the GRAM (Globus Resource Allocation Manager) service to run the job in the remote resource indicated by the Node_Server.
- Node_Server: It contains a database with information about all the nodes available for execution of jobs in a given instant of time, and the tasks already running on the `VHTP`. It is in charge of node management joining or leaving the `VHTP`, and assignment of nodes to users. It communicates with the Input_Point to provide resources and inform of resource changes.
- Nodes: Machines made available to the `VHTP` for the execution of jobs. Each node contains an activity daemon (AD), which notifies the Node_Server the availability of that node for processing remote tasks.

As it is shown in Figure 2.1, the Node_Server keeps updated two different information tables, one for the nodes and the other for the executions management. The information contained in the table of nodes consists of the name of the real node, the power computing weight (node computing capability relative to the fastest node in the platform), some useful flags to inform about enable/disable and active/inactive state, and a list with the identification number (tid) of every execution having an active process in the remote node. On the other hand, the table of executions stores the list of tasks corresponding to each execution, information on the status of each process running on remote nodes (active/sleep/finished), and information on those remote nodes, such as *task load index* parameter. The *task load index* allows the user to control his request for resources depending on the requirements of each task. This parameter will be explained in depth later on.

The primary concern of our project is to develop low–intrusive components and easy–to–use interfaces in order to make the use of the virtual platform more attractive for *donors* and users. All the components have been programmed in C to minimize their impact on nodes

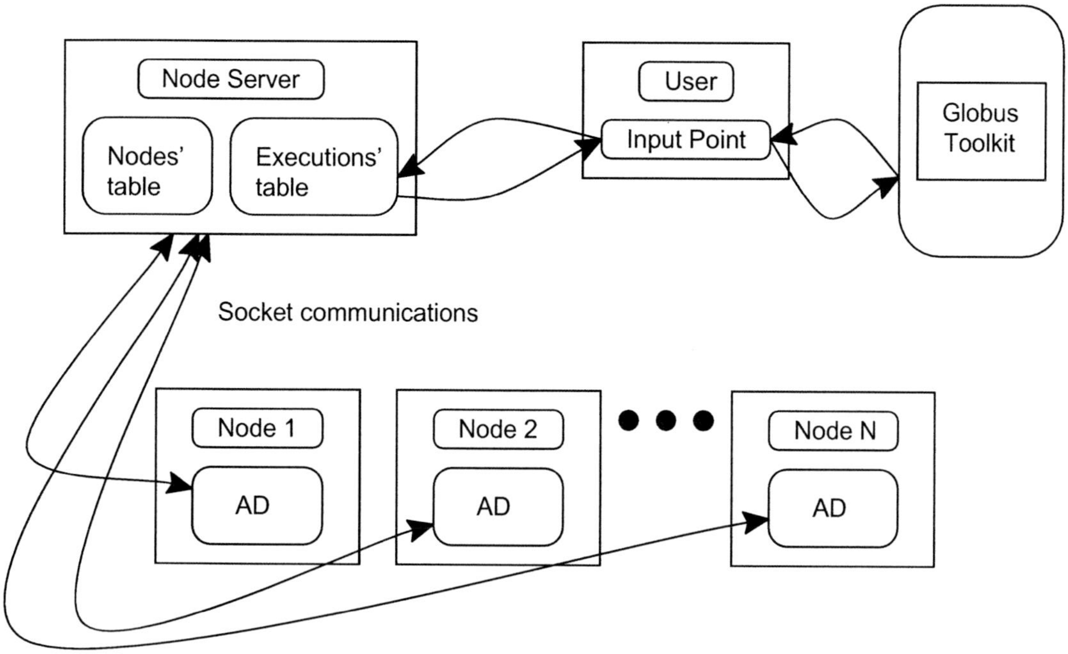

FIG. 2.1. *System architecture*

made available to the VHTP. The communications among all the components are carried out through a socket layer using a light custom designed protocol.

Our system is not prepared to perform checkpointing. This means that, when a task is migrated, it should be restarted again in the new placement. Unfortunately, the work done in the previous node is lost. Checkpointing provides fault tolerance, allowing an application to restart from the most recent snapshot in the event of a service interruption. However, there are several problems with checkpointing capability. On one hand, not all the applications can be re–linked with a checkpointing library. On the other hand, even if the job is able to checkpoint, it may not have the time or the resources it needs to successfully complete a checkpoint. Finally, even if the checkpoint can be performed, it frequently generates significant load on the network. For all these reasons, instead of the checkpoint feature, we advocate to make an effort to minimize the probability of process migration. This minimization is obtained through the application of a double strategy. First, not all the available machines are included as part of the Grid as explained in Section 2.1. Second, as will see in Section 2.2, we propose a CPU scheduler policy which attempts to minimize the occurrence of migrations.

2.1. Monitoring resources. The activity daemon is in charge of the activity monitoring. Its role is to decide either if a node is available to be added to the VHTP system or not. One important thing to bear in mind is that, unlike other recent experiences in coordinating parallel processing on distributed systems [20], we do not allow both local and remote jobs to run together in a node. The reason is that we want to ensure at all times that the resources taken up do not compromise the local usage of the machine. This is done in order to make the VHTP system more attractive to potential users and *resource donors*. Besides, we try to succeed in mapping tasks to available nodes where they can stay for a while avoiding frequent migration to other nodes.

In order to fulfill this double objective two parameters are used: the *timetable* and the *owner workload*. The *timetable* is defined by the owner of the node and avoids the daemon to communicate node availability for short periods of time causing constant tasks migrations. The activity daemon evaluate the *owner workload* to ensure that the local user will not be damaged, either because he has decided to work after his usual work-hours, or to leave a background execution on his machine.

Timetable. Local user of a potential node of the VHTP should define a variable number of intervals where the machine is donated to become a virtual node of the Grid. For instance, an user working in his laboratory during the morning, will donate the machine during evenings and nights. Other approaches try to *predict* future behavior of CPU resources [21]. Instead of using user information, these approaches use heuristics based on information about the behavior of CPU in previous days and recent availability. Selecting the node that has been available for the longest time should cause fewer migrations than a random selection. This solution release the donor from defining the timetable, however, the computational cost of the solution is larger and the prediction hit rate lower. We combine both solutions, by applying the timetable policy first, in order to decide if a machine can be a potential node in the virtual environment or not, and the historical behavior of the machine when the node is already part of the platform and the scheduler is allocating new tasks, as we will explain in Section 2.2.

Owner workload. The activity daemon checks the local CPU load subtracting the possible contribution from processes executed by users of the VHTP. If the CPU load does not exceed a given percentage (usually 20% of the total), then the node is added to the virtual group of the VHTP (by means of a message to the Node_Server). If the workload exceeds that percentage, and the node is already part of the virtual group, the activity daemon will ask the Node_Server to disable it.

The timetable parameter diminishes the probability of nodes leaving to attend owners (by making the owner to *predict* the unoccupied timetable of his machine). The CPU load information ensures a node will be removed from the Grid when the owner requires it. Both parameters are checked periodically, so that in case the status of the local machine changes, the corresponding message (enable/disable) is sent to the Node_Server. Then, the Node_Server takes the appropriate actions, it sends a process to that node, in case of an "enable" message, or it migrates the processes running in that node to any other available one, in case of a "disable" message. Moreover, the activity monitor informs periodically the Node_Server about the CPU usage and workload of every node in the virtual group. This information will be a key factor to implement our scheduling policy, as set out below.

This development results in a low–intrusive application for the donor and, however, it provides sufficient features for our purposes.

2.2. CPU scheduling. The Node_Server is in charge of resources scheduling. At the request of an Input_Point, the Node_Server decides where to map the new task so that a good load balance and a minimization of the migration on the whole system could be achieved.

The code for the Node_Server consists basically of an infinity loop that receives messages, and takes decisions based on the received message and its source. The Node_Server of the VHTP has to maintain open two communications channels at the same time, one for reception of messages (*enable/disable* from the distributed nodes, or *request/finished* from the users of the Grid), and the other to send messages to users reporting on their requests and migrations.

If a user submits more tasks than available nodes then more than one process is assigned to some nodes. Besides, in case that during the execution any available node becomes disabled, the Node_Server will perform a new scheduling among the new virtual group to migrate the tasks that were running previously in that node.

The heuristic employed follows a similar approach as the one proposed for the SVG project [11], however some of the features addressed now deal with the previous handicaps of the project. We avoid, as far as possible, putting restrictions on the heterogeneity of the nodes and the network used. Also, the users have not free access to all the machines, except by means of the VHTP. This can be achieved using the Globus capabilities.

One of the goals of the customized scheduler is that, in our case, the users are allowed to control their requests for resources, according to the requirements of each task i, by giving a *task load index* (t_i). The task load index is an estimate of the computational require ments of the task. The scheduler normalizes the task load index provided by the user in the following way:

$$q_i = \frac{t_i}{\max_{j=1}^{M}\{t_j\}} \qquad i = 1, \ldots, M$$

where M is the number of tasks in the bunch. If the user does not provide this index, the normalized task load index is set to the one by default for every task.

On the one hand, it is important to quantify the processing capability of every node to perform a suitable scheduling process that ensures a good load balance. Different nodes may have different computing capabilities. We make use of the *power weight* concept [22] to refer to a node's computing capability relative to the fastest node in the platform:

$$W_j(A) = \frac{S_j(A)}{\max_{k=1}^{N}\{S_k(A)\}} \qquad j = 1, \ldots, N$$

where N is the number of nodes and $S_j(A)$ is the speed of node j to solve an application of size A on a dedicated system.

In addition, we should also take into account the present workload at each node. The metric used is the *load average* (LA), defined as follows in terms of the *node load index* (Q^j):

$$LA_j = \frac{Q^j}{W_j(A)}, \quad Q^j = \sum_{k=1}^{T} q_k, \quad j = 1, \ldots, N$$

where T is the number of tasks running on processor node j, and q_k is the *normalized task load index.*

On the other hand, the task migration minimization objective (either due to node failure or due to unexpected local workload) is achieved taking into account the historical behavior of the nodes. During the distribution of new tasks a parameter called *On–Percentage* (OP) is used:

$$OP_j = \frac{T^j_{\text{available}}}{T^j_{\text{donated}}} \qquad j = 1, \ldots, N$$

where T_{donated} is the total time the node is donated to the VHTP, and $T_{\text{available}}$ is the real time the node is up and available as a virtual node.

Finally, the heuristic used by the scheduler consists in minimizing for each node of the Grid what we have called sum of *Heuristic Parameters* (HP):

$$HP_j = \frac{LA_j}{OP_j} \qquad j = 1, \ldots, N$$

It is easy to realize that the larger the load average and the lower the on–percentage are in a node, the larger the heuristic parameter will be. This means there is little probability for the selection of that node during task distribution.

3. Experimental Evaluation. In order to evaluate the behavior of the monitoring and scheduling tools proposed in this paper on the virtual platform we performed a distributed execution of two scientific applications, a coarse-grain parallel application and a message–passing (MPI) one. Note that most of other available management packages do not allow, or do not perform properly, inter-process communication; our approach allows the execution of MPI codes.

3.1. Applications. We have tested two real applications, already developed in our group, that can benefit from this new shared node policy: image modeling using Gibbs distributions [10] and the STEM–II Air Quality Model simulation [5].

The first application consists of a bunch of sequential independent tasks. Fixing in advance appropriate initial parameters for Gibbs functions may be difficult and it is usually found by trial and error; the more processors we use to run different Gibbs Samplers with different parameters from different start points, the faster we will achieve the convergence of the sampling algorithm for an image. The idea of this application is to explore in a parallel way the solution space.

The STEM–II is an Eulerian air quality model which simulates transport, chemical transformations, emissions and depositions processes in a integrated framework. This program has been parallelized previously to be run in a multicomputer using the message passing interface (MPI) [16]. It has been executed on the VHTP using MPICH-G2 [7], the Grid–enable version of MPICH. This application is computationally intensive and the parallelization gave rise to loosely coupled tasks with relatively small number of communications compared with the computational kernels. For instance, initially, using the original sequential code for a simulation of a complete day, 31 hours of execution time (more than one day) was needed. Using 8 processors we are able to reduce a day simulation to only 7 hours.

3.2. Virtual platform. Currently, our experimental virtual platform consists of 14 computing nodes. However, it may grow easily by joining other user PCs available in our department. The nodes have different processor and memory characteristics, although, all of them are based on the Intel architecture. The CPU speed range from 450 MHz to 1.9 GHz and the RAM memory from 128 MB to 1GB. With regard to the network characteristics, there are two different networks interconnecting the nodes, a Fast Ethernet network with a maximum bandwidth of 100 Mbps, and a Ethernet network with a bandwidth of 10 Mbps. Figure 3.1 shows the network configuration. Finally, the operating system running in these computers is Linux Debian, and MPICH is the message passing interface library available for parallel applications.

Table 3.1 shows the main characteristics of the different machines in the VHTP system. The *computer weight* (W) can be calculated executing on each node the applications to be run in the experimental platform. For each program and each machine the speed ratio is obtained, defined as:

$$SR_{ji} = \frac{\max_{i=1}^{P}(T_{ji})}{T_{ji}}$$

where j and i represent the application and the machine considered respectively, and P is the number of computer nodes. The computer weight for each machine is calculated using the geometric mean of the ratios obtained for each application:

$$W_i = \sqrt[n]{SR_{1i}SR_{2i}\dots SR_{ni}}$$

where n is the number of applications; in our case n is equal to 2. Finally, the power weight is rounded up to a multiple of 1/4. The SPEC benchmarks [13] can be used to obtain this

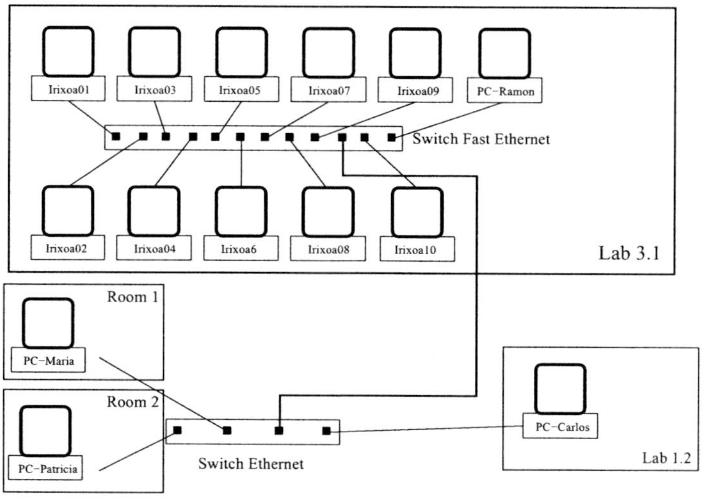

FIG. 3.1. *Network configuration of the experimental VHTP*

Machine	CPU (MHz)	Memory (MB)	W
irixoa01	800	128	1.25
irixoa02	800	128	1.25
irixoa03	800	128	1.25
irixoa04	800	128	1.25
irixoa05	800	128	1.25
irixoa06	800	128	1.25
irixoa07	800	128	1.25
irixoa08	800	128	1.25
irixoa09	800	128	1.25
irixoa10	800	128	1.25
pc-ramon	933	1024	1.50
pc-maria	600	512	1.25
pc-patricia	1900	512	1.75
pc-carlos	450	512	1.00

TABLE 3.1
Description of the "potential" nodes in the VHTP

computer weight if the applications to be executed on the VHTP system are not known in advance, or if they vary in the time.

3.3. Results. Good performance results are expected when the infrastructure is used to schedule large number of tasks, with the goal of putting unused processor cycles to work. If the tasks are loosely coupled or independent the number of communications among processor nodes will be small, and thus efficiency will be high. If the number of communications grows, the efficiency will decrease due to the network characteristics, its capacity limits or the fact that network resources can be oversubscribed.

We carry out different experiments in the VHTP. First experiment aims to show the good load balance obtained by the scheduler. In this experiment, we executed the Gibbs Sampler from different start points, which means different tasks running on the VHTP. Specifically we have tested the platform for 7, 16 and 23 start points. Figures 3.2, 3.3 and 3.4 show snapshots of the VHTP state in a given instant of time during the execution of Gibbs application for the three different situations. These diagrams show the CPU load for the available machines in the VHTP. Note that only 11 machines are available to launch remote

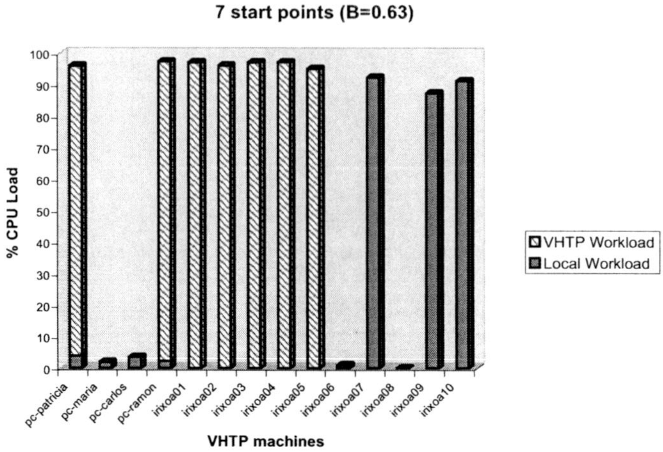

FIG. 3.2. *Gibbs Sampler with 7 start points.*

executions, the other three "potential" machines of the VHTP are unavailable because of their owners' local workload.

It can be seen from the Figures that when the local workload exceeds a maximum or the owner is working on its machine, the node becomes unavailable for the VHTP. In the experiment at hand this occurs in nodes irixoa07, irixoa09 and irixoa10.

The different tasks are distributed by the scheduler among all the available machines according to the heuristic algorithm, taking into account the load of each individual node in a give instant of time, the task load index, and the computational power (*power weight*) of the node. When the Gibbs Sampler application is launched using 7 start points, that is 7 different and independent tasks, the tasks are allocated in different machines (see Figure 3.2). When the application is launched using 16 start points, more than one task is allocated to the same node in some cases (see Figure 3.3), that is, some of the nodes execute one task while other ones execute two tasks. Finally, when 23 start points are launched, we can see that most of the nodes execute two tasks, but the most powerful nodes (pc-patricia and pc-ramon with W_j=1.75) execute three tasks, and the slowest node (pc-carlos with W_j=1.00) executes only one (see Figure 3.4).

The *balance rate* (B) obtained for each situation is also shown in Figures 3.2, 3.3 and 3.4. This parameter was measured as the rate between the maximum execution time and the minimum one on each of the VHTP machines, that is, $0 < B \leq 1$, corresponding $B = 1$ to a perfect load balance. One interesting fact can be extracted from the results of this experiment: the most tasks we provide to the scheduler the better it can balance the amount of work among the nodes. This is specially true if, as in our platform, the computational power is quite different from one node to another.

In a second experiment the response of the VHTP using an application involving message–passing among processors was analysed. The MPI STEM-II application was used for this experiment. The simulation on a fixed number of processors was executed, considering different load situations in the VHTP system. Initially, we evaluated a simulation of the STEM–II model using up to 8 processors. Results shown a performance degradation using more than 4 nodes due to the network overhead introduced by the message–passing operations. Thus, the diagrams in this section show results for the STEM–II simulation running on 4 processors. The different load situations were obtained launching at the same time the Gibbs application with different number of start points. Figures 3.5, 3.6 and 3.7

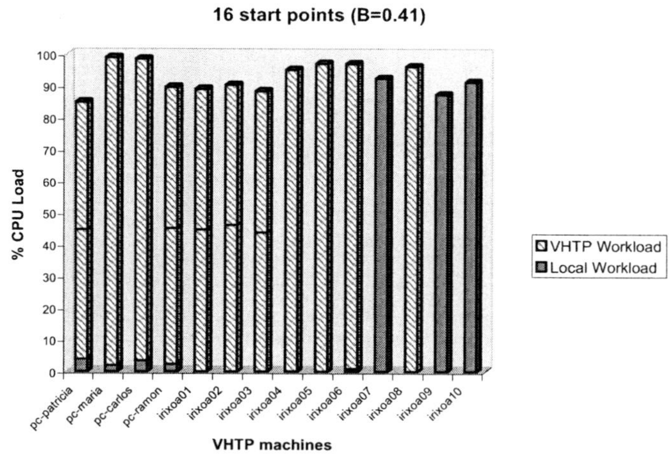

FIG. 3.3. *Gibbs Sampler with 16 start points.*

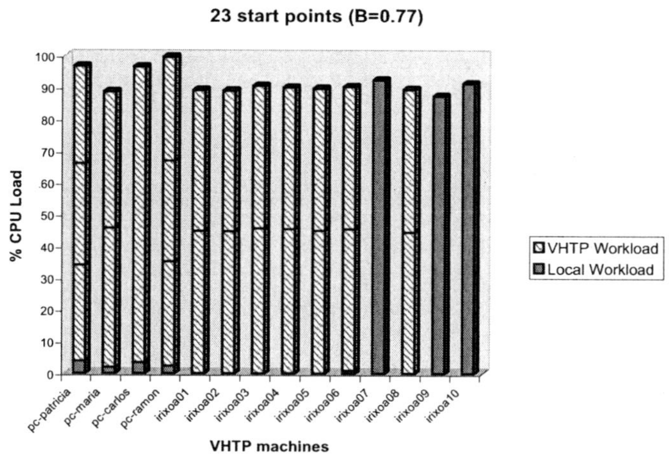

FIG. 3.4. *Gibbs Sampler with 23 start points.*

show load balance behavior among the available nodes for each of the situations considered: light (3 start points), medium (10 start points) and high (19 start points) workload.

Timing results obtained for both applications were also analysed. Time and speedups for the Gibbs and the STEM-II programs are shown in Tables 3.2 and 3.3 respectively. The total time shown in these tables represents the elapsed time from the point when the program is sent to the VHTP (from user local machine) until it completely finishes. For the Gibbs applications the speedup is calculated as:

$$Speedup = \frac{\max_{i=1}^{P}(T_i)}{\frac{\sum_{i=1}^{P} Ts_i}{P}} \tag{3.1}$$

where P is the number of available machines in the VHTP system, T_i is the execution time consumed by the i machine in processing all its assigned tasks, and Ts_i is the execution time consumed by machine i for processing all the considered start points. Note that the best speedup corresponds to the situation when a large number of tasks is launched. It is easy

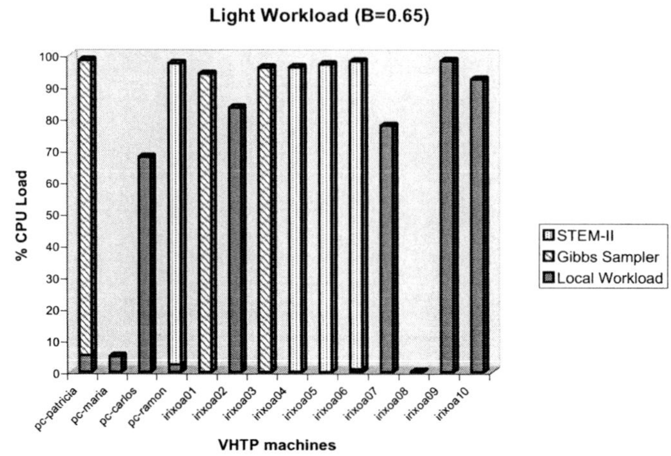

FIG. 3.5. *STEM–II simulation and Gibbs Sampler application. Light workload*

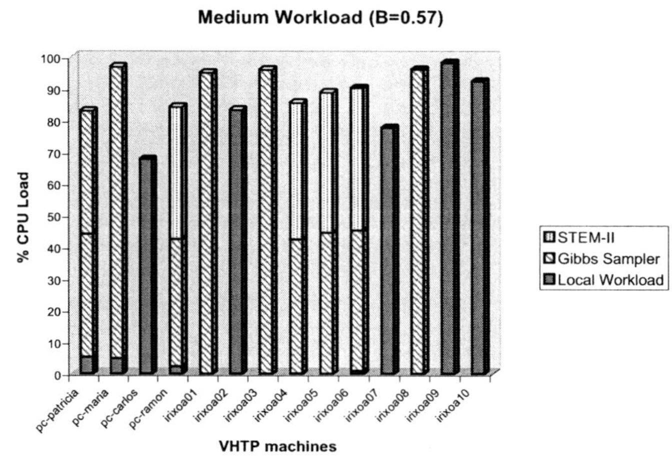

FIG. 3.6. *STEM–II simulation and Gibbs Sampler application. Medium workload*

to think that the optimal situation would be achieved when the number of nodes are large enough to attend all the requests. However, if the computational power is quite different among the available nodes, better performance may be achieved when more than one task is placed in the fast nodes. For instance, in the 23 start points situation three tasks were launched to node pc-patricia while only one were allocated to pc-carlos. However, node pc-patricia finishes three tasks in the same amount of time as pc-carlos finishes only one task, so the speedup achieved turns out to be higher for this situation.

Table 3.3 shows the results for the STEM-II program. The speedup is calculated using the equation:

$$Speedup = \frac{max_{j=1}^{4}(T_j)}{\frac{\sum_{i=1}^{P} Ts_i}{P}} \tag{3.2}$$

where now T_j is the execution time consumed by processor j to process its part of the

Exper.	Start Points	Total Time (s)	Speedup
Gibbs Sampler	7	12130	5.89
	16	29820	5.48
	23	35120	6.69

TABLE 3.2
Total time and speedup for the Gibbs Sampler algorithm

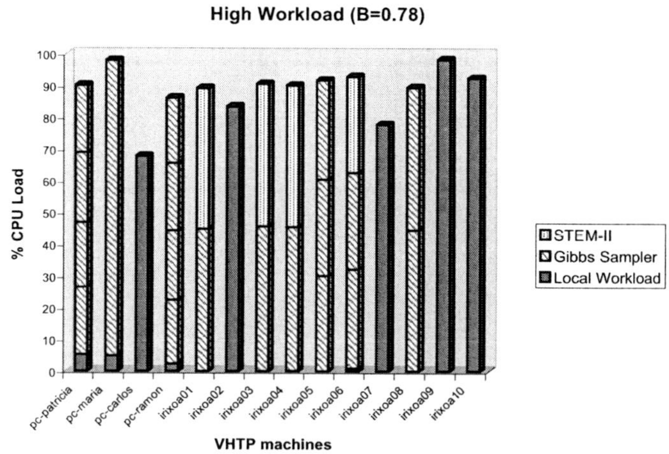

FIG. 3.7. *STEM–II simulation and Gibbs Sampler application. High workload*

parallel STEM-II code, and Ts_i is the execution time consumed by machine i to process the sequential STEM-II program. The results may vary depending on the network connecting the used nodes. These results were taken when all the nodes involved in the MPI execution were linked through a fast ethernet. However if a heterogeneous network (fast ethernet and 10 Mbps ethernet) is used the results will be slightly different. For instance, in the case of light workload situation the achieved speedup will be 1.89.

In this experiment the number of processed tasks is always the same and, therefore, the best result corresponds to the light workload situation. In fact, when the workload increases the speedup goes down. However, the aim is to efficiently exploit the computational resources of our virtual platform. This goal is better achieved by a high workload situation.

Finally, to point out the low–intrusive feature of the management tools, the average CPU cost of the activity daemons and the Node_Server were measured. Since the platform O.S. was Linux, the statistics given in the process information pseudo–filesystem were taken into account to check the percentage of CPU occupied by these tools. In the case of Node_Server, the CPU percentage used was only 0.00012% of the total load in the machine, measured in a period of 30 minutes. The activity daemons uses a percentage of only 0.00016% in each machine in the same time period.

4. Related Work. An important number of research and commercial packages for resource management and scheduling across clusters of machines have been proposed recently: LSF [15], Condor [21], Nimrod [2], PBS [17], Codine [6], LoadLeveler [19], etc. Unfortunately, these packages do not support all the necessary features required for our virtual platform (security issues or transfer of data files between systems with different file systems,

Exper.	Workload	Total Time (s)	Speedup
STEM–II (4 proc.)	Light	920	2.61
	Medium	1640	1.46
	High	2710	0.89

TABLE 3.3
Total time and speedup for the STEM–II program

among others).

Globus middleware provide a set of low-level protocols for resource access and secure connectivity. These facilities have been used for the implementation of several resource management packages for Grids, examples being Nimrod/G and Condor/G, the Grid-enable versions of Nimrod and Condor respectively.

Nimrod/G [1] is a very specific package tailored for running parametric applications over computational Grids, with particular emphasis on developing scheduling schemes based on the concept of computational economy.

Condor/G [9], as our proposal, is specifically aimed at utilizing free resources, but currently it does not suppport the management of MPI applications. This is the main difference between Condor/G and our approach, although it is not the only one. We have developed an *ad hoc* scheduler using an own heuristic (see Section 2.2). We pursue two main objectives with this work. First, we aim to increase the global throughput by means of a good load balance over component nodes. Second, we aim to minimize the process migration probability, instead of providing a checkpointing mechanism, because frequent job migrations can generate significant load on the network. Other differences can be found in the monitoring process, as pointed in Section 2.1. For instance, the strategy to *predict* the future availability of CPU resources is different in both architectures. Condor/G studies the availability in the same hour on the previous days to try to predict future behavior, while our approach simply asks the machine owner to predict his/her work–timetable (see Section 2.1). This latest solution is costless for the activity daemon, and the prediction is more accurate. Finally, the objective of our proposal unlike Condor is to develop low-intrusive tools. The overhead introduced by our approach is far lesser than the overhead introduce by Condor/G, see for instance [4, 14].

5. Conclusions and Future Work. This paper describes the architecture of a High Performance Virtual Platform made up of the idle resources available in a given instant of time in our labs, and discusses the implementation of low–intrusive monitoring and scheduling tools designed for CPU management in such a platform. We have employed a heuristic method, using quantified and deterministic heterogeneous system information for the scheduling algorithm. Our objective is to obtain a good load balance and to minimize the occurrence of migration. Both, sequential and parallel MPI applications can be executed on our system.

The main idea is that the job scheduling is not an user matter, but a system matter. The system should decide how to distribute the jobs among the idle nodes on the Grid, taking into account parameters like workload on each node.

The results obtained running two different applications, a sequential image processing application and a parallel air quality model simulation, were satisfactory. Monitoring and scheduling tools perform efficiently the task distribution among idle nodes and achieve good workload balance at a very low cost. Results prove that Grid technology is a powerful tool to derive profit from available computational distributed resources.

We have focused our work in management of CPU resources, mainly because of the characteristic of our applications, where communications between processors are not a critical factor. However, management of network resources is also a key task in batch scheduling systems, specially in platforms with different network features as in our virtual platform. Thus, network management will be worthwhile future work.

REFERENCES

[1] D. Abramson, J. Giddy, and L. Kotler, *High performance parametric modeling with Nimrod/G: Killer application for the global Grid?*, in Proceedings of the 14th International Conference on Parallel and Distributed Processing Symposium (IPDPS-00), pp. 520–528. IEEE Press., May 2000.

[2] D. Abramson, R. Sosic, J. Giddy, and B. Hall, *Nimrod: A tool for performing parameterised simulations using distributed workstations*, in Proceedings of the 4th IEEE Symposium on High Performance Distributed Computing, August 1995.

[3] J. Almond and D. Snelling, *UNICORE: uniform access to supercomputing as an element of electronic commerce*, in Future Generation Computer Systems, 15(5–6):539–548, Oct. 1999.

[4] J. Basney, *Network and CPU co-allocation in high throughput computing enviroments*, PhD thesis, University of Wisconsin-Madison, 2001.

[5] G. Carmichael, L. Peters, and R. Saylor, *The STEM-II regional scale acid deposition and photochemical oxidant model - I. An overview of model development and applications*, in Atmospheric Environment, 25A(10):2077–2090, 1991.

[6] *Codine*, in http://www.hu-berlin.de/rz/compsv/codine.html.

[7] I. Foster and N. T. Karonis, *A Grid-Enabled MPI: Message passing in heterogeneous distributed computing systems*, in Proceedings of the 1998 ACM/IEEE SC98 Conference. ACM Press and IEEE Computer Society Press, 1998.

[8] I. Foster and C. Kesselman, *Globus: A metacomputing infrastructure toolkit*, in The International Journal of Supercomputer Applications and High Performance Computing, 11(2):115–128, 1997.

[9] J. Frey, T. Tannenbaum, I. Foster, M. Livny, and S. Tuecke, *Condor-G: A computation management agent for multi-institutional Grids*, in Journal of Cluster Computing, 5:237–246, 2002.

[10] S. Geman and D. Geman, *Stochastic relaxation, Gibbs distributions, and the Bayesian restoration of images*, in IEEE Transactions on Pattern Analysis and Machine Intelligence, 6(6):721–741, 1984.

[11] P. González, J. R. Luaces, J. A. Becerra, R. J. Duro, and I. López, *Managing distributed resources in the SVG project*, in Proc. of the Euromicro PDP'02, pp. 139–146, 2002.

[12] A. S. Grimshaw, W. A. Wulf, and the Legion team, *The Legion Vision of a Worldwide Virtual Computer*, in Communications of the ACM, 40(1):39–45, Jan. 1997.

[13] J. L. Henning, *SPEC CPU2000: Measuring CPU performance in the new millennium*, Computer, 33(7):28–35, July 2000.

[14] M. Litzkow, T. Tannenbaum, J. Basney, and M. Livny, *Checkpoint and migration of UNIX processes in the condor distributed processing system*, Technical Report CS-TR-1997-1346, University of Wisconsin, Madison, April 1997.

[15] *Load Sharing Facility*, in http://www.platform.com.

[16] J. Mouriño, M. Martín, R. Doallo, D. Singh, F. Rivera, and J. Bruguera, *The STEM-II Air Quality Model on a distributed memory system*, in Proceedings of the 2001 ICPP Workshops, pp. 85–92, sept. 2001.

[17] *Portable Batch System*, in http://www.openpbs.org/.

[18] *SETI@home*, in http://www.setiathome.ssl.berkeley.edu.

[19] J. Skovira, W. Chan, H. Zhou, and D. Lifka, *The EASY — LoadLeveler API project*, in Lecture Notes in Computer Science, 1162:41–47, 1996.

[20] F. Solsona, F. Giné, F. Molina, P. Hernández, and E. Luque, *Implementing and analysing an effective explicit coscheduling algorithm on a NOW*, in Lecture Notes in Computer Science, 1981:75–88, 2001.

[21] T. Tannenbaum and M. Litzkow, *The Condor distributed processing system*, in Dr. Dobb's Journal, 20(2):40–48, February 1995.

[22] X. Zhang and Y. Yan, *Modeling and characterizing parallel computing performance on heterogeneous networks of workstations*, in Proceedings of the Seventh IEEE Symposium on Parallel and Distributed Processing, pp. 25–34, 1995.

In: Parallel and Distributed Scientific and Engineering Computing ISBN 1-59033-956-8
Editor: Y. Pan and L.T. Yang, pp. 177-190

A GRID-BASED RPC SYSTEM FOR MEDICAL IMAGING

M. BERTERO* , P. BONETTO*, L. CARRACCIUOLO†, L. D'AMORE‡, A. R. FORMICONI§, M. R. GUARRACINO† , G. LACCETTI‡ , A. MURLI‡,† , AND G. OLIVA†

Abstract. In the last decades, diagnosing medical images has heavily relied on digital techniques. As a consequence, huge amounts of data produced by modern instruments need to be processed, organized, and visualized in a suitable response time. Many efforts have been devoted to the development of digital systems which archive and distribute image information across a hospital and provide web access to avoid the expensive deployment of a large number of such systems. However, this approach does not solve problems related to the increasing demand of high performance computing and storage facilities, which cannot be placed within a hospital.

In this work we describe MedIGrid, an application that enables nuclear doctors to transparently use high performance computers and storage systems for the PET/SPECT (Positron Emission Tomography/Single Photon Emission Computed Tomography) image processing, management, visualization and analysis. MedIGrid is the result of the joint efforts of a group of researchers committed to the development of a distributed application to test and deploy new reconstruction methods in clinical environments. The outcomes of this work include a set of platform independent software tools to read medical images, control the execution of computing intensive tomographic algorithms, and explore the reconstructed tomographic volumes.

In the following we describe how the collaboration among different research groups has resulted in the integration into a single framework of several components that span from medical devices, to hardware computing systems and software modules. The results of our work will be presented and discussed.

Key words. Distributed computing, Medical imaging, Grid-aware application, Middleware tools, Image processing and visualization.

1. Introduction. In the last decades, new imaging systems, such as computer tomography, ultrasound, digital radiography, magnetic resonance imaging, and tomographic radioisotope imaging, have revolutionized medical diagnosing providing the clinician with new information about the interior of human body that had never before been available.

Many efforts have been devoted to the development and deployment of so-called electronic Picture Archiving and Communications Systems (PACS) which archive and distribute any kind of information related to the huge amount of data acquired by medical instruments - such as quantitative results or interpretations of the specialist - across the hospitals [7, 12]. However, several difficulties are associated with the actual deployment of such systems. PACS workstations are expensive, run proprietary software, and have limited computing and storage capabilities. Moreover, a large number of workstations is usually needed to satisfy the requirements of the institution.

The use of proprietary software may have a strong influence on diagnosis. Indeed, since the algorithms involved in image reconstruction are kept secret by the manufacturer of the medical acquisition device, the results of the same analysis may vary among different instruments. Furthermore, it is not possible to exchange data acquired by different instruments since their format is also proprietary. Such limits slow down the impact of algorithms advances on software products, since only the producer of the equipment decides which changes and optimization the next software release will address.

Another limit of PACS is related to the limited computing power of the control workstation, that restricts the number of usable reconstruction techniques to the ones with the lowest computation complexity. Similarly, to cope with the usually limited storage capabilities, once 2D data are stacked up into 3D images they are deleted: the entire information in the volume data set is lost forever, barring its future use.

*Department of Computer and Information Science, University of Genoa, Italy
†Institute for High Performance Computing and Networking - CNR, Naples, Italy
‡Department of Mathematics and Applications, University of Naples Federico II, Italy
§Department of Clinical Phisiopatology, University of Florence, Italy

PACS workstations cannot be easily deployed in several locations because they are fairly expensive and they require dedicated hardware for image display. Nuclear medicine workstations are typically too complex; they often require considerable software setup and maintenance and they only partially solve the outlined problems.

Delocalization of diagnostic acquisition instruments from processing power and storage facilities seems a viable way to overcome such difficulties. The maintenance and management of high performance computing and storage equipment needs skills that are not usually found in hospitals and specially equipped computing centers. On the other hand, end-users of such applications are not distributed systems experts; this has led to hide as much as possible the difficulties related to the use of high performance geographically distributed platforms and needed to manage, catalogue and process this huge amounts of data.

Here we focus on three-dimensional *Single Photon Emission Computed Tomography* (SPECT), which is a popular acquisition technique in most nuclear medicine departments, due to its fairly low costs compared to other approaches. The object of SPECT is to reconstruct an unknown radioactivity distribution inside the body from projection data consisting of the number of photons collected on a (usually planar) collimated detector placed at various angles around the body. 3D SPECT is a generalization of conventional 2D tomography allowing the reconstruction of volumes from a set of 2D conic projections from different angles of view. Actually, SPECT is an inherently 3D imaging modality, because the photons collected in a point of the planar detector come from a diverging cone through the unknown 3D radioactivity source. In this work we are concerned with a specific SPECT device, a CERASPECT system, which is used for brain imaging. Projections data are affected by the attenuation of the photons through the body, therefore an accurate projection matrix must take into account both collimator blur and attenuation. In this case, a straightforward inversion of the projection operator is not possible. The classical approach to the tomographic image reconstruction problem is the *filtered back projection method* (FBP) [23], which is based on direct Fourier inversion. While FBP is relatively fast, it suffers from a number of limitations. It assumes that measurements are samples of Radon Transform and thus ignores the effects of blurring and attenuation; hence iterative algebraic methods must be used.

As basic acquisition model we consider the so called Blurred Radon Transform [6] in which the kernel is usually modelled with sufficient accuracy by a Gaussian–shaped PSF. This model introduces additional difficulties due to the fact that the parameters that characterize the bell-shaped PSF have to be tuned according to the experimental conditions, and depend on the geometric system response [15].

In the last ten years the world wide web has been accepted by the scientific community as an efficient and reliable tool to distribute and access services with existing or specifically developed protocols. In the meantime, such services and protocols aren't any longer capable of providing the coordination and sharing capabilities needed by the development of the newest applications that use distributed resources. In this context the use of technologies for computational grids [18] can solve problems related to authentication, discovery, dynamic allocation and all other aspects connected to remote resources access. Such technologies provide the software infrastructure for scientific computing.

In this work we describe MedIGrid, a grid collaborative environment useful to nuclear doctors, that enables the transparent use of geographically distributed computing and storage resources. By taking advantage of the grid middleware software, MedIGrid enables new ways for doctors to conduct diagnosis, obtaining coordinated resource sharing and problem solving in a dynamic, multi-institutional virtual organization [19].

MedIGrid provides the following benefits:

- it promotes the creation of a virtual organization sharing resources on a computational grid;

- it enables transparent use of remote resources;
- it promotes the development of open source scientific software, in an easy and fast way;
- it makes the distribution and installation of software on remote resources an easy task;
- it supports the distant collaboration between doctors.

This work is organized as follows: Section 2 motivates the MedIGrid structure explaining the challenges faced along the implementation of the application; Section 3 details the software architecture of the system explaining the interaction among the various components; Section 4 describes the advantages that derive from the solution of those problems; Section 5 overviews the state of the art and describes related research projects and products, highlighting the differences with MedIGrid; Section 6 presents future possible development and, finally, in Section 7 conclusions are drawn.

2. MedIGrid Overview. In this section we describe MedIGrid by a simple case study and elucidate how we solved the problem of delocalizing the acquisition equipment from the computing and storage elements.

Let's consider the case of a radiologist who has to edit an analysis in order to complete a medical report that will be passed over to the nuclear doctor: he needs to access data sets produced by medical instruments and decide the kind of reconstruction needed; he may also want to consult a distant colleague to setup the reconstruction and share the results with him. Probably, in a near future he will need to access that report and the associated data again to evaluate the evolution of the patient's state during that time.

The situation is described in Figure 2.1: when a patient is under analysis, scanned data are saved on a storage server. At the end of this phase, the doctor visualizes the raw data and decides, with the help of a graphical user interface (GUI), the reconstruction method to use along with its related parameters such as the boundaries of the reconstruction volume. This information is stored in a metadata file. He can now authenticate himself within MedIGrid. Authentication is based on an encrypted certificate stored on the machine from which he is accessing the data. With a single password, the certificate is decrypted and used to create a proxy credential with limited time validity. Such credential will be used for all subsequent operations involved in the process. MedIGrid will now transfer the raw data and the file containing the metadata, from the storage server to the high performance computing system. This file transfer uses SSL encryption to guarantee data privacy. Once the data are copied, a checksum is performed to ensure no corruption occurred. At this point, a job is queued to the local scheduler: its purpose is to execute the reconstruction, transfer the data back to the storage server, and return to the doctor whether the job completed successfully or not; in the latter case the state of the computation is also reported, whereas in the first case, the user can access the reconstructed data and analyze its content with the help of a GUI.

3. Software Architecture. In this section we describe in detail both middleware and application software used in the implementation of MedIGrid. More specifically, both the various components and their interaction will be described.

3.1. Globus. The Globus Toolkit [16] has been chosen as the middleware software upon which to build the application. In particular, we used the following services:

- GASS (Globus Access to Secondary Storage System) [5] allows the application to access data stored on any remote filesystem by specifying the position and the transfer protocol with the URL syntax `prot://hostname:port/path`.
- GSI (Grid Security Infrastructure) [8] allows secure authentication and communication over an open network, mutual authentication across organizations bounds and single sign-on authentication with X.509 certificates.

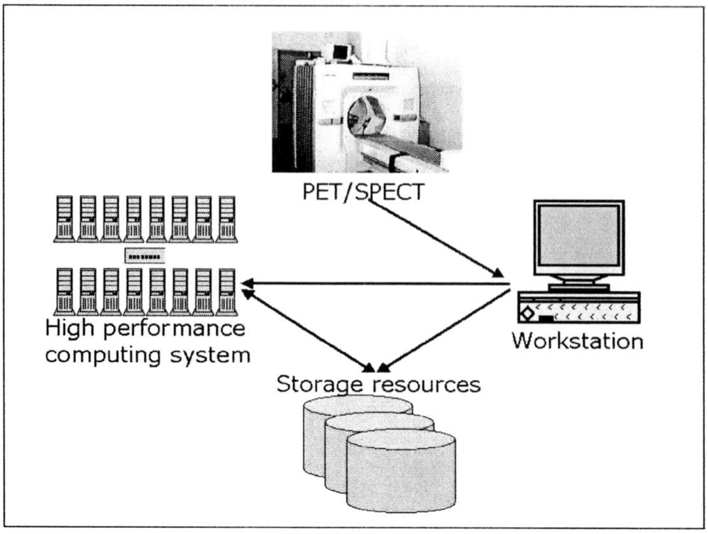

FIG. 2.1. *MedIGrid Application*

- GRAM (Globus Resource Allocation Manager) [17] manages the requests for resources for remote application execution, allocates the required resources, and monitors the jobs during their execution.

3.2. Repository. The repository is the system that manages both raw data as acquired by the medical equipments and the data that was already processed. It is implemented integrating the Globus services for the authentication and the data transfer with MedIMan.

3.3. MedIMan. The application manager is composed of a set of procedures developed at the ICAR-CNR section of Naples, that coordinates all grid operations: authentication, I/O servers activations, file transfers, data consistency checks, reconstruction jobs submissions. The first step for the user is authentication. Each user owns a X.509 certificate signed by a Certification Authority trusted by all the organizations involved in the virtual organization. Such certificate is crypted and stored in a directory to which the user has access. Using Globus line command `globus-proxy-init` the user provides a password to decrypt the certificate and to generate a proxy with a limited time validity. That proxy will be used for all subsequent authentications on the machines used by the application. The advantage of using proxies is that the certificate is never transmitted through the network; moreover, the proxy has a time validity in the order of hours, while the certificate is usually valid for months: in case a malicious user gains access to the proxy, he will not be able to generate new credentials from that proxy, which means that he won't gain access to new resources. At this point, the doctor uses the GridReconstruction graphical user interface, described hereafter, to provide the reconstruction parameters, which will be stored in a metadata file, and to transparently start the file transfer service and the job submission. Third party file transfer functionality is provided by Globus by means of its GASS module. The application invokes a GASS server activation on both the repository and the supercomputer where the data reconstruction will take place. The data transfer uses an https protocol, which provides SSL tunneling of the data. GASS provides a tool for secure data transfer, but no mechanism for error detection. It has been necessary to implement a simple checksum mechanism to detect transmission errors and to restart data transfer when needed. The metadata and raw data file are transferred together with a script that will take care of clean up, error detection, reconstruction program execution and transmission of reconstructed data back to the repository. Once the file transfer has been completed with success, a job is submitted by the Globus GRAM module, which performs all authentication steps needed on the supercomputer and queues the script execution request to the local queue. When reconstruction is terminated with success, the script activates the file transfer servers again, in order to have the data transmitted back. Once again error check is performed and the script informs the doctor that his job has been successfully completed. In case of error the script reports to the user the state of computation and the eventual partial reconstruction obtained in order to let him resubmit the task.

3.4. MedITomo. The basic mathematical description of SPECT imaging relates the observed data u_0 with the original image u through a linear model [6]:

$$u_0(s,\phi,z) = \int\int\int u(\mathbf{x},z')\kappa(s-\mathbf{x}\cdot\theta, \mathbf{x}\cdot\theta^{\perp}, z-z')\mathrm{d}\mathbf{x}\mathrm{d}z' \tag{3.1}$$

where $u_0(s,\phi,z)$ is the distribution of the tracer concentration relative to projection angle ϕ, and $\mathbf{x} = \{x, y\}$ are the plane coordinates where the 2D projections of the body of the patient is represented by a disk centered at the origin; z-axis is the axis of rotation of the detectors; $\theta = \{\cos\phi, \sin\phi\}$, ϕ being the projection angle of the detector plane with respect to a fixed position, s is the radial distance and $\theta^{\perp} = \{-\sin\phi, \cos\phi\}$. The kernel κ models the physical structure of the measurement device which introduces an unavoidable blurring effect due to the fact that the photons pass through the holes of a collimator. This model is called the Blurred Radon Transform [6], where the integration kernel κ, which is usually called *Point Spread Function (PSF)*, differs from the Radon's one for several reasons: the PSF is no longer an impulse function, it is defined on the projection plane as a function of two variables, s and z, and it depends on the source-detector distance $t = \mathbf{x}\cdot\theta^{\perp}$. In particular, a realistic model is

$$\kappa(s,t,z) = \kappa_0(s,t)\kappa_0(z,t), \quad \text{with} \quad \kappa_0(z,t) = \frac{1}{\sigma(t)\sqrt{2\pi}}\exp\left[-\frac{z^2}{2\sigma^2(t)}\right]$$

and

$$\sigma = \sigma_{\min} - \frac{\sigma_{\max}-\sigma_{\min}}{2r}(t-r), \quad \text{with} \quad t\in[-r,r]$$

$r, \sigma_{\min}, \sigma_{\max}$ being given constants. Typical values for these parameters are $\sigma_{\min} = 3, \sigma_{\max} = 8, r = 192, R = 95$.

In operator form the above mathematical model of 3D SPECT imaging can be stated as follows:

$$u_0 = \mathcal{K}u + \eta \tag{3.2}$$

where η models Poisson noise, $\mathcal{K}$ is a linear operator, the unknown vector u represents the 3D image, and u_0 is the acquired data, the so-called *3D sinogram.* From this formulation, it is evident that SPECT imaging belongs to the class of linear inverse and ill posed problems. Indeed, due to the compactness of the operator $\mathcal{K}$ the computation of $\mathcal{K}^{-1}$ affects noise amplification with the risk of obtaining un-useful solutions. This kind of problems has been widely investigated. The regularization approach produces an estimate, u^{λ} of u as the solution of

$$u^{\lambda} = \mathrm{argmin}_u\{||\mathcal{K}u - u_0|| + \lambda\mathcal{R}(u)\} \tag{3.3}$$

where $\mathcal{R}(u)$ is the regularization functional and λ is a parameter controlling the regularization term relative to the residual norm. The functional $\mathcal{R}(u)$ is a measure of the "regularity" of the solution, in the sense that functions with random oscillations are more penalized than smooth functions with a regular behavior.

MedITomo, developed at the Dept. of Fisiopatologia Clinica, University of Florence, is the software library of computational routines that apply to the reconstruction of SPECT images from projection data. The reconstruction algorithms in the package are based on the Conjugate Gradient (CG) and on the Ordered Subset Expectation Maximization (OSEM) methods. The routines are written in FORTRAN and in ANSI C. The parallel software [1], developed at the Department of Mathematics and Applications, University of Naples Federico II, in collaboration with ICAR-CNR section of Naples, is based on the standard message passing interface, MPI.

In the following we give an overview of the software library. It is organized in packages: beside the computational routines, each package contains the header file for setting the input parameters, the input data file and the output data file. The reconstruction algorithms are supplied as the following subroutines:

- `2d+1tomo_fan_cg` CG based reconstruction algorithm for a fan-beam geometry of the collimator.
- `2d+1_fan_tv+cg` CG based reconstruction algorithm for a fan-beam geometry of the collimator. The reconstruction technique has been regularized by using a TV regularization functional.
- `2d+1tomo_fan_emosn` EM based reconstruction algorithm for a fan-beam geometry of the collimator.
- `3dtomo_par_cg` CG based reconstruction algorithm for a parallel geometry of the collimator. The underlying mathematical model is the so called fully 3D.
- `3dtomo_fan_cg` CG based 3D reconstruction algorithm for a fan beam geometry of the collimator.
- `3dtomo_fan_cg+tv` CG based 3D reconstruction algorithm for a fan beam geometry of the collimator. The reconstruction algorithm has been regularized by using the TV regularization functional.
- `3dtomo_fan_emosn+tv` EMOS based 3D reconstruction algorithm for a fan beam geometry of the collimator. The reconstruction algorithm has been regularized by using the TV regularization functional [2, 10].

The prefix 3d or 2d+1 of each Package means that the underling mathematical model is the fully 3D or the "approximation 2D+1" [6].

3.5. A set of plugins for ImageJ. According to the ImageJ philosophy we have organized our tools in terms of Java, platform independent plugins, that can be freely downloaded either from the ImageJ plugin page (http://rsb.info.nih.gov/ ij/plugins) or from DISI site (http://www.disi.unige.it/person/BerteroM/MedNuc). The ensemble of tools leads the user through the main operations that can be applied to medical data: import and read, control the execution of tomographic reconstruction algorithms, explore, analyze and display the reconstructed volumes. Most of our plugins were originally designed for data acquired by tomographic devices, with particular reference to the PET / SPECT scanners located at the S.Martino Hospital at Genoa and at the Careggi Hospital at Florence [6, 3, 15]. However, this does not prohibit to also use some of them on data collected by other sources or on any kind of 3D images. The discussion is organized in three sections, according to the different "nature" of the various tools: reconstruction, visualization and utilities plugins.

3.5.1. Reconstruction plugins. These plugins are basically graphical interfaces from which two external procedures can be started to reconstruct a tomographic set of scintigraphic data without leaving ImageJ. The external procedures are the result of a past project on tomographic reconstruction [6, 3, 15, 14]; they are written in Fortran and C and, hence, although they can be (locally or remotely) called from any computational node, they

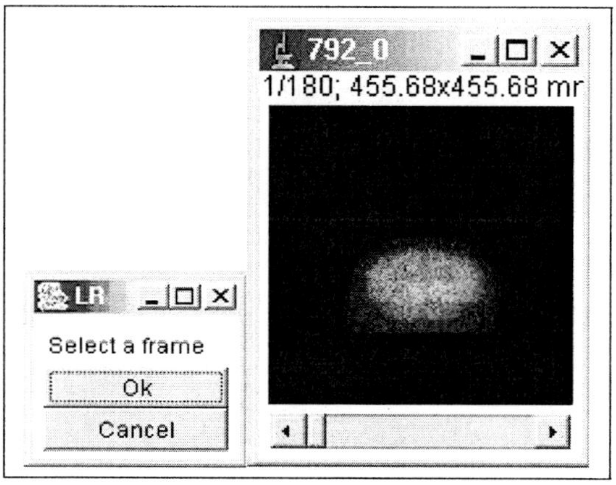

FIG. 3.1. *The stack of lateral projections on which the user can select a specific projection by moving the slide bar at the bottom of the window on the left.*

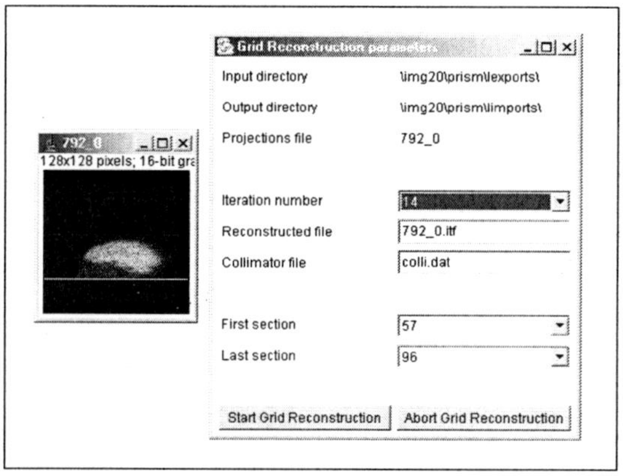

FIG. 3.2. *LocalReconstruction. Selection of the planes to reconstruct (left) and setting of the reconstruction paramenters (right).*

are strictly connected to the specific platform they were designed for. One can easily guess that two plugins were written, one for a local and another for a remote execution of the reconstruction procedures respectively. The common properties of both plugins include i) the visualization of a stack of lateral projections related to the study to be reconstructed (Figure 3.1, left) ii) the possibility to select a specific projection (Figure 3.1, right) on which the user can subsequently choose the lower and upper limits of the data subset to reconstruct (Figure 3.2, left), thus avoiding the time consuming reconstruction of the entire volume, and iii) a dialog through which the user can set all required parameters (Figure 3.2 right, for the specific case the reconstruction is performed locally).

LocalReconstruction locally starts an iterative, reconstruction procedure, based on the OSEM algorithm (Ordered Subset Expectation Maximization) and on an accurate mathematical model of the acquisition device and of the blurring effects due to the collimators [6]. The execution can take place either on the very same machine from which it was started, or on a machine on the local network. Figure 3.2, on the right, shows the ImageJ plugin dialog box through which the user can specify the necessary parameters to run the reconstruction.

GridReconstruction remotely calls an iterative, Least Square reconstruction procedure, based on the CG (Conjugate Gradient) and written in Fortran [14]. The execution takes place on a remote machine, for which the reconstruction procedure was appropriately

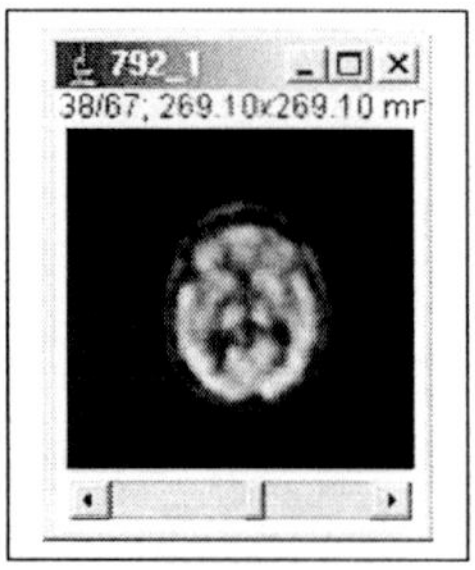

FIG. 3.3. *A brain volume as shown from within ImageJ. The user can move through the individual transaxial slices by sliding the bar at the bottom of the window.*

compiled. The ImageJ plugin dialog box is very similar to the one shown on the right of Figure 3.2. In order to take full advantage of the benefits offered by remote executability, we have written a parallel implementation of the reconstruction procedures [25] in order to make it possible to run them on a high performance class supercomputer, which in our case is a Beowulf.

3.5.2. Visualization plugins. These tools are designed to display, analyze and represent 3D image volumes in different ways. The first two items we discuss can be used on a rather wide range of image types: the examples included below are referred to the brain volume shown in Figure 3.3. The latter two plugins were designed for cardiological and renal studies respectively: they have a very special significance in the context of our project since they were specifically requested to us by a group of physicians in order to integrate some other software they were already using in their daily practice, and they thus represent the first newborns resulting from a direct interaction between our group and members of the medical environment.

MIP/TIP computes a sequence of lateral projections of a volume, usually consisting of transaxial planes, according to the Maximum Intensity Projection (MIP) method: this scheme requires the volume to be rotated in a stepwise way, with the lateral projections being added together and then normalized at each step [27]. Each lateral component can also be weight corrected according to its distance from the front plane (see the depth correction checkbox, Figure 3.4, left). Alternatively, one can consider the Total Intensity Projection rather than the Maximum one (see the checkbox in the dialog shown in Figure 3.4 on the left). The resulting projections are inserted into a new stack to which a pseudo color map is applied, and that can be regularly displayed from within the main ImageJ kernel (Figure 3.4, right). The resulting stacks can also be exported as AVI movies in which each view is treated as a frame. The combined use of MIP and TIP helps at a visual, qualitative inspection of the patient's data.

OrtView offers an alternative way to display a 3D image: given a volume and the coordinates of a point within that volume, the three orthogonal planes - transaxial, coronal and sagittal - passing through that very point are shown. The user can interact with the image by clicking on a desired location on one of the three panels and thus changing the focus spot and updating the views. Further processing can be applied to the volume by selecting one of several choices from the pull down menus. Such choices include axial smoothing, interpolation, rotation, contrast correction and displaying of the three active cuts combined together into a single image. A snapshot of the plugin is shown in Figure 3.5.

CardProfile computes and displays the maximum values along the rays passing through a point of a (usually cardiological) volume selected by the user. On the basis of the results it computes and plots some statistical values.

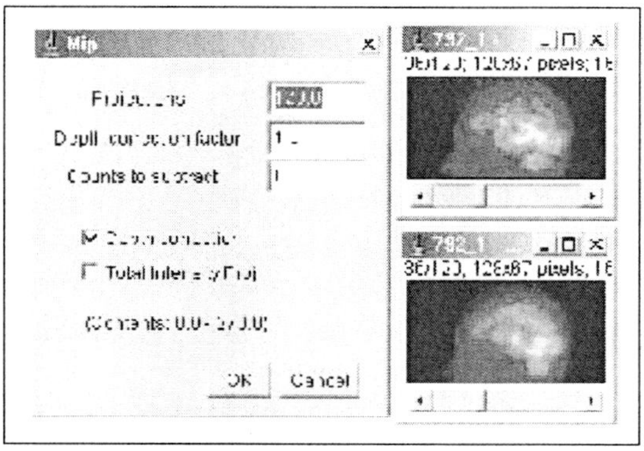

FIG. 3.4. *MIP/TIP. The dialog box (left), a maximum (top right) and a total (bottom right) intensity projection for the example volume shown in Figure 3.3.*

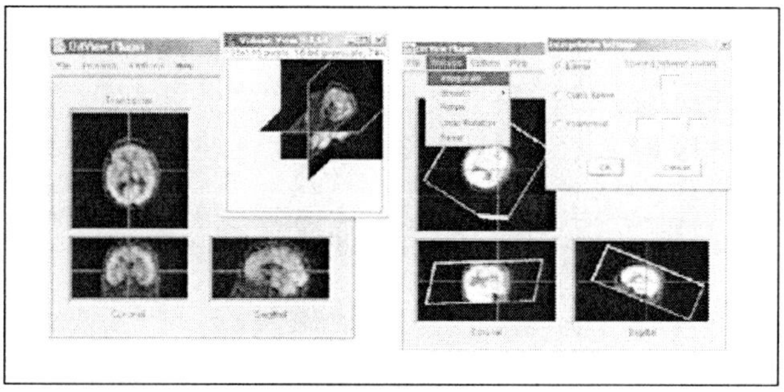

FIG. 3.5. *OrtView. Three orthogonal cuts of the volume shown in Figure 3.3, along with a combined view of all planes (left). After rotation (right); the interpolation popup dialog box is also shown.*

RenalConv reads and displays a sequential, renal study acquired by a Picker Gamma Camera, and saves it in the proprietary format of the Cure imaging package used for a quantitative processing of renal scintigraphies at the Niguarda Hospital at Milan.

3.5.3. Utilities plugins. The final set of plugins consists of tools meant to facilitate the user in his daily, ordinary use of ImageJ and that hence most directly respond to the purposes of our work: by providing the medical personnel with a valuable aid in its routine use of ImageJ (starting from the very basic operations such as file reading), they help the medical community in quickly getting familiar with a new environment, and thus being willing and open to cooperate with the research community by trying out and providing feedback on new tools and methods. FileOpener and RawFileOpener load several images simultaneously by letting the user multiply selecting them from a "File open" dialog box. The first plugin opens images in some standard format such as jpg, tiff of gif. The latter imports raw data by asking for the necessary parameters such as volume dimension, a possible header size, and the number of planes for a 3D data set. GePetOp loads a DICOM study acquired by a PET GE. A study consists of a collection of .dcm files, one for each transaxial slice, with all files related to the same data being located in a common directory and having a name that fulfills specific rules. GECardPetOp is very similar to GePetOp, but it can only be applied to tomographic, sequential, usually cardiological, DICOM studies acquired by a General Electric PET device. In order to be loaded into ImageJ, such datasets need a renaming of all filenames they consist of, according to either a spatial or a temporal order, as chosen by the user.

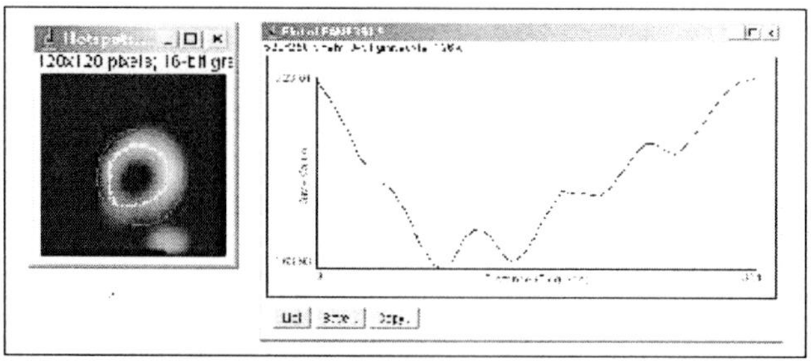

FIG. 3.6. *CardProfile - A cardiological image (left) and a histogram of the gray values plotted as a function of their distance from a point selected by the user (right).*

4. MedIGrid Features. The scenario we described has all the characteristics of a distributed application, where members of a virtual organization share their competence and resources. In this application such competence have provided the means to develop computational kernels for image reconstruction, port the latter onto parallel computer, design graphical user interfaces and visualization tools, and integrate all these modules into a distributed computing environment.

The shared resources are the medical equipment, a storage server and a parallel computer: the PET/SPECT instrument is owned and managed by the Policlinico Universitario Careggi at Florence, the storage equipment by ICAR-CNR at Naples, and the Beowulf class supercomputer by the Department of Mathematics and Applications at the University of Naples Federico II. All this appears to the user as a single commodity resource. Nevertheless, each component of the system can still be used for its original purpose. During a user session, resources are dynamically and transparently acquired and released to fit to the current situation. The application is composed of a dynamic set of processes that are executed on computers belonging to the virtual organization, and uses various different resources.

The application modularity has allowed the use of services available through the web and developed in the context of other scientific applications with similar requirements, thus promoting a community of scientific software developers, that collaborate in the development of the application.

Another important point is that only Open Source software is used, which allows to quickly debug single application components, since the entire organization has access to the source code. Furthermore, it is easy to distribute software, and its installation is not an issue. Last, in such an environment distant collaboration among doctors is natural since the application is pervasively accessible from any location. The approach proposed also provides a way to overcame the limits in the diagnosis process outlined in section 1. Indeed, in an open environment the results of the image reconstruction only depend on the algorithm adopted, which is freely chosen by the doctor, and its implementation is provided by the virtual organization. If a new algorithm is conceived, it can be implemented and used by everyone in the community. The increased computing power encourages the users to use more complex algorithms and the standard ones take shorter wall-clock execution times. The added storage capabilities make it possible to store data for future reuse, thus providing a more powerful tool and a deeper insight, as discussed in section 6.

5. Related Work. The MedIGrid application represents a new tool for medical diagnosis providing new insight into what can be done within a distributed collaborative environment. Overcoming the limits of the diagnosis process reveals new frontiers as well as new challenges and problems, the solution of which could lead to an even more powerful tool: considering that the realization of virtual organizations has up to day become possible with de facto standard software tools what will happen when more and more institutions decide

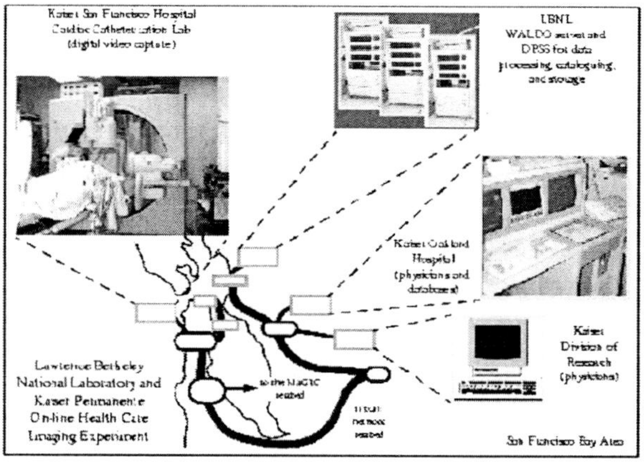

FIG. 5.1. *Waldo application*

to take part to such a community? What are the added features that a wider community can provide? What are the problems related to the management of a complex environment in which a variety of different human, hardware and software resources meet?

Those questions have been only partially answered by completed and ongoing projects, and some of those aspects challenge research communities not strictly related to medical problems. Indeed, many national and international projects are facing the fascinating challenges related to the use, allocation, scheduling and mapping issues in dynamic, multi-institutional, virtual organizations. In the following, an overview of some of those projects is given.

WALDO (Wide Area Large Data Objects) [18, 24] is an application to store medical data. As shown in Figure 5.1, it is based on a distributed database capable of managing large quantities of data, which are visualized on a remote workstation through a browser. Mechanisms such as network cache are used to access data from specific applications.

Since data are asynchronously produced by different sources, the WALDO architecture provides mechanisms to flexibly handle data storage, security and access integrity. Moreover, a data catalog is also provided.

The basic components are data collection tools, image processing and reconstruction tools for different medical analysis, software to manage issues related to security and protection, and application oriented graphical user interfaces to access data. Such a GUI provides the means to pervasively access data.

Kaiser [22] is based on the Waldo project and its aim is to use on-line instruments as data source. In particular, cardio-hagiographical data are collected by a scanner, sent to storage servers, and finally redistributed by WALDO to be accessed from other hospitals. The difference with MedIGrid is that image processing and reconstruction tools are not integrated within the environment, in order to use them in the different hospitals where data are analyzed.

Within NPACI alliance there is Telescience [29], a project devoted to the investigation of tomographic applications. As stated on the website, the project is merging technologies for remote control, grid computing, and federated digital libraries of multiscale, cell-structure data. The objective is to provide a complete tele-instrumentation solution that will connect scientists desktops to remote instruments, distributed databases, high-performance analysis environments, and experiment planning. Products of the project are Globus-enabled tomography (GTOMO) codes for simple back projection and iterative restoration, which is being used by the NASA Information Power Grid and further developed by Argonne National Laboratory (synchrotron x-ray tomography), and the Telescience Portal to remotely access and

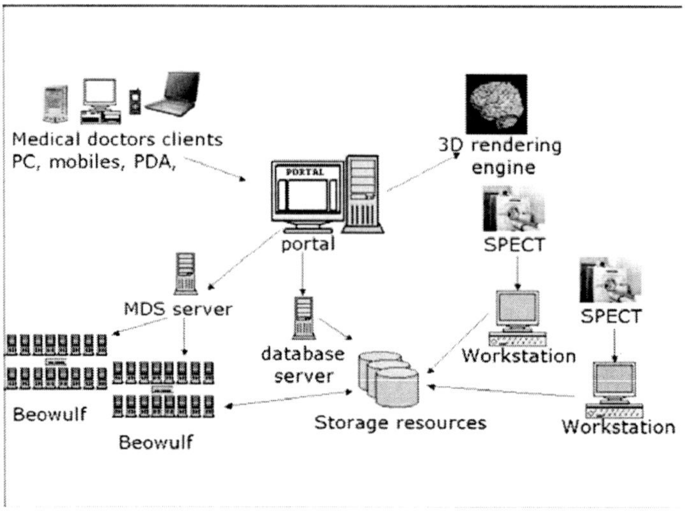

FIG. 6.1. *Future implementation*

control instruments, manage data, and control batch jobs with a single login and password. Key features of the portal include personalized user information, collaboration tools such as chat and shared white boards, automatic storage of data with the Storage Resource Broker, and job tracking tools. Our project differs with Telescience in that it is designed in order to let doctors share the progresses made by new reconstruction and processing techniques.

6. Future Work. The research carried out has highlighted many ways to complete or to improve the implemented application (Figure 6.1). The probably most interesting extension is to provide the application with a tool for its pervasive use. This can be achieved with a web portal. A user equipped with an Internet access and a web browser can use the portal to request image reconstructions, monitor the state of submitted jobs, visualize reconstructed images to complete his medical reports. With the integration of web technologies, visualization software and grid software tools, it is possible to implement a collaborative diagnostic tool which enables a pervasive access to MedIGrid. The implementation represents a challenge from the point of view of security, authentication, privacy and web-grid interface [28].

A catalogue of both raw and reconstructed data produced by a variety of acquisition devices, as well as metadata regarding the patient, medical reports, diagnosis produced over the years, represent a rich starting set of data on which to carry out statistical studies, and compare old and new reconstruction techniques. The management of such data is a challenging task, in particular from the point of view of efficient distribution and storage.

To increase application scalability dynamic resource discovery and allocation is needed [13], which allows to reserve resources on the grid in the most economic way.

Navigation and visualization tools [21] need to be grid-enabled both with the use of techniques like data staging, caching and asynchronous striping, that help hiding variable latency and transfer speeds, and with algorithms capable to adapt to the dynamic behavior of the computing environment. Such methods improve distant collaboration and make data steering possible.

7. Conclusions. MedIGrid, a grid enabled application for medical diagnosis has been described. It has been developed with the aim of facilitating and optimizing reconstruction, display and analysis of medical images. Feedback from the medical community has proven these tools to be useful in a clinical environment. A further point of interest of the tools we have developed is their free availability.

From these points we conclude that future work must be oriented towards making scientific materials as widely accessibly to the community as possible: beside developing code in an Open Source environment, this also means optimizing the performance and the simplicity of use. In this way it will represent a possible contact point between the basic science and the medical communities.

8. Acknowledgments. This work was partially founded by Italian National Research Council through Agenzia 2000 grant *Grid Computing and Applications*, by Italian Ministry for Education, University and Research through Special Grant for Strategic Research Y1999 *Grid Computing: enabling technologies and applications for e-science*, and FIRB grant *GRID.it: Enabling Platforms For High-Performance Computational Grids Oriented To Scalable Virtual Organizations.*

REFERENCES

[1] L. Antonelli, M. Ceccarelli, L. Carracciuolo, L. D'Amore, and A. Murli, *Total Variation Regularization for Edge Preserving 3D SPECT Imaging in High Performance Computing Environments*, Lecture Notes in Computer Science, 2330 (2002), pp. 171–180.

[2] L. Antonelli, L. Carracciuolo, L. D'Amore, and A. Murli, *Il funzionale di Totale Variazione nella ricostruzione di dati 3D SPECT mediante l'algoritmo di EM-OSn*, ICAR-CNR Tech. Rep. TR-02-01, 2002.

[3] D.L.Bailey, F.Zito, M.C.Gilardi, A.R.Savi, F.Fazio, and T.Jones, *Performance comparison of a state-of-the-art Neuro-SPECT Scanner and a dedicated Neuro-PET Scanner*, E. J. of Nuclear Medicine, 21 (1994), pp. 381–387

[4] D. Baldini, P. Clavini, and A. R. Formiconi, *Image reconstruction with conjugate gradient algorithm and compensation of the variable system response for an annular SPECT system*, Phys. Medica, 14 (1998), pp. 159–173.

[5] J. Bester, I. Foster, C. Kesselman, J. Tedesco, and S. Tuecke, *GASS: A Data Movement and Access Service for Wide Area Computing Systems*, Sixth Workshop on I/O in Parallel and Distributed Systems, (1999), pp. 78–88.

[6] P. Boccacci, P. Bonetto, P. Calvini, and A. R. Formiconi, *A simple model for the efficient correction of collimator blur in 3D SPECT imaging*, Inverse Problems, 15 (1999), pp. 907–930.

[7] S. Bryan G. C. Weatherburn, J. R. Watkins, et al., *The benefit of hospital-wide picture archiving and communication system : a survey of clinical users of radiology services*, Br. J. Radiol, 72 (1999), pp. 469–478.

[8] R. Butler, D. Engert, I. Foster, C. Kesselman, S. Tuecke, J. Volmer, and V. Welch, *A National-Scale Authentication Infrastructure*, IEEE Computer, 12 (2000) pp. 60–66.

[9] C.S. Butler and M.I. Miller, *'Maximum a posteriori estimation for SPECT using regularization techniques on massively parallel computers*, IEEE Trans. on Medical Imaging, 12 (1993), pp. 84–89.

[10] L. Carracciuolo, L. D'Amore, and A. Murli, *Sviluppo di software parallelo per la ricostruzione di dati 3D SPECT basato sull'algoritmo di EM-OSn*, ICAR-CNR Tech. Rep. TR-02-02, 2002.

[11] C.M. Chen, S.Y. Lee, and Z.H. Cho, *Parallelization of the EM algorithm for 3D PET image reconstruction*, IEEE Trans. on Medical Imaging, 10 (1991), pp. 513–522.

[12] C. Creighton, *A literature review on communication between picture archiving snd communication systems and radiology information systems and/or hospital information systems*, J. Digital Imaging, 12 (1999), pp. 138–143.

[13] S. Fitzgerald, I. Foster, C. Kesselman, G. von Laszewski, W. Smith, and S. Tuecke, *"A Directory Service for Configuring High-Performance Distributed Computationsr.* Proc. 6th IEEE Symp. on High-Performance Distributed Computing (1997), pp. 365–375.

[14] A.R. Formiconi, A. Passeri, and A. Pupi, *Compensation of spatial system response in SPECT with conjugate gradient reconstruction technique*, Phys Med Biol, 34 (1989), pp. 69–84.

[15] A.R. Formiconi, A. Passeri, and P. Calvini, *Theoretical determination of the collimator geometrical transfer function of reconstruction of SPECT data*, IEEE Trans. Nucl. Science, 46 (1999), pp. 1075–1080.

[16] I. Foster and C. Kesselman, *Globus: A Metacomputing Infrastructure Toolkit*, Intl J. Supercomputer Applications, 11 (1997), pp. 115–128.

[17] I.Foster, C. Kesselman, C. Lee, R. Lindell, and K. Nahrstedt, *A Distributed Resource Management Architecture that Supports Advance Reservations and Co-Allocation*, A. Roy. Intl Workshop on Quality of Service, (1999).

[18] I. Foster and C. Kesselman, *The Grid. Blueprint for a new computing infrastructure*, Morgan Kaufmann, San Francisco, 1999.

[19] I. Foster, C. Kesselman, and S. Tuecke, *The Anatomy of the Grid: Enabling Scalable Virtual Organizations.* Intl J. Supercomputer Applications, 15 (2001), pp. 200–222.

[20] A.O. Freier, P. Karlton, and P.C. Kocher, *Secure Socket Layer 3.0*, Internet Draft. IETF, 1996.

[21] M.R. Guarracino, G. Laccetti, and D. Romano, *Browsing Virtual Realty on a PC Cluster*, Proc. of Cluster 2000, IEEE Computer Society Press (2000), pp. 201–208.

[22] W. Johnston, G. Jin, C. Larsen, J. Lee, G. Ho, M. Thompson, B. Terney, and J. Terdiman, *Real Time Generation and Cataloguing Data-Objects in Widely Distributed Environments*, Internationa Journal of Digital Libraries, 1997.

[23] A. C. Kak and M. Slaney, *Principles of Computerized Tomographic Imaging*, IEEE Press, 1988.

[24] J. Lee, B. Tierney, and W. Johnston. *Data Intensive Distributed Computing: A Medical Application Example*, HPCN 99.

[25] A. Murli, L. D'Amore, L. Carracciuolo, P. Boccacci, and P. Calvini, *Parallel Software for 3D SPECT imaging based on the 2D+1 approximation of collimator blur*, Ann. Univ. Ferrara - Sez. VII - Sc. Mat., Suppl. to XLV, 1-0, 2000.

[26] A. Passeri, A. R. Formiconi, M. T. De Cristofaro, A. Pupi, and U. Meldolesi, *High performance computing and networking as tools, for accurate emission computed tomography reconstruction*, E. Journal of Nuclear Medicine, 24 (1997), pp. 390–397.

[27] Y.Sun and D.L.Parker, *Performance analyses of Maximum Intensity Projection algorithm for display of MRA images*, IEEE Trans. Medical Imaging, 18 (1999), pp. 1154–1169.

[28] G. von Laszewski, I. Foster, J. Gawor, W. Smith, and S. Tuecke, *CoG Kits: A Bridge between Commodity Distributed Computing and High-Performance Grids.* ACM 2000 Java Grande Conference, 2000.

[29] http://www.npaci.edu/Alpha/telescience.html

[30] *Requirements for grid-aware Biology Applications*, DataGrid-10-D10.1, available at DataGrid web site, 2001.

In: Parallel and Distributed Scientific and Engineering Computing ISBN 1-59033-956-8
Editor: Y. Pan and L.T. Yang, pp. 191-207

GRID ENVIRONMENT WITH WEB-BASED PORTAL ACCESS FOR AIR QUALITY MODELLING

BARBARA CHAPMAN, HARI DONEPUDI, YUPENG LI, PRIYA RAGHUNATH, YONGHONG YAN, BABU SUNDARAM* AND JIWEN HE†

Abstract. Air Quality Modelling is a recent important application that addresses several modern environmental health concerns. It requires considerable compute power to build, deploy and analyze the results of an air quality model and efforts to develop such applications can benefit from the availability of a computational grid. In this paper we discuss the needs of an air quality modelling project and describe the campus grid environment that we have built to support this effort. The environment includes a portal with a number of features that go beyond the functionality provided by major existing portals.

Key words. Computational grids, Air quality model, Grid portals, Resource management, OGSA, Customizable portals, Globus, Resource policies, Workflow

1. Introduction.

Advanced scientific and engineering problems require a large, pervasive and reliable supply of computing resources. Such requirements cannot always be satisfied by a single organization. A Computational Grid is a virtual organization [1] that combines computational resources from different administrative domains. They may be built to meet the needs of a very large application or project, or they may be constructed to improve resource provision to a group of users, often by increasing the quantity and kind of resources available to individuals. Campus grids are such virtual organizations consisting of resources owned by various labs and departments on a university campus that may be collectively put to use. In an effort to provide better services in our necessarily limited budget, as well as to enable computations such as the one described in this paper, we have begun to collaborate with our HPC Center to build such a grid on our campus.

A number of problems must be solved if a variety of resources in different administrative domains are routinely deployed in concert. One of these is the need to enable users to login to all machines as if they formed a single, jointly managed heterogeneous cluster. Another is to provide help for submitting jobs to one or more machines in this grid in a location-transparent manner; this involves being able to transfer files between different storage resources on the grid, and starting jobs on behalf of the user, typically via a local scheduling system. Since data and other code is frequently transferred between different domains, security concerns must also be addressed. Portable grid software [2, 3], so-called *middleware* that provides much of this functionality, is widely available today and is maturing rapidly; its deployment can provide a viable strategy for institutions such as ours to meet service goals via a grid. However, in addition to the administrative and organizational challenges that have to be met – these include such issues as providing system-wide user identification and management – progress must be made in the provision of user-level grid services if grids are to be routinely used. Middleware solves these problems at a relatively low level; yet users demand more transparency in their interactions with "the grid".

Web based portals provide users with a convenient, ubiquitous and intuitive interface that acts as a single point of access (single sign-on) to a grid and its resources. In addition to serving as a login window, a portal may enable the submission and management of scientific applications in a grid. If carefully designed, it can shield users from the heterogeneity of grid hardware and the complexities of the grid software, as well as resource-specific or scheduler-specific configuration details. There are a large number of on-going efforts attempting to

*Department of Computer Science, University of Houston, Houston, TX, 77204-3010 (Email:chapman@cs.uh.edu)
†Department of Mathematics, University of Houston, Houston, TX, 77204-3008

provide a unified, web-based single point of access to a set of grid resources. However, many such efforts are either specific to an application (area) or a grid environment.

Air quality modelling (AQM) [4] attempts to provide precise and reliable air quality forecasts for a given geographical region and time frame. A number of on-going projects are working to develop such models based upon meteorological as well as chemical processes. They have large-scale computational requirements during both development and deployment phases, and may need to be executed within a strict timeframe. In this paper we describe an interdisciplinary AQM project at our university and show how we are working to meet its computational requirements. Our efforts include building a computational grid on our campus in order to harness the available resources for its execution, and developing and deploying a complete customized version of a general-purpose portal that supports a variety of project tasks including project management, job submission and monitoring, and the subsequent viewing of a job's runtime behavior. We have designed the software used to create the portal environment in a manner that enables us to rapidly build custom portals for projects that intend to use the capability of the grid. One of the challenges that this work entails is the need to adapt to evolving standards for the provision of grid services. We also discuss the emerging Open Grid Service Infrastructure (OGSI) standard [5] and indicate how we are attempting to take it into account.

In the following, we first describe the AQM project in Section 2 below, which briefly describes the applications at the heart of this project and the campus grid that we have built to help meet their execution needs. We then discuss portals for accessing grid functionality and state the main requirements of the AQM project in this respect. Afterwards, Section 4 introduces EZ-Grid, our portal system that has been customized to support AQM. We conclude by briefly discussing related work and our plans for the future.

2. Air Quality Modelling. Every day, the average adult breathes over 3,000 gallons of air. Children breathe even more air per pound of body weight and are thus more susceptible to air pollution. Millions of people live in areas where urban smog, very small particles, and toxic pollutants pose serious health concerns. Long-term exposure to air pollution can cause chronic health concerns, such as cancer and damage to the body's immune, neurological, reproductive, and respiratory systems. Air pollution can be wide-ranging as well as persistent. Many air pollutants, such as those that form urban smog and toxic compounds, remain in the environment for long periods of time.

Many on-going efforts aim to provide precise and reliable air quality forecasts for different areas and some [6, 7] have been put into daily public service. Most forecast systems possess similar frameworks, but different modelling components are chosen for basic functionalities. These modelling components are usually compute-intensive numerical programs parallelized via MPI. Scripting languages are generally deployed to integrate and automate the Fortran or C simulation codes running on supercomputers. This approach usually lacks flexibility and impedes system development because the heterogeneity of different execution environments has to be dealt with at the user level.

2.1. Air quality studies at University of Houston. The Air Quality Modelling (AQM) project of the Institute for Multidimensional Air Quality Studies (IMAQS) at the University of Houston analyzes the air quality in the Greater Houston area and works with national, state and local leaders to provide solutions for Houston's air quality problems, which have resulted in several violations of the ozone standard between 1997 and 1999.

One of the tasks of this project is to develop and apply state-of-art air environmental models and provide precise and reliable air quality forecasts for the Greater Houston Area. There are three major components (Figure 2.1) in our forecast system: a numerical weather forecast system, MM5 [8, 9, 10, 11] which may be replaced by a more advanced model WRF [12, 13], an emission inventory processing package, SMOKE [14, 15, 16], and the chemical

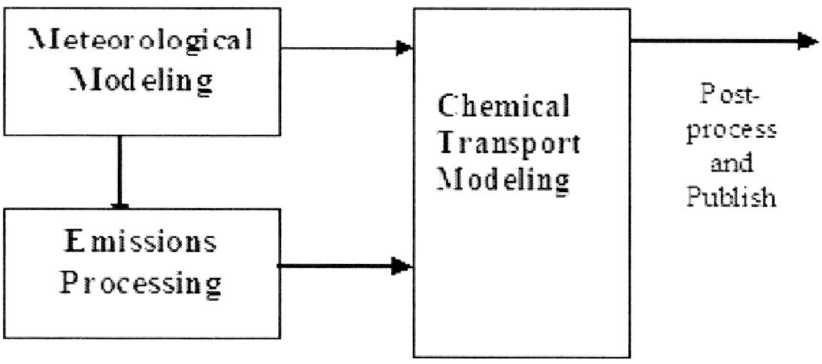

FIG. 2.1. *General application framework for air quality modelling.*

transport model, CAMx [17] or CMAQ [18]. To forecast air quality, several application subsystems, each with multiple processing steps (Figure 2.2), must interact. Large amounts of computing resources are needed on a daily basis. Different parts of the software system must routinely run on different platforms within the campus grid that we describe below. For example, we are currently using the popular weather code MM5 for limited area weather forecasting and reanalysis. In order to prepare the meteorological data as input to the emissions and chemical transportation subsystems, the NCEP input data for MM5 itself must be obtained, preprocessed to create the initial conditions, the simulation performed and post-processing tasks carried out. For a typical setup of the daily forecast of the greater Houston area, MM5 runs on 20 processors of a cluster of Sun SMPs and takes more than 15 hours. The size of the output data produced is more than 3 GB; this data is subsequently transferred to another machine on campus and visualized. Before and after the simulation, several pre- and post-processing steps are performed. The total cost in terms of CPU time as well as storage of results exceeds the amount of available resources at our centrally located HPC Center. Participants come from different research groups and managing the jobs that they individually launch, as well as the output they generate, is a non-trivial task.

2.2. Target environment. Air quality studies including weather and air quality forecasts always demand huge amounts of computing resources. UH has both large and small computational clusters connected through optical fiber across the campus; we exploit their availability by operating a number of different systems, including those at the High Performance Computing Center (HPCC), in a campus-wide grid. The campus grid (Figure 2.3) currently consists of a heterogeneous cluster of Sun SMPs and an SGI visualization system, including a total of 9 TB storage, at the university's HPC Center, along with a cluster of Sun SMPs in Computer Science and several Sun workstations and Linux clusters operated by the Math Department and Geophysics Department. The AQM effort has access to two additional Myrinet-based 64 node Intel clusters and 5 TB storage for further experimentation. This grid is available to a cross-section of faculty and is deployed for both research and teaching. The AQM project and its team members are among the heaviest users of the campus grid.

The campus grid is divided into several different administrative domains corresponding to the owner of the hardware; each domain may contain multiple clusters with a shared file system. In our environment, all basic grid services, such as security and authentication,

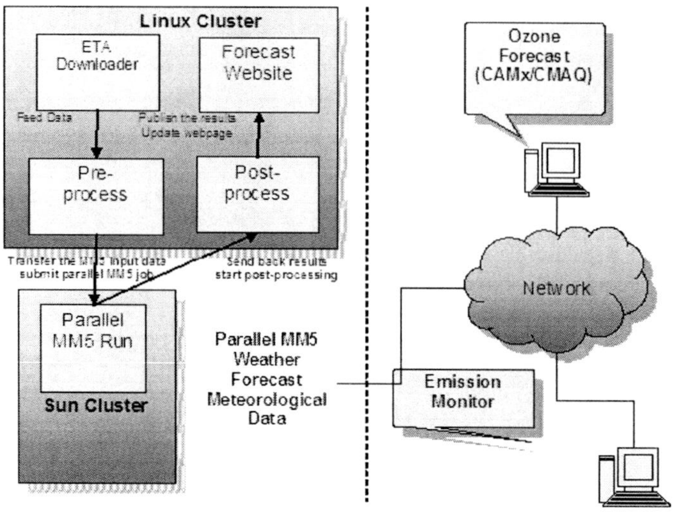

FIG. 2.2. *Real-time MM5 weather forecast at UH*

resource management, static resource information, and data management, are provided by the freely available Globus toolkit [2], an implementation of a standard set of services for building a grid. Sun Grid Engine (SGE), another free software package, has been installed to manage the resources within the individual administrative domains. We outline their features below. Users may interact with the grid by using Globus and SGE functions directly or they may use our portal (as described in Section 4) to exploit the grid's resources.

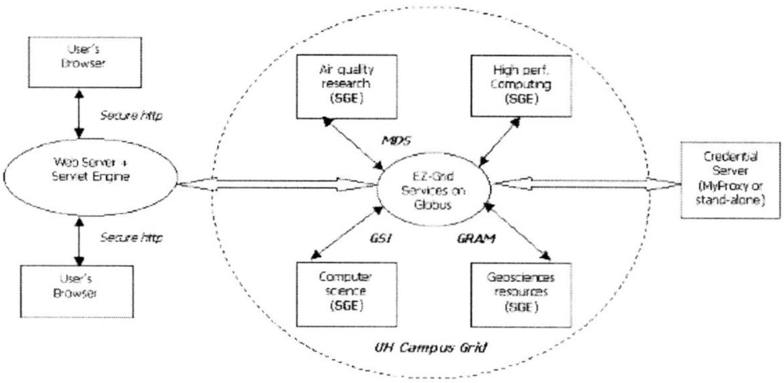

FIG. 2.3. *University of Houston Campus Grid Setup*

2.3. Grid Software, Globus and Sun Grid Engine. The Globus project has pioneered fundamental technologies for building computational grids that harness geographically distributed hardware and software resources. It is widely distributed and is available on a large number of platforms. Thus it forms the basis of many on-going efforts to provide a computational grid, and is considered to be standard infrastructure. Globus middleware is provided as a toolkit of functions that may be used individually or together. They provide the following three major services:

- *resource management* (GRAM) [19], which accepts a job submitted to the grid via a script in Globus' own scripting language, RSL, and passes it on to the resource management system on the selected target for actual queueing and execution, thereby acting as an interface to various kinds of scheduling systems,
- *data management* (GASS, GSI-FTP and GridFTP) [20, 21] that primarily serves to transfer data between different locations on the grid, so that this does not have to be performed by the user before and after jobs are submitted, and
- *information services* (MDS) [22] which provide detailed (static) information on the resources configured in the grid. For compute resources, this comprises hardware details, operating system, other software configurations and more.

These three services are built on top of the underlying Grid Security Infrastructure (GSI) [23], whose functions include single/mutual authentication, encrypted communication and credential delegation. It is essential for security as well as for accounting that a job is associated clearly with the user who submitted it. User access rights and permissions will be used to determine whether and with what priority a job is executed on the machine selected by the user. In the main, PKI (Public Key Infrastructure) has been used for the underlying authentication.

Earlier versions of Globus (GT1,2.x) adopted a toolkit-based approach to realizing grid infrastructure. Globus Toolkit 3 (GT3) is an emerging major revision of this software that aims to provide Globus functionality in the form of web services. It uses technologies such as the Simple Object Access Protocol (SOAP) [24] and Web Services Description Language (WSDL)[25] to enable the creation, management and discovery of grid service instances in a secure and fault-resilient manner. GT3 is based upon Open Grid Services Architecture (OGSA) and related specifications (OGSI), emerging standards which attempt to define what a service must provide if it is to function as a grid service; we describe OGSI in Section 4.4 further below.

Sun Grid Engine (Enterprise Edition) [26] is the local job scheduler and resource manager at each administrative domain of our campus grid. SGE manages heterogeneous collections of machines that share files, possibly via NFS. It provides a variety of mechanisms for specifying domain-specific access priorities and can handle job submissions to an architecture rather than an individual machine. Globus resource management interfaces with SGE as follows. When the user submits a job via RSL, the GRAM component of Globus processes the script and determines the target machine as well as the location of input files; an RSL script will generally specify the kind of job and the name and location of the executable as well as of the input and output files. The local GRAM typically interacts with the GRAM components installed on the corresponding platforms in order to handle data transfers and to dispatch job submission requests to the scheduler managing the selected resources; the scheduler starts the job locally in accordance with the domain-specific scheduling policy, evaluating any arguments passed to it by the job. It also reports resource usage information to the Globus information service.

We have created a job manager to enable interaction between Globus and SGE so that the above functions can be performed. Its task is to do the following: First, it parses the job resource request made via the Globus scripting language (RSL) or via our portal (see below) and uses this to submit job requests to the SGE `qmaster` daemon in the appropriate domains. If necessary, it will send callbacks to client systems. Finally, it will automatically transfer output files to other grid systems using GASS if remote locations have been specified.

With the help of the job manager, different cluster resources can be selected based on their loads and their high-level scheduling and reservation policies. The job manager collects resource usage information from the local resource manager, which records and is able to provide a variety of status information about the cluster.

Certificates form the basis of the authentication process: when a job is submitted to a machine on the grid, the embedded certificate will enable GSI to identify the owner of the job. An independent certification authority (CA) for the campus grid is managed by HPCC. Certificates are issued to the users when their grid accounts are set up. Existing Globus CA or other trusted CA credentials may be exported to the credential repository using secure `http` sessions. Our model for handling credentials is explained further below (Section 4).

For many application scientists, it is a daunting task to deal with a grid infrastructure; we therefore provide a portal interface to simplify interactions with grid services. In the next section, we discuss portal technology and the specific support required for the AQM project. Our EZGrid software [27, 28] provides web-based access to the grid, interfacing Globus features and providing additional support, and is described afterward.

3. Grid Portals. In general, user interaction with existing grid environments is relatively low-level. Job submission is a cumbersome process that typically requires the use of scripts and job description languages. Grid middleware tools like Globus provide command line tools to interact with grids, which are not user-friendly. The user is responsible for selecting the target platform and for describing the location of files. However, information needed in order to identify suitable target resources is usually only partially available. Grid portals assist users from the scientific community by making available a high-level interface that may provide a variety of services to support the deployment of applications on a grid. Basic features include support for identifying oneself to the grid, and displays of the information available to support resource selection, as well as forms for submitting jobs and subsequently monitoring their progress. Much more is being addressed in emerging portals, which may contain any of the following: services for resource and application discovery, construction and submission of workflow and single executable jobs, automated target resource selection (brokerage), file handling, error handling, management of projects, maintenance of data, maintenance of user profiles and access control, and more. For broad usability, a portal should be able to function in conjunction with Globus software: Globus provides interfaces known as CoG kits to the popular portal-building languages to simplify their construction. An important requirement of all portals is that they must guarantee security of user code and data.

3.1. Current portal projects. There are many efforts to provide unified web-based access to a collection of high performance computing resources. Most of them either provide a general set of grid services that are not directly applicable to complex scientific application needs, and which do not satisfy all the requirements of user-grid interactions, or they are specific to an application or organization and thus not suitable as a generic grid portal. Here, we mention just a few significant grid portal efforts.

PUNCH [29] provides users with a visualized view of computational resources that span multiple administrative domains by performing resource allocation for jobs transparently. It is thus very easy to use. But it is based on custom middleware rather than Globus, and this software must be installed on strategically distributed machines (servers) in the grid. Software is pre-installed; accredited users may run only those applications that have been made available on the grid. Also, PUNCH uses virtual accounts that require the user environment (files and data) to be transparently moved to the actual execution location. This may cause significant performance degradation in lower bandwidth environments.

Websubmit [30] is another web-based portal that gives access to applications available on a set of HPC resources while hiding the complexities of the underlying operating system. It provides form (web)-based job submission and file transfer capabilities to users. But like PUNCH, it is not based on Globus and does not benefit from components of the toolkit, such as GSI [23]. It has been implemented using CGI scripts based on Tcl that are known to have poorer performance and portability than do Java-based web applications. Moreover, it supports only the Loadleveler batch system.

UNICORE [31] aims at providing a uniform and seamless, web-based access to grid HPC resources to carry out tasks such as job preparation, submission and monitoring. It relies on its own server modules that manage job execution on various resources. Hence, this project also does not employ Globus middleware services although interoperability initiatives are underway. UNICORE does not target provision of resource status information and requires special client and gateway software for accessing its services.

The Gateway [32] portal provides generic services such as job submission, file transfer and information services using CORBA-based [33] middleware that makes use of the services provided by Globus and a database backend. A high level Gateway API is provided that allows users to build complex tasks. But this portal also has a few drawbacks. In particular, it requires the gateway server to be running on each resource. It does not include support for resource brokerage so that a user must manually select the resources on which a job is to be run. The Gateway security infrastructure uses the CORBA standard. CORBA was not designed for high performance computing and does not provide the desired performance levels.

The XCAT [34] science portal allows grid application programmers to create scripts for complex distributed computations and to package these applications with simple interfaces for others to use. It differs from the other efforts described above, as it requires each user workstation to act as a portal with its own personal web server that is capable of running application scripts and launching remote applications for a user. For each application there is also the extra burden of packaging applications and developing an application manager (although this process is simplified by using scriptable components). Resource brokerage is not yet fully supported. GSI and MDS [22] are the only components of Globus that are used.

3.2. Toolkits for grid portals. Portals are critical for user acceptance of grids. As a result, there are already a few toolkits available to assist those developers who intend to build a grid portal. These toolkits provide the basic features required in such an effort. Here, we describe two important toolkits, GPDK [35] and GridPort [36, 37].

GPDK and GridPort/Hotpage both aim to provide generic, reusable common components to access the grid services provided by Globus. The generic services include security, simple job submission, file transfer and information services. GPDK leverages common commodity technologies such as Java beans and servlets to provide interoperability with existing technologies. It is designed using the Model-View-Controller (MVC) paradigm to provide modular and flexible portal software. GridPort is based on server side Perl modules, which have poorer performance and portability than Java-based applications, using the Perl CoG kit. The most attractive feature of GPDK is that it provides an extensible library and a template portal that can be easily extended to provide new capabilities for customized portals. However neither of these toolkits provide support for job management, resource brokerage or a broad range of information to aid the user in such tasks as selecting a target environment for a specific job. Portals such as [38, 39] have been developed based on GPDK, while [40, 41] and [42] are based on GridPort. The GRB [43] portal is similar to the Hotpage portal in terms of services provided and technology used.

3.3. Portal support for AQM. A comprehensive user environment is needed by AQM and other similar projects to assist in the efficient management and deployment of various applications and computing resources. As with other early adopters of grids, there is a demand for more transparency when dealing with the execution environment, and therefore for a more comprehensive set of services at a high level. In addition to portal support for the "standard" functions provided by Globus, the AQM project has identified the following features that are highly desired for a custom grid environment:

- The AQM project will benefit from a web-based user interface which offers easy access to computational and data resources to grid users with different roles such as researchers, administrators, and project leaders. An interface that is cognizant of the various participants, their roles and activities, can provide multiple levels of user support including but not limited to acting as a single point of access to grid and project resources. It may also permit a personalized view of resources, applications, credentials, GUI preferences and more.
- The project participants need to be able to define sequences of tasks involving meteorological forecasts, or to couple forecasting, emissions processing, and chemical transport simulation. Some of these tasks must be started at a given time. Workflow support at the user level and the ability of the underlying system to provide advance reservation of resources are thus essential features of a grid environment that will enable AQM users to conveniently and flexibly combine the different computational tasks needed to achieve such a complicated goal. A high-level interface is also necessary for the convenient definition, scheduling and submission of simple jobs as well as jobs that may entail complex dependencies between its components.
- For the AQM project, automated resource brokerage can be used to automatically and transparently select suitable resources to test the environment model configurations and find optimal setups for different geographic and seasonal conditions. By coupling with tools for data mining and data visualization, a grid environment can be enhanced to efficiently access and analyze the vast amounts of observational data and simulation results.
- For a research project such as the air quality study, in which the activities rely heavily on numerical simulation tools and computing resources, the grid environment may help the researchers improve their collaboration and help the project leaders to better manage members' research activities by recording and analyzing the usage history of the computing resources and modelling tools.

4. EZ-Grid Portal. EZ-Grid is an ongoing project to develop technologies that facilitate the utilization of grids and their supporting services, primarily by simplifying user interaction with such services and by providing automated versions of standard tasks. EZ-Grid software can be used to build a generic interface for working on a grid, or it can be used to create a custom grid environment. The project also aims to provide a more complete set of user-level grid services in accordance with the demand for simplification of grid activities.

4.1. Basic functionalities. The EZ-Grid portal provides the following basic services required for user interaction with the grid, in a graphical environment:

- *Job specification and submission*: Means for the user to specify and submit a job, including the location of input and output files and compute needs; arguments may be passed to SGE in our local setup. Automated translation of these into Globus RSL is followed by job submission to GRAM.
- *Job management*: Storage and retrieval of relevant user and application profile information, history of job executions and related information. Application profiles consist of metadata that characterize frequently run jobs.
- *File handling*: Transparent authentication with and browsing of remote file systems that are part of the grid resources is supported. Data can be securely transferred between grid resources using the GSI-enabled data transport services and GridFTP.
- *Data archive maintenance*: this feature allows users to organize, locate and use the huge amount of data typically produced by scientific applications.
- *Single sign-on*: Globus proxy (temporary identity credential) creation using Grid Security Infrastructure and X509 certificates. This allows the user to seamlessly

establish his or her identity across all campus grid resources by providing the portal identity and passphrase. Upon sign-on, the user's Globus proxy is generated on the portal server; and used for subsequent authentication with the grid resources using GSI. All communications are carried out over secure `http` channels.

Our campus grid's credential server provides a repository for user credentials, such as the X509 certificate [44] and key pairs and proxies. In our current campus grid setup, we have adopted a stand-alone credential server model to allow users to access grid services with unlimited mobility. Alternatively, a MyProxy [45] server can be used to act as an online repository for user proxies. However, this adds an upper limit to the mobility of the users, due to the limited lifetime of the Globus proxies delegated. Appropriate mapping of the portal accounts to proxies allows users to perform single sign-on and to access grid resources. The portal supports the export of encrypted keys from the user to the credential server using secure `http` sessions. In some scenarios, the credential server can also be used to generate the user credentials, thus ensuring enhanced security by not exposing the private keys.

4.2. Advanced functionalities. Here we describe several features that are not yet provided by other existing grid portals but which are necessary for scientific applications. The first three are offered by the EZ-Grid portal and the remaining two are currently under development:

- *Comprehensive resource information*: Status information on grid resources, both static (hardware and software information) and dynamic attributes (CPU loads, job queue and status information). Static information is obtained primarily from Globus Information services (MDS); dynamic scheduler information and queue details are retrieved from SGE using our information subsystems. Additional information provided graphically includes application profiles and job execution histories, as mentioned above.
- *Resource brokerage*: Automatic and transparent selection of a set of available target resources that match the user job requirements. The resource brokerage uses the resource information, the usage control services (see below) and the scheduler specific interfaces to make resource choices based on the job specifications. The goal of this brokering process could be budget-based or deadline-based or both. Accordingly, the broker is expected to choose resources with the lowest cost or with the fastest execution time. The brokering process is split into a series of stages in which the potential set of resources is progressively narrowed down to ultimately identify the best resource for the given job specification. It starts by filtering based on static resource information, including the application profile, which needs no interaction with the remote resources. Then, the policy-based evaluation determines which resources are available to the user and the cost; this too incurs little or no interaction with remote resources. After these initial stages are carried out, network parameters such as available bandwidth and latency are assessed; these are critical if large datasets must potentially be transferred. For those resources that are thus considered most likely candidates, any additional history information about previous job submissions is fetched from the remote resource and analyzed. Finally, the scheduler interfaces at the remote resource are queried to obtain dynamic information about the work queues and the current loads in order to estimate job run times.
- *Precise usage control*: Policy-based authorization and accounting services to assist in examining and evaluating usage policies of the resource providers. Policies on system usage set up and enforced by the provider may focus on diverse issues such as security, priority, class of acceptable jobs and users, quality of service and avoidance of misuse. They may need to be flexible; for example, it may be appropriate

to modify the priorities for a particular job according to changes in the dynamic environment. Tools are provided for the administrators of grid resources to specify and enforce policies at the grid environment level. The user may view this information while making job submissions [46]. The policies are part of the information that is evaluated as part of the brokerage process.

- *Customizable user profile*: a customizable view of resources, applications and personalized contents. Personalized user information includes not only basic information such as the name, email address etc. but also the desired display of information about resources, credentials, portal GUI preferences and settings associated with the user. We are modifying our EZ-Grid portal so that it will be able to provide user-specific GUI customization, including desired color palette and background colors, help information for personal interests, and so on.
- *WorkFlow management*: support for the specification of multi-executable jobs, where the executables interact in a potentially non-trivial manner. The AQM work requires workflow support so that the different parts of jobs with multiple codes can be started at appropriate times. Current work focusses on building a GUI that helps users to create, store, run and monitor complex tasks and applications. We intend to enable the user to graphically construct workflow jobs via easy drag-and-drop operations. Workflow specifications can then be stored and scheduled, as needed, to automatically run jobs periodically or at a specified time. We plan to leverage recent and developing technologies such as GridAnt [47] for realization of the workflow management.

4.3. EZ-Grid implementation. The two most common technologies for building web-based applications are CGI/PERL and JSP/Servlets/Java Beans. Traditionally, web applications were built using CGI/PERL technology. CGI is a standard for interfacing external programs with information servers such as a web server. The server submits client requests encoded in URLs to the appropriate registered CGI program, which executes them and returns results back to the server. CGI programs are executable programs that run on the web server; although they are usually written in PERL, they can be written in any available scripting language or programming language that can run on a web server, including PERL, TCL, and Unix shells. A grid portal can be developed by writing CGI programs that make use of Globus PERL CoG kit scripts. An alternative to this approach is to use Java technologies such as servlets, Java beans and JSP. Java Servlet technology provides web developers with a simple, consistent mechanism for extending the functionality of a web server based on the power of the Java language. It offers a component-based, platform-independent method for building web-based applications. The EZ-Grid implementation is based on Java Servlets because they have the following advantages over traditional CGI applications:

- Efficiency: With CGI, a new program is created for every `http` request, but with Java servlets a new thread is spawned instead of a new program for every request. This approach reduces server memory requirements and saves time by instantiating fewer objects.
- Enhanced functionality: Java servlets may exploit the power of the Java programming language and talk directly to the web server, whereas regular CGI programs cannot, at least not without using a server-specific API. Communicating with the web server makes it easier, for instance, to translate relative URLs into concrete path names. Multiple servlets can also share data, making it easy to implement database connection pooling and similar resource-sharing optimizations. Servlets can also maintain information from request to request, simplifying strategies for session tracking and caching of previous computations.

- Portability: Java servlets are more portable than CGI programs because they are written in Java's standard API. Servlets are supported directly or by a plug-in on virtually every major web server.
- Security: CGI programs are mostly executed as shell scripts and different shells may treat symbols like '\' differently. Any errors caused by inappropriate use of such symbols may lead to unexpected results and server crashes. Also, Java has more stringent checks for memory binding and types than is performed for CGI.
- Convenience: Java servlets provide more convenient methods for reading and setting `http` headers, handling cookies, tracking sessions, and many other such high-level utilities.

The Apache Struts Web Framework [48] encapsulates the MVC paradigm to provide structures and common web functionalities that greatly speed up web application development with JSP/Java Beans and improve the performance of the final product. JSP [49] provides multiple ways to use templates in web-site building. In EZ-Grid, the web-page template is maintained in a single place and is included dynamically upon viewing, allowing the web application front end to be easily integrated with any web portal interface design. Currently, the EZ-Grid web application contains more than 40 JSP files. However, these files use only two design templates. If the portal is to be customized for use by an institute, company or project, the web pages must be redesigned to incorporate the desired user background and meet specified needs. This might include, for example, a logo, help information or adding a news section to the web pages with articles that are closely related to their research topics. Unless care is applied, it might be necessary to revise the whole 40 JSP pages to suit the needs of this project. But, as the EZ-Grid portal deploys a dynamic template built using Struts template tag library, which makes the layouts of web pages much more flexible and maintainable, the new portal can be developed by changing just a few layout files. Figure 4.1 contains some sample JSP code segments that show how easy it is to customize the portal's web page appearance to suit particular user needs using this dynamic template technique. The webmaster who deploys or maintains the portal can easily customize it by designing or updating one or two template files; in the example, the file modified is *template.jsp*. The webmaster needs to make sure that the following three header lines required by EZ-Grid appear as part of the JSP headers for every new template he or she creates

```
<%@ taglib uri="/template" prefix="template" %>
<%@ taglib uri="/WEB-INF/app.tld" prefix="app" %>
<app:checkLogon/>
```

and then use the `template:get` tags provided by the Struts framework to control which part of the EZ-Grid portal interface should go into the design template. No other JSP pages ever need to be changed. The EZ-Grid related tags are underlined in the figure. The first of these is `<template: get name="EZ-GridJavaScripts"/>`, which denotes the EZ-Grid related Javascripts. The remaining three denote the header, content (forms etc. implementing the actual EZ-Grid functionalities) and EZ-Grid related footer respectively. This facility gives the webmaster the ability to change the appearance of the web-pages while retaining the EZ-Grid portal functionalities. It is important to notice that, even though all the template files are JSP files, the webmaster does not need to know JSP and can use any popular web development tool such as Dreamweaver to design the template page.

Figure 4.2 shows how the EZ-Grid architecture is layered and also indicates its interaction with other middleware tools and resource management systems. The presentation layer consists of HTML/JSP web pages containing a customizable GUI to provide users with convenient and useful graphical interfaces. The web application service layer uses the Struts framework to organize/model the generic web application services in the standard MVC paradigm. The so-called business logic consists of Java classes implementing the ac-

```
File : template.jsp

<%@ page contentType="text/html; charset=iso-8859-1" language="java"
import="java.sql.*"%>
<%@ taglib uri="/template" prefix="template" %>
<%@ taglib uri="/WEB-INF/app.tld" prefix="app" %>
<app:checkLogon/>
<html>
<head>
<title>AQMG   EZ-Grid Portal</title>
<meta http-equiv="Content-Type" content="text/html; charset=iso-8859-1">
<template:get name="EZ-GridJavaScripts"/>
</head>

<body>
<table width="100%" border="0" cellpadding="0" cellspacing="0">
  <tr>
    ... more code  ...
    <td width="72%">
      <template:get name="EZ-GridHeader"/>
    </td>
  </tr>
  <tr>
    <td colspan="2">
      <template:get name="EZ-GridContent"/>
    </td>
  </tr>
  <tr>
    <td colspan="2">
      <template:get name="EZ-GridFooter"/>
    </td>
  </tr>
</table>
</body>
< html>

File : editJobProfile.jsp

<%@ taglib uri="/template" prefix="template" %>
<template:insert template="template.jsp">
  <template:put name="EZ-GridJavaScripts" content="jobprofilejs.htm"/>
  <template:put name="EZ-GridHeader" content="appheader.htm"/>
  <template:put name="EZ-GridContent" content="mainMenuPart.jsp"/>
  <template:put name="EZ-GridFooter" content="appfooter.htm"/>
</template:insert>
```

FIG. 4.1. *Dynamic templates in EZ-Grid*

tual services required by the EZ-grid portals such as single sign-on, job submission, file transfer, etc. The business logic makes use of the services provided by the Grid Service Interface, which is actually a layer that consists of a standardized encapsulation of the grid services provided by the Globus toolkit. Finally, the Database access layer provides methods for accessing databases as needed. Note that although this is not shown in the diagram, EZ-Grid interacts both directly and indirectly (via Globus) with the resource manager.

4.4. OGSI. With the growing interest in grids and their commercial development and deployment, the lack of accepted standards for interoperability between diverse grid computing technologies used in individual organizations [50] became a major impediment to progress. The integration of dynamic business applications in the form of web services was sought. In a grid environment, means must be provided to support the dynamic discovery of services and to exploit other related tools. The Open Grid Services Architecture (OGSA) provides a generic grid system architecture that leverages web services technologies and enhances existing grid technologies and tools to realize "grid services". Such grid services are based, though not exclusively, upon SOAP, WSDL and other web services concepts to enable wide-scale resource sharing with no tight coupling to any specific protocols, thereby avoiding associated deficiencies. OGSI is a concrete technical specification being drafted by the OGSI

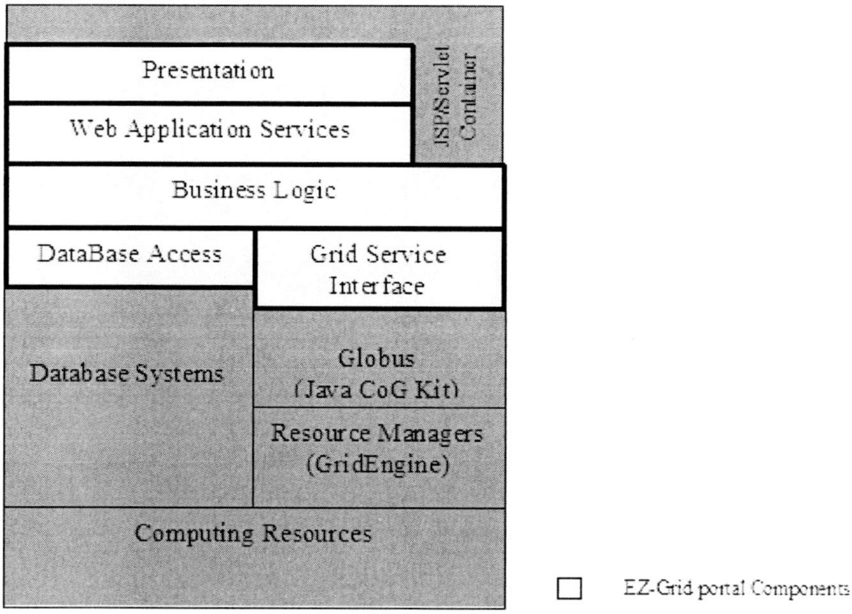

FIG. 4.2. *EZ-Grid Portal Architecture*

working group of the Global Grid Forum (GGF) [57] that provides the basic conventions for implementing grid services. It defines mechanisms for creating, managing and exchanging information among grid services. A grid service should be an addressable instance that has facilities to achieve its creation and its information introspection, manage its lifetime, and provide for its invocation. Grid service handles (GSH) (global URI names) and Grid service references (GSR) (WSDL document with the specifics of the bindings to facilitate service invocation) facilitate naming, identifying and invoking specific grid service instances. Grid services may be persistent or transient. Mechanisms have been defined for soft-state lifetime management to enable authorized clients to extend, shorten or immediately destroy grid service instances. Typically, client applications/programs will be isolated from the web service invocation by an interface that acts on behalf of the client to perform argument marshalling, message routing and invoking of appropriate bindings on the server side.

Version 3 of the Globus toolkit (GT3) provides a reference implementation in Java for the current grid service specifications and a container to create and invoke basic Globus toolkit services such as GRAM and GSI or other OGSI compliant grid services. The core of GT3 provides the basic OGSI functionality to enable reuse by grid service programmers. The client and the server side implementations are JAX-RPC [51] compliant and the stubs for the service interfaces are generated using automated tools. This makes it relatively straightforward for a programmer who knows the conventions to implement and offer additional OGSI-compliant services.

4.4.1. OGSI compliance in EZ-Grid. The OGSI specification has defined a few portTypes that can be extended to create OGSI-compliant Grid services. They capture the most common behavior expected from distributed computing components. The service interfaces are translated into WSDL specifications (portTypes) and are used to generate stubs for the clients for introspection and invocation.

Put simply, the designer of OGSI-compliant components should combine and extend a combination of GridService portTypes (a base interface definition that captures the behavior expected of all grid services), optional portTypes (such as Factory, ServiceGroup and so on) and other application-specific portTypes. OGSI-compliant services should inherit from the ServiceSkeleton class (that is part of the GT3 core) and implement the WSDL portTypes exposed in the interface specification of the service as well. The major portal services of EZGrid such as information services, job submission and monitoring services have been reengineered to be compliant with the OGSI specification. Interfaces have been created to support lifetime management, state introspection and more, and they inherit from the ServiceSkeleton class as required. The interface with Sun Grid Engine complies with the Master Managed Job Manager Factory Service instances (MMJFS) and job manager instances of GT3.

OGSA and the related specifications are still undergoing refinement and are therefore subject to change. We are closely monitoring GGF developments to ensure that our portal services will be compliant with the most recent specifications for grid services.

5. Related Work. There are several other air-quality or meteorological studies which have begun to take advantage of grid technologies. The Modelling Environment for Atmospheric Discovery project [52, 53] supported by NCSA focuses on retrospective analysis of hurricanes and severe storms using the TeraGrid [54], integrating computation, grid workflow management, data management, model coupling, data analysis/mining, and visualization. CrossGrid [55] meteorological applications [56] analyze archived operational data from a mesoscale model. Meteorological reanalysis of databases, which include homogeneous meteorological information from a single numerical weather prediction model integrated over decades, will also be performed. The system will include an atmospheric pollution chemistry module.

6. Conclusions and Future Work. Grid environments enable new infrastructures such as "virtual organizations" that seamlessly aggregate distributed and dynamic collections of resources. Campus grids provide good opportunities for researchers to solve computationally demanding problems in science and engineering. However, simplified access to grid services is essential for computational scientists to fully utilize the advantages. Grid portals enable users to gain web-based access to grid resources and services. They may be used to perform single sign-on, view resource status information, submit jobs and manage data.

The EZ-Grid portal project addresses these issues and provides a single web-based interface for performing standard grid tasks. The adaptation of the portal to meet specific project or individual user interface needs is relatively straightforward. It has enabled researchers in our AQM project to automate the process of specifying and starting complex jobs that utilize a variety of hardware resources on our campus. Ongoing work extends our current functionality to support additional needs of this project and of other computational projects at our university. Future work includes development of strategies for increased fault-tolerance and maximum performance gains to meet the needs of time-critical applications. With an increasing user demand for insulation from the complexities of a heterogeneous and distributed grid environment, portals such as EZ-Grid and their services will become increasingly sophisticated.

HiPCAT is a consortium of leading research institutions in Texas that share advanced technologies and resources to simulate new methods of computing and collaboration. The University of Houston participates in this initiative. The future HiPCAT portal will provide authenticated users with information on the grid resources, including static and dynamic information on their status and the job queues. We intend to collaborate with our HiP-CAT colleagues so that EZ-Grid functionality may be part of this environment and AQM applications can be deployed in this larger computational grid.

Acknowledgements. This work is being performed as part of a Sun Center of Excellence in Geosciences. We wish to thank our colleagues within this Center and the staff of the HPC Center for their support for this initiative. We would also like to thank Sun MicroSystems^{TM} for their support and guidance.

REFERENCES

[1] I. Foster, C. Kesselman and S. Tuecke, *The Anatomy of the Grid: Enabling Scalable Virtual Organizations*, in International Journal of Supercomputer Applications, 15(3), 2001.

[2] I. Foster and C. Kesselman, *Globus: A metacomputing infrastructure toolkit*, in International Journal of Supercomputer Applications 11(2): 115-128.

[3] Andrew S. Grimshaw, William A. Wulf, James C. French, Alfred C. Weaver, Paul F. Reynolds Jr, *Legion: The Next Logical Step Toward a Nationwide Virtual Computer*, Technical Report No. CS-94-21. Department of Computer Science, University of Virginia. June 1999

[4] Institute for Multidimensional Air Quality Studies (IMAQS): http://www.aqm.uh.edu

[5] I. Foster, C. Kesselman, J. Nick and S. Tuecke, *The Physiology of the Grid: An Open Grid Services Architecture for Distributed Systems Integration*, Globus Project, 2002, www.globus.org/research/papers/ogsa.pdf.

[6] *EPA: Guideline for Developing an Ozone Forecasting Program* `http://www.epa.gov/ttn/oarpg/t1/memoranda/foreguid.pdf`

[7] P. C. Manins, M. E. Cope, G. D. Hess, P. F. Nelson, K. Puri, N. Wong and M. Young, *The Australian Air Quality Forecasting System: prognostic air quality forecasting in Australia*, Clean Air, 36 (2): 43-48.

[8] *Mesoscale Model (MM5)*, Pennsylvania State University, National Center for Atmospheric Research, `http://www.mmm.ucar.edu/mm5`

[9] J. Dudhia and J. Bresch, *A global version of the PSU-NCAR mesoscale model*, Mon. Wea. Rev., 130: 2989-3007, 2002.

[10] G. Grell, J. Dudhia, and D. Stauffer, *A Description of the Fifth-Generation Pennsylvania State/NCAR Mesoscale Model (MM5) NCAR/TN-398+STR*, NCAR Tech Notes

[11] J. W. Nielsen-Gammon, *Initial Modeling of the August 2000 Houston- Galveston Ozone Episode*, A Report to the Technical Analysis Division, Texas Natural Resource Conservation Commission, December 19, 2001

[12] J. Michalakes, J. Dudhia, D. Gill, J. Klemp and W. Skamarock, *Design of a next- generation regional weather research and forecast model: Towards Teracomputing*, World Scientific, River Edge, New Jersey, 117-124, 1998.

[13] J. Michalakes, *Weather Research and Forecast Model 1.2: Software Design and Implementation*, internal draft documentation, October 2002.

[14] *Sparse Matrix Operator Kernel Emissions (SMOKE) Modeling System*, `http://www.emc.mcnc.org/products/smoke/`

[15] Z. Adelman and M. Houyoux, *Processing the National Emissions Inventory 96 (NEI96) version 3.11 with SMOKE*, the Emission Inventory Conference: One Atmosphere, One Inventory, Many Challenges, 1-3 May, Denver, CO, U.S. Environmental Protection Agency, 2001.

[16] Vukovich, J. McHenry, C. Coats and A. Trayanov, *Supporting Real-Time Air Quality Forecasting using the SMOKE modeling system*, Denver, CO, EPA Emissions Inventory Conference, April 30-May 2, 2001.

[17] *Comprehensive Air quality Model with extensions (CAMx)*, `http://www.camx.com/`

[18] D. Byun, J. Pleim, R. Tang, and A. Bourgeois, *Meteorology-Chemistry Interface Processor (MCIP) for Models-3 Community Multiscale Air Quality (CMAQ) Modeling System*, Washington, DC, U.S. Environmental Protection Agency, Office of Research and Development.

[19] K. Czajkowski,I. Foster, N. Karonis, C. Kesselman, S. Martin, W. Smith and S. Tuecke, *A Resource Management Architecture for Metacomputing Systems*, in Proceedings of the IPPS/SPDP '98 Workshop on Job Scheduling Strategies for Parallel Processing, Orlando, USA, 30 March 1998.

[20] W. Allcock, J. Bester, J. Bresnahan, A. Chervenak, I. Foster, C. Kesselman, S. Meder, V. Nefedova, D. Quesnel and S. Tuecke, *Data Management and Transfer in High-Performance Computational Grid Environments*, In Proceedings of the Parallel Computing 2001, Naples, Italy, 4-7 September 2001.

[21] J. Bester, I. Foster, C. Kesselman, J. Tedesco and S. Tuecke, *GASS: A Data Movement and Access Service for Wide Area Computing Systems*, Proceedings of the 6th Workshop on I/O in Parallel and Distributed Systems, Atlanta, USA 5 May 1999.

[22] K. Czajkowski, S. Fitzgerald, I. Foster and C. Kesselman, *Grid Information Services for Distributed Resource Sharing*, In Proceedings of the 10th IEEE International Symposium on High-Performance Distributed Computing (HPDC-10), IEEE Press, San Francisco, USA, 7-9 August

2001.

[23] I. Foster, C. Kesselman, G. Tsudik and S. Tuecke, *A Security Architecture for Computational Grids*, Proceedings of 5th ACM Conference on Computers and Security, San Francisco, USA, 3-5 November 1998.

[24] *Simple Object Access Protocol (SOAP), Version 1.2*, http://www.w3.org/TR/soap12-part0/

[25] *Web Services Description Language (WSDL), Version 1.2*, http://www.w3.org/TR/wsdl12/

[26] *Sun Grid Engine, Sun Microsystems 2002*, http://www.sun.com/software/gridware

[27] B. M. Chapman, J. He, Y. Li and B. Sundaram, *A Computational Environment for Air Quality Modeling in Texas*, In: W. Zwieflhofer (Ed.), Use of High Performance Computing in Meteorology, World Scientific Publishing Co., 2003

[28] B. M. Chapman, H. Donepudi, J. He, Y. Li, P. Raghunath, B. Sundaram and Y. Yan, *An OGSI-Compliant Portal for Campus Grids*, 10th ISPE Int. Conf. on Concurrent Engineering, Portugal, July 2003 (to appear)

[29] N. H. Kapadia, J. A. B. Fortes, M. S. Lundstrom, and D. Royo, *PUNCH: A Computing Portal for the Virtual University*, International Journal of Engineering Education (IJEE). In special issue on Virtual Universities and Engineering Education. Vol. 17, No. 2.

[30] J. E. Koontz, R. P. McCormack, and J. E. Devaney, *WebSubmit: a paradigm for platform independent computing*, Proceedings of the Workshop on Seamless Computing, Reading, England, September, 1997.

[31] M. Romberg, *The UNICORE architecture: Seamless access to distributed resources*, Proceedings of the 8th International Symposium on High Performance Distributed Computing HPDC-8, August 1999.

[32] T. Haupt, E. Akarsu, G. Fox, A. Kalinichenko, K.-S. Kim, P. Sheethalnath, and C.H. Youn, *The Gateway System: Uniform Web Based Access to Remote Resources*, In ACM 1999 Java Grande Conference, 1–7, San Francisco, CA, June 1999.

[33] *CORBA: Common Object Request Broker Architecture*, http://www.corba.org.

[34] S. Krishnan, R. Bramley, D. Gannon, M. Govindaraju, R. Indurkar, A. Slominski, B. Temko, R. Alkire, T. Drews, E. Webb, and J. Alameda, *The XCAT Science Portal*, Proceedings of Supercomputing 2001

[35] *Grid Portal Development Kit (GPDK)*, http://www-itg.lbl.gov/grid/projects/GPDK/

[36] *SDSC GridPort Toolkit*, http://gridport.npaci.edu/

[37] M. Thomas, S. Mock, and J. Boisseau, *Development of Web Toolkits for Computational Science Portals: The NPACI HotPage*, The 9th IEEE International Symposium on High Performance Distributed Computing, Pittsburgh, August 2000.

[38] NASA Information Power Grid, https://portal.ipg.nasa.gov

[39] M. Russell, G. Allen, G. Daues, I. Foster, T. Goodale, E. Seidel, J. Novotny, J. Shalf, W. Suen, and G. Von Laszewski, *The Astrophysics Simulation Simulation Collaboratory: A Science Portal Enabling Community Software Development*, Proceedings of Tenth IEEE International Symposium on High Performance Distributed Computing, August 2001(submitted)

[40] *LAPK Portal: The laboratory for Pharmacokinetics Modeling*, https://gridport.npaci.edu/LAPK

[41] *GAMESS Portal The laboratory for Pharmacokinetics Modeling*, https://gridport.npaci.edu/GAMESS

[42] *The DSG grid portal web page*, https://159.csm.port.ac.uk/dsgPortal/

[43] G.Aloisio, M.Cafaro, P.Falabella, C.Kesselman and R.Williams, *"Grid Computing on the Web using the Globus Toolkit"*, Proc. HPCN Europe 2000, Amsterdam, Netherlands, Lecture Notes in Computer Science, Springer-Verlag, N. 1823, 32-40, 2000

[44] S. Tuecke, D. Engert, I. Foster, M. Thompson, L. Pearlman and C. Kesselman, *Internet X.509 Public Key Infrastructure Proxy Certificate Profile*, IETF, Draft draft-ietfpkix-proxy-01.txt, 2001.

[45] J. Novotny, , S. Tuecke and V. Welch, *Initial Experiences with an Online Certificate Repository for the Grid: MyProxy*, The Tenth IEEE International Symposium on High Performance Distributed Computing, August, 2001

[46] B. Sundaram and B. M. Chapman, *Policy Engine: A Framework for Authorization, Accounting Policy Specification and Evaluation in Grids*, 2nd International Conference on Grid Computing, Nov 2001.

[47] S. Krishnan, P. Wagstrom and G. von Laszewski, *GSFL: A Workflow Framework for Grid Services*, In Preprint ANL/MCS-P980-0802, Argonne National Laboratory

[48] *The Apache Struts Framework web page*, http://jakarta.apache.org/struts.

[49] *The Java Server Pages web page*, http://java.sun.com/products/jsp

[50] I. Foster, C. Kesselman, J. Nick and S. Tuecke, *Grid Services for Distributed System Integration*, Computer, 35(6), 2002. http://www.globus.org/research/papers/ieee-cs-2.pdf

[51] *Java API for XML Processing 2001*, http://java.sun.com/xml/jaxp/index.html

[52] R. Wilhelmson, K. Droegemeier, S. Graves, M. Ramamurthy, D. Haidvogel, B. Jewett, J. Alameda and D. Gannon, *Modeling Environment for Atmospheric Discovery. MEAD*, Preprint - Annual American Meteorological Society Meeting - February, 2003

[53] *MEAD*, http://www.ncsa.uiuc.edu/expeditions/MEAD/
[54] *TeraGrid Project*, http://www.teragrid.org/
[55] *CrossGrid Project*, http://www.crossgrid.org
[56] *CrossGrid Meteorological Applications*, http://www.eucrossgrid.org/Presentations/IST2002_meteo.zip
[57] *Global Grid Forum (GGF)*, http://www.ggf.org

In: Parallel and Distributed Scientific and Engineering Computing ISBN 1-59033-956-8
Editor: Y. Pan and L.T. Yang, pp. 209-219

COORDINATION IN UTILITY MANAGED MULTI-AGENT GROUPS

FERNANDA BARBOSA*, JOSÉ C. CUNHA†, OMER F. RANA‡, AND STEVEN J. LYNDEN§

Abstract. A two stage approach to co-ordination in a multi-agent society is presented. The first stage involves agents learning to co-ordinate their activities based on local and global utility – the latter being assigned by an Environment Service Node. Each agent aims to maximise its local utility over a single-step or finite horizon, subject to reinforcements being received from the ESN. An agent may reveal all or partial state to the ESN, and does so through specialised function operators. Groups are formed by agents trying to identify partners which enable them to achieve a higher local utility. Subsequent interactions with the group are structured and managed via `GroupLog` – an approach for supporting interactions between agents within a community. An example based on resource sharing within a Computational Grid is used to illustrate how the two approaches may be combined.

Key words. Multi-agent systems, Co-ordination, Group models, Computational grids.

1. Introduction and Related Work. As the complexity of distributed systems has increased, de-centralized co-ordination has become an important goal. The emerging trend away from Client/Server-based approaches to Peer-2-Peer (P2P) systems, indicates the need for providing co-ordination techniques which are more dynamic, can scale, and do not necessitate a fixed structure. Generally, in P2P systems, it is the grouping of peers that is important, rather than the activities that must be undertaken by each peer – a good survey of concerns can be found in [8]. Establishing pre-defined co-ordination strategies may not be appropriate in these systems, and the "cookbook" approach applied in existing systems may be of limited use. Rasmusson [10] provides a survey of different co-ordination approaches in the context of multi-agent systems, and classifies these into a number of coarse-grained categories: (1) Game Theoretic, (2) Market-Oriented Programming based approaches, (3) Contract and Commitment based approaches, and (4) those based on Social Conventions. These categories employ a number of different themes, such as planning/reasoning, utility, and learning (for instance), to support co-ordination. It is also possible to combine themes, for instance, having social conventions (contracts) to constrain the behavior of selfish agents. An 'agent' in this work is used to identify a resource provider or a resource user, where interaction between the two are based on a policy.

The WALRAS algorithm [11] provides one approach for co-ordination based on utility, although this is in the context of very specific constraints on how the utility function (monotonicity, for instance) is calculated and assigned. This research, closely related to the first theme in our work, is based on the assumption that each agent owns resources, and can trade these in a market-place. Interaction does not take place directly between the agents, but via resource "prices" managed by them. There is no aspect of commitment in this approach, as agents can dynamically change their behaviors (and hence interaction patterns with others), based on prices for particular resources in the market. Although a useful and important paradigm within a dynamic environment where agents may have conflicting local goals, this approach may not be able to guarantee useful behaviors if commitments made by agents change often (as the market changes). In this approach, it is also not possible to guarantee that agents will continue to participate in a given market over a particular period of time (this may be important in the context of supply-chains, for instance, where agents need to commit for a particular period of time).

*Department of Computer Science, Faculty of Science and Technology, Universidade Nova de Lisboa, Portugal (fb@di.fct.unl.pt).
†Department of Computer Science, Faculty of Science and Technology, Universidade Nova de Lisboa, Portugal (jcc@di.fct.unl.pt).
‡Department of Computer Science, Cardiff University, UK (o.f.rana@cs.cardiff.ac.uk).
§Department of Computer Science, Cardiff University, UK (s.j.lynden@cs.cardiff.ac.uk).

We use a two layer approach for managing agents – the first is based on a utility model to co-ordinate agents, and create agent communities. This model assumes the agents are non-cooperative, and are interested in maximizing their local utilities. The incentives for agents to create groups is therefore based on them maximizing their own local utilities through the collaboration with their group peers. The second layer is then based on managing this group, once it has been formed. The duration over which participants of a group can remain stable is determined by the dynamicity of the environment in which they operate (although we do not address this issue in this paper). This layer assumes that agents within a group trust and cooperate with other members of a group – and that an entire group may be viewed as a single entity. The approach provided is also a demonstration of how two different styles of co-ordination (and implementation) may be combined to yield a system that can support: (1) both selfish and cooperative agents, (2) selective disclosure of internal state – by combining tuple space ideas [5] and messaging, and (3) the concept of time horizons to maintain group structure. Hence, initially agents do not commit to any particular actions, and operate in a selfish manner. They may subscribe to a number of different communities – and based on the utility they receive from these communities, decide to stay or leave. The second phase involves some commitment from the agents to continue to work collectively over a particular period of time. This is controlled by the concept of a "time horizon" in our approach.

1.1. The LEAF model. The LEAF model is aimed at supporting co-ordination between agents based on utility assignment [7]. The co-ordination of agents in this model is seen as a mechanism to enable agents to work collectively to solve a single problem – as part of a group/community. Co-ordination in this model is implicit, in that an agent will try to collaborate with those other agents which improve its own local utility. However, the community is not pre-defined, each agent must learn to select possible partners based on how well it performs with such partners as a group. Hence, if an agent works well with a particular set of other agents, then it is allocated a higher utility. Each community or group is managed by a special purpose agent (ESN), which maintains information about the community as a whole (compared to each agent managing only its own properties). An important part of LEAF is to enable each ESN to determine the "value" of the contribution made by each agent to some overall goal of the community. An agent may participate in one or more communities, based on the particular capabilities it brings to the community. However, each community may provide a set of commitments that the agent must adhere to – some of these may restrict membership of other communities.

In LEAF, the concept of utility is divided into two categories: performance utility and functional utility. Performance utility is parameterized by implementation dependent performance related aspects of agent behavior, such as memory used, CPU requirements, and speed of execution. Performance utility is therefore related to the usage of particular computational resources by an agent, in its goal to improve its local utility. Functional utility on the other hand is related to the problem solving ability of an agent. Functional utility is characterized by a value function in the local learning algorithm used by the agent (these could include mean-squared error, minimal-distance, etc.). The balance between these two aspects allows us to obtain a trade-off between the accuracy of problem solving vs. the execution time required to reach a particular answer. This trade-off is also influenced by the types of communities within which an agent may decide to participate. For instance, two communities may be trying to solve similar problems, however one community manager assigns a high utility to its participants if they reach an approximate result quickly, whilst another assigns a high utility for reaching an accurate result, even if it requires a longer execution time (or greater resource consumption). The utility assignment approach in LEAF is motivated by the belief that practical system issues become as relevant as problem solving capability of agents in real-world systems.

1.2. The GroupLog model. The GroupLog model is a co-ordination model for collective agent based systems [2]. It is based on the notion of group, a cooperating entity whose definition is important to model the agents cooperation in a flexible and well-structured manner and to hide low-level management of co-ordination activities.

The GroupLog model supports multi-agent systems through the specification of: (1) individual agents; (2) inter-agent communication patterns; and (3) cooperation behaviours. The model defines two main program structuring entities: agents and groups of agents.

The agent notion aims at capturing the computation aspect and its encapsulation within an autonomous entity. Through the group notion, GroupLog can be seen as supporting two forms of co-ordination: objective and subjective. On one hand, groups specify the organisation and structuring of an agent space into distinct sets. Several inter-agent communication patterns are supported: point-to-point, multi-cast, and multiple shared tuple spaces. Furthermore, it allows the modelling of dynamic systems, where agents can dynamically enter and leave such cooperating groups. On the other hand, each group can be seen as an agent, with well–defined internal behavior and communication interface. So, the group notion can be used to model the social behaviors of its members, which act as cooperating entities.

A GroupLog system contains concurrently executing agents able to: (1) communicate through interface predicates, and (2) join groups to co-ordinate their activities.

1.2.1. Agents in GroupLog. The specification of an agent consists of:

- The name of the agent, which defines its type;
- The list of interface predicates, which can be invoked by others agents;
- The agent program, consisting of a set of predicates and a set of definitions for interface, creation and elimination rules.

An instance of an agent of a given type has a unique identifier (e.g. *resource(1)* instance *1* of agent of type "resource"). The creation and elimination of agent instances are dynamic. In the agent creation, the instance takes an initial configuration. At each point in the computation, the agent instance has a current configuration. The interface predicates define the visible "entry points" of an agent that can be invoked from the outside environment. The communication with an agent can be one–to–one or one–to–any. In one–to–one communication, the destination agent and its interface predicate are explicitly cited. In one–to–any communication, we only need to specify the agent type and the interface predicate, because this is a form of selective communication targeted at all instances of the specified type.

An agent exhibits a well defined behavior, depending on its current configuration and on the invoked interface predicate. There is a non empty set of interface rules associated with each interface predicate. Each interface rule specifies:

1. The current configuration, that the agent instance must have at the moment that the interface predicate is invoked;
2. The signature of the interface predicate;
3. The pre-actions, the actions that the agent must execute before changing to a new configuration;
4. The new agent configuration for the instance, after having executed the pre-actions;
5. The post-actions, the actions that the agent must execute after changing to a new configuration.

At the predicate invocation, the evaluation of the first three conditions (1,2,3) as well as the transition to a new configuration (4) correspond to an atomic step in the invoked agent. This means any other invocations made to this agent remain suspended until this agent has completed such an atomic step, i.e. until it is available again for further interactions. If the first three conditions are satisfied, the agent instance changes to a new configuration.

An invocation of an interface predicate suspends if the invoked agent is busy evaluating a previous invocation, or if the invoked agent has not a current configuration as defined by the interface rule (condition 1).

Given the current configuration of an agent and an invoked interface predicate, there is a (possibly empty) set of rules which are **enabled** by that configuration. These are the rules of that interface predicate that satisfy the current agent configuration. All other rules are **disabled** for that configuration. This notion of disabled rules represents the rules that cannot be used by an invoked interface predicate due to the current agent configuration. If there is an enabled interface rule, the communication is accepted by the invoked agent, so the agent executes the pre-actions and changes its current configuration to the new agent configuration as defined by the rule. This configuration transition is non reversible and the agent becomes available for further interactions with other agents. After the transition, the agent executes the post-actions defined by the rule. These actions are performed concurrently with further interactions involving the invoked agent and other invoker agents. This corresponds to an implicit spawning of a concurrent thread, internal to the invoked agent. An interaction ends when the invoked agent finishes to execute the post-actions.

One–to–any communication proceeds in two steps:

1. The communication suspends until there is an available agent instance (i.e. such that the instance is currently waiting for interactions) with an enabled interface rule for the interface predicate invocation;
2. If multiple instances are found in step 1, one is selected in a non–deterministic way and the communication with the selected instance proceeds as in one–to–one communication.

Agent termination. An instance of an agent can be cancelled by the predefined interface predicate *kill*, or implicitly cancelled by an interface rule with no new agent configuration and post-actions. This implies the forced cancellation of all communications involving this agent (both suspended and ongoing).

1.2.2. Group of agents in GroupLog. The need for structuring the space of agents and supporting agent co-ordination motivated the definition of groups as dynamic entities. Cooperation relies on two basic forms of communication: (1) access to a shared group state, based on the Linda model [5]; and (2) direct communication through interface predicates. Each group of agents is itself viewed as an agent, so it has a name, an interface and a program. The interaction with the group is done in the same way as an agent. Associated with each interface predicate, there is a set of interface rules which define the group behavior. Additionally, a group has the following attributes:

Group membership The group is a composition of agents, called its members. The group membership changes dynamically, so the agents can enter or leave the group. A group hides its members from the outside but allows the redirection of communication to them through the group interface predicates. The internal concurrency to a group is explicitly defined by its members. An agent can belong to one or more groups, so the agent can inspect the list of its groups and the list of members of its groups;

Shared group state The shared group state is a multi–set of atoms. The members of the group may interact by accessing the shared group state, i.e. by reading and writing state elements (or tuples). The predefined predicates - **rd**, **ts**, **in** e **out** allow, respectively, to read, test, take and write the state elements of a group. The predicates *ts* and *out* are non–blocking.

Inside the group, co-ordination is now facilitated by accessing the shared group state or via direct communication (via interface predicates). Besides using the interface predicate of other agents, each member can communicate with other members in the same group through an one-to-many communication. This communication allows the interaction involving the members of a given group, which provides a form of multi-cast. The use of multi-cast allows agents to minimize the number of messages they need to exchange with each other.

2. Co-ordination in Dynamic Communities. Co-ordination within a community of agents in our approach is achieved through a two phase process. The first phase involves agents learning to form mutually beneficial communities, managed by Environment Service Nodes (ESNs). Each ESN is responsible for validating the usefulness of an agent to a given community, and achieves this by allocating a utility to each participant within the community that it manages. In the first phase, agents may subscribe to a number of concurrent communities (and hence ESNs), and get allocated utility from each one of these ESNs. Utility is based on two related aspects of an agent: (1) functional utility – a utility value an agent receives based on its problem solving capabilities, and (2) performance utility – a utility value based on the resource usage of an agent. It is important to note that utility is only useful if the source of the activity that leads to high utility (high reward) is deterministic (given a stationary environment). Hence, an underlying assumption is that agents will be able to determine the source of high/low utility. Each agent aggregates utility received from different ESNs – and uses this to decide whether or not it should remain within a particular community. In the first phase, agents therefore learn to choose between the available communities – and do not reveal their internal properties to other agents within their community. Direct interaction between agents is possible, and achieved through FIPA-ACL messages. There is no shared state within the community. Coordination between agents in this phase is regulated through utility assigned via the ESN. At the end of this phase, a data structure containing: (1) the list of agents present within a community, (2) the utility value allocated to each agent, (3) the group utility as calculated by the ESN, (4) the service types managed by each agent, and (5) the agent types, are passed on to the next phase.

The second phase involves agents being more cooperative, and revealing their internal properties through a shared group state, or via a direct one-to-one interaction. The shared space is a data structure that is made available to all participants within a community (i.e. a group managed by an ESN). The data structures contain attributes obtained from the first phase, and contain properties of each agent (such as its identity, its utility, etc.) and the group state (such as group utility).

The following notation is used to define participants of a community:

1. The set $A = \{A^1, ..., A^s\}$ of agents.
2. One or more Environment Service Nodes (ESNs).
3. FIPA platform agents: the directory facilitator agent (DF) and the agent management service (AMS).
4. The set $Tup = \{Tup^1, ..., Tup^n\}$ of tuples, where each tuple represents some property of a given agent community.

The DF and AMS services need to be shared by participants, and discovery is supported by mapping agent properties to addressing information managed by the DF. The following definitions are made:

Agent Service Types A set of service types $T = \{T^1, ..., T^m\}$ are defined for all available groups. A valid agent must implement a service type – for instance, `leaf.cg.data` may define a specific type of agent managing data. Agent type definitions are globally consistent, allowing other agents, and the ESN, to make assumptions about an agent's capabilities and behavior once the agent's service type is known. Agents must register their service type with the local platform DF (to be FIPA compliant).

Observable Property Set For each service type T^i, an observable property set O^i is defined as a set of dynamic properties belonging to agents implementing service type T^i. Each property has a globally unique name and a value associated with it.

O^i is observable in the sense that an agent of type T^i can be required to inform the ESN of the values of each property in O^i. These properties are primarily used in the first phase – whereby agents may restrict access to all their internal properties to the ESN. In the second phase, agents may also restrict access to their internal state to the observable property set. Hence, the total state of an agent consists of $O^i \cup L^i$ – where L^i represents the non-observable, local properties.

Global Utility Function The global utility function, U_g, rates the overall performance of a peer community.

Local Utility Functions Local utility functions are assigned by the ESN to agents. The local utility function assigned to agent A^i is referred to by U_l^i.

2.1. Utility management. Utility assignment relies on the assumption that agents are trying to maximize some local metric – and often work with uncertain knowledge about other agents. This is different from plan based systems, where agents must interact with each other to fulfill a given overall goal. Utility assignment and management is achieved using the LEAF toolkit [7]. Co-ordination in LEAF is based on the utility function assignment techniques of COIN [12], and support for this is incorporated into the LEAF infrastructure – and builds on FIPA-OS [9]. The essential concept is that machine learning based agents can learn to maximize their personal local utility functions, which are assigned to agents with the aim of engineering a system in which improvements made to local utility are beneficial to the system globally. This concept is inherited from the COIN framework – and requires agents to undertake local optimizations based on a reward they receive for their operations. Global utility is therefore based on the observable property sets of the agents that comprise the agent group.

The set of observable properties required by the ESN from each agent implementing service type T^i is defined as $O_g^i \subseteq O^i$, where O_g^i may be empty if no parameters are required from agents with a particular service type. In many cases, multiple instances will exist of certain service types, meaning that the global utility function must be able to handle parameters with multiple values. On start-up, the ESN distributes local utility functions to all agents. For every agent A^i, its local utility function U_l^i will depend on a number of parameters. Each parameter of U_l^i is either (a) a member of O^i, or (b) must be supplied by the ESN. Parameters falling into category (b) for agent A^i are defined by the set R_l^i. If the ESN assigns the utility function U_l^i, it is then responsible for dynamically updating the parameters R_l^i. Utility may be calculated by an agent based on each action that it takes, or averaged over a sum of states. Hence, an agent may use one of the following models:

- Finite Horizon – optimize expected reward for next 'h' state updates:

$$E\left(\sum_{t=0}^{h} U^t\right) \tag{2.1}$$

  using this update scheme, the agent group exists for only 'h' states, and is then disbanded. Hence, over its lifetime, an agent may belong to different groups (managed by different ESNs).
- Infinite Horizon – long-run reward expected by the agent. In this case, the agent may not get an initially high utility, but expect to improve utility over a given number of time/states:

$$E\left(\sum_{t=0}^{\infty} \gamma^t U^t\right) \tag{2.2}$$

where γ^t is a discounting rate for future states. Using this scheme, the agent group remains intact forever – and utility update is primarily within each group by the ESN.

- Averaged Finite Horizon (gain optimal policy)

$$lim_{h\to\infty} E\left(\frac{1}{h}\sum_{t=0}^{h} U^t\right) \tag{2.3}$$

this is midway between an Infinite Horizon and a Finite Horizon scheme – whereby the further away the reward, the less important it is to an agent. Using this, an agent may be able to optimize its utility over the "medium" term.

Hence, the kind of update mechanism in place is influenced by the rate of change of the environment in which the agent exists. This can also be determined by a user – and we assume an infinite horizon at present (section 3 discusses the impact of this parameter with reference to a particular example). This parameter also influences interaction between phase 1 (managed by LEAF) and phase 2 (managed by `GroupLog`). Local and global utility functions are designed with default parameters, so that the functions can still be computed if some parameters are unavailable. For the first phase, interactions are as follows:

1. The ESN must locate agents, and determine their service types via the FIPA service descriptions which agents are required to specify when they register with the platform DF agent.
2. The ESN must inform all agents of each type T^i of the observable properties O^i_g that it needs to compute U_g.
3. Each agent of type T^i must dynamically inform the ESN of the values of the observable properties O^i_g.
4. The ESN must dynamically inform each agent A^i of the values of the parameters R^i_l in order for local utility functions to be computed.
5. The ESN must dynamically obtain from agents any additional observable property values it needs to perform (4). This is necessary because some parameters in R^i_l may be dependent on the observable properties of other agents. The set of additional observable properties which must be obtained for this purpose from agents of service type T^i is defined as O^i_a.

The above updates (steps 3,4,5) can take place either periodically, or whenever an observable property/parameter changes. This is an application specific issue that is decided depending on the amount of communication that would be present in each case.

2.2. Group management. Once an initial group has been established based on LEAF, it is now managed by the `GroupLog` system. A **G**roup**L**og system contains concurrently executing agents able to: (1) communicate through interface predicates, and (2) shared state made available to all members of a group. The data structures created by LEAF are now used to initialize `GroupLog`, and consist of the following:

- Each agent of the group identified in LEAF is now a member of a `GroupLog` group.
- The interface of an agent represents service types managed by an agent.
- The shared state of a group managed by GroupLog will contain a collection of tuples. These represent the state of each agent on the completion of LEAF, and the utility information managed by the ESN. The following tuples are used:

```
Tup1=global_utility_function(F)
Tup2=service_types(List_Service_Types)
Tup3=observable_properties(Agent_ID,
                           Properties)
```

```
Tup4=service_attributes(Service_Type,
                        List_Properties)
```

The number of tuples depend on the parameter types that must be made publicly available by each agent and group.

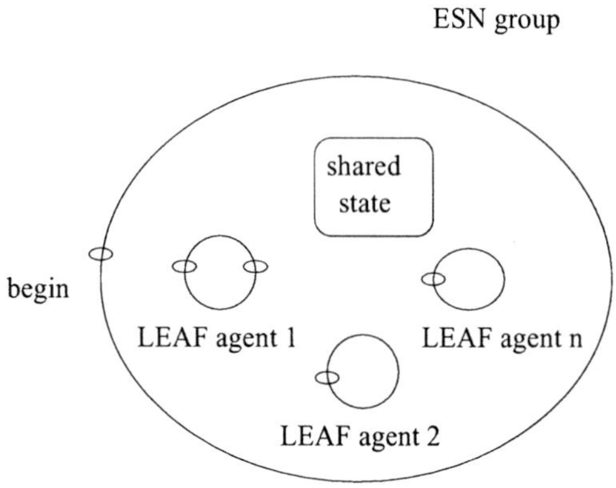

FIG. 2.1. *Sharing of data structures and agent properties between LEAF and GroupLog*

Fig. 2.1 illustrates how data structures are transformed between LEAF and `GroupLog`. The properties of each LEAF agent are now made public via the shared space, and a `begin` predicate may be used to initiate execution within a group.

3. Example: Resource Sharing in Computational Grids. We use an example to illustrate the two phases of our approach. Consider an application utilizing resources (computational and data) in multiple administrative domains. We assume that such an application requires multiple computational and data resources to execute successfully – and there is no one domain that offers all of these resources. This application may be divided into a number of tasks (with dependencies defined using a task graph) – all of which must be executed to successfully complete the application. Resource domains may be defined based on an IP sub-mask, or as logical domains implemented using middleware such as Globus [6]. In this example, each administrative domain can offer multiple resources – and is represented as a group managed by an ESN – hence, we can perceive different groups as *esn*(D_i), which represents the *esn* node for the ith group. We assume that there are 's' ($s \geq 1$) participants in each group. We also consider that each resource owner obtains a monetary benefit by providing access to their resource by external tasks. The greater the utilization of the resource, the greater will be the monetary profit that the resource owner can collect over a given period of time. Hence, initially resource providers within a particular group are interested in maximizing the utilization of their resources, and therefore may act in a selfish manner. However, if an application manager were to make collective use of resources within a particular domain – the combined monetary reward for the entire group will improve.

Resource owners may also wish to participate in multiple logical domains, evaluating the utility assigned by the *esn* managing the group. Hence, an *esn(domainA)* is composed of different resource providers, and each one offers a particular role (service type) in the group (eg data provider, processor provider, etc.). The group as a whole will have a global utility, along with a local utility for each member of the group. The *esn* calculates local utility for each member of the group – based on the observable properties revealed to the *esn* by each provider (this includes parameters such as number of jobs processed (throughput), time per job (response time), and utilization). Combining these three parameters (with a greater emphasis on utilization) into a utility measure, allows the *esn* to assign a reward to the resource provider for each application (or collections of applications) that the resource provider participates in. Each resource provider, on the other hand, will also aim to choose application tasks that are likely to improve its local utilization – thereby increasing its reward.

The utility values assigned by each group are then aggregated by the resource provider, to determine its current local utility. Utility value may be provided by the *esn* for a particular group either for every task executed by the resource provider, or for a collection of tasks. In this case, co-ordination is achieved by the resource provider deciding which group to join based on rewards received – and is therefore implicit based on the decision taken. Co-ordination decisions are made at this stage to form groupings of providers who can work together more effectively (and hence get better rewards from the *esn*). Once these decisions have been made, what results is a "team", that may now work more effectively together – this is phase 1 of our approach, and achieved through LEAF.

Once a team has been formed, it is now important to enable team members to share information more readily. To achieve this, each team member must register itself and some of its properties into a shared state. Communication between team members is now facilitated through the shared space (via a list of common predicates) – or via direct communication (via common predicates maintained by each participant through their interface). Fig. 3.1 illustrates the organization of a domain. In this second phase, group members have a greater trust in each other, and operate in a more cooperative manner.

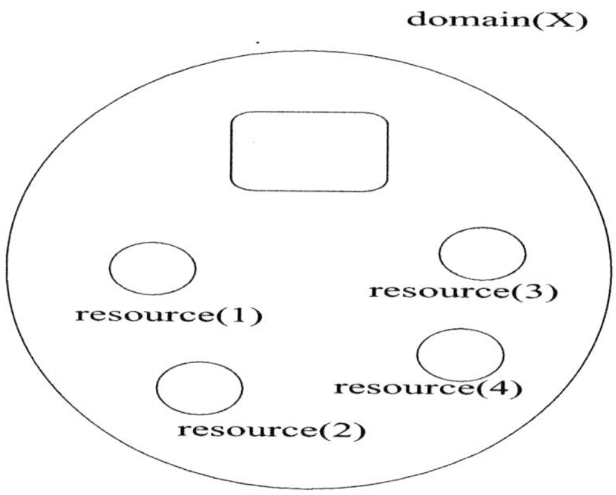

FIG. 3.1. *Domain Organisation*

Discussion. The actions taken by a resource provider are dependent on the environment within which the provider (and the *esn*) are situated. It is likely that the same action taken by a provider, within the same group, may lead to different rewards. Hence, each provider within a team may base its involvement on an *expected* reward after a given number of task executions. Our analysis above assumes that the provider commits to participate in a number of concurrent applications (and would base its reward on this assumption). It is also possible, however, for a provider to leave mid way through the execution of an application, and therefore the expected reward must be calculated over a finite horizon. There are two particular scenarios associated with this: (1) a provider leaving does not have an impact on the other participants in the team, (2) a provider leaving causes an impact on the other providers in the team – and hence the *esn* has to adjust reward for other participants. Case (2) can therefore lead to unbalanced teams – and the ESN must decide how rewards must be given to agents within this context.

The `add` and `delete` predicates in `GroupLog` can be used to support providers leaving and entering groups. Once a new provider joins a group, others are made aware of its presence via the shared space.

4. Conclusion and Future Work. A mechanism to support co-ordination in dynamic multi-agent communities is provided, based on a two phased approach. The first phase involves co-ordinating selfish agents, which try to maximize their local utilities. The agents reveal very little about their internal state at this stage, and have imprecise knowledge of other participants. The second phase involves co-operative agents, which are able to reveal more details about their internal state, and are able to use a shared space to exchange data. The first phase is implemented using the LEAF system, and the second using the `GroupLog` system. Interaction between these is achieved using a set of common data structures – which enable the structure being created through LEAF to be instantiated as a `GroupLog` group. At present, these two systems exist on their own, and a stronger coupling and interaction between them is being implemented. `GroupLog` has been implemented using PVM-Prolog [4], and existing work includes creating a Java interface to this. LEAF has been implemented using Java, and builds on the FIPA-OS implementation from Emorphia. LEAF is also being deployed within the AgentCities consortium [1].

Another aspect being explored is the time period over which a group must remain – a factor dictated by the type of environment within which the group exists. Our scenario's range from having the group active over a finite horizon (limited number of states), to an infinite horizon (the group structure does not change over the total lifetime of all agents in the group). The exact factor that determines which of these two schemes is most appropriate is not explored here. A simple example based on resource sharing in a Computational Grid is used to demonstrate the concepts involved – although the ideas presented here are applicable in a number of other domains.

Acknowledgments. The authors wish to thank the CITI/FCT-UNL and the Portuguese FCT/MCT Foundation.

REFERENCES

[1] THE AGENTCITIES CONSORTIUM, in Web site `http://www.agentcities.org/`. Last Visited: September 2002.

[2] FERNANDA BARBOSA AND JOSÉ C. CUNHA, *A Coordination Language for Collective Agent Based Systems: GroupLog*, in Applied Artificial Intelligence Journal, Special Issue: Coordination Models and Languages in AI, A. Omicini and G. A. Papadopoulos, eds., Taylor & Francis, 15(1)(2001), pp. 59–78.

[3] M. D. BEYNON, T. KURC, A. SUSSMAN, AND J. SALTZ, *Optimizing Execution of Component-based Applications using Group Instances*, in Proc. of IEEE CCGrid conference, Brisbane, Australia, 2001.

[4] JOSÉ C. CUNHA AND RUI F. P. MARQUES, *Distributed Algorithm Development with PVM-Prolog*, in Proc. of 5th Euromicro Workshop on Parallel and Distributed Processing, IEEE Computer Society Press, London, UK, 1997, pp. 211–215.

[5] D. GELERNTER, *Generative Communication in Linda*, in ACM Transactions on Programming Languages and Systems, 7(1), 1985, pp. 80–112.

[6] ARGONNE NATIONAL LABORATORY, *The Globus Project*, in Web site `http://www.globus.org/`. Last visited: April 2003.

[7] S. J. LYNDEN AND O. F. RANA, *The LEAF Tookit*, in Web site `http://www.cs.cf.ac.uk/User/S.J.Lynden/leaf/`. Last visited: April 2003.

[8] DEJAN S. MILOJICIC, V. KALOGERAKI, R. LUKOSE, K. NAGARAJA, J. PRUYNE, B. RICHARD, S. ROLLINS, AND Z. XU, *Peer-to-Peer Computing*, HP Labs, Technical Report HPL-2002-57, 2002.

[9] S.J. POSLAD, P. BUCKLE, AND R. HADINGHAM, *The FIPA-OS Agent Platform: Open Source for Open Standards*, in Proc. of Workshop on Scalability in MAS, T. Wagner and O. F. Rana, eds., ACM Autonomous Agents Conference, Barcelona, Spain, 2000.

[10] L. RASMUSSON, *Decentralized Coordination for Open Distributed Systems*, Technical Report, Swedish Institute of Computer Science, Box 1263, 164 29 Kista, Sweden, 2001.

[11] M. P. WELLMAN, *A Market-Oriented Programming Environment and its Application to Distributed Multicommodity flow problems*, in Journal of Artificial Intelligence Research, 1, August 1993.

[12] D. Wolpert and K. Tumer, *An Introduction to Collective Intelligence*, in Handbook of Agent Technology. AAAI Press/MIT, 2001.

Index

A

agent software, 161
AgentCities consortium, 218
air quality model, 163, 168, 174, 191, 193
air quality modelling project, 191
algorithms, 3, 5, 26, 35, 36, 42, 46, 48, 51, 60, 63, 69, 85, 86, 88, 91, 94-96, 103, 104, 119, 123, 128, 129, 177, 182, 186, 188
antiferromagnetic (AFM) layer, 99
application clusters, 147, 148

B

BLAS3 routines, 99, 103
block preconditioners, 9, 11

C

CA model, 85, 86
catalysts, 85
cellular automaton, 88, 96
chemical industry, 85
chromosomes, 69
communication overhead, 16, 44, 47, 63, 64, 79, 80, 81, 131-134, 139
compiler, 5, 23, 52, 60, 64, 71
computational capacity, 163
Computational Grid, 189, 191, 205, 209, 216, 218
computational grids, 11, 13, 20, 21, 178, 194
computational performance, 16-18, 20, 21, 104
concurrency, 85, 92, 148, 212
Constrained density functional theory, 99
Constrained Local Moment, 99
convergence, 9, 11, 13, 16, 18-21, 26, 27, 101, 105, 120, 140, 168
CPU management, 174
Cray T3D, 51, 52
Cray T3E, 51, 52, 64, 101, 105
cyclic distribution, 40-47

D

data distribution, 64
data mining, 147, 198
density functional theory, 99
discrete Fourier transform, DFT, 3-5, 99, 100
disease gene, 69, 83
distributed applications, 129, 152
distributed Krylov iterative solvers, 9
distributed memory, 3, 5, 7, 47, 48, 51, 131, 132, 144, 175
distributed memory computer, 3, 5, 7
distributed memory machines, DMMs, 51, 52, 55, 64, 131, 132
distributed memory parallel computers, 47
division, 35, 36, 38-44, 47, 48, 76, 77, 93, 127, 129
dynamic global service lists, 161
dynamic Monte Carlo algorithms, 85
dynamic virtual high throughput platform, 163

E

Emorphia, 218
engineering, 3, 23, 51, 147, 191, 204, 214
enhanced service, 23
Environment Service Node, ESN, 209, 210, 213-217
error detection, 161, 180

F

fast Fourier transform (FFT), 3, 35
ferromagnetic, FM, 99

G

genetic linkage, 82-84
genetic programs, 69
global communications, 99
global matrix transposition, 7
global Schur complement system, 12, 21
globus, 180, 205, 206, 218

GNU MP, 35, 48
grid computing, 187
grid environment, 191, 192, 196, 198, 200, 202, 204
grid portals, 197, 199, 202
grid resolution, 9, 11, 14, 19-21
grid services, 192, 193, 196-199, 202-204
grid technology, 161
GroupLog system, 211, 215, 218

H

high performance platform, 83
HiPCAT, 204
Hitachi SR8000, 35, 36, 45-48
hypercube, 5

I

infrastructures, 147, 204
integrity, 147, 158, 161, 187
interactive model reduction, 31
interface programs, 23
Internet, 23, 147, 188, 190, 206
Iron-Manganese, FeMn, 99-101, 103, 105, 106, 107
IT world, 147
iteration counts, 16-18, 20, 21

J

Java interface, 218
job queues, 204
job scheduling, 174

L

large scale quantum mechanical simulations, 99
large sparse linear systems, 9
LEAF model, 210, 214-218
legacy software, 70, 83
linear systems, 9, 13, 20-25, 27, 28, 31-33
Linkage/Fastlink, 69
Linkmap, 69-79, 81, 83, 84
Linkmap program, 69, 76-78, 83
Linux machines, 23
load balance, 47, 132, 133, 142, 143, 145, 164, 166, 167, 169-171, 174
load imbalance, 51, 64, 104, 131, 132, 134, 135, 139, 140, 143, 144
Locally Selfconsistent Multiple Scattering, 99

M

magnetic multilayer storage, 99
magnetic structure, 99, 100, 107, 108
magnetism, 101
migration, 131, 134, 135, 139-143, 165-167, 174, 175
model magnetic structures, 99
model reduction, 23-28, 30-33
monitoring, 151-154, 156, 158, 161, 163, 164, 168, 174, 192, 196, 197, 204
MPFUN package, 35
MPI, 16, 24, 42, 47, 51-59, 64, 72, 74, 80, 84, 105, 109, 112, 113, 116, 118, 168, 170, 173-175, 182, 192
MPI applications, 174
mpi parallel air quality model simulation, 163
multiple family input, 83
multiplication, 35, 36, 38, 40, 42, 45-48, 77

N

natural sciences, 51
neighborhood occupations, 85
NetSolve, 23, 31, 32
network congestion, 7
Newton iteration, 35, 39, 47
Numerical analysis, 51
numerical reliability, 31
numerical tool, 69

O

OGSA, 191, 195, 202, 204
operating system, 23, 27, 148, 150, 154-157, 168, 195, 196
Origin 2000, 69, 76, 83, 84

P

parallel algebraic preconditioners, 9, 11, 16, 19, 21
parallel algorithms, 35, 95
parallel cluster, 23
parallel implementation, 3, 6, 35, 36, 47, 51, 52, 60, 63, 64, 69, 70, 127, 145, 184
parallel model reduction library, 26
parallel platform, 31, 69, 83
parallel simulation, 85, 88, 89, 95
parallelization, 3, 5-7, 36, 37, 69, 70, 83, 85, 95, 96, 168
pARMS, 9, 16, 17, 20, 21
partition, 25, 53, 70, 73, 85, 86, 90, 92, 93, 104, 105
PDEs, 9, 11, 13, 15, 21
Performance modelling, 51, 161
portability, 51, 127, 143, 197
portable communication, 51
preconditioned Krylov solvers, 9
PVM, 51, 53-59, 64, 105, 119, 121, 123, 125, 127-130, 218

Q

quality of service, 147, 160, 161, 189, 199

R

read head devices, 99
reduction, 23-28, 30-33, 39, 51, 55, 59, 77, 127, 131, 132, 134, 143, 144
relaxations, 99
remote model reduction service, 23
resource management, 164, 194, 195, 201
responsiveness, 147
routines, 16, 23-27, 31, 48, 99, 103, 104, 106, 182
RPC interface, 31
runtime formulas, 52, 57, 64
runtime libraries, 51

S

scatter, 51, 55, 56, 58, 102
scheduling, 70, 155, 157, 158, 163, 164, 166, 167, 168, 173-175, 187, 191, 195, 198
Schur complement techniques, 9, 11, 21
science, 23, 105, 147, 189, 197, 204
scientific computing, 23, 51, 178
Scientific computing, 51
selfish agents, 218
semantic grids, 161
serial code, 7, 70
SGI Origin 2000 machine, 69
simulation, 21, 24, 69, 70, 74, 75, 85-91, 93-96, 99, 105, 109, 112, 131-135, 140, 142-145, 158, 163, 168, 170, 172-174, 192, 193, 198
software code, 9
spin dynamics, 99, 100, 102, 105, 108
square root operations, 35, 36, 41, 44, 47
subdomains, 9-13, 16, 20, 21, 133-135, 140, 141
subtraction, 35, 36, 38, 40, 47, 77
surface reactions, 85, 88, 94-96

T

task allocation, 69, 73
Time Warp, 85
timelines of system behavior, 161
troubleshooting, 148, 151-154, 157, 158, 160, 161

U

Unix based distributed application clusters, 147
user data, 31
user interface needs, 204

W

web browser, 23, 188
web service, 23, 25, 27, 31, 148, 195, 202
workflow, 196, 200, 204
workstations, 36, 69, 70, 131, 132, 143, 144, 163, 175, 177, 178, 193
world wide web, 23, 178